The Le   # HALESOWEN COLLEGE LIBRARY

The Lecturer's   and teachers
in universities   r, the *Toolkit*
addresses a bro   elps develop
many facets of

     Built around   is outcomes-
focused. Build   strengthened
emphasis on as   al age, when
students can ge   ge includes:

- how stud
- designing
- lectures i
- making s
- resource-
- looking a
- challenge

     Fully updat   and flexible
resource for ev

Phil Race is a Visiting Professor at Plymouth University and at University Campus, Suffolk, and
Emeritus Professor of Leeds Metropolitan University. He is a Principal Fellow of the Higher Education
Academy, and a National Teaching Fellow. He continues to travel widely in the UK and abroad giving
conference keynotes and running staff development workshops in universities and colleges. His other
publications include *Making Learning Happen* (2014) and *How to Get a Good Degree* (2007). For
further information, visit www.phil-race.co.uk.

The Lecturer's Toolkit

A practical guide to assessment,
learning and teaching

Fourth edition

Phil Race

 Routledge
Taylor & Francis Group

LONDON AND NEW YORK

Fourth edition published 2015
by Routledge
2 Park Square, Milton Park, Abingdon, Oxon OX14 4RN

and by Routledge
711 Third Avenue, New York, NY 10017

Routledge is an imprint of the Taylor & Francis Group, an informa business

© 2015 Phil Race

First edition published 1998 by Routledge
Third edition published 2006 by Routledge

British Library Cataloguing in Publication Data
A catalogue record for this book is available from the British Library

Library of Congress Cataloging in Publication Data
Race, Philip.
The lecturer's toolkit: a practical guide to assessment, learning and teaching / Phil Race. – Fourth edition.
    pages cm
  Includes bibliographical references and index.
  1. Lecture method in teaching – Handbooks, manuals, etc.
  2. College teaching – Handbooks, manuals, etc. I. Title.
  LB2393.R33 2015
  371.39′6–dc23   2014025640

ISBN: 978-1-138-78644-8 (hbk)
ISBN: 978-1-138-78645-5 (pbk)
ISBN: 978-1-315-76727-7 (ebk)

Typeset in Times
by HWA Text and Data Management, London

MIX
Paper from
responsible sources
FSC® C013604

Printed and bound by CPI Group (UK) Ltd, Croydon, CR0 4YY

Contents

Figures

Tables

Preface to the fourth edition

Things have changed very significantly since I prepared the third edition of this *Toolkit*. Developments have included the creation of massive open online courses (MOOCs), a huge increase in what's available on the internet, the widespread use of social media for communication (not least between students), and with students in many parts of the world paying for their own higher education, increased expectations regarding the student experience in universities and colleges.

The roles of the lecturer have moved far beyond just preparing and giving lectures. Disintermediation is happening – students are no longer dependent on lecturers providing them with information – they can find it themselves on the internet. The ethos of the lecture room has changed beyond recognition – it is no longer the place for students to go to get all the material they need to study successfully. Most information nowadays is gathered by students online rather than from handouts or even textbooks and journal articles – many of these are now available electronically. The lecture is now to help students see the big picture – but particularly to inspire and motivate them to go away and get down to learning with all the resources now available to them – not least each other.

We now live in an age dominated by league tables, with institutions vying for positions in world-ranking tables, competing to attract and retain students, competing for funding, and with the quality of the student experience regarded more seriously than ever before. Disintermediation, however, has not led to the demise of the human teacher in higher education, even if it has dramatically reduced the information-giving part of the job – the process that used to be described as 'transmit–receive'. The lecturer's job has become more complex, and student expectations continue to increase. There is now a vast evidence-base of literature on all aspects of learning, assessment, feedback and teaching, and increased pressure to emulate best practice as researched in the literature.

This *Toolkit* aims to help you to underpin and develop further your professional practice as a teacher in higher education. It is essentially a practical book, and although the contents are intended to be useful to new lecturers, I found with the earlier editions that many experienced practitioners found the book a source of practical suggestions, as well as food for thought and reflection. There continues to be pressure on university lecturers not just to be excellent researchers, but also to be professionally trained and qualified at supporting students' learning, motivating students and giving them useful feedback on their learning, and designing and implementing assessment. This pressure comes from all sides: from students, from colleagues, from funding agencies and from institutional managers. With students in many countries increasingly contributing towards the funding of their higher education, they are becoming much more aware of their status as consumers, and their right to demand high quality in the ways that their learning, teaching and assessment are implemented. In many countries including the UK, students' views are now collected systematically through a National Student Survey (or similar process) each year, and the findings of such surveys are regarded very seriously (and competitively) as indicators of the learning experience of students and the teaching quality of institutions.

What does this edition cover, and why?

There are seven chapters in this fourth edition. Each chapter is written to be relatively complete in itself. References are collected at the end of the book. Most of the book links to the central agenda of the factors underpinning successful learning introduced in Chapter 1, and I hope that you will find this a useful start to whichever parts of your professional practice you decide to review and develop first. Each chapter is prefaced by some intended outcomes, which tell more about the particular purposes the chapters are intended to serve. Each chapter is also prefaced by one or more 'pre-quotes' to set the scene for what is to follow. I have also added 'pause for thought' episodes at various points of the book, to give you the opportunity to stop and reflect on various key aspects of teaching, learning and assessment.

Chapter 1, 'How students *really* learn', aims to get you thinking about the fundamental processes which underpin your students' learning. After reviewing just some of the ways learning is addressed in the literature at large, in this chapter I ask you to interrogate your own learning (past or present), and draw out seven straightforward factors which need to be catered for in making learning truly learner-centred. All of these factors are things that you can take into account in any of the learning, teaching and assessment contexts your students are likely to encounter. This chapter also includes some suggestions on expressing and using learning outcomes, and developing students' competences.

Chapter 2, 'Designing assessment and feedback to enhance learning', is the most extensive – and probably the most important – part of this *Toolkit*. Of all the things that lecturers do, I believe it is assessment and feedback from lecturers that most profoundly influence the ways that students go about their learning. Yet I continue to meet many lecturers for whom the burden of marking students work and giving them feedback has spiralled right out of control, so the thrust of this chapter is to explore ways of maintaining or increasing the *quality* of assessment and feedback at the same time as streamlining the *amount* of these important aspects of the job of the lecturer. My intention in this chapter is to alert you to some of the tensions between effective learning and assessment, and to encourage you to diversify your approaches to assessment, so that as many as possible of your students will be able to use a range of assessment formats to show themselves at their best.

In this chapter, I offer critical comments about two of the main assessment devices still around – traditional exams and essays – and offer you 'pause for thought' exercises to reflect on the extent to which they are fit for purpose. I have added to this chapter discussion of the pros and cons of a variety of ways of getting feedback to students. The chapter ends with a section on involving students in their own assessment, to deepen their learning and make them more aware of how assessment works in other contexts.

Chapter 3, 'Lectures in the digital age', has been developed to address the changed nature of the large-group teaching session, at a time when students get the vast majority of the information they use for their studies outside the lecture room. Nowadays, with massive open online courses (MOOCs) available to all, and some of the best lecturers in the world accessible online, for example in TED-talks, the 'everyday' lecture faces strong competition. The chapter explores ways to design large-group teaching situations so that students' learning during them is optimised. Especially for those new to lecturing, the thought of standing up before a large group of students can be somewhat intimidating. The thrust of the chapter is about thinking through what your *students* will be doing during a large-group session, and planning ways that they can be involved, and making the most of the opportunities in large groups for students to get feedback on how their learning is progressing. The chapter includes a range of suggestions aiming to help you make large-group teaching work for your students, and suggestions about using technology in lecture rooms.

Chapter 4, 'Making small-group teaching work', explores ways of getting students to participate effectively. Small-group learning situations can be deep learning experiences for students, but need skilful facilitation to get the most out of the opportunities they provide. This chapter focuses on the processes which can be used to help all students to engage in small-group learning situations. The chapter also looks at the place of academic tutorials in higher education, at a time when for a variety of reasons it is increasingly difficult to provide the quality or quantity of such student–staff encounters.

Chapter 5, 'Resource-based learning in the digital age', starts by reviewing how present day online learning has developed from the roots of open and flexible learning processes, and aims to encourage you to make the most of the wide range of learning resources that are available to support learning, including MOOCs, and online lectures and podcasts. With larger numbers of students at university, and lecturers increasingly under higher workloads, the role of resource-based learning pathways or elements in higher education continues to grow in significance. In this chapter, I offer particular advice for those wishing to adapt existing resources to optimise their usefulness to their own students, and for those setting out to design new learning resource materials for their students. The chapter continues by helping you to interrogate how effectively students learn both from print-based resources, and from electronic resources using the ever-widening range of communication and information technologies available.

Chapter 6, 'Looking after yourself', is to help *you* to survive! It includes a range of suggestions to help you take control of your time, workload, stresses and so on, and on preparing for appraisal. There are also suggestions about how to go about gathering feedback from your students about their experience of higher education in general, and your teaching in particular. Several feedback methods are illustrated, each with their own advantages and drawbacks.

Chapter 7 on 'Challenges and reflections' continues the theme of your own survival, and starts by addressing seven challenges now facing teachers in higher education, including the increased importance of helping students to avoid plagiarism, the importance of considering the student experience across whole programmes rather than just within modules, the increasing expectation for experienced teachers in higher education to demonstrate their excellence in competitive awards frameworks, and the expectations regarding getting work published, not least relating to pedagogic development. Finally, the *Toolkit* ends with a range of ideas (and templates) on how you can set about not only reflecting on your practices of teaching and assessment, but also capturing evidence of such reflections to aid your own further development as a practitioner in higher education.

Acknowledgements

I am grateful for feedback from thousands of lecturers at the workshops I run, in the UK and abroad, and to countless colleagues who have emailed and tweeted me with comments and suggestions. Such feedback continues to help me to develop the ideas and suggestions throughout this *Toolkit*. I am also indebted to large numbers of students, with whom I continue to run interactive sessions on developing their learning skills, as I continue to find that working with students is vital to help me think more deeply about teaching and assessment.

I am particularly grateful to my wife Sally Brown, with whom I continue to discuss ideas in assessment, learning and teaching, and whose passion for creative, pragmatic and student-centred approaches remains an inspiration to me in my work.

Phil Race
June 2014

Chapter 1

How students really learn

The tertiary education sector is an area of current very rapid and unpredictable change, with universities and colleges reviewing and often implementing radical alterations in the ways they design, deliver and assess the curriculum, taking into account not just innovations in how content is being delivered and supported, particularly through technological means, but also the changing relationships between academics and their students. The role of the teacher in higher education needs to be reconsidered, when students can freely access content worldwide, and seek accreditation and recognition of learning by local, national or international providers.

(Sally Brown, 2013)

Intended outcomes of this chapter

When you have worked through this chapter, you should be better able to:

- equip yourself for the rapidly developing role of the lecturer, by focusing clearly on how learning really happens;
- avoid unnecessary jargon and old thinking, when helping your students to learn effectively;
- identify seven factors, in straightforward language, which underpin student learning;
- address these factors in your day-to-day work with students;
- help your students to gain control over these factors;
- design or modify intended learning outcomes associated with your teaching, so that they align constructively with evidence of achievement, teaching approaches, assessment criteria, and feedback mechanisms.

This chapter underpins just about everything else in this *Toolkit* – whatever else we do, our job as lecturers is to do everything we can to make learning happen. The chapter is in four main sections:

- *Never mind the teaching – feel the learning!* This section ranges briefly around some of the ideas in the vast literature about how human beings are thought to learn – some ideas are better than others!
- *Factors underpinning successful learning:* this is an account of an evidence-based approach I have used over some decades now, working out how learning happens using the language of learners themselves and their teachers.
- *Developing students' competences:* some thoughts about competence – and the opposite?
- *Positioning the goalposts – designing and using learning outcomes:* making learning outcomes work for students – it's *their* targets we're talking about.

The model of learning developed in this chapter comes from hundreds of thousands of people's responses to some straightforward questions about their own learning. I stress that this is a *model* and not a theory. It's become known as the 'ripples on a pond' way of thinking about learning, because the factors all affect each other – it's not a cycle – a mere cycle does no justice to how complex the human brain actually is.

Never mind the teaching – feel the learning!

There is no single ideal way to teach – it would be very boring for learners if we all did exactly the same things! Whatever sort of training we think about, or whatever sort of educational experience we consider, the one thing they all need to have in common is that they lead to effective learning, otherwise everyone's time is being wasted. However, whatever teaching approaches we choose to use, it's worth stopping to think about exactly how students learn, so we can help them succeed to learn from our actions – and perhaps more important – from each other.

As will be seen throughout this book, the job of the lecturer is far more complex than just 'lecturing'. It's essentially about facilitating learning – causing learning to happen – often then leading to measuring evidence of achievement of learning thereby accrediting learning. Carl Rogers was one of the early advocates of the facilitation of learning, and wrote of essential qualities of teachers thus:

> Perhaps the most basic of these essential attitudes is realness or genuineness. When the facilitator is a real person being what he is, entering into a relationship with the learner without presenting a front or facade, he is much more likely to be effective. This means that the feelings which he is experiencing are available to him, available to his awareness, that he is able to live these feelings, be them, and able to communicate them if appropriate. It means that he comes into a direct personal encounter with the learner, meeting him on a person-to-person basis. It means that he is being himself, not denying himself. Seen from this point of view it is suggested that the teacher can be a real person in his relationship with his students. He can be enthusiastic, he can be bored, he can be interested in students, he can be angry, he can be sensitive and sympathetic. …
> Thus, he is a person to his students, not a faceless embodiment of a curricular requirement, nor a sterile tube through which knowledge is passed from one generation to another.
>
> (Rogers, 1983, p. 106)

(Sorry about the male pronoun – shows how long ago this was written – but the point Rogers makes stands well the test of time here.)

The human species is unique in its capacity for learning – that is why our species has evolved as much as it has. The record of human beings engaging in learning goes back to the dawn of civilisation (and for quite some time before either of the words 'education' or 'training' were invented). Yet much that has been written about *how* we learn tends to have language that is unfamiliar and sometimes even alienating to most of the people who want to learn, or need to learn, or indeed to those who wish to cause learning to happen.

In the main part of this chapter, my intention is to share with you the results of my work over the last three decades, working with hundreds of thousands of lecturers, trainers, teachers and learners, probing them about how their learning *really* happens. There emerge seven factors which seem to underpin successful learning at any age, in any part of the world, in any discipline, and by just about any human being! That's a bold claim, but those of you who have followed my journey thus far, in previous editions of this *Toolkit* or in Race (2005a, 2010, 2014) will know how this way of thinking about learning has developed and consolidated over the years.

The seven factors I will explain in this chapter prove to be a very tangible basis upon which to build a strategy for designing lectures, tutorials and student assignments, and also for developing learning materials, including computer-based and online learning resources, and indeed massive open online courses (MOOCs) much discussed at present.

However, before taking the practical look at learning mentioned above, there follows a short review of just a few of the recent ideas in the wide literature now available about learning, and to put these into perspective one or two thoughts from much longer ago.

Recent thoughts on theories and models of learning

Introducing his collection *Contemporary theories of learning,* Knud Illeris (2009) suggests:

> During the last 10–15 years, learning has become a key topic, not only for professionals and students in the areas of psychology, pedagogy and education, but also in political and economic contexts. One reason for this is that the level of education and skills of nations, companies and individuals is considered a crucial parameter of competition in the present globalised market and knowledge society. It is, however, important to emphasise that the competitive functions of learning are merely a secondary, late-modern addition to the much more fundamental primary function of learning as one of the most basic abilities and manifestations of human life.
>
> (Illeris, 2009, p. 1)

A number of models have been put forward to explain the processes of learning, or the ways that people acquire skills. There have been two main schools of thought on how learning happens. The behaviourist school takes as its starting point a view that learning happens through stimulus, response and reward, in other words a conditioning process. The stimulus is referred to as an 'input', and the learned behaviours as 'outputs'. It can be argued that the now widespread emphasis on expressing the curriculum in terms of intended learning outcomes derives from the behaviourist school of thinking, and that clearly articulated assessment criteria are an attempt to define the learning outputs.

The other main approach is the cognitive view, which focuses on perception, memory and concept formation, and on the development of people's ability to demonstrate their understanding of what they have learned by solving problems. One of the most popular approaches of the 'cognitive' school arose from the work of Lewin (1952) and was extended by Kolb (1984) in his book *Experiential Learning: Experience as the source of learning and development.* Kolb's model identifies that most of what we know we learn from experience of one kind or another, and then breaks this down into four stages, turning them into a learning cycle.

Bruner et al. (1956), however, criticised some of the cognitive approaches as follows, reminding me of the views of Carl Rogers which started this chapter:

> A final point relates to the place of emotion and feeling. It is often said that all 'cognitive psychology', even its cultural version, neglects or even ignores the place of these in the life of mind. But it is neither necessary that this be so, nor at least in my view, is it so… Surely emotions and feelings are represented in the process of meaning making and in our constructions of reality.
>
> (Bruner et al., 1956, in Illeris, 2009, p. 167)

Wenger (1998), following up the social dimensions of learning in his book *Communities of practice: learning, meaning and identity,* suggests that:

Learning has traditionally been the province of *psychological* theories.

Behaviourist theories focus on behaviour modification via stimulus–response pairs and selective reinforcement. … Because they completely ignore issues of meaning, their usefulness lies in cases where addressing issues of social meaning is made impossible or is not relevant.

Cognitive theories focus on internal cognitive structures and view learning as transformations in these cognitive structures. Their pedagogical focus is on explanation, recombination, contrast, inference, and problem-solving.

Constructivist theories focus on the processes by which learners build their own mental structures when interacting with an environment. Their pedagogical focus is task-oriented. They favour hands-on self-directed activities oriented towards design and discovery.

Social learning theories take social interactions into account, but still from a primarily psychological perspective. They place the emphasis on interpersonal relations involving imitation and modelling, and thus focus on the study of cognitive processes by which observation can be a source of learning.

(quoted in Illeris, pp. 216–17)

Then Wenger goes on to suggest the advantages of *activity* theories, *socialisation* theories and *organisational* theories over these traditional ways of thinking about learning.

Meanwhile, Coffield et al. (2004) in a large-scale systematic review of various models of learning were very critical of the Kolb learning cycle (which is still widely cited) and said:

Kolb clearly believes that learning takes place in a cycle and that learners should use all four phases of that cycle to become effective. Popular adaptations of his theory (for which he is not, of course, responsible) claim, however, that all four phases should be tackled and in order. The manual for the third version of the LSI is explicit on this point: 'You may begin a learning process in any of the four phases of the learning cycle. Ideally, using a well-rounded learning process, you would cycle through all the four phases. However, you may find that you sometimes skip a phase in the cycle or focus primarily on just one' (Kolb 1999:4). But if Wierstra and de Jong's (2002) analysis, which reduces Kolb's model to a one-dimensional bipolar structure of reflection versus doing, proves to be accurate, then the notion of a learning cycle may be seriously flawed.

(Coffield et al., 2004)

Coffield et al. also reviewed in detail the strengths and weaknesses of various learning styles, instruments and models, some deriving from Kolb's work, and were very critical of the 'learning styles' approach, going as far as to ask 'Should research into learning styles be discontinued, as Reynolds (1997) has argued?', quoting Reynolds: 'Even using learning style instruments as a convenient way of introducing the subject [of learning] generally is hazardous because of the superficial attractions of labelling and categorizing in a world suffused with uncertainties' (Reynolds, 1997, p. 128 in Coffield et al., 2004).

A further criticism of many of the approaches to thinking about learning was neatly made by Peter Jarvis in his chapter 'Learning to be a person in society':

As a sociologist, I recognised that all the psychological models of learning were flawed, including Kolb's well-known learning cycle, in as much as they omitted the social and the interaction.

(in Illeris, 2009, p. 23)

Going much further back in time, another important approach was that of Ausubel (1968), who in his book *Educational Psychology: A cognitive view,* placed particular emphasis on starting points, and asserted:

The most important single factor influencing learning is what the learner already knows. Ascertain this and teach him accordingly.

(Ausubel, 1968, p. 235)

I like nowadays to think of 'learning incomes' as well as learning outcomes. The more we know about what our students can already do, where they've already been, their hopes, fears and hang-ups, the better we can help them to learn. Many practices now common in training can be matched to the cognitive psychology approach of Ausubel, and his ideas of the need for 'anchoring' concepts, advance organisers (such as what we now commonly refer to as learning objectives or statements of intended learning outcomes), and clearly structured learning material. This can be regarded as bringing together useful elements of the cognitive and behaviourist ways of thinking about learning. Skinner (1954), in a journal article entitled 'The science of learning and the art of teaching', presented one of the seminal papers for the behavioural school, and paid particular attention to the importance of repeated practice, and the use of rewards to help appropriate responses to be retained. The present way of designing curriculum around intended learning outcomes grew from the 1950s and 1960s when behavioural objectives ruled, and one of the most influential publications was the Bloom et al. *Taxonomy of Educational Objectives,* volume 1 *The Cognitive Domain,* published in 1956.

Yrjo Engestrom, known for his discussion of 'expansive learning' suggests:

Any theory of learning must answer at least four central questions: (1) Who are the subjects of learning – how are they defined and located? (2) Why do they learn – what makes them make the effort? (3) What do they learn – what are the contents and outcomes of learning? (4) How do they learn – what are the key actions and processes of learning?

(quoted in Illeris, (2009, p. 53) at the start of a chapter summing up Engestrom's discussion of 'expansive learning' as an activity-theoretical re-conceptualisation)

More recently, Biggs and Tang (2011) in successive editions of *Teaching for Quality Learning at University* have brought together a comprehensive survey of the links between teaching and learning in higher education making a powerful case for 'constructive alignment' – systematically linking intended learning outcomes, choices of teaching methods, evidence of achievement of the outcomes and assessment methods and criteria. 'Joined-up thinking' could be another term for constructive alignment, perhaps.

The profound influence of assessment design on approaches to learning was brought into sharp relief by Gibbs (1999) in his chapter in *Assessment Matters in Higher Education* edited by Brown and Glasner, and developed further in Gibbs (2010). Meanwhile the importance of the role of formative feedback, has been addressed by Knight and Yorke (2003), and developed in great detail by Sadler, who also delves deep into the real problems which exist in trying to quantify learning in terms of marks and grades, in a wide-ranging series of contributions to the literature from 1998 to the present time.

Deep, surface or strategic learning?

Much of the discussion about learning revolves around three or four words which describe different (though overlapping) ways of going about the process of learning. In their chapter entitled 'The link between assessment and learning', Dunn et al. introduce the topic of approaches to learning thus:

Many researchers have distinguished between different cognitive levels of engagement between learning tasks. Perhaps most widely referred to is the distinction between a *surface approach,* in which a relatively low level of cognitive engagement occurs, and a *deep approach,* where a relatively high level of cognitive engagement with the task takes place. In a surface approach to a learning task, the student perceives that it is necessary to remember the body of knowledge. Mostly this would involve the need to rote-learn and then recall the facts concerned. Of course there are many situations where this kind of approach to learning task is appropriate – such as perhaps learning the chemical tables. At the other end of the spectrum is a deep approach to a learning task, where the student perceives that it is necessary to make meaning of the content concerned, to be able to appraise it critically and to be able to apply the knowledge to other contexts or knowledge domains.

(Dunn et al. 2004, pp. 9–10)

So what sorts of learning are we as lecturers aiming to encourage? The most frequent response is 'deep learning'. But what *is* deep learning? Possibly really making sense of the topic concerned, and linking it well to all the other things around? This is more likely to be the case when *researching* a topic, and when lots of time is spent focusing on it, and when there is plenty of time to get one's head around it bit by bit. But a problem comes to light if we ask ourselves 'what are we really *measuring* with most of our forms of assessment?', and the answer is much more likely to be 'surface learning', or indeed 'strategic learning'.

'Surface learning' is looked down upon. It is regarded as the poor relation of deep learning. But in this age where information is so easy to download, store, file and carry around with us, we're hardly likely to 'learn' that information in ways which used to be necessary in the past. In most avenues of life, we can depend on having the information we need readily available, so we don't see the need to carry it around in our heads any more. It is indeed useful to be quick and accurate at *finding* and *re-finding* information however. There is a tendency to keep in our heads only what we need fairly immediately, and we all tend to use our memories for information which is 'sufficient to the day' – and in students' case 'sufficient to the exam day' perhaps. It can be argued that much of modern life only requires 'surface learning', as we can so easily get back to important or relevant information as and when we may need it. As always, however, there can be unintended consequences of progress.

Pause for thought
Nowadays, most people rarely pick up a hard-copy dictionary, unless learning a language and translating. We can enter a word (even spelled incorrectly) into our laptop, tablet or phone using Google, or many available online dictionaries, and quickly get a range of explanations, illustrations, examples – everything we might need. But not quite. What do we miss out?

One thing we can miss is the *other* words which are close in an alphabetical list to the word or phrase we are looking for. In the days of traditional dictionaries, a not-insignificant amount of learning tended to happen when our eyes strayed beyond our original search. With today's focused online dictionaries, that is unlikely to occur any more.

But another term creeps in: 'strategic learning'. This is about making conscious choices about what to learn relatively 'deep', and what only merits deliberate 'surface' learning. It is probably a sign of how intelligent our students are, that they seem to get increasingly keener to ration the time and energy they put into learning things according to the need to do so. When learning is to be assessed in some way, they are looking for how best to get as many as possible of the available marks. This applies to just about every form of assessment, exams, essays, reports, presentations, dissertations, theses, interviews, and so on.

It should come as no surprise to us that there is now a lot of evidence showing that 'strategic learners' tend to be not only more successful than surface learners, but also do better in many aspects of life than deep learners too. So what exactly *is* strategic learning? I have argued in recent years (e.g. Race, 2014) that:

> We could regard it as making informed choices about when to be a deep learner, and when to be a surface learner. It could be viewed as investing more in what is important to learn, and less in what is less important to learn. It could be regarded as setting out towards a chosen level of achievement, and working systematically to become able to demonstrate that level of achievement in each contributing assessment element. It can also be argued that those learners who go far are the strategic ones, rather than the deep ones. It can be argued that they know *when* to adopt a deep approach, and when it is sufficient to adopt a surface approach.
>
> (Race, 2014, p. 79)

Many of the sources referred to above inform the view of learning that this chapter will now propose. However, I continue to argue that much of the literature on learning is presented using language and concepts which most students and teachers find different from their everyday experience, and in this chapter (and throughout this *Toolkit*) a more pragmatic approach is sought, to inform appropriately teaching, learning and assessment practices. The approach outlined in this chapter is based on asking students (and others) questions about their own learning, and then analysing their responses (to date from hundreds of thousands of people from a wide range of disciplines, professions and vocations) to identify primary factors which influence the quality of learning. These factors, as you will see in this book, can be addressed consciously and directly both by students and teachers. Students can be helped to gain control over the factors, and teachers can plan their teaching to maximise the learning payoff associated with each factor.

Learning and intelligence

If the word 'learning' has caused countless different attempts to describe human behaviour and mental functioning, the word 'intelligence' can be argued to be equally problematic. There are numerous so-called 'intelligence tests', but what exactly do they measure? Most likely, skill at performing within the limits which define the tests, and under the conditions in which these tests are being used. A breath of fresh air was introduced by Howard Gardner, in his book *Frames of Mind: The theory of multiple intelligences* (2011), summing up his idea that there are several different kinds of intelligence. From his earlier work, Gardner (1993) in his work on 'multiple intelligences' starts by regarding intelligence as 'the capacity to solve problems or to fashion products that are valued in one or more cultural setting'. Whatever *intelligence* may be, it should not be thought of as simply being the capacity to perform well in particular assessment-related contexts or environments – for example intelligence must be much more than merely the capacity to do well in time-constrained, unseen written examinations, or even to use 3,000 words or so to construct a written argument or review. Gardner's work usefully subdivides *intelligence* into multiple facets:

- linguistic – use of language – words;
- mathematical-logical – patterns, deductive reasoning, logic and numbers;
- musical – compose, perform and appreciate musical patterns, sound and rhythm;
- bodily – kinaesthetic – use of whole body or parts of the body – coordination of movements;
- spatial – recognising and using patterns of space – images – parking the car, crystallography;
- interpersonal – working with other people, understanding their motivations, intentions and desires;

- intrapersonal – self-awareness, understanding oneself, and recognising one's feelings, fears and motivations;
- naturalist – awareness of the natural environment, sustainability;
- spiritual/existential – embracing aesthetic, unseen and spiritual dimensions; faith and religion;
- moral – ethics, humanity, value of life;
- bestial – communicating effectively with animals.

There's a lot more to the human species than just words. That's why I worry whenever I see the phrase 'neuro-linguistic programming', and it's not just the 'programming' that feels somewhat sinister in discussion of human thinking! Any one person's intelligence can be regarded as a fairly unique blend of several of Gardner's facets. Any learning experience is likely to involve several of these, adding to the picture of each individual student being quite unique in their overall approach to learning, but without all the difficulties discussed by Coffield et al. (2004) when thinking about learning styles. At last, perhaps, we're working towards a map upon which just about every aspect of human learning can be placed, and which spans the cognitive, behavioural, social and emotional aspects of human thinking and behaviour.

Factors underpinning successful learning – an evidence-based approach, using the language of learners themselves

One of the problems common to some, if not most, of the theories of learning referred to above is that they tend to be written using educational or psychological terminology – jargon. This does not mean that they are wrong, but it does mean that they are not particularly valuable when we try to use them to help our students to learn more effectively, or to help ourselves to teach more successfully. The remainder of this chapter is intended to provide you with a jargon-free, practical approach to enquiring into how learning happens best, which you can share with your students, and which you can use to inform all parts of your own work supporting students' learning.

Getting people to think of something they have learned successfully is a positive start to alerting them to the ways in which they learn. It does not matter what they think of as the successful learning experience of their choice – it can be work-related, or a sporting achievement, or any practical or intellectual skill. Try it for yourself – answer the pair of questions which follow now before reading on.

Question 1
(a) Think of something you're good at – something that you know you do well. Jot it down in the space below.

(b) Write below a few words about *how* you became good at this.

Most responses to question 1(b) are along the lines of:

- practice (by far the most common answer);
- trial and error;

- just doing it;
- repetition;
- having a go;
- experimenting;
- playing.

We all learn an immense amount in early childhood, seemingly effortlessly, by playing. Then all too soon, learning seems to be relegated to 'work'. This is tragic and unnecessary! All answers to question 1(b) boil down to 'learning-by-doing' in one way or another, a strong factor underpinning how most people learn. There's nothing new about this – it's already been called experiential learning for long enough – but let's stay with short words like *doing* for the present. 'Trial and error' is also important. Learning through one's mistakes is one of the most natural and productive ways to learn almost anything. Sadly, our educational culture – and particularly our assessment culture – leaves little room for learning from mistakes. Too often, mistakes are added up and used against students! Next, another question, to probe another dimension of successful learning.

Feeling the learning

The matter of *feelings,* as noted by many writers from Rogers to Jarvis, is something which has not been sufficiently explored by the developers of theories of learning. Feelings are as much about what it is to be human as any other aspect of humanity. There is a lot of discussion about student motivation (particularly when there is a *lack of motivation*), but perhaps too little energy has been invested in exploring the *emotions* upon which motivation depends. A relatively simple question yields a wealth of information about the connection between feelings, emotions and successful learning. Try it for yourself.

Question 2
(a) Think of something about yourself that you feel good about – a personal attribute or quality perhaps. Jot it down in the space below.

(b) Write below a few words about how you *know* that you can feel good about whatever it is. In other words, what is the *evidence* for your positive feeling?

Most responses to question 2(b) are along the lines of:

- feedback;
- other people's reactions;
- praise;
- seeing the results.

Therefore (unsurprisingly) feedback is an important underpinning factor to most people's learning.

Receiving positive feedback

It is useful to follow up our exploration of the importance of positive feelings with some thoughts about how students can be helped to *receive* positive feedback. In some cultures, including that of the UK, there is quite a strong tendency to shrug off compliments and praise, or to resort to the defence strategy of laughter! The effects of this behaviour detract from the value of the positive feedback in the following ways:

- the positive feedback is often not really taken on board;
- the person giving the feedback may feel rejected, snubbed or embarrassed;
- the ease of giving further praise may be reduced.

Helping students (and others) to confront these possibilities can be useful in developing their skills to derive the maximum benefit from positive feedback. For example, simply replying along the lines 'I'm glad you liked that' can make all the difference between embarrassment, and feedback effectively delivered and received.

When extended to the domain of critical feedback, further dividends are available. It can be very useful to train students (and ourselves!) to thank people for critical feedback, while weighing up the validity and value of it. This is much better than resorting to defensive stances, which tend in any case to stem the flow of negative feedback, usually before the most important messages have even been said.

Doing + feedback = successful learning?

Though these two elements are essential ingredients of successful learning, there are several further factors which need to be in place. Some of these are easier to tease out by asking a question about *unsuccessful learning*. Try it for yourself now, then read on.

Question 3

(a) Think, this time, of something that you *don't* do well! This could have been the result of an unsatisfactory learning experience. Jot down something you're *not* good at in the space below.

(b) Now reflect on your choice in two ways. First, write a few words indicating what went wrong when you tried to learn whatever-it-was.

(c) Next, try to decide whose fault it was (if anyone's of course) – does any blame rest with you, or with someone else (and if so, whom?).

Typical responses to question 3(b) include:

- I did not really *want* to learn it;
- I couldn't see the point;
- I couldn't get my head round it;
- The light just wouldn't dawn.

As for whose fault it may have been that the learning was not successful, many people blame themselves, but a significant number of respondents blame particular teachers, lecturers, trainers or instructors – and can usually remember the names of these people, along with a lot of what they did to damage motivation.

Wanting to *learn*

If there's something wrong with one's motivation, it's unlikely that successful learning will happen. However, motivation (despite being very close to 'emotion') is a rather cold word; *wanting* is a much more human word. Everyone knows what 'want' means. Also, *wanting* implies more than just motivation. *Wanting* goes right to the heart of human urges, emotions and feelings. When there's such a powerful factor at work helping learning to happen, little wonder that the results can be spectacular. We've all been pleasantly surprised at how well people who really *want* to do something usually manage to do it. If people want to learn, all is well. Unfortunately, the *want* is not automatically there. When subject matter gets tough, the *want* can evaporate quickly. When students don't warm to their teachers, or their learning environments, their *want* can be damaged.

Making sense of what one has learned – digesting – realising – 'getting my head around it'

We are thinking here about making sense of what has been learned, and also the learning experience – and also making sense of feedback received from other people. *Digesting* can be thought of as sorting out what is important in what has been learned, and extracting the fundamental principles from the background information. *Digesting* is also about discarding what's not important. It's about putting things into perspective. *Digesting,* above all else, is about establishing a sense of *ownership* of what has been learned. It's about *far more* than just reflection. Students often describe digesting as 'getting my head around it'. They sometimes explain it as 'realising'. When one has just *realised* something, one is then able to start to *communicate* the idea to other people – tangible evidence that learning has been successful. And looking ahead to assessment, we can only ever try to measure what *comes out* of learners, what they *communicate.* We can never really find out what they 'know' or what they 'understand' other than through what they *show.*

Thousands of people have answered the three questions we've looked at so far, and even written their answers down. The people asked have covered all age ranges, occupations and professions. It is not surprising to discover that very different people still manage to learn in broadly similar ways, and that people's answers have remained very similar across all the years I've now been posing these questions, even when the learning environments have changed dramatically. After all, learning is a *human* process – it matters little whether you're a human trainer, a human student, or a human manager. In face-to-face training, or large-group-based education, students are already surrounded by people who can help with the *making sense* stage – most importantly, each other. This remains the case when learning online, as with the ease of communication using social media, learners rarely feel alone. When students put their heads together informally to try to make sense of a difficult idea or problem, a lot of making sense and realising occurs.

Now another question!

For the next question, let's return to successful learning, but this time without that vital 'want'.

> **Question 4**
> (a) Think of something that you did in fact learn successfully, but at the time you did not *want* to learn it. Probably it is something that you're now glad you learned. Jot something of this sort below.
>
>
> (b) Write down a few words about 'what kept you at it' – in other words the alternatives that worked even when your *want* to learn was low or absent.

A wide range of things are cited by respondents to question 4(b), but common factors keeping different students going include:

- strong support and encouragement;
- determination not to be seen to get it wrong or fail;
- simply *needing* to learn the thing concerned, so that something else would be achievable.

Needing to learn – a substitute for motivation?

Responses to question 4 often highlight that a successful driving force for learning is *necessity*. There are some subjects where it can be very difficult to generate in students a strong *want* to learn, but where it may be quite possible for us to explain to them convincingly why they really do *need* to learn them. For example, for many years I taught students chemical thermodynamics. Few (normal!) students *want* to get to grips with the Second Law of Thermodynamics, but many *need* to get their heads round it. When students have ownership of a *want* to learn, there is little that we need to do to help them maintain their motivation. However, helping students to gain ownership of the need to learn something is a reasonable fallback position, and can still help students to learn successfully.

Five of the factors underpinning successful learning

From my analysis of thousands of people's answers to the four straightforward questions we've explored so far in this chapter, five of the principal factors underpinning successful learning can be summarised as follows.

1 *Wanting*   motivation, interest, enthusiasm
2 *Needing*   necessity, survival, saving face
3 *Doing*   practice, repetition, experience, trial and error
4 *Feedback*   other people's reactions, seeing the results
5 *Making sense* getting one's head round what has been learned.

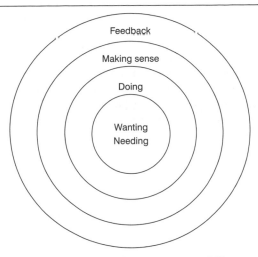

Figure 1.1 'Ripples on a pond': the first five factors underpinning successful learning

How do these factors interact with each other?

The human brain is not a computer that works in a linear or pre-programmed way all the time. Nor do we just go round in circles. Our brains often work at various overlapping levels when, for example, solving problems or making sense of ideas. The *wanting* stage needs to pervade throughout, so that *doing* is wanted, *feedback* is positively sought, opportunities for *making sense* are seized, and so on. Perhaps a more sensible model would have *wanting* at the heart, and *feedback* coming from the outside, and *doing* and *making sense* occurring in an overlapping way as pictured in Figure 1.1.

In various publications over recent years, including the previous editions of this book, I have argued that these factors all continuously affect each other, and that a way of thinking about them is to liken them to 'ripples on a pond'. Perhaps learning can be started by some *wanting,* where the bounced-back ripples from the external world constitute the *feedback* and continue to influence the *doing.* The effects of the *feedback* on the *doing* could be thought of as enabling *making sense* to happen. The main benefit of such a model is that it removes the need to think about learning as a unidirectional sequence. The model has about it both a simplicity and a complexity – in a way mirroring the simultaneous simplicity and complexity in the ways in which people actually learn.

Using the model

Probably the greatest strength of the *wanting/needing, doing, feedback, making-sense* model of learning is that it lends itself to providing a solid foundation upon which to design educational and training programmes. If you look at any successful form of education and training, you'll find that in one way or another, all of these factors underpinning effective learning are addressed. Different situations and processes attend to each of the factors in different ways.

For example, *wanting* is catered for by the effective face-to-face lecturer who generates enthusiasm. Enthusiasm is very infectious. Have you ever learned anything really well from someone who was clearly bored with it? *Wanting* can also be invoked by carefully worded statements showing the intended learning outcomes, which capture the students' wishes to proceed with their learning. The wanting can be enhanced by the stimulation provided by attractive colours and graphics in online or computer-based learning materials. What if there's no *wanting* or *needing* there in the first place? Perhaps feedback can, when coupled with learning-by-doing and making sense, cause the ripple to move back into the centre, and create some motivation. Learning-by-*doing* is at the heart of any good learning programme, and equally in any well-designed flexible learning package or online course.

Feedback is provided by tutors, or by the responses to exercises or self-assessment questions in flexible learning materials, or on-screen in online learning environments, or simply by fellow-students giving feedback to each other. Feedback can be regarded as the process that prevents the whole 'ripple' simply dying away, as feedback interacts with the *making sense* and *doing* stages, and keeps the learning moving.

The one that's all too easy to miss out is *making sense*. This is something we can't do to our students, only they can make sense of things. However, all experienced tutors know how important it is to give students the time and space to make sense of their learning and to put it into perspective. Similarly, the best learning packages cater for the fact that students need to be given some opportunity to practise with what they've already learned, before moving on to further learning.

How can we increase students' motivation?

In many educational institutions, staff grumble that students' motivation is not what it used to be. There are students who simply don't seem to *want* to learn. There are students who don't seem to see why they may *need* to learn. They seem less willing to sit at our feet and imbibe of our infinite wisdom. And nowadays in many parts of the world, students are often paying a lot to be at a university (or their parents or grandparents are paying!). There are some students who even seem to believe that we are paid to do their learning for them – and it can certainly be argued that we're paid to do everything we reasonably can to make sure that their learning is successful.

Why is motivation often low?

There are many reasons for increased incidence of low levels of student motivation, including:

- There are many more students in our higher education system. We still have those students who are keen to learn, but they are diluted by students whose motivation is much less, and who would not have come into our system some years ago. The proportion of students who know exactly *why* they're in higher education seems to have decreased.
- More students enter higher education to satisfy other people's expectations of them, rather than through their own motivation to succeed. Some are coaxed, cajoled or pressed by parents and others, and come in as a duty rather than as a mission.
- There is a great culture shock on moving from school to higher education – all those distracting temptations, and the scary unprecedented freedom. Many students are unprepared for the increased responsibility for their own learning that higher education places upon them.
- Students are much more 'grown up' than they used to be. Their lifestyle expectations have increased. This means that problems with finances and difficulties with relationships take a greater toll on the energies of more students than used to be the case.
- The rigours of our academic systems can mean that there may be no chance of remediation for poor assessed work, and failure can breed irrecoverably low motivation.

What are the symptoms of low motivation?

Some symptoms of failing motivation appear to us as in-class behaviours, others we see evidence of as out-of-class behaviours, with yet more symptoms reflecting students' perceptions about ourselves. For online learning, the symptom is drop-out or non-completion – usually less than 10 per cent of starters on a MOOC are likely to complete.

SOME IN-CLASS SYMPTOMS OF LOW MOTIVATION:

- coming to class late and/or leaving early, or indeed not turning up at all;
- talking to friends in class about other things;
- looking out of the window, scribbling, drawing, doodling, texting, and generally fiddling with mobiles, laptops and tablets;
- not being engaged in classrooms or lecture theatres, not asking questions, not being willing to answer questions, nor volunteering responses when invited;
- diverting lecturers from the main issues;
- coming in without pens, paper, books, calculators, and so on;
- taking a longer break than is intended during long sessions, or failing to return at all;
- yawning, looking disinterested, and avoiding eye contact;
- inappropriate social interactions in class (compare back row of cinema!).

SOME OUT-OF-CLASS SYMPTOMS OF LOW MOTIVATION:

- consistent absence without explanation or reason;
- inadequate preparation towards class work;
- handing in hasty last-minute work – botched, or not handing in any work;
- drifting for hours online, without achieving any real learning;
- low quality individual and/or group work;
- damaging each other's attitude;
- work avoidance strategies – giving in too easily to doing only unimportant tasks and putting off doing important ones;
- ignoring lecturers out of class;
- being found not to have contributed to group tasks – doing only what's necessary for coursework marks, but not doing other things;
- not buying books, nor using library resources;
- not downloading essential resources from the module web-pages – or (even more often) downloading them, but never opening the files.

IS SOME OF IT OUR FAULT?

Some explanations of low student motivation point in our direction! The charges against us include:

- our seeming indifference to time-of-day factors – Friday afternoon classes, students' need for an early afternoon snooze after lunch;
- students' experiences of the unevenness of the pressure of work – e.g. weeks go by with nothing to hand in, then a deluge of hand-in dates;
- some students feeling that they've been labelled by us already as low-achievers, and taking all slightly critical feedback as reinforcement of their lowered self-esteem;

- seating plans too rigid and predictable, room quality, the overall learning environment being scruffy or un-enthusing;
- the teachers they meet – our own looks, sounds, level of enthusiasm, perceived lack of understanding about how learning really happens and the effects of the learning environment;
- more able students feeling that they are undervalued and under-challenged, and that we spend too long catering for the lower-fliers;
- insufficient acceptance on our part of a basic human need for students (like children) to win at least some of the battles.

How can we tackle low motivation?

The following suggestions are tactics, rather than solutions. However, choosing tactics can be our first steps towards building a strategy to counter the malaise of poor student motivation. You will already have your own tactics to add to (or supersede) the ones suggested below.

1 **Accept that motivation is a real problem.** Pretending that low motivation doesn't exist does not make it disappear. Treating it as an issue to be addressed jointly with students increases the chance that they will recognise it themselves, and (as only they can) make adjustments to their rationale for being in higher education.

2 **Recognise the boundary conditions of the problem.** Low motivation is essentially a problem with full-time students, rather than with part-timers. Low motivation is essentially a problem with younger students, rather than mature returners. When we have large mixed-ability, mixed-age classes containing full-timers and part-timers together, the range of motivation is even more of a problem to all concerned.

3 **Remember that students can have difficult lives.** First-year students may be far from home, family, friends, familiar streets, for the first extended time so far. For some, it's like being on remand – they've been sent there by other people. Some delight in their new environment, others are homesick, but all are expending a lot of their energy adjusting their lives. The differences between school and university are more profound than perhaps they were when we were new students.

4 **Accept that many young people are rebels.** It's a natural enough stage of growing up. But this means that they aren't so keen to please us, and may be more willing to be sullen, uncooperative and passive. In our consumer-led society (and students are consumers) they are less likely to try to hide their dissatisfaction. None of this means that they aren't intelligent, or that they lack potential.

5 **Seek different kinds of feedback from students.** We already seek lots of feedback, but often with repetitive, boring devices such as tick-box questionnaires, where students don't really tell us anything other than their surface responses to too-often-asked structured questions about our teaching. Ask students how they feel about topics, rooms, online work, assignments, and us! Ask for words, not just rankings.

6 **Make it OK to be demotivated.** Students sometimes feel that their low morale is yet another failure, and it becomes a self-fulfilling prophecy. All human beings (ourselves included) have peaks and troughs in motivation, and students need to see that (for example) success can breed more success.

7 **Don't expect students to be passionately interested in things they haven't yet got their heads around.** The passion often comes with making sense of subject matter, and this often comes with experience and interaction, so concentrate on the learning-by-doing, peer feedback, and in-class involvement. Don't lecture to a group as if every member of it is entirely switched on, when we know all too well that this isn't the case.

8 **Don't presuppose that our own topic is the most fascinating thing in the life of all the students we see.** A few may end up researching in this topic, but for most it is just another stepping stone to a qualification that they are going to use for something quite different to our own particular field. Make it an interesting stepping stone, but don't expect all the students to take it as seriously as we perhaps do.

9 **Concentrate on their learning, rather than our teaching.** Think more carefully when teaching about what will be going on in their minds, rather than the information in our minds that we'd love to transfuse to our students. Knowledge is not infectious, and is much more than mere information. Enthusiasm is, however, infectious – we can try to transmit this.

10 **Keep assessment in perspective.** The assessment students do for us sits alongside all the other assessed tasks they do for all their other teachers. Don't let students' lives be dominated by assessed work, to the exclusion of the natural joy of learning.

11 **Spend more time helping all students to become better learners.** Don't regard it as someone else's business. Don't assume that students should already be skilled learners. Help students to gain more control over how they learn, so that they have a greater ownership over what they learn. Above all, continue to help them to address *why* they are learning, and *how best* to go about their studies.

12 **Spend more energy on praising.** Students (like ourselves) respond well to positive feedback. Ticks aren't enough. It's all too easy for us to spend our limited time on giving constructive critical feedback, but if there is not enough praise there, this just seems like condemnation to demotivated students.

13 **Continue being a student.** Perhaps a requirement for employment as a teacher in higher education should be that we too should always be enrolled on an academic programme as students, and that we should see our studies through to assessment. And we should have the opportunity to fail or succeed, just like our students. Therein lies the essence of understanding students' motivations.

Two more factors underpinning successful learning

We've already looked at four questions about how people learn, and identified five straightforward factors arising from hundreds of thousands of people's responses to these questions. We've explored how these factors do not work in a particular sequence or cycle, but interact with each other concurrently. We've also looked at what can go wrong with motivation, and some of the things we can do to enhance the *want* to learn. But I argue that learning is not complete until two more stages have been achieved. The first of these can be linked to people's responses to question 5 below.

Question 5
(a) Think of something which you've helped other people to learn. This could include teaching people, coaching them, training them and so on. Think back particularly to the first time you explained it to other people, particularly by putting it into spoken words.
(b) To what extent did you find that you 'had your own head around it' much better after putting it into spoken words that first time? Choose one of the following options:
- Very much better
- Somewhat better
- No better.

Verbalising: putting it into spoken words – teaching, explaining coaching

Question 5(a) is eagerly embraced by just about anyone whose work includes teaching, training, or coaching. Furthermore, even those whose job does not include these things readily recall explaining things to other people, including colleagues and children.

Question 5(b) leads to a vast majority of respondents choosing the 'very much better' option. The key additional factor is *verbalising*. This is about putting it into spoken words to other people. In other words, we've never really made sense of something properly until we've spoken it. This is bad news for anyone just studying alone at a desk or a computer! There's something about putting it across to other people that causes us to get our heads around it deeper. We could rationalise that this causes all the factors we've looked at so far to resonate deeply and quickly – we're *doing,* we're *getting feedback* from those we're explaining things to, we're *making sense* ever more deeply, and we're interacting with others' *want* and *need* as we go.

The fact that this sixth factor necessarily involves other people brings to the fore what was missed by so many earlier, clumsy models and theories of learning – the social dimension is now present. But there's still something missing. Let's go straight on to the final question.

People have no difficulty picturing this scene. We've all checked up about whether those we're explaining things to have 'got it', and the vast majority of people vote for 'very much better' when it comes to question 6(b). In other words, we all 'get our heads around something' considerably more deeply every time we try to measure whether other people's learning has succeeded. It's the acts of *making judgements* or *applying criteria* to other people's evidence of achievement which helps each of us deepen our own learning that last bit more.

Once more, we could argue that the act of assessing causes the other six factors we've already considered to resonate much more strongly, and that the social dimension of learning is strongly involved. Therefore, the picture of the factors underpinning successful learning is completed by showing *verbalising* and *assessing* as two further ripples which are needed when something is learned much more fully (Figure 1.2).

Figure 1.2 The seven factors underpinning successful learning

Question 6
(a) Think of something which you've helped other people to learn. This could include teaching people, coaching them, training them and so on. Think back particularly to the first time you explained it to other people, particularly by putting it into spoken words.

(b) To what extent did you find that you 'had your own head around it' much better after putting it into spoken words that first time? Choose one of the following options:
- Very much better
- Somewhat better
- No better.

Sadler (2010a) writes convincingly on how we need to get our students verbalising, and making judgements to deepen their learning.

> Students need to be exposed to, and gain experience in making judgements about, a variety of works of different quality... They need planned rather than random exposure to exemplars, and experience in making judgements about quality. They need to create verbalised rationales and accounts of how various works could have been done better. Finally, they need to engage in evaluative conversations with teachers and other students. Together, these three provide the means by which students can develop a concept of quality that is similar in essence to that which the teacher possesses, and in particular to understand what makes for high quality. Although providing these experiences for students may appear to add more layers to the task of teaching, it is possible to organise this approach to peer assessment so that it becomes a powerful strategy for higher education teaching.
>
> (Sadler, 2010a, p. 544)

Developing students' competences

Let's stand back from what we've already thought about in this chapter, and go back to the central purposes of everything we do when teaching, or designing learning resources for students. We intend to help them to become more competent. The competences we are addressing are not just those relating to skills which students will be able to demonstrate to us, nor are they all amenable to our usual assessment processes and practices. The competences include those connected with thinking, creativity, originality, enterprise, employability, entrepreneurship, problem-solving, and so on, as well as those linked to mastery of defined areas of knowledge. Sadler (2013b) cautions us about adopting simplistic checklist approaches to competence measurement:

> Decomposing competence into manageable (or even atomised) components in order to facilitate judgments may have some interim value in certain contexts, but the act of decomposition can obscure how a practitioner would work the various bits in together to form a coherent whole. Judgments of competence can properly take place only within complex situations, not in the abstract, and not componentially.
>
> (Sadler, 2013b, p. 13)

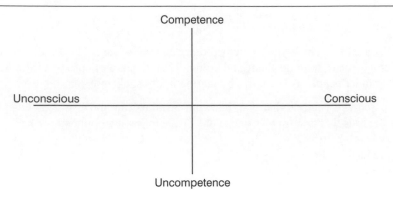

Figure 1.3 Conscious–unconscious, competence–uncompetence

As with many other recommendations from Sadler's work, it is best to help students to become aware of how best to develop their own competences; the approach shared in the next part of this chapter parallels what we've already discussed about letting students in to how learning really happens.

What's the opposite of competence? 'Incompetence' is the word which immediately comes to mind. Unfortunately, incompetence is a word with negative associations, so some time ago I coined the word 'uncompetence' to mean not-yet-competent, less threatening than incompetence. This is why I developed a model of conscious versus unconscious competence and uncompetence, see Figure 1.3.

The 'target' box

We want to help our students to become consciously competent. This can be regarded as the target box on the competence–uncompetence matrix. Please see Figure 1.4. The more we can help students to be *aware* of their competences, the better their motivation. In other words, conscious competence links to the *wanting* to learn factor. It breeds confidence. We can address this by expressing intended learning outcomes as clearly as we can, so that students are aware when they have reached the position of achieving these outcomes, and know that they are able to demonstrate their achievement of them to us when we assess their performance.

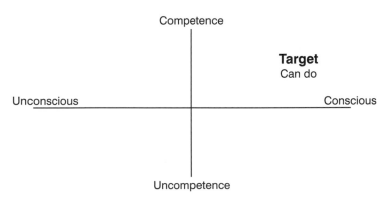

Figure 1.4 Conscious competence: the 'target' box

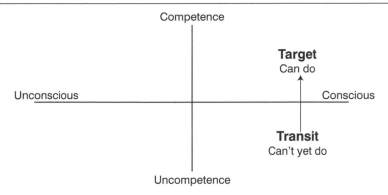

Figure 1.5 Conscious uncompetence: the 'transit' box

The 'transit' box

There's nothing wrong with 'conscious uncompetence'. Indeed, knowing what one can't yet do is usually an essential step towards becoming able to do it. Of course, many unconscious uncompetences don't even need to be addressed, including all the things one does not need to become able to do, and so on. It is only those conscious uncompetences which relate to the topics to be learned which need to be moved towards the target box on the diagram in Figure 1.5.

When the intended learning outcomes are clear, it is easier for students themselves to work out what they can't yet do, and they can often turn their conscious uncompetences into competences without further help. However, as teachers we can often help students to gain feedback which gives them a lot more detail of exactly how they should go about moving out of the transit position. Similarly, students can gain a great deal of feedback from each other about how best to make the move.

Unconscious uncompetence – the 'danger' box

This is about not knowing what one can't yet do. For most learners (students, but also ourselves), it's the things we don't know we're not yet good at which pose the greatest threat. It could be argued that the art of teaching is about helping students to find out what lies hidden in their 'danger' boxes on this diagram!

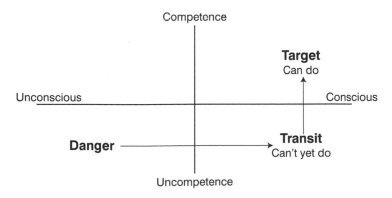

Figure 1.6 Unconscious uncompetence: the 'danger' box

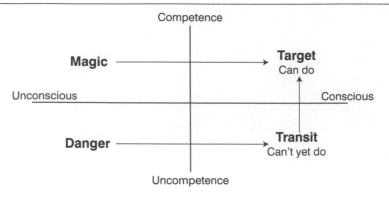

Figure 1.7 Unconscious competence: the 'magic' box

Clear expressions of intended learning outcomes can help students to see that there are things they hadn't yet identified that they needed to become able to achieve. However, even more help can be brought to bear by assessment and feedback, where we (and indeed fellow students) contribute to giving students information about what they didn't know that they couldn't yet do. Please see Figure 1.6.

It is of course possible for students to jump straight from the 'danger' position to the 'target' one, but then it can be argued that their learning is not nearly so deep as it would have been if they had been alerted to the detail of exactly what it was that they didn't know they couldn't yet do, then tackling the situation consciously and addressing the problem.

It is increasingly recognised that an important function of higher education is to help students to develop their key transferable skills. Some of the most important of these are those connected with becoming self-sufficient, autonomous learners. Ideally, we need to be training students toward becoming able to probe for themselves what might lie in the danger box in their learning.

Unconscious competence – the 'magic' box?

Fortunately, we've all got unconscious competences as well as conscious ones. Many skilful teachers don't actually *need* to be aware of exactly wherein lies the success of their teaching. Students who can already achieve learning outcomes don't necessarily have to *know* that they are already in a position to do so. However, it can be argued that the transition from the 'magic' box to the 'target' one is a useful part of the learning process. For example, the excellent teacher who finds out *why* his or her teaching is successful is in a much better position to help others emulate that success. Similarly, students who find out about their unconscious competences are in a better position to build up their confidence, and to draw from that gain in self-understanding reflective processes that they can use in their conscious learning. See Figure 1.7.

It can be a little unsettling to translate unconscious competences into conscious ones. It can be compared to being able to ride a bike, and wobbling when becoming aware of the processes involved. However, the learning which accompanies this sort of transition can be of value when applied to new learning scenarios.

More importantly, most students find that when they are alerted to the things they did not realise that they could already do well, they gain confidence and self-esteem. As teachers, we need to remind ourselves that our work is not just about telling students what they need to do, but equally about alerting to students to strengths they already have – their 'learning incomes' perhaps. Positive feedback is a powerful aid to motivation, and where better to direct our positive feedback than to the things that students may not have realised deserved our praise.

Confidence and self-concept

Students from non-traditional academic backgrounds are likely to find their confidence levels are further undermined if their beliefs in their own abilities to succeed are undermined by conceptions about themselves which have made it difficult for them to achieve academically in the past.

Clegg, in Peelo and Wareham (2002) citing Dweck, argues that there is a high correlation between self-concept and achievement and this depends on whether students see their capabilities as being set in stone or malleable to change through hard work and strategic approaches. They discuss two positions that students can adopt in regard to their own abilities; first, that intelligence is fixed (an entity theory of intelligence, as evidenced by IQ scores) and that there is very little they can do to improve themselves, and second, that ability is malleable and that hard work can lead to high achievement (an incremental theory of intelligence):

> The personal commitment an individual makes to a theory of intelligence is indicative of their self perception. Students who subscribe to an entity theory of intelligence believe that failure is the final point, the outcome of their achievements. They need 'a diet of easy successes' (Dweck, 2000: 15) to confirm their ability and are fearful of learning goals as this involves an element of risk and personal failure. Assessment for these students is an all-encompassing activity that defines them as people. If they fail at the task, they *are* failures. Challenges are a threat to self-esteem as it is through being seen to be successful that these students define themselves. ...Perhaps predictably, those students who believe that intelligence is incremental have little or no fear of failure. A typical response from such a student is 'The harder it gets, the harder I need to try'. These students do not see failure as an indictment of themselves and [can] separate their self-image from their academic achievement. When faced with a challenge, these students are more likely to continue in the face of adversity because they have nothing to prove.
>
> (Clegg, in Peelo and Wareham, 2002, p. 176)

Carole Dweck, more recently in a transcript of an interview which is available online, discusses the inadequacy of 'knowing' in a rapidly changing environment, where new information becomes available every second and is accessible so readily:

> The things you know today are not enough. Facts change, new challenges arise, and so you can never think, 'I know this' and call it done. To do so would assume that the question stays static or that the knowledge set necessary for solving a problem is permanently the same. To say 'I know' is to assume that your ideas are non-revisable, and that the question or problems haven't shifted.
>
> (Dweck, 2013)

Self-beliefs, whether concerning knowledge or intelligence, are remarkably persistent and can interfere powerfully in how a student responds to negative comments in feedback from tutors; Clegg (2002) continues:

> Blaming oneself for failure indicates an incremental theory of intelligence. Students believe they could have done something to avoid failure and will try harder next time. ... In other words, students choose how they interpret feedback and failure so as to lessen the emotional damage. Students deny the validity of teacher, peer and professional judgement if it disagrees with their own self concept.
>
> (Clegg, in Peelo and Wareham, 2002, p. 177)

Positioning the goalposts – designing and using learning outcomes

So far, this chapter has been about *how* learning can be caused to happen. All of this is academic unless we also link it to *what* is intended to be learned, including thinking about why, when and where. That's where learning outcomes come in. Indeed, Biggs and Tang (2011) place intended learning outcomes at the centre of their model of constructive alignment.

Learning outcomes represent the modern way of defining the content of a module or course. The old-fashioned way was simply to list topic headings, and leave it to the imagination of the lecturer exactly what each heading would mean in practice, and how (or indeed if) each part of that would be assessed in due course. Nowadays, expressions of learning outcomes are taken to define the content, level and standard of any course, module or programme. External scrutiny interrogates assessment criteria against learning outcomes to ensure that the assessment is appropriate in level and standard to the course or module. Even more importantly, however, learning outcomes can be vitally useful to students themselves, who (with a little guidance) can be trained to use the expressed learning outcomes as the targets for their own achievement.

Why use learning outcomes?

- Well-expressed statements of intended learning outcomes help students to identify their own targets, and work systematically towards demonstrating their achievement of these targets.
- Learning outcomes are now required by quality assurance bodies, professional bodies, in the review and validation of educational programmes around the world.
- Learning outcomes can provide one of the most direct indicators of the intended level and depth of any programme of learning, helping students and others to choose the most appropriate modules.

Where can learning outcomes be useful to students?

Learning outcomes should not just reside in course validation documentation (though they need to be there in any case). They should also underpin everyday teaching–learning situations. They can be put to good use in the following places and occasions:

1 In student handbooks and programme web pages, so that students can see the way that the whole course or module is broken down into manageable elements of intended achievement, and set their own targets accordingly;
2 At the start of each lecture, for example on a slide, so that students are informed of the particular purposes of the occasion;
3 At the end of each lecture, so that students can estimate the extent to which they have travelled towards being able to achieve the intended outcomes associated with the lecture;
4 At suitable points in the briefing of students for longer elements of their learning, including projects, group tasks, practical work and field work;
5 On each element of resource materials issued (usually online) before, during or after lectures, to reinforce the links between the content of the session and students' intended learning;
6 On tasks and exercises, and briefings to further reading, so that students can see the purpose of the work they are intended to do;
7 On the first few screens of each online learning sequence that students study independently (or in groups).

Designing and using learning outcomes

It is natural enough that professional people such as lecturers may feel some resistance to having the content of their teaching 'pinned down' by pre-expressed statements of intended learning outcome. However, the rationale for using them is so strong that we need to look at some practical pointers which will help even those who don't believe in them to be able to design them reasonably successfully. It is in the particular public context of linking learning-expressed outcomes to assessment criteria that most care needs to be taken. The following suggestions are based on many workshops I have run helping lecturers to put into clear, everyday words the gist of their intentions regarding the learning they intend to be derived from a particular lecture, or a practical exercise, or a tutorial, or students' study of a journal paper, an online resource and so on – *each and every* element which makes up a programme of study.

1 **Work out exactly what you want students to be able to do by the end of each defined learning element.** Even when you're working with a module that is already expressed in terms of learning outcomes, it is often worth thinking again about your exact intentions, and working out how these connect together for different parts of students' learning.

2 **Keep thinking in terms of evidence.** Learning outcomes essentially should point towards the evidence of achievement needed to show that they've been successfully mastered. When students know what they're going to be expected to show for their achievement, they're much more likely to get there.

3 **Link the evidence of achievement of learning outcomes strongly to assessment.** Whether the assessment is in the form of traditional exams, online activities or ongoing coursework, it is important that students themselves can see how the learning outcomes spell out their targets for achievement.

4 **Make the outcomes personal.** Don't say, for example, 'students will be expected to…'. It's much better to use the word 'you' when referring to students. 'When we've completed this lecture, you should be able to compare and contrast particle and wave models of radiation' is better than stating 'the expected learning outcome of this lecture is that students will …'. Similarly, use the word 'you' when expressing learning outcomes in student handbooks, web pages, handouts, laboratory briefing sheets, and so on. Students need to feel that learning outcomes are for them – not just for other people.

5 **Work imaginatively with existing learning outcomes.** There may already be externally defined learning outcomes, or they may have been prescribed some time ago when the course or programme was validated. These may, however, be written in language which is not user-friendly or clear to students, and which is more connected to the teaching than to the learning process. You should be able to translate these outcomes, so that they will be more useful to your students.

6 **Match your wording to your students.** The learning outcomes as expressed in course documentation may be off-putting and jargonistic, and may not match the intellectual or language skills of your students. By developing the skills to translate learning outcomes precisely into plain English, you will help the outcomes to be more useful to students, and at the same time it will be easier for you to design your teaching strategy.

7 **Your intended learning outcomes should serve as a map to your teaching programme.** Students and others will look at the outcomes to see if the programme is going to be relevant to their needs or intentions. The level and standards associated with your course will be judged by reference to the stated learning outcomes.

8 **Remember that many students will have achieved at least some of your intended outcomes already.** When introducing the

intended learning outcomes, give credit for existing experience, and confirm that it is useful if some members of the group already have some experience and expertise which they can share with others.

9 **Be ready for the question 'why?'.** It is only natural for students to want to know why a particular learning outcome is being included. Be prepared to illustrate each outcome with some words about the purpose of including it.

10 **Be ready for the reaction 'so what?'.** When students, colleagues, or external reviewers still can't see the point of a learning outcome, they are likely to need some further explanation before they will be ready to take it seriously.

11 **Work out your answers to 'what's in this for me?'.** When students can see the short-term and long-term benefits of gaining a particular skill or competence, they are much more likely to try to achieve it.

12 **Don't promise what you can't deliver.** It is tempting to design learning outcomes that seem to be the answers to everyone's dreams. However, the real test for your teaching will be whether it is seen to enable students to achieve the outcomes. It's important to be able to link each learning outcome to an assessable activity or assignment.

13 **Don't use words such as 'understand' or 'know'.** While it is easy to write (or say) 'when you have completed this module successfully, you will understand the Third Law of Thermodynamics', it is much more helpful to step back and address the questions: 'how will we know that they have understood it?', 'how will they themselves know they have understood it?', and 'what will they be able to do to *show* that they have understood it?'. Replies to the last of these questions lead to much more useful ways of expressing the relevant learning outcomes.

14 **Don't start at the beginning.** It is often much harder to write the outcomes that will be associated with the beginning of a course, and it is best to leave attempting this until you have got into your stride regarding writing outcomes. In addition, it is often much easier

to work out what the 'early' outcomes actually should be once you have established where these outcomes are leading students towards.

15 **Think ahead to assessment.** A well-designed set of learning outcomes should automatically become the framework for the design of assessed tasks. It is worth asking yourself 'how best can I measure this?' for each draft learning outcome. If it is easy to think of how it will be measured, you can normally go ahead and design the outcome. If it is much harder to think of how it could be measured, it is usually a signal that you may need to think further about the outcome, and try to relate it more firmly to tangible evidence that could be assessed.

16 **Keep sentences short.** It is important that your students will be able to get the gist of each learning outcome without having to re-read them several times, or ponder on what they really mean.

17 **Consider illustrating your outcomes with 'for example ...' descriptions.** If necessary, such extra details could be added in smaller print, or in brackets. Such additional detail can be invaluable to students in giving them a better idea about what their achievement of the outcomes may actually amount to in practice.

18 **Test-run your learning outcome statements.** Ask target-audience students 'what do you think this really means?', to check that your intentions are being communicated clearly. Also test your outcomes statements out on colleagues, and ask them whether you have missed anything important, or whether they can suggest any changes to your wording.

19 **Aim to provide students with the whole picture.** Put the student-centred language descriptions of learning outcomes and assessment criteria into student handbooks and module web pages, or turn them into a short self-contained leaflet to give to students at the beginning of the course. Ensure that students don't feel swamped by the enormity of the whole picture! Students need to be guided carefully through the picture in ways that

allow them to feel confident that they will be able to succeed a step at a time.

20 **Don't get hung up too much on performance, standards and conditions** when expressing learning outcomes. For example, don't feel that such phrases as 'on your own', or 'without recourse to a calculator or computer', or 'under exam conditions' or 'with the aid of a list of standard integrals' need to be included in every well-expressed learning outcome. Such clarifications are extremely valuable elsewhere, in published assessment criteria. Don't dilute the primary purpose of a learning outcome with administrative detail.

21 **Don't be trivial!** Trivial learning outcomes support criticisms of reductionism. One of the main objections to the use of learning outcomes is that there can be far too many of them, only some of which are really important.

22 **Don't be bullied into ritualistic module templates.** For example, 'rules' that there will only be three learning outcomes per module are simply silly. Some topics need quite a lot of relatively brief but different learning outcomes to describe the intended learning well, while other topics may only have one or two such outcomes.

23 **Don't try to teach something if you can't think of any intended learning outcome associated with it.** This seems obvious, but it can be surprising how often a teaching agenda can be streamlined and focused by checking that there is some important learning content associated with each element in it, and removing or shortening the rest.

24 **Don't write any learning outcomes that can't (or won't) be assessed.** If it's important enough to propose as an intended learning outcome, it should be worthy of being measured in some way, and it should be *possible* to measure.

25 **Don't design any assessment task or question that is not related to the stated learning outcomes.** If it's important enough to measure, it is only fair to let students know that it is on their learning agenda.

26 **Don't state learning outcomes at the beginning, and fail to return to them.** It's important to come back to them at the end of each teaching–learning element, such as lecture, self-study package, or element of practical work, and so on. Turn them into checklists for students, for example along the lines 'Check now that you feel able to …' or 'Now you should be in a position to …'.

Conclusions about learning

For too long, learning has been considered as a special kind of human activity, requiring its own jargon and vocabulary. It's not! To learn is to be human. Nor does learning require particular kinds of room, desk, silence, or other environmental conditions – learning can happen anywhere. My main point is that *wanting/needing, doing, feedback* and *making sense* are so close to the essence of being human that it's possible to keep these processes firmly in mind when designing educational courses, training programmes, learning resources and open learning materials. Moreover, and more importantly, it's important to ensure that students get lots of opportunity to deepen their learning by *verbalising* it, talking to each other in class and beyond the classroom, putting what they have learned into spoken words. And perhaps crucially, we need to ensure that students have plenty of practice at *assessing* their own – and each other's – learning so that they further deepen their learning by making judgements and applying criteria to evidence of learning. This is perhaps our best chance to help students to link the fundamental factors explored in this chapter to something that is usually inextricably linked to learning: assessment.

Furthermore, we need to remember that learning is done *by* people – not *to* them. In other words, it is useful to use a model of learning which students themselves can understand. Moreover, it is important to use a model of learning which students themselves *believe in*. The *wanting/needing, doing, feedback, making sense, verbalising, assessing* model can easily be introduced to students by asking them the questions used earlier in this chapter, and they then gain a sense of ownership of the model. Similarly, students themselves readily identify with the competence–uncompetence model illustrated in this chapter, and find it helpful in taking more control of their own learning. It often comes as a pleasant surprise and a welcome relief that there is not something mystical or magical about how people learn.

Having paid due regard to *how* students (and of course we ourselves) learn, it's vital to become very skilled at putting into clear, unambiguous words our descriptions of *what* is to be learned. Writing learning outcomes is not an activity that can be done off the cuff. Expressions of intended learning outcome need to be drafted, edited, discussed, refined, and continuously reviewed, if we are to define our curriculum in ways which will stand up to the increasing levels of external scrutiny of our professional practice.

Learning is about human achievement. Students are at the heart of learning – all learning can be regarded as student-centred (sadly not all teaching is student-centred!). For achievement to be recognised and accredited, it has to be evidenced. Our closest encounters with students are usually when we try to measure their achievement, and provide feedback to them to help them to develop it even further. That's why the next chapter is on assessment and feedback – whatever else we do, we need to get these right if we're going to do students' learning justice.

Chapter 2

Designing assessment and feedback to enhance learning

On assessment:

> Assessment of student learning is a fundamental function of higher education. It is the means by which we assure and express academic standards and has a vital impact on student behaviour, staff time, university reputations, league tables and, most of all, students' future lives. The National Student Survey (in the UK), despite its limitations, has made more visible what researchers in the field have known for many years: assessment in our universities is far from perfect.
>
> (HEA, 2012, p. 7)

> Assessment is a central feature of teaching and the curriculum. It powerfully frames how students learn and what students achieve. It is one of the most significant influences on students' experience of higher education and all that they gain from it. The reason for an explicit focus on improving assessment practice is the huge impact it has on the quality of learning.
>
> (Boud and Associates, 2010, p. 1)

And on feedback:

> Higher education teachers are often frustrated by the modest impact feedback has in improving learning. The status of feedback deserves to be challenged on the grounds that it is essentially about telling. For students to become self-sustaining producers of high quality intellectual and professional goods, they must be equipped to take control of their own learning and performance. How can students become better at monitoring the emerging quality of their work during actual production? Opening up the assessment agenda and liberating the making of judgments from the strictures of preset criteria provide better prospects for developing mature independence in learning.
>
> (Sadler, 2013b)

Intended outcomes of this chapter

When you've explored the ideas in this chapter, and tried out the most appropriate ones in the context of your own teaching and assessment, you should be better able to:

- design assessment processes and instruments which will be integral to your students' learning;
- reduce the assessment burden on yourself and on your students;
- interrogate your assessment processes, practices and instruments to ensure that they are valid, reliable, authentic and transparent;

- give more and better feedback to more students in less time;
- diversify the assessment processes and instruments you use, so that the same students are not repeatedly disadvantaged by just a few of these;
- involve students in appropriate elements of their own assessment, to deepen further their learning.

This is the longest chapter in the *Toolkit*. This is partly because most lecturers actually spend far more time marking students' work and designing feedback for them, than they spend on preparing and giving lectures. But it's also because there is nothing more important than assessment – if we get that wrong we damage students' futures. And getting assessment and feedback right are the hardest things we do. The chapter is therefore divided into four main parts as follows:

1 *Putting assessment and feedback into perspective:* exploring the implications of some of what we can learn from the huge literature of evidence-based practice around assessment.
2 *Pros and cons of sixteen assessment processes:* a detailed comparison of a range of different ways to go about assessing students' evidence of achievement of intended learning outcomes, including a detailed and critical probe into essays and exams.
3 *Making formative feedback work:* a discussion of various ways of going about helping students to benefit from feedback on their assessed work.
4 *Involving students in their own assessment:* rounding off much of what has been discussed in this chapter and the previous one, with some suggestions for getting students to deepen their learning by being involved in their own and each other's assessment, using self- and peer-assessment.

The chapter also contains two essays you can try your hand at marking, a quiz about what exams really measure, and various other tools which may help you to reflect on your own choices of assessment processes.

Putting assessment and feedback into perspective

This is probably the most important chapter in this *Toolkit*, and addresses the most important and intimate interactions of lecturers and students: assessment and feedback. Often, in fact, lecturers spend more time and energy on assessing students' work and providing feedback for students, than on preparing and delivering teaching. I am therefore starting the chapter with some detailed references to some of the most important recent publications about assessment and feedback, before we begin a point-by-point exploration of what we can do to live up to some of the recommendations which have been made about radically overhauling assessment in higher education.

Whether we think of ourselves as lecturers, or teachers, or facilitators of learning, the most important thing we do for our students is to assess their work. This is why, in this book, I have gone straight into assessment after thinking about learning. It is in the final analysis the assessment we do that determines their diplomas, degrees, and future careers. One of the most significant problems with assessment is that just about all the people who do it have already survived having it done to them. This can make us somewhat resistant to confronting whether it was, when we experienced it at the receiving end, valid, fair, authentic and transparent, and explains why so many outdated forms of assessment still permeate higher education practice today.

Over the last decade, many of us have seen our assessment workload grow dramatically, as we work with increasing numbers of students, who are ever more diverse. Consequently, the time we have available to devote to assessing the evidence of achievement arising from each student has reduced. Even those methods and approaches which used to work satisfactorily with relatively small numbers of students are now labouring as we try to extend them to a mass higher education context. It is therefore more important than ever to review the way we design and implement our assessment.

Brown and Glasner began the conclusion of their edited collection *Assessment Matters in Higher Education* with the words:

> Assessment does matter. It matters to students whose awards are defined by the outcomes of the assessment process; it matters to those who employ the graduates of degree and diploma programmes; and it matters to those who do assessing. Ensuring that assessment is fair, accurate and comprehensive – and yet manageable for those doing it – is a major challenge. It is a challenge which has been grappled with by many … Despite the fact that there is a considerable body of international research about assessment and related issues, we experiment largely in ignorance of the way others have effected positive change, and we have limited opportunity to learn from the lessons of others.
>
> (Brown and Glasner, 1999)

Their book is a good place from which to work backwards through the literature on innovative assessment during the last decade of the twentieth century, and more recently Knight and Yorke (2003) explore in depth some of the things that are still going wrong in assessment at the opening of the present century, and the collection edited by Peelo and Wareham (2002) confronts both the experiences of students who fail, and the ways in which assessment in higher education can be regarded as failing students.

But even now, we have not learned the lessons which are presently available from a very substantial literature on how best to design assessment and feedback. In *A marked improvement,* published in 2012 by the Higher Education Academy in the UK, collecting together the wisdom and experience of a distinguished group of experts on assessment, the following warning is sounded:

> Assessment practices in most universities have not kept pace with the vast changes in the context, aims and structure of higher education. They can no longer do justice to the outcomes we expect from a university education in relation to wide-ranging knowledge, skills and employability. In a massified higher education sector where tutor–student ratios have gradually been eroded, students can remain confused about what is expected of them in assessment. Efforts to make this transparent through learning outcomes, assessment criteria and written feedback have proved no substitute for tutor–student interaction and newer groups of students are particularly likely to need this contact.
>
> (HEA, 2012, p. 7)

In Chapter 1 of this *Toolkit*, I looked at feedback as a fundamental process underpinning successful learning. Indeed, feedback on not-yet-successful learning can be even more important, as learning by trial and error is a perfectly valid way to learn. Unfortunately, the assessment culture within which higher education systems currently work tend to reward successful learning with credit, and to equate not-yet-successful learning with failure. The accompanying feedback culture tends all too often to take the form of giving students critical feedback when things go wrong, and precious little comment when things go right. In this situation, the feedback which students receive can be almost as damaging to their motivation as the label of failure that we pin on their not-yet-successful learning.

My overall aim in this chapter is to challenge your thinking on how best to assess students' learning, and how to optimise the impact of our feedback on students' learning – whether that learning has proved successful or not. I hope too to provide food for thought to enable you to confront the difficulties in order to move towards making assessment demonstrably fair, valid, authentic and reliable. As a prelude to this chapter, I would like to share some overarching thoughts and questions about teaching, learning and assessment, and the relationships between these processes. Then I will outline some 'concerns' about unseen written examinations, and about continuous assessment. The remainder of this chapter is intended to offer some thoughts about sixteen particular forms of assessment, each with its pros and cons, and with some suggestions for making each work better, to improve student learning.

What are the main purposes of assessment?

The UK Quality Assurance Agency for Higher Education preface the chapter on 'Assessment of students and the recognition of prior learning' of the *UK Quality Code for Higher Education* with this explanation:

> Assessment is a complex topic since it involves two distinct aspects. First, it forms an essential element of the learning process. Students learn both from assessment activities and from their interaction with staff about their performance in those activities. This interaction has two elements: a focus on their learning and the extent to which that has been demonstrated in the assessment, and a focus on furthering their learning, which may itself subsequently be assessed. The latter element is often referred to as 'feedforward'.
>
> Second, it is the means by which academic staff form judgements as to what extent students have achieved the intended learning outcomes of a programme, or of an element of a programme. These judgements form the basis for the grading of student performance through the allocation of marks, grades and (where applicable) classification, and (provided the learning outcomes have been met) for the award of the credit or qualification to which the programme leads.
>
> (QAA, 2013, p. 3)

This neatly shows that assessment and feedback need to be driving learning in appropriate directions, but assessment also needs to be capable of being the basis for the achievement of standards and the award of qualifications. Ideally, these two purposes need to be served at the same time, but some of the problems experienced with assessment are when the two purposes are not addressed in harmony. Boud et al. (2010) go further in their influential publication *Assessment 2020: Seven propositions for assessment reform in higher education* by proposing that students themselves should be involved in assessment much more intimately and productively than has been done in the past, and that assessment is not only the business of academics. They propose that getting students involved in assessing is a prerequisite for enabling them to produce work of optimum quality as follows:

> Assessment is the making of judgements about how students' work meets appropriate standards. Teachers, markers and examiners have traditionally been charged with that responsibility. However, students themselves need to develop the capacity to make judgements about both their own work and that of others in order to become effective continuing learners and practitioners.
>
> Assessment plays a key role in both fostering learning and the certification of students. However, unless it first satisfies the *educational* purpose of ensuring students can identify high quality work and can relate this knowledge to their own work, the likelihood that they will reach high standards themselves is much reduced.
>
> (Boud et al., p. 1)

Throughout this chapter, I suggest ways of helping students get their heads around how assessment works, not only so that they can optimise their performance in various assessment contexts, but also so that they can deepen their learning while in education, and far beyond.

The language of assessment

In any discussions of assessment, most of the following words appear: validity, reliability, authenticity, transparency and inclusiveness. It's worth explaining briefly a few of the key terms relating to assessment at this point. A fuller description of many of these terms is provided shortly, under the heading 'Values for assessment'.

- *Validity* is about whether the particular assessment format under consideration is the most appropriate for the intended purpose. In other words, is it the best way of measuring evidence of achievement of the related intended learning outcomes?
- *Reliability* is about how well different assessors would agree on the mark or grade awarded for a particular piece of students' work. This is also, of course, about *fairness* and indeed *justice* as perceived by students and others.
- *Authenticity* is about how well the assessment correlates to the sorts of things students need to be able to do in their career after leaving the educational institution. It's about the *real-world* relevance of the assessment activity.
- *Transparency* is particularly about how well students can see how the assessment works in practice, and how marking occurs. Professional bodies also are keen to see this.
- *Inclusiveness* is about how well the assessment can be taken by a range of candidates with additional learning needs, including dyslexia, dyspraxia and so on. It is about minimising unfair discrimination towards candidates with particular needs.

Alongside these factors, it is important to consider how *manageable* each particular type of assessment proves in practice – in other words how much time it takes for marking and moderation to be done, and indeed how much time and energy it needs from students themselves.

And finally, there's the issue sometimes referred to as *veracity* – in other words, who did it? (In workshops, I can't resist calling this the 'whodunit?' factor!) This is about the extent to which it can be guaranteed that no plagiarism, copying or cheating has occurred. In exams, for example, this issue can (normally) be regarded as 'safe', but in word-processed assessed coursework, reports, dissertations and theses it can be 'unsafe'!

Sally Brown (2015) describes quite graphically the problems we have regarding veracity as follows:

> We need to be confident that the work submitted is the students' own. A chilling anonymous article in the *Times Higher Education* of 1 August 2013 describes the work of a 'freelance ghost-writer' who writes essays and dissertations to order, with little risk of discovery. All writers are carefully vetted by the agency (they must be Oxbridge or elite UK Russell group graduates and submit sample assignments before being accepted for work) and rely mainly on Wikipedia and Google books to write assignments for a pre-specified grade, as outstanding work submitted by a mediocre student would raise suspicion. The ghost writer is well-versed in avoiding plagiarism detection services, which in any case, since these assignments are personalised for each client, are unlikely to show up through Turnitin or other software. Some clients are lazy, others are desperate and yet others know their written English isn't up to scratch to get good marks. From time to time spelling

errors or short poorly written sections are added in, just as a cabinet maker faking antiques will rough up the edges of a piece of furniture to age it.

(Brown, 2015, p.114)

Perhaps it's not all about deliberate unfair conduct, and the ways in which people handle information have changed irreversibly? Rhodri Marsden suggests in a newspaper article:

The learning process is being radically reshaped, to a point where the notion of plagiarism is becoming foggier, and not one that's automatically synonymous with cheating.

(Marsden, 2014)

He also quotes broadcaster Vicky Beeching as having said:

I have recently heard someone refer to the Internet as our 'outboard brain' and now it's surely a question of making a difference in the world by applying that pool of resources.

(Marsden, 2014)

It can be argued that the ready availability of source materials on all subjects imaginable has changed how we regard reference materials. I do not agree that the learning process itself has been 'radically reshaped' however, but agree that how people view other people's work has altered probably irreversibly.

Returning to the wider picture of assessment, in this chapter I offer various practical suggestions regarding how assessment can be improved, particularly so that assessment can be:

- more *valid,* measuring that which we really intend to measure, rather than 'ghosts' of students' real learning;
- more *reliable* and *consistent,* moving away from the subjectivity that can cause assessment to be unfair;
- more *transparent,* so that students know where the goalposts are, and so that external reviewers can see clear links between intended learning outcomes as spelled out in course documentation, and assessment criteria applied to students' work;
- more *authentic,* bridging the gap between what students do in assessed contexts at university, and what they need to do in the world outside when in employment;
- more *diverse,* so that individual students are not disadvantaged unduly by particular forms of assessment;
- more *manageable,* both for our students and for ourselves;
- more useful in terms of *feedback,* so that students' learning is enhanced;
- more successful in promoting *deep* learning, so that students get a firmer grasp of the important theories and concepts underpinning their learning.

Values for assessment

The ten values described below can be regarded as a framework to ensure that assessment is fit for purpose both for students themselves and for those involved in assessing. As will be seen throughout this chapter, these values are quite difficult at times to achieve in practice, and some of the most widely-used forms of assessment fall significantly short regarding some of the values proposed here. Also, sometimes a given form of assessment proves able to live up to *some* of the values, but at the expense of other values.

Assessment should be valid. Assessment should measure evidence of achievement of the intended learning outcomes in the best way possible. It should assess what it is that you really want to measure. For example, when attempting to assess problem-solving skills, the assessment should not be dependent on the quality and style of the production of written reports on problem solving, but on the quality of the solutions devised.

1 **Assessment should be reliable.** This is essentially about standards, fairness and justice. If we can get the task briefings, assessment criteria and marking schemes right, there should be good inter-assessor reliability (when more than one assessor marks the work), as well as good intra-assessor reliability (assessors should come up with the same results when marking the same work on different occasions). All assignments in a batch should be marked to the same standard. (This isn't the same as the strange notion of benchmarking, which implies that assignments should hit the same standards in every comparable course in existence – which proves to be an interesting but quite unachievable idea.)

2 **Assessment should be transparent.** Students should know how it works, preferably by having become well-practised at applying assessment criteria on their own and each other's work. There should be no hidden agendas. There should be no nasty surprises for students. Students should not be playing the game 'guess what's in our assessors' minds'. Students should also know what can be expected in line with the intended learning outcomes as published in their handbooks and course web pages, and the links between these outcomes and the assessment criteria should be plain to see by students themselves (as well as by external scrutineers such as professional bodies, or quality assurance agencies).

3 **Assessment should be authentic.** Assessment should link as far as is reasonably practicable to the sorts of activities which students may expect to meet in the wider world of employment, and under conditions relating to day-to-day performance in the profession or vocation towards which they are heading. Assessment should not be 'artificial hoops to jump through' on the way to a qualification.

4 **Assessment should motivate students to learn.** It should not be something they fear or dread. Assessment should help them to structure their learning continuously during their studies, not just in a few critical weeks before particular assessment climaxes. Students should not be driven towards surface or 'reproductive' learning because of the ways their learning is to be assessed. They should not find themselves 'clearing their minds of the last subject, in order to make room for the next subject'. Assessment should allow students to self-assess and monitor their progress throughout a course, and help them to make informed choices about what to learn, how to learn it, and how best to evidence the achievement of their learning.

5 **Assessment should be inclusive.** Students should have equivalence of opportunities to succeed even if their backgrounds or experiences are not identical. Students should not be disadvantaged by particular learning needs, or different educational history. To make assessment inclusive often means that reasonable adjustments should be made to particular assessments to cater for students with special needs, and allow them to evidence their achievement of the intended learning outcomes in ways that are suitable for them.

6 **Assessment overall should be sufficiently diverse, not to disadvantage students who do not cope well with one particular form of assessment.** Each and every form of assessment disadvantages *some* students. Some thrive on exams, some on essays, some on oral presentations, some on problem-solving, and so on. There should be sufficient variety in the bigger picture of assessment to allow all students opportunities to show their learning under optimal conditions.

7 **Assessment should be formative – even when it is primarily intended to be**

summative. Assessment is a time-consuming process for all concerned, so it seems like a wasted opportunity if it is not used as a means of letting students know how they are doing, and how they can improve. Assessment that is mainly summative in its function (for example when only a number or grade is given) gives students very little information, other than frequently confirming their own prejudices about themselves.

8 **Assessment should be timely.** There is a great deal of research evidence that students benefit greatly by having some early feedback on how they are doing, and adjust their efforts accordingly. Conversely, if we leave assessment till too late, students who fail are frequently so discouraged that they drop out, or lose motivation.

9 **Assessment should be incremental.** Assessment that occurs only at the end of a learning programme is not much use in providing feedback, and also leads to the 'sudden death' syndrome, where students have no chance to practise before they pass or fail. Ideally, feedback to students should be continuous. There is sense therefore in enabling small units of assessment to build up into a final mark or grade. This avoids surprises, and can be much less stressful than systems when the whole programme rests on performance during a single time-constrained occasion.

Seven propositions for assessment reform: Boud and Associates (2010)

I have already quoted from the underpinning principles of the propositions for assessment reform produced by Boud and a wide range of associates (including notably Royce Sadler whose work I've referred to often in this *Toolkit*, and Gordon Joughin, known for his convincing advocacy of the value of oral assessment compared with written assessment) in Australia in 2010. These propositions are now widely adopted far beyond Australia, as their applicability ranges widely around the English-speaking world. It is worth giving the skeleton of the entire set of seven propositions here, and encouraging readers to download the whole document (it is only four pages) for the supporting detail and for suggestions about how to go about addressing the respective proposed reforms. Boud et al. propose that:

Assessment has most effect when...

1 **Assessment is used to engage students in learning that is productive**
   - assessment is designed to focus students on learning;
   - assessment is recognised as a learning activity that requires engagement on appropriate tasks.

2 **Feedback is used to actively improve student learning**
   - feedback is informative and supportive and facilitates a positive attitude to future learning;
   - students seek and use timely feedback to improve the quality of their learning and work;
   - students regularly receive specific information, not just marks and grades, about how to improve the quality of their work.

3 **Students and teachers become responsible partners in learning and assessment**
   - students progressively take responsibility for assessment and feedback processes;
   - students develop and demonstrate the ability to judge the quality of their own work and the work of others against agreed standards;
   - dialogue and interaction about assessment processes and standards are commonplace between and among staff and students.

4 **Students are inducted into the assessment practices and cultures of higher education**
   - assessment practices are carefully structured in early stages of courses to ensure students make a successful transition to university study in their chosen field;

- assessment practices respond to the diverse expectations and experiences of entering students.

5 **Assessment for learning is placed at the centre of subject and programme design**
   - assessment design is recognised as an integral part of curriculum planning from the earliest stages of course development;
   - assessment is organised holistically across subjects and programmes with complementary integrated tasks.

6 **Assessment for learning is a focus for staff and institutional development**
   - professional and scholarly approaches to assessment by academic staff are developed, deployed, recognised and rewarded by institutions;
   - assessment practices and the curriculum should be reviewed in the light of graduate and employer perceptions of the preparedness of graduates;
   - assessment of student achievements is judged against consistent national and international standards that are subject to continuing dialogue, review and justification within disciplinary and professional communities.

7 **Assessment provides inclusive and trustworthy representation of student achievement**
   - interim assessment results used for feedback on learning and progress do not play a significant role in determining students' final grades;
   - evidence of overall achievement to determine final grades is based on assessment of integrated learning;
   - certification accurately and richly portrays graduates' and students' achievements to inform future careers and learning.

(Boud and Associates, 2010, pp. 2–3)

This paper by Boud and Associates is having major impact not least because its authors cover all the main institutions in Australia and several from other parts of the world; all are practitioners who are very closely involved with the development of assessment and feedback in their institutions, and are regarded as 'knowing what they are talking about' when it comes to assessment and feedback in higher education. It is remarkable how well this paper links to other developments in the UK and elsewhere on 'assessment *for* learning' including the work of the UK Centres for Excellence in Assessment at Northumbria University and Oxford Brookes University. All of these works agree about putting students at the centre of assessment, rather than them being passive recipients at the end of assessment processes.

A view about assessment from students themselves

In the UK, the National Union of Students published the 'NUS Charter on Assessment and Feedback' also in 2010. This contains ten principal recommendations on assessment, each with explanatory detail as reproduced below (the full document can be downloaded from http://www.nusconnect.org.uk/asset/news/6010/FeedbackCharter-toview.pdf).

1 **Formative assessment and feedback should be used throughout the programme.** Assessment should be used as part of the learning process, as well as a tool to measure understanding and application. Formative assessment and feedback is critical to the development of learning and should be integrated into the curriculum in a strategic way. You should consider how to capture and formalise ongoing feedback in practical courses such as art and design. Wherever appropriate, there should be formative feedback before the assessment deadline for taught postgraduate students and for undergraduate dissertations.

2 **Students should have access to face-to-face feedback for at least the first piece of assessment each academic year.** For most

students, a discussion about their work is the most productive form of feedback they can receive. At the start of each academic year, it is crucial that students are given an opportunity to discuss their work with a tutor to enable them to set goals for the coming year. As well as helping students to develop their learning, this can act as a progression monitoring tool for the institution. If face-to-face feedback is impossible (e.g. due to distance or part-time learning), technology can be used to facilitate a discussion between tutor and student.

3 **Receiving feedback should not be exclusive to certain forms of assessment.** Traditionally, summative feedback is usually only given on written essays and some forms of practical work. But students need feedback on all forms of assessment they come across in order to develop their learning. In the recent NUS/HSBC Student Experience Report, 90 per cent of students say they would like feedback on exams, compared with only 12 per cent who currently receive written comments and 9 per cent who receive verbal feedback. Most courses rely on exams as the summative assessment – it is therefore important that students receive feedback on these, especially in exams prior to finals.

4 **Feedback should be timely.** Timely feedback is a key concern of students, with the NUS/HSBC Student Experience Report showing that almost a quarter of students have to wait more than five weeks to receive feedback. Students should usually receive personalised feedback within three weeks of the assessment submission deadline. There could also be generalised group feedback on the key learning areas that affect most students within one week of the assessment.

5 **Students should be provided with a variety of assessment methods.** In many courses there is too much reliance on exams or long essays as the sole form of assessment. There should be greater innovation in assessment, including the use of technology, and students should be involved in helping to design their own assessment. Similarly, not all subject disciplines use peer and self-reflective feedback – these methods should also be encouraged.

6 **There should be anonymous marking for all summative assessment.** NUS research shows that where anonymous marking has been introduced there has been an improvement in the marks of women, black and Asian students and among some other student groups. Anonymous marking provides reassurance for students and staff against the perception of discrimination. Where anonymous marking is not possible, especially in the arts, there should be stringent measures to blind double mark, or use external examiners.

7 **Students should be able to submit assessment electronically.** While this will not be possible in every case, this increased flexibility will support part-time and distance learners as well as other non-traditional students, such as those with caring responsibilities or those who commute to university. Ultimately, the flexibility of electronic submission will benefit all students and will help to ensure that assessment methods respond to the changing expectations of digitally-literate students.

8 **Students should be supported to critique their own work.** Students should not be overly reliant on feedback from tutors. One of the key skills developed in higher education is the ability to critique, and students should be supported to be able to review their own work and that of fellow students. Developing students' abilities to peer review and self-reflect is an important skill for future employment, as well as deepening their own learning.

9 **Programme induction should include information on assessment practices and understanding marking criteria.** Assessment standards and marking criteria are not readily understood by students. Students should be given an induction on what is expected of them academically on their course, in order for them to produce high-quality work. Some students

can be unwittingly engaged in academic misconduct, or plagiarism, through simple misunderstandings of what is expected, and how to reference properly. Good inductions and study skills sessions prior to major assessment would aid students' understanding of these issues. Academic misconduct guidelines could also be translated into the languages of any large student groups at an institution.

10 **Students should be given the choice of format for feedback.** Students want feedback in a variety of formats, including verbal, written and electronic. At the start of the year students should also be able to state their preferred form of summative feedback. This provides a useful focus for a meeting with a personal tutor, while giving students a choice in the form of feedback; and making the feedback more physically accessible to them. This approach should ensure that all students, no matter whether they are full-time, part-time or distance learners, will have easy access to their feedback. Regardless of format, the feedback should always be written in plain English, and be legible and clear.

The views of students are interesting, not only in how strongly they match many of the propositions of Boud et al., but in some of the other things that students include in their requests about assessment and feedback. It is particularly noteworthy that they say 'assessment standards and marking criteria are not readily understood by students'.

Radically overhauling and re-designing assessment and feedback in higher education is a daunting task, but HEA (2012) express desirable benefits which may be achieved thereby, not least by increasing the proportion of formative assessment and feedback:

> Where programmes plan for more formative assessment and feedback, there is a better chance that a greater proportion of students pass modules at their first attempt, thereby saving staff time in relation to demand for extra support, resits, appeals and complaints. Improved pass rates and reduced attrition bring obvious financial benefits for institutions and positive outcomes for students. Overall, a radical review of assessment can bring cost savings and better use of teaching resources.
>
> (HEA, 2012, p. 11)

Having 'scoped the task' of overhauling the design of assessment in higher education, let us now proceed to a step-by-step analysis of some of the things we need to address, starting with establishing a sound rationale for assessment.

Why should we assess? A rationale for assessment

Staff and students spend a great deal of time and energy on matters linked to assessment, and we need to keep in mind a variety of reasons for doing so. This can help to clarify which particular methods are best suited for our purposes, as well as helping to identify who is best placed to carry out the assessment, and when and where to do it. Some of the most common reasons for assessing students are listed below. You might find it useful to look at these, deciding which are the most important ones in the context of your own discipline, with your own students, at their particular level of study.

1 **To guide students' development.** The feedback students receive helps them to build on their strengths, and address weaknesses. Many forms of formative assessment can be useful to students to help to diagnose errors or weaknesses, and enable students to rectify mistakes. Nothing is more demotivating than struggling on getting bad marks and not knowing what

is going wrong. Effective assessment lets students know where any problems lie, and provides them with information to help them to put things right. The more effective and timely we can make the feedback we provide, the greater is the likelihood that students will adjust their learning appropriately.

2 **To define standards.** The best way to estimate the standard of an educational programme is to look at the intended learning outcomes, and the specifications of evidence of achievement expected from students. Then look at the various ways in which students' achievement is measured. The standard of the course is most closely shown by the assessment tasks, and illustrated by the quality of students' work in response to such tasks.

3 **To allow students to make timely and realistic decisions about whether they are up to the demands of a course or module.** Students sometimes choose a module because they are interested in part of the subject, but then find that substantial parts of the module are too difficult for them, or not interesting enough. When the assessment profile of the module is clearly spelled out in advance, students can see how much the part they are interested in actually counts in the overall picture, and can be alerted to other important things they may need to master to succeed in the module.

4 **To allow students to check out how well they are developing as learners.** Assessment does not just test subject-specific skills and knowledge, but provides an ongoing measure of how well students are developing their learning skills and techniques. Students themselves can use assessment opportunities to check out how they are developing their study skills, and can make adjustments as appropriate.

5 **To classify or grade students' achievements.** There are frequently good reasons for us to classify the level of achievements of students individually and comparatively within a cohort. Assessment methods to achieve this will often be summative and involve working out numerical marks or letter grades for students' work of one kind or another. However, continuous assessment

processes can address classifying or grading students' achievement, yet continue to provide opportunities for formative developmental feedback along the way.

6 **To give us feedback on how our teaching is going.** If there are generally significant gaps in student achievement, this indicates deficiencies in the learning which has happened, and can point toward shortcomings in the teaching of the areas concerned. Most experienced teachers in higher education can give accounts of how they have developed their teaching approaches to address matters which arose in earlier assessment episodes.

7 **To cause students to get down to some serious learning.** While high-quality learning can be achieved in the absence of any forthcoming assessment, in practice most students are caused to put effort into their learning when preparing for their evidence of achievement to be measured in one way or another.

8 **To add variety to students' learning experience.** Utilising a range of different assessment methods spurs students to develop different skills and processes. This can promote more effective – and enjoyable – teaching and learning, and can help us to ensure that all students can demonstrate their strengths in those assessment contexts they find most comfortable and appropriate for them.

9 **To help us to structure our teaching and constructively align learning outcomes to assessments.** While 'teaching to the exam' is regarded as poor practice, 'learning for the exam' can still be useful learning! Assessment can help both staff and students focus on what is important, prioritising learning outcomes and consolidating the expectations of evidence of achievement of the outcomes.

10 **To allow students to place themselves in the overall class picture.** Students can get a great deal of feedback from each other – often far more than their teachers can give them. Assessment can give students a frame of reference, whereby they can compare their achievements with those of their peers. Assessment helps them to find out how they are placed in the cohort, and can

motivate them to make adjustments to get into a better position.

11 **To provide statistics for the course, or for the institution.** Educational institutions need to provide funding bodies and quality assurance agencies with data about student achievement and progression, and assessment systems need to take account of the need for appropriate statistical information. In the present 'age of league tables' the end-use of at least some of the statistical information needs to be kept in mind.

12 **To lead towards a licence to practise.** In some professions, a degree or other qualification is taken as a measure of fitness to practise. It then becomes particularly important to ensure that validity and authenticity are achieved in the design of the assessment processes and instruments.

Concerns about assessment: we can't go on like this!

Boud et al. (2010) are in no doubt: the status quo in assessment is not an option. In their words:

> Universities face substantial change in a rapidly evolving global context. The challenges of meeting new expectations about academic standards in the next decade and beyond mean that assessment will need to be rethought and renewed.
>
> (Boud et al., 2010, p. 1)

Before it is possible to persuade people to review what they are presently doing, and to consider implementing changes, it is useful to take a critical look at whether current practices actually work as well as we think they do. Therefore I continue this chapter with a critical review of the two principal areas of assessment which most students encounter: traditional time-constrained, unseen written exams, and assessed coursework. In each case I will list some general concerns, starting with concerns about the links between these kinds of assessment and the factors underpinning successful learning drawn from Chapter 1 of this book: wanting to learn, needing to learn, learning-by-doing, learning through feedback and making sense of what has been learned, and also the need for students themselves to gain experience in *verbalising* and *assessing* their own learning before it is formally assessed by us. For most of the concerns, I will add hints at how the repercussions they cause be ameliorated – or at least confronted.

Finally in this section on 'concerns' I move on briefly to the increasingly prevalent climate of standards and benchmarks, and quote Sadler's (2014) paper positing whether or not attempts to prescribe or define standards are doomed to be futile! However, despite all these concerns and doubts, assessment needs to go on, so later in the chapter I offer a range of practical pointers suggesting how even the most traditional methods of assessment can be put to good use, as well as exploring the pros and cons of a variety of alternative ways of measuring students' evidence of achievement.

Concerns about traditional exams

Much has been written about the weaknesses of traditional examinations – in particular time-constrained unseen written exams. In many subject disciplines, this assessment format seems to be at odds with the most important factors underpinning successful learning. Moreover, there is abundant evidence that even in discipline areas where the subject matter is well defined, and answers to exam questions are either correct or incorrect, assessors still struggle sometimes to make exams valid, reliable, authentic or transparent to students. In disciplines where the subject matter is more discursive, and flexibility exists in how particular questions can be answered well, it can be even harder to achieve demonstrable reliability (and that means fairness) in assessment, even when validity is well achieved.

Overall in higher education at present, with staff time under more pressure than ever before, there is evidence of a drift back to reliance on exams, which have been argued to be one of the more time-efficient and cost-effective methods of assessment, where it is fairly easy to achieve fairness and reliability, and with the added bonus that plagiarism or cheating cause fewer headaches to markers than in many other forms of assessment. However, when one takes into account the time it takes to design, set, mark, moderate, and process the results of exams, I remain sceptical of the time-efficiency of traditional exams compared with many alternative forms of assessment.

Some of the principal concerns that can be expressed about unseen written exams are summarised below. Half of the fourteen concerns below are conflicts between this kind of exam and the seven factors underpinning successful learning which we considered in Chapter 1. It could be said that unseen written exams are diametrically opposed to these factors working successfully. Several of the remaining concerns relate to our own procedures for marking students' exam scripts.

1 **Exams don't do much to increase students' 'want' to learn.** Students often make choices in modular schemes strategically, so that they avoid this kind of assessment if they can. This can lead them to choose subjects in which they are less interested than those which they fear to select because they will be subjected to exams. Ask students for words that come to mind at the mention of exams. Words include 'dread', 'looming', 'fear', 'scared' and 'threat' far more often than 'challenge' or 'pleasure'.

2 **Exams are not often a good way of alerting students to what they really need to learn.** Admittedly, students will often only get down to serious learning when an impending exam causes them to revise actively, but the fact that in unseen exams the actual assessment agenda has to be guessed at rather than worked towards systematically means that the resultant learning can be unfocused, and the assessment judgement becomes too dependent upon the success of the agenda-guessing.

3 **Exams are not ideal occasions for learning-by-doing.** Though students may do a lot of learning *before* formal unseen written examinations, their actual experiences of learning *in* such situations is extremely limited. In other words, a note could be placed on the door of the exam room stating 'exam cancelled; you've already done all the learning that this exam could have caused'! The learning payoff during an assessment element should be considered more – assessment *as* learning rather than mere assessment *of* learning. It is therefore worth our while revisiting our testing processes to search for forms of assessment which are in themselves better learning experiences.

4 **The amount of feedback that students receive about exams is far from optimal.** Most systems require marked exam scripts to be regarded as secret documents, not to be shown to students on any account! It is worth asking what reasons underlie this philosophy. You might have noticed that among the student demands in their charter in 2010 was a request for feedback on exams. It is useful to reconsider the value that students can derive from seeing their marked examinations papers, where it should be possible to be able to demonstrate to students that the examination marking has indeed been reliable, fair and valid. Moreover, the natural process of learning from mistakes should always be accommodated, even when the assessment judgements have already been taken down to be used in evidence against the candidates.

5 **Exams tend not to do much to help students make sense of what they have learned.** While there may be a significant amount of making sense of concepts and theories during the time leading up to exams, the assessment experience itself does little to help students to gain any further deepening of their grasp of these. One of the consequences of modularising the curriculum can be that some subject matter is

introduced too close to an impending exam for the content to be satisfactorily digested.

6 **Written exams don't do much for learning through** *verbalising.* However, practising putting learning into spoken words pays enormous dividends even when the eventual testing is written. We need therefore to encourage students not to study for exams in solitary silence, but to work for at least some of the time explaining answers to likely questions to each other (or anyone else who will listen).

7 **Written exams don't encourage students to learn by** *assessing.* The tendency is for students to do what they can and hope for the best. However, the more we can encourage students to practise making judgements on their answers to typical exam questions, the better they can make similar judgements while they are answering questions in exams. The more they know about how marks are gained and lost, the better they can structure their efforts towards doing written exams successfully.

8 **We mark exam scripts in a rush.** Most staff who mark exams agree that the task usually has to be completed in haste, in preparation for timetabled exam boards. The situation has been worsened by modularisation and semesterisation developments in most institutions, which give tighter turn-round intervals between examinations and progression to the next element of study. While our marking may still be relatively fair and reliable (at best), it can be shocking to students who have spent a great deal of time preparing for unseen written exams to find out that their scripts are marked so hastily.

9 **Unseen written exams can lead to us placing too much emphasis on unimportant factors in candidates' answers.** For example, factors such as quality of handwriting, or neatness of overall presentation of scripts can influence examiners, consciously or subconsciously. Many students nowadays are much more comfortable composing essays or reports using a keyboard, and adjusting their writing on-screen, cutting and pasting to bring their writing to a logical or coherent whole; this is well nigh impossible to do well with pen and paper, against the clock, in a threateningly silent environment. Moreover, there's a factor we don't see but that students know all too well – speed of handwriting.

10 **We're often tired and bored when we mark exam scripts.** Because of the speed of marking, and the pressure to do the task well, we may not be functioning at our best while undertaking the task. Our fairness can suffer. We can suffer from 'halo' effects after marking an excellent answer, and the reverse after marking a poor one.

11 **We're not good at marking objectively.** There is abundant data on the problems both of inter-assessor reliability and intra-assessor reliability, particularly with the more qualitative or discursive kinds of exam answer.

12 **Unseen written exams tend to favour candidates who happen to be skilled at doing exams!** We've created an examinocracy! If we look at exactly what skills are measured by unseen written exams, the most important of these from students' point of view turns out unsurprisingly to be the techniques needed to do unseen written exams, and the same students can get rewarded time after time! This skill may have little to do with the competences we need to help students to develop to become professionals in the subject disciplines they are learning.

13 **Unseen written exams force students into surface learning, and into rapidly clearing their minds of previous knowledge when preparing for the next exam.** Students are encouraged to clear their brains of the knowledge they have stored for each exam in turn. This of course is quite contrary to our real intentions to help students to achieve deep learning.

14 **There are many important qualities which are not tested well by traditional exams.** For example, unseen written exams are limited or useless for measuring teamwork, leadership, and even creativity and lateral thinking, all of which have their parts to play in heading towards graduateness.

Two final concerns are expressed by Gibbs (2010):

> Exams can have the effect of concentrating study into a short intense period at the end of the course with, for example, little study of lecture notes until many weeks after the lecture.
>
> (Gibbs, 2010, p. 10)

> Teachers rarely set tests or exam questions with the deliberate intention of inducing a surface approach, but they do often allow students to accumulate enough marks to pass without ever doing anything more sophisticated. For students, that may be all the encouragement they need.
>
> (Gibbs, 2010, p. 23).

Despite all these concerns, there is a lot we can do to make exams work better or in different ways, for example open-book exams, open-notes exams, time-unconstrained exams, in-tray exams, OSCEs and so on. Some discussion is given later in this chapter, and further developed by Race (2010, 2014).

Enough for the moment about traditional exams; not all is well, however, with continuous assessment either: read on!

Concerns about continuous assessment

Having made a broadside about the limitations of unseen written exams, I have to admit that such exams have advantages as well, particularly that in their own way they can be fair to candidates, and they are not subject to most of the problems of plagiarism, unwanted collaboration, and so on which can affect the assessment of coursework. Let me proceed to further balance the picture by expressing some parallel concerns about continuous assessment – including assessment of essays and reports.

1 **If students are under too much coursework-related pressure, their 'want' to learn is damaged.** When almost everything that students do, as part of their learning, is measured, they naturally adopt strategic approaches to their learning, and only concentrate on those things that are going to be assessed. If some work is recommended as purely for formative purposes or practice, it gets short shrift with students. In many disciplines, we need to ensure that students' assessed coursework is focused on quality of learning, and is not unnecessarily burdensome regarding quantity.

2 **Continuous assessment does not always alert students to important aspects of their need to learn.** For example, when continuous assessment is repetitive in format (too many essays or too many reports), students may indeed become better able to deliver in these formats, but their overall learning is not deepened in ways that could be achieved by matching each assessment format to the nature of the particular achievements of the intended learning outcome intended to be assessed.

3 **The range of learning-by-doing may be too narrow.** For example, repetitive use of formats such as essays and reports narrow the scope of students' learning, and tend to favour inordinately those students who happen to master the skills associated with the format at the expense of other students who have been more successful at learning the subject itself.

4 **Coursework feedback may be eclipsed by marks or grades.** Students pay most attention to their scores or grades when they get back marked work, and often are quite blind to valuable feedback which may accompany their returned work. A way out of this problem is to return students' work with feedback but without grades in the first instance, then get them to self-assess their own grades. Most students' self-assessments (when they are primed with clear assessment criteria, linked

to clear statements defining the intended learning outcomes) are within 5 per cent or one grade point of the tutor's assessment, and it is possible to allow students' own grades or scores to count. It is well worth talking to the few students whose self-assessment is at odds with our own assessment, and alerting them to the blind spots which could have caused them to overestimate the worth of their work, or (this happens more often) to boost their self-esteem by reassuring them that their work was worth more than they believed it to be.

5 **Students may not have the opportunity to make sense of the feedback they receive.** Particularly when there is a delay in getting feedback to students, they may already have moved on to learning other topics, and they don't then make learning from the feedback available to them a priority. Modularisation and semesterisation have both in their own ways contributed to making delays in receiving feedback more significant, related to the overall learning timescales involved. Sometimes students only receive feedback after they've finished a module altogether, and rarely give that feedback more than a passing glance.

6 **Coursework is usually written (or word-processed).** Coursework is still largely dependent on what comes out of a pen or from fingers on keyboards. This can discourage students from the useful learning they might have achieved by *verbalising* their achievement before putting fingers to keyboard or pen to paper.

7 **Even in coursework, students often have little idea how exactly assessors' minds are going to work.** In other words, coursework can contrive to deprive students of the opportunity to learn by *assessing,* applying criteria to their work as they compose it. Involving students in self- and peer-assessing the kinds of work used in assessed coursework can address this concern.

8 **It is now very difficult to detect unwanted collaboration.** Particularly with assignments submitted in word-processed formats, it is difficult if not impossible to detect every instance of plagiarism or copying. Whether marking essays or practical reports, if there are several lecturers or graduate teaching assistants involved in marking them, students who have copied can be quite skilled at making sure that different people mark their respective work, minimising the chance that the collaboration is detected. The most skilful plagiarists will always evade our detection!

9 **Too much of our time may be involved in fairly routine kinds of marking.** In many courses, lecturers continue to try to use the same continuous assessment processes that worked quite well when student numbers were much smaller (or when they themselves were students!). With large numbers of students, it is essential that human assessment and feedback should be reserved for higher-level agendas, and that computer-delivered assessment formats (in those curriculum areas where they can be designed well) should be exploited to provide assessment and feedback on relatively routine matters. There has already been a significant growth in the use of computer-aided assessment (or e-assessment) in many subject disciplines, saving a great deal of assessor time, while (when used well) providing a great deal of feedback to students, often very quickly.

10 **Students may not be aware of the criteria used to assess their work.** When students are practised in interpreting and making use of assessment criteria, the standard of their assessed work rises dramatically. Alerting students to the detail of the assessment agenda is regarded by some staff as a move towards 'spoonfeeding'. However, it can be argued that enabling students to demonstrate their full potential is a desirable goal. Involving students in self-assessment of suitable elements of their own work, and in peer-assessment of appropriate assignments, can help students to gain a substantial understanding of the way that their work is assessed by tutors. Moreover, there is an increased level of expectation that assessment criteria can be closely linked to the achievement of expressed learning outcomes,

and students themselves can make good use of these ways of clarifying the assessment agenda.

11 **Students often get the balance wrong between continuous assessment and exams.** Students feel the pressure to submit coursework by stated deadlines, and may still be working on such work at a late stage in their studies on a particular module, when they would be better advised to cut their losses regarding that coursework and prepare for important exams. This particularly happens when students who fall behind in writing up practical work, continue to try to get this work finished and handed in, when they may be better advised to spend their remaining time making sure that they are well prepared for forthcoming formal exams.

12 **Learning may become driven by assessment, and students may only do those things that are assessed.** Earlier in these concerns, it was mentioned that students tend to adopt strategic approaches to their learning. Such approaches can be made beneficial if the nature and range of the assessed tasks are adjusted to make *all* the learning that students do in their assessed work as relevant as possible to the intended learning outcomes. In particular, it can help to reduce the size of many of the assessments. A well-designed essay plan (for example a mind-map, alongside a short written introduction, and a concise summary or conclusion) can present (say) 90 per cent of the thinking that would have taken ten times as long to write (and to mark) in a full essay.

Once again, Gibbs (2010) neatly sums up an important dimension of the picture as follows:

> It is a common observation of higher education teachers that if coursework is taken away from a module because of resource constraints, then students simply do not do the associated studying; for example students will rarely write unassessed essays. It is argued that you have to assess everything in order to capture students' time and energy. There are several problems with this rationale.
>
> (Gibbs, 2010, p. 5)

Tony Harland (2012) usefully sums up another concern about assessed coursework as follows:

> By and large, higher education has replaced the stress of one final examination with the stress of multiple in-course assessments on top of a smaller exam. We have substituted one intense period of revision with the anxiety that comes from an insidious trickle of small assessments. Contemporary students always seem to have assessment on their mind, whether or not there is an assignment due, an online test to do, an essay, a short mid-term test, a laboratory check-out test and so on. At least the final exam was something that had to be dealt with sometime in the future and this allowed students more space and freedom to study as they wished until that time.
>
> (Harland, 2012, p. 114)

All of these concerns about continuous assessment provide a timely reminder that whatever else we do, the balance between end-point and continuous assessment needs to be achieved with due care, and the *quantity* of assessment may need to be reduced substantially to gain better learning.

Concerns about standards

Sadler (2011) usefully identifies the dilemma as follows:

> The tension between the freedom of academics to grade the achievements of their students without interference or coercion and the prerogative of higher education institutions to control grading

standards is often deliberated by weighing up the authority and rights of the two parties. An alternative approach is to start with an analysis of the characteristics necessary for a system to exhibit integrity in grading academic achievement, and treat the establishment and maintenance of academic standards as a problem to be solved.

(Sadler, 2011, p. 103)

Part of the problem is the freedom of assessors to grade achievements. To some extent this grading is always going to be subjective, and the reliability (fairness) of assessment is always at some degree of risk. In the UK's *QAA Quality Code* (2013), 'Indicator 4' requires of institutions that:

Higher education providers assure themselves that everyone involved in the assessment of student work, including prior learning, and associated assessment processes is competent to undertake their roles and responsibilities.

(QAA, 2013, p. 11)

In their amplification of this Indicator, though QAA hesitate to prescribe directly that academic staff should have had particular training in assessment, however their supporting comments include:

Assessment processes are implemented effectively when all staff involved have the necessary knowledge and skills, have received the appropriate development or training to fulfil their specific role, and are clear about their remit and responsibilities. Higher education providers identify what is appropriate for each role and how competence will be demonstrated, recognising that assessment involves different roles, each of which may be carried out by a variety of staff.

(QAA, 2013, p. 11)

In the present climate where attempts to benchmark assessment standards seem endemic, it is worth pausing to reflect whether this will ever be realistically possible. Royce Sadler (2014) captures the problem very well in his abstract to an online paper 'The futility of attempting to codify academic achievement standards':

Internationally, attempts at developing explicit descriptions of academic achievement standards have been steadily intensifying. The aim has been to capture the essence of the standards in words, symbols or diagrams (collectively referred to as codifications) so that standards can be: set and maintained at appropriate levels; made broadly comparable in different specified contexts; and generally shared and understood better by assessors, academic program directors, students, employers, quality assurance agencies and the public at large. The scale of this practice ranges from rubrics for single assessment tasks to national standards statements used as academic performance benchmarks for graduates from academic programs. A critical analysis shows that the underlying assumptions of this process are fundamentally flawed. Codifications are inherently incapable of meeting the requirements because key terms lack the necessary attributes. A fundamentally different material form of representation is therefore necessary if the original intentions are to be realised.

(Sadler, 2014, p. 273)

One of my aims in this important chapter of the *Toolkit* is to help you to be more aware of many of the problems and challenges involved in designing fit-for-purpose assessment, both to meet institutions' obligations and to do students justice. We continue by putting sixteen forms of assessment under the microscope in terms of validity, reliability, authenticity, manageability – and the extent to which they allow feedback to help learners to improve.

Pros and cons of sixteen assessment processes

Assessment can take many forms, and it can be argued that the greater the diversity in the methods of assessment, the fairer assessment is to students. Each and every one of the forms of assessment I consider in this chapter can be claimed to disadvantage those students who do not give of their best in the particular circumstances in which it is used. Therefore, diversifying assessment so that students experience a range of assessment methods evens out the situation, and increases the chance that all students will be able to demonstrate their best performance in at least some of the formats. The art of assessing therefore needs to embrace several different kinds of activity. I would like to encourage colleagues to broaden the range of assessment processes (and to reduce sometimes quite dramatically the *size* of at least some individual assessments – for example a 300-word argument instead of a 3,000-word essay, and so on), and I have tried to provide practical suggestions about how to maximise the benefits of each of a number of methods I have addressed below.

It must be added, however, that *rehearsal* is critically important to students encountering any new or different kinds of assessment from those to which they have become accustomed. Students develop their own ways of coping with, and preparing for the kinds of assessment they already know. To show themselves at their best in any unfamiliar kinds of assessment, they need time to adjust their preparation approaches, as well as the ways in which they provide evidence of their learning in these different circumstances.

In the next part of this chapter, I will look systematically at each of sixteen forms of assessment, listing a few advantages, some disadvantages, and I will offer some suggestions (sometimes a few, sometimes a lot) for making the particular assessment device work better. None of these lists should be considered as anything more than a starting point. Nor should the sixteen kinds of assessment I happen to have chosen be taken as representative of a sufficiently diverse range of assessment processes. Some of this discussion is further developed in Race et al. (2005), Brown and Race (2012) and particularly now in Race (2014).

I Traditional unseen, time-constrained written exams

Traditional unseen written exams still make up the lion's share of assessment in higher education, though in some disciplines, for example mathematics, engineering and sciences courses, this situation is considerably balanced by the inclusion of practical work, projects and other contributions to the evidence on the basis of which we grade and classify students. Despite growing concern about the validity and fairness of traditional exams, for all sorts of reasons they will continue to play a large part in the overall assessment picture. Despite many concerns about exams, I have tried in the following discussion to suggest a number of ways that the use of exams can be improved. I have given more suggestions about setting exam questions than for setting any of the other types of assessment explored in this chapter as, in general, good practice in writing exam questions overlaps with, or extends across, many of the other types.

Nowadays, this kind of exam does not have to be constrained to handwritten answers, but keyboards and computers can be used, and with suitable invigilation such exams can be conducted online. With computers or online environments there are of course significant complications regarding access to information or data from outside the exam, and typing speeds and accuracy may interfere with performance.

Advantages

- *Exams are relatively high on transparency.* Most students have experienced them before, and have a reasonable idea of how they work, and indeed have fared relatively successfully with exams to get into higher education in the first place.
- *Exams can be reasonably high on reliability.* Where rigorous moderation of marking is in place, and where high-quality marking schemes are designed and adhered to, the fairness of exam marks can be reasonably well assured.
- *Relatively economical.* Exams can be more cost-effective than many of the alternatives (though this depends on the duration of the exams, and on economies of scale when large numbers of students are examined, and also on how much time and money needs to be spent to ensure appropriate moderation of assessors' performance). However, any form of assessment can only be truly said to be cost-effective if it is actually *effective* in its contribution to students' learning.
- *They don't have to be long!* In higher education it is still common to have exams of two or three hours duration, but with different kinds of structured question it is possible to have a much shorter exam and still test a great deal.
- *Equality of opportunity.* Exams are demonstrably fair in that students have all the same tasks to do in the same way and within the same timescale. (However, not all things are equal in exams – ask any hay-fever sufferer, or candidate with additional needs such as dyslexia, or with menstrual problems.)
- *We know whose work it is.* It is easier to be sure that the work being assessed was done by the candidate, and not by other people. For this reason, exams can be considered to be an 'anti-plagiarism assessment' device, and although there are instances of attempting to cheat in exam rooms, good invigilation practice and well-planned design of the room (and the questions themselves) can eliminate most cheating.
- *Teaching staff are familiar with (long!) written exams.* Familiarity does not always equate with validity, but the base of experience that teaching staff already have with traditional unseen exams means that at least some of the problems arising from them are well known, and sometimes well addressed.
- *Exams cause students to get down to learning.* Even if the assessment method has problems, it certainly causes students to engage deliberately with the subject matter being covered by exams, and this can be worthwhile particularly for those more difficult topics where students may not otherwise spend the time and energy that is needed to make sense of the subject matter.

Disadvantages

- *Written time-constrained exams are often 'low' regarding validity.* In many subjects, exams are not the best way of getting from students evidence of achievement of the intended learning outcomes – oral assessment can be much more valid. However, in some subjects (maths, science, engineering), exams can be a valid way of allowing students to demonstrate their skills at problem-solving and numerical manipulation.
- *Speed of handwriting and legibility may be what is really measured.* In an age where far less than formerly is handwritten, and where most writing is done through a keyboard, handwritten exams may discriminate significantly against those who are not used to writing with a pen!

- *Where answering questions is computer-based, speed and accuracy of typing/keyboarding may be too important.* This may be as serious as the disadvantages regarding speeds/legibility of writing in handwritten exams.
- *Students get little or no feedback on their exam performance.* Their work preparing for and sitting exams is therefore wasted as far as feedback is concerned. Though it can be argued that the purpose of exams is measurement rather than feedback, the counter-argument is that most exams, to some extent, represent lost learning opportunities because of this lack of feedback. Add to this picture the fact that most exam markers write comments on the scripts anyway, for those who may be moderating the standard or the marking, and these comments are wasted as far as students are concerned (while in practice, students are often fascinated when they have the chance to see this kind of comment on their answers). Where students are given the opportunity to see their marked scripts (even with no more feedback than seeing the subtotals and total marks awarded along the way), they can learn a great deal about exactly what went wrong with some of their answers, as well as having the chance to receive confirmation regarding the questions they answered well.
- *Badly set exams encourage surface learning.* Students consciously clear their minds of one subject as they prepare for exams in the next subject. In many discipline areas, it is inappropriate to encourage students to put out of their minds important subject matter, where they will need to retain their mastery for later stages in their studies.
- *Exam technique is too important.* Exams tend to measure how good (and fast) students are at answering exam questions, rather than how well they have learned. The consequence is that those students who become skilled at exam technique are rewarded time after time, while other students who may have mastered the subject material to a greater degree may not get due credit for their learning if their exam technique repeatedly lets them down, or if they 'shoot themselves in the foot' by running off at great detail about something they're really interested in, failing to leave time to answer the rest of the questions properly.
- *Exams only represent a snapshot of student performance, rather than a reliable indicator of it.* How students perform in traditional exams depends on so many other factors than their grasp of the subject being tested. Students' state of mind on the day, their luck or otherwise in tackling a good question first, their state of health, and many other irrelevant factors creep in.

Helping students themselves to tune in to what written exams actually measure

Table 2.1 presents an exercise which can be given to students to alert them to some of the many factors which can affect their performance in exams. Even better, it can be useful as a class discussion exercise, allowing students to question tutors about some of the items on the agenda. The exercise can also be valuable in its own right to those setting and marking exams, as an indicator of the extent to which exams are achieving their desired goals. You might well wish to add to (and subtract from) the forty questions presently in the table.

Setting unseen written exam questions: some practical suggestions

Many experienced lecturers remember with some horror the first time they put pen to paper to write exam questions. Sometimes they felt well equipped to do so, as they had been involved in exams as candidates for most of their lives, and thought that it was quite straightforward to write good questions. But then the realisation dawned that the words and tasks used in exam questions could determine students' future careers,

Table 2.1 Factors measured by written exams

Which factors are measured by written exams?	Measured very well	Measured to some extent	Not really measured
How much you know about your subject on the day			
How much you don't know about your subject on the day			
How well you've been concentrating in related lectures			
How conscientiously you've done suggested tasks between lectures			
How widely you've read around the subject			
How long you've spent online working at the subject			
How well you've kept the published intended learning outcomes in mind as you studied			
How well you've studied information about the assessment criteria			
How often you've practised assessing your own answers to typical exam questions			
How much you've learned from tutor-feedback on coursework assignments			
How well you've kept your head down working on your own at the subject			
How much you've talked to others about the subject and learned from them			
The quantity of revision that you have done			
The quality of revision that you have done			
How intelligent you are			
How determined you are to get a really good mark			
How well you maintain your concentration during the exam			
How much 'polishing' work you've done the night before			
How well you keep your cool in the run up to the exam			
How well you keep your cool on the day of the exam			
How unruffled you remain if things go wrong while attempting a question			
How well you resist getting carried away when you know a lot about a question			
How good your memory is			
How good you have been at question spotting			
How carefully you read each question before choosing to attempt it			
How fast you think			
How fast you write			
How legible your handwriting is			
How well you manage your timing as you answer questions			

continued ...

Table 2.1 continued

Which factors are measured by written exams?	Measured very well	Measured to some extent	Not really measured
How much practice you've had at thinking through how to answer exam questions			
How much practice you've had at actually writing answers to exam questions			
How carefully you re-read the questions while you're answering them			
How wisely you choose the questions that you attempt			
How well you leave time to re-read and edit your answers			
How well you keep exactly to the questions in your answers			
How well you set out your answers to the questions			
How skilled you have become at solving problems			
How easy you make it for the marker to see how exactly you've worked out things in your answers			
How carefully you read your own answers after writing them			
How well you edit/improve your answers after reading them			

prospects, incomes and lifestyles. Often, only when marking the exam scripts do lecturers first become aware of just how sensitively the questions need to be designed, and how clearly the assessment criteria and marking schemes need to be laid out to anticipate as many as possible of the different ways that even the most unambiguous looking question can turn out to be answered in practice. The suggestions below can help to spare you from some of the headaches which can result from hastily written exam questions.

1 **Aim towards writing shorter exams!** Remember that long exam questions tend to measure students' legibility and speed of handwriting (or keyboarding), rather than mastery of the subject. Always ask yourself 'is an answer to this exam question the best way for students to show that they've achieved the relevant learning outcome(s)'.

2 **Remember that in an exam question, you've normally only got print on paper.** There is no 'tone of voice' or body-language or any other means of clarifying what the question really means, or how you intend students to structure their answers.

3 **Whatever else your question is, students are very keen that it's *fair*.** External examiners are keen on this too. There should be no tricks or hidden depths. Check carefully that each question is clearly linked to the course documentation which students have.

4 **Don't write questions on your own!** Make sure you get feedback on each of your questions from colleagues. They can often spot whether your question is at the right level more easily than you can. Having someone else look at one's draft exam questions is extremely useful. It can be better still when all questions are discussed and moderated by teams of staff. Where possible, draft questions *with* your colleagues. This allows the team to pick the best questions from a range of possibilities, rather than use every idea each member has.

5 **Ask colleagues: 'what would you say this question really means?'** If they tell you anything you hadn't thought of, you may need to adjust your wording a little. Try this out on students too.

6 **Get one or two colleagues to *do* your questions!** Sometimes even sketch answers can be helpful. This may be asking a lot of busy colleagues, but the rewards can be significant. You will often find that they answered a particular question in a rather different way than you had in mind when you designed the question. Being alerted in advance to the ways that different students might approach a question gives you the opportunity to accommodate alternative approaches in your marking scheme, or to adjust the wording of your question so that your intended or preferred approach is made clearer to students.

7 **Have your intended learning outcomes in front of you as you draft your questions.** It is all too easy to dream up interesting questions which turn out to be tangential to the learning outcomes. Furthermore, it is possible to write too many questions addressing particular learning outcomes, leaving other outcomes unrepresented in the exam.

8 **Keep your sentences short.** You're less likely to write something that can be interpreted in more than one way if you write plain English in short sentences. This also helps reduce any discrimination against those candidates whose second or third language is English.

9 **Work out what you're really testing.** Is each question measuring decision-making, strategic planning, problem solving, data processing (and so on), or is it just too much dependent on memory? Most exam questions measure a number of things at the same time. Be upfront about all the things each question is likely to measure. In any case, external scrutiny of assessment may interrogate whether your questions (and your assessment criteria) link appropriately with the published learning outcomes for your course or module.

10 **Don't measure the same things again and again.** For example, it is all too easy in essay-type exam questions to repeatedly measure students' skills at writing good introductions, firm conclusions, and well-structured argu-ments. Valuable as such skills are, we need to be measuring other important things too.

11 **Include data or information in questions to reduce the emphasis on memory.** In many subjects, case-study information is a really good way of doing this. Science exams often tend to be much better than other subjects in this respect, and it is appropriate to be testing what candidates can *do* with data rather than how well they remember facts and figures.

12 **Make the question layout easy to follow.** A question with bullet points for separate parts can be much easier for (tense) candidates to interpret correctly than one which is just several lines of continuous prose.

13 **Don't overdo the standards.** When you're close to a subject, it's easily possible that your questions get gradually harder year by year. For example, in exams including quantitative questions, there is the danger that numerical problems become more difficult in each successive exam, partly because of the wish to stretch students a little further than did the worked examples they may have seen in lectures, or the problems students tackled online or in tutorials or coursework assignments.

14 **Write out an answer to your own question.** Don't leave this till after the exam has been taken – that's just going to make marking much harder work. A prepared answer is handy when you come to mark answers, but also you'll sometimes find that it takes *you* an hour to answer a question for which candidates have only half an hour. Lecturers setting problem-type questions for students often forget that familiarity with the type of problem profoundly influences the time it takes to solve it. Students who get stuck on such a question may end up failing the exam more through time mismanagement than through lack of subject-related competence.

15 **Decide what the assessment criteria will be.** Check that these criteria relate clearly to the syllabus intended learning outcomes. Make it your business to ensure that students themselves are clear about these intended outcomes, and emphasise the links between

these and assessment. When students are aware that the expressed learning outcomes are a template for the design of assessment tasks, it is possible for them to make their learning much more focused.

16 **Work out a tight marking scheme.** Imagine that you are going to delegate the marking to a new colleague. Write it all down. You will find such schemes an invaluable aid to share with future classes of students, as well as colleagues actually co-marking with you, helping them to see how assessment works.

17 **Use the question itself to show how marks are to be allocated.** For example, put numbers in brackets to show how many marks are attached to various parts of the question (or alternatively, give suggested timings such as 'spend about ten minutes on Part 2').

18 **Try your questions out.** Use coursework and student assignments to do pilot runs of potential components of your future exam questions, and use or adapt the ones that work best for exams.

19 **Proofread your exam questions carefully.** Be aware of the danger of seeing what you *meant,* rather than what you actually *wrote*! Even if you're very busy when asked to check your questions, a little extra time spent editing your questions at this time may save you many hours sorting out how to handle matters arising from any ambiguities or errors which could have otherwise slipped through the proofreading process.

Designing marking schemes

Making a good marking scheme can save you hours when it comes to marking a large pile of scripts. It can also help you to know (and show) that you are doing everything possible to be uniformly fair to all students. As your marking schemes will normally be shown to people including external examiners and quality reviewers, it's important to design schemes in the first place so that they will stand up to such scrutiny. Well-prepared marking schemes can also be enormously valuable to students themselves, to aid them practise making informed judgements on their own, and each other's answers to typical questions.

The following suggestions should help.

1 **Write a model answer for each question.** (I suggested that you should have done this when you set the question, of course.) This can be a useful first step towards identifying the mark-bearing ingredients of a good answer. It also helps you see when what you thought was going to be a 30-minute question turns out to take an hour! If you have difficulties answering the questions, the chances are that your students will too! Making model answers and marking schemes for coursework assignments can give you good practice for writing exam schemes.

2 **Make each assessment decision as straightforward as possible.** Try to allocate each mark so that it is associated with something that is either present or absent, or right or wrong, in students' answers.

3 **Aim to make your marking scheme usable by a non-expert in the subject.** This can help your marking schemes be useful resources for students themselves, perhaps in next year's course.

4 **Aim to make it so that anyone can mark given answers, and agree on the scores within a mark or two.** This is to maximise *reliability* (fairness) of assessment in due course. It is best to involve colleagues in your piloting of first-draft marking schemes. They will soon help you to identify areas where the marking criteria may need clarifying or tightening up.

5 **Allow for 'consequential' marks.** For example, when a candidate makes an early mistake, but then proceeds correctly thereafter (especially in problems and calculations),

allow for some marks to be given for the ensuing correct steps even when the final answer is quite wrong.

6 **Pilot your marking scheme by showing it to others.** It's worth even showing marking schemes to people who are not closely associated with your subject area. If they can't see exactly what you're looking for, it may be that the scheme is not yet sufficiently self-explanatory. Extra detail you add at this stage may help you to clarify your own thinking, and will certainly assist fellow markers.

7 **Think ahead to 'honourable exceptions'.** Ask yourself whether your marking scheme is sufficiently flexible to accommodate a brilliant student who hasn't strictly conformed to your original idea of what should be achieved. There are sometimes candidates who write exceptionally good answers which are off-beam and idiosyncratic, and they deserve credit for these.

8 **Consider having more than 20 available marks for a '20-mark question'.** Especially in essay-type answers, you can't expect students to include all the things you may think of yourself. It may be worth having up to 30 or more 'available' marks, so that students approaching the question in different ways still have the opportunity to score well.

9 **Look at what others have done in the past.** If it's your first time writing a marking scheme, looking at several other people's ways of doing them will help you to focus your efforts. Choose to look at marking schemes from other subjects that your students may be studying, to help you tune in to the assessment culture of the overall course.

10 **Learn from your own mistakes.** No marking scheme is perfect. When you start applying it to a pile of scripts, you will soon start adjusting it. Keep a note of any difficulties you experience in adhering to your scheme, and take account of these next time you have to make one.

Marking examination scripts to optimise reliability

Reliability is about fairness. The research literature on assessment shows that some kinds of exam question are not at all reliable – especially essay-type questions. The following suggestions may help you approach the task of marking exam scripts efficiently, while still being fair and helpful to students.

1 **Be realistic about what you can do.** Marking scripts can be boring, exhausting and stressful. As far as constraints allow, don't attempt to mark large numbers of scripts in short periods of time. Put scripts for marking into manageable bundles. It is less awesome to have ten scripts on your desk and the rest out of sight than to have the whole pile threatening you as you work.

2 **Scan through a number of scripts before you really start marking.** It's useful to get a feel for the overall standard of the answers before you get deep into the scripts themselves. This can help you to pitch your marking at the right level from the outset and save you the painful task of having to go back and make significant adjustments to your marking of the first few scripts.

3 **Avoid halo effects.** If you've just marked a brilliant answer on a script, it can be easy to go into the *same* student's next answer seeing only the good points and passing over the weaknesses. Try to ensure that you mark each answer dispassionately. Conversely, when you look at the *next* student's answer, you may be over-critical if you've just marked a brilliant one.

4 **Watch out for prejudices.** There will be all sorts of things which you like and dislike about the style and layout of scripts, not to mention handwriting quality. Make sure that each time there is a 'benefit of the doubt' decision to be made, it is not influenced by such factors.

5 **Recognise that your mood will change.** Every now and then, check back to scripts

you marked earlier, and see whether your generosity has increased or decreased. Be aware of the middle-mark bunching syndrome. As you get tired, it feels safe and easy to give a middle-range mark. Try as far as possible to look at each script afresh.

6 **Remind yourself of the importance of what you're doing.** You may be marking a whole pile of scripts, but each individual script may be a crucial landmark in the life of the student concerned. Your verdict may affect students for the rest of their careers.

7 **Take account of the needs of second markers.** Many universities use a blind double-marking system, in which case you should not write any comments or numbers on the scripts themselves, to avoid prejudicing the judgement of a second marker (unless of course photocopies have already been made of each script for double-marking). You may find it useful to use post-it notes or assessment pro formas for each script, so you are able to justify the marks you give at any later stage. Such aide-memoires can save you having to read the whole scripts again, rethinking how you arrived at your numbers or grades.

8 **Make notes to explain your assessment decisions to second-markers.** These may be even more necessary to justify your decisions when necessary to external examiners, or to help you re-visit a particular script when a student ends up on a borderline or in case of appeals.

9 **Compose feedback for students too.** In most exams, the system may not allow you to write on the scripts the sort of feedback you would have given if the questions had been set as assessed coursework. However, students may still need feedback, and making notes for yourself of the things you would have explained about common mistakes can help you prepare some discussion notes to issue to students after the exam, or can remind you of things to mention next time you teach the same subjects.

10 **Devise your own system of tackling the marking load.** You may prefer to mark a whole script at a time, or just Question 1 of every script first, and so on. Do what you feel comfortable with, and see what works best for you.

11 **Provide feedback for yourself and for the course team.** As you work through the scripts, note how many students answered each question, and how well they performed. You may begin to realise that some questions turned out to have been very well written, while others could have been framed better. You will find out which questions proved to be the hardest for students to answer well, even when all questions were intended to be of an equal standard. Such feedback and reflection should prove very useful when designing questions next time round.

12 **Set aside time for a review.** Having marked all the scripts, you may wish to capture your thoughts, such as suggestions about changes for part of the course or module, or the processes used to teach it. It is really useful, however tired you feel, to write a short draft report on the marking as soon as you have completed it. Otherwise, important things which are still fresh in your tired mind will all too quickly evaporate away.

Using exam questions as class exercises

Answering exam questions well is still one of the principal skills which students need to develop to succeed in their studies in most subjects. In our attempts to increase the learning payoff of taught sessions, we can help students to develop their exam skills by making use of past exam questions. The following suggestions may help you to build related activities into your lectures and tutorials – but don't try to implement more than two or three of these suggestions with any one cohort – you haven't got time!

1 **Let a class have a try at an exam question under exam conditions.** Then ask students to exchange their answers, and lead them through marking their work using a typical marking scheme. This helps students to learn quickly how examiners' minds work. It is well worth using the whole of at least one lecture slot for such an exercise; the learning payoff for students is likely to be considerably more than if you'd just spent an extra hour with one small element of their curriculum.

2 **Issue two or three old exam questions for students to try in preparation for a tutorial.** Then lead them through assessing their work using a marking scheme during the tutorial. Ask them to prepare questions on matters arising from the exercise, both on subject content and requirements for exams, and use their questions to focus tutorial discussion.

3 **Display an exam question on-screen in a large-group lecture.** Ask students in groups to brainstorm the principal steps they would take in the way they would approach answering the question. Then give out a model answer to the question as a handout, and talk the class through the points in the model answer where marks would be earned. It can also be useful to give out a flawed answer, and get the students to see the weaknesses in this. All this can be achieved in less than half of the overall time of a typical lecture, and you may be surprised at the levels of interest and attention which students pay to such elements in a lecture slot.

4 **In a lecture or a tutorial, get students in groups to think up exam questions themselves.** You can base this on work they have already covered, or on work currently in progress. Where possible, display each of these in turn, giving feedback on how appropriate or otherwise each question is in terms of standard, wording, length and structure. (You will get many questions this way which you can later use or adapt for next year's exams or future coursework assignments!)

5 **Use exam questions to help students to create an agenda.** In a lecture or tutorial, give out two or three related exam questions as a handout. Ask students in groups to make lists of short questions that they don't yet know the answers to. Then allow the groups to use you as a resource, quizzing you with these questions. You don't have to answer them all at once – for some your reply will be along the lines 'We'll come to this in a week or two', and for others 'You won't actually be required to know this'.

6 **Get students to make marking schemes.** Give them a typical exam question, and ask groups of students to prepare a breakdown of how they think the marks should be allocated. Discuss each of these in turn with the whole group, and give guidance to how closely the marking schemes resemble those used in practice.

7 **Get students to surf the net.** Ask them to find appropriate exam questions on the subjects they are studying. Suggest that they work in twos or threes, and bring the questions they find to the next class session. You can encourage them to download the questions they find, and then assemble a question bank on a course web page.

8 **Ask students in groups to think up a 'dream' question.** Ask the groups to make bullet-point lists of the ten most important things that they would include in answers to these questions. These questions will give you useful information about their favourite topics.

9 **Ask students in groups to think up 'nightmare' questions.** With these, you can open up a discussion of the causes of their anxieties and traumas, and can probably do a lot to allay their fears, and point them in the right direction regarding how they might tackle such questions if needed.

10 **Ask students to think of way-out, alternative questions.** Suggest that they think of questions which are not just testing of their knowledge and skills, but which get them to think laterally and creatively. This encourages deeper reflection about the material they are learning, and will probably give you some interesting ideas to use in future exams.

2 Open-book exams

In many ways these are similar to traditional exams, but with the major difference that students are allowed to take in with them sources of reference material. Alternatively, candidates may be issued with a standard set of resource materials that they can consult during the exam, and are informed in advance about what will be available to them, so that they can prepare themselves by practising to apply the resource materials. Sometimes, in addition, the 'timed' element is relaxed or abandoned, allowing students to answer questions with the aid of their chosen materials, and at their own pace.

There is the possibility of an online equivalent of an open-book exam, where in a computer-based exam all students are provided with the same range of online resource materials. You can choose whether or not to inform them in advance of the range of materials they will be able to consult as they answer the questions.

Advantages

Open-book exams have many of the advantages of traditional exams, with the addition of:

- *Less stress on memories!* The emphasis is taken away from students being required to remember facts, figures, formulae and other such information.
- *Questions can be used which would not be possible in traditional exams.* For example, where it would have been quite inappropriate to expect students to remember all the detail of a wide range of information, open-book exams can test how well they can navigate provided information, and pick out trends, review alternative points of view and so on.
- *Higher on authenticity.* Open-book exams are closer to the real-world situation where relevant information can be assembled and consulted when tackling problems.
- *There is less emphasis on reproducing things.* There is no point in an open-book exam just writing out extracts from the available materials, and questions can get candidates to go deeper into making judgements, comparing sources, prioritising options and so on.
- *Retrieval skills can be measured.* It is possible to set questions which measure how well students can use and apply information, and how well they can find their way round the contents of books and even databases.
- *Slower writers helped?* If coupled with a relaxation in the timed dimension (e.g. a nominal '2-hour' paper where students are allowed to spend up to three hours if they wish), some of the pressure is taken away from those students who happen to be slower at writing down their answers (and also students who happen to think more slowly).

Disadvantages

- *Not enough books or resources!* It is hard to ensure that all students are equally equipped regarding the books they bring into the exam with them. Limited stocks of library books (and the impossibility of students purchasing their own copies of expensive books) means that some students may be disadvantaged.
- *Open-book exams require different sorts of exam questions.* It would not be enough simply to ask students to *find* things in the available resource-materials, and questions need to probe what students can actually *do* with the resource materials.
- *Estimating timing is not as straightforward as in 'normal' exams.* It can be hard to anticipate how long is a reasonable time to allow for students to undertake a task with resource materials available, as part of the time needs to be spent navigating the materials, detracting from the time available to actually answer the questions.

- *Reliability can be compromised.* Where different students have access to different resources, their work can reflect the range or quality of resources they have available, rather than the quality of their learning.
- *More desk space is needed.* The tables in traditional exams are normally quite small, allowing a venue to accommodate quite large numbers of students. Students necessarily require considerably more desk space for open-book exams if they are to be able to use several sources of reference as they compose their answers to exam questions. This means fewer students can be accommodated in a given exam room, and therefore open-book exams are rather less cost-effective in terms of accommodation and invigilation.
- *Speeds of reading and of writing may limit candidates' performance.* Marks can only be awarded on the basis of what candidates manage to do with the question, and when they have to spend significant time on browsing the resource materials, they have less time to do themselves justice in their written answers.

Setting open-book exam questions

Many of the suggestions already offered regarding traditional exam questions still apply. In addition:

1 **Decide whether to prescribe the books or articles students may employ.** This is one way round the problem of availability of books. It may even be possible to arrange supplies of the required books or articles to be available in the exam room.
2 **Consider compiling a source-collection for the particular exam.** Check on copyright issues, and see if it is cost-effective to put together a set of papers, extracts, data and other information from which students can find what they need to address the questions in the particular exam.
3 **Set questions which require students to do things with the information available to them,** rather than merely summarising it and giving it back.
4 **Provide rehearsal opportunities.** Where students have not met open-book exams before, they need at least some practice to familiarise themselves with the approach they need to adopt. It can be useful to provide a dry-run, asking students to time themselves accordingly when doing a set task with

particular resource materials on their own, and bring their results to a class session where they are guided through marking their own (or each other's) work, helping them to see what may constitute a good response to the question.
5 **Make the actual questions particularly clear and straightforward to understand.** The fact that students will be reading a lot during the exam means that care has to be taken that they don't read the actual instructions too rapidly.
6 **Focus the assessment criteria on what students will have done with the information,** and not just on them having located the most relevant or appropriate information.
7 **Plan for shorter answers.** Students doing open-book exams will be spending quite a lot of their time searching for, and making sense of, information and data. They will therefore write less per hour than students who are answering traditional exam questions 'out of their heads'.

3 Open-notes exams

These are similar to open-book exams described above, but this time students are allowed to bring into the examination room any notes that *they* have prepared for the purpose. In other words, we are talking about a situation of 'legitimised crib-notes'! Your first thought may be that this is all very strange, but in fact such exams can work surprisingly well. Many of the advantages and suggestions for open-book exams continue to apply – the following additional matters arise.

Advantages

- *Students can achieve a very significant learning payoff by simply making the notes in the first place.* The act of making revision summaries can have high learning payoff. It is best not to place stringent limits on the amount of materials which students can bring in. Those who bring in everything they have ever written about your topic will be disadvantaging themselves in that it will take them much longer to search for the relevant parts of their notes, compared with students who have been really selective in summarising the important parts of your topic.
- *Higher on authenticity.* In real-world contexts, people usually have the opportunity to assemble the information they need before undertaking a task.
- *The emphasis on memory is reduced, allowing competence to be tested more effectively.* Open-notes exams can also spread candidates' abilities out more fairly, as the better candidates will have made better notes in the first place.
- *Drafting out answers to likely questions is legitimised.* This may enable students to do 'better-quality' revision as they prepare for this kind of exam.
- *You can write shorter questions.* When it is up to the students to ensure that they have with them important information or data, you don't have to put so much into the questions themselves.

Disadvantages

- *Students need rehearsal at preparing for open-notes exams.* They may take two or three practice runs to develop the art of making comprehensive but manageable summaries of the important data or information you intend them to make available to themselves.
- *Candidates whose open notes were not very suitable are penalised quite severely.* Some of these candidates may have been better at answering traditional exam questions with no notes.
- *Extra desk space is needed, just as for open-book exams.*
- *We're thinking of paper-based notes, including print-outs.* In practice nowadays, students are more likely to prefer to make computer-based notes, and may find it much easier to search their notes electronically rather than by browsing pages physically.

Designing open-notes exams

1 **Think of giving a topic menu in advance.** This can save candidates from trying to prepare open notes on everything they have learned about your topic. It does, of course, also mean that you are letting them off the hook regarding trying to learn some of the things that you *don't* include in your menu.

2 **Consider having an inspection process.** For example, let it be known that yourself or your colleagues will be keeping an eye on the range and content of the open notes, or even that they may be temporarily retained after the exam.

3 **Give students some practice at writing open notes.** For example, set a coursework task where students prepare open notes to a given specification (length, number of references quoted and so on) on a given topic, then facilitate peer-assessment of the open notes in class (ideally having each participant assessing at least two peers' notes) on quality, depth,

and coverage. Students learn a great deal from seeing each other's ways of going about the task, helping them to make much better open notes where they are to be used for 'real' exams.

4 Structured exams: for example multiple-choice questions

These include multiple-choice exams, and several other types of formats where students are not required to write 'full' answers, but are involved in making true/false decisions, or identifying reasons to support assertions, or fill in blanks or complete statements, and so on. It is of course possible to design mixed exams, combining free-response traditional questions with structured ones. Some kinds of structured exams can be computer-based, either online synchronously in a normal 'exam' environment, or synchronously but at different locations (with appropriate invigilation). Software can be used both to process students' scores and to provide feedback to them. In the following discussion, I will concentrate on the benefits and drawbacks of multiple-choice and multiple-response questions. Many of the same points also apply at least in part to other types of structured exam questions, such as true–false, short-answer, and sequencing questions.

Advantages

- *Greater syllabus coverage can be achieved.* It is possible, in a limited time, to test students' knowledge of a much greater cross-section of a syllabus than could be done in the same time by getting students to write in detail about a few parts of the syllabus.
- *Multiple-choice exams can be high on validity.* In other words, they can be a better way of measuring whether candidates have made sense of a topic, than just asking candidates to write out things that they know.
- *Multiple-choice exams can be high regarding reliability.* The possibilities of unfair subjectivity in marking are eliminated.
- *Multiple-choice exams can be high regarding authenticity.* In many disciplines, the ability to make decisions between options can be closer to real-world tasks.
- *Multiple-choice exams can test how fast students think,* rather than how fast they write. The depth of their thinking depends on how skilled the question-setters have been.
- *Students don't have to waste time writing out complex things like equations.* For example, questions can already show, for example, formulae, definitions, equations, statements (correct and wrong) and students can be asked to select the correct one, without having to write it out for themselves.
- *Staff time and energy can be reduced dramatically.* With computer-based assessment platforms, or optical mark readers for paper-based answer scripts, it is possible to mark multiple-choice exams very quickly and cost-effectively, and avoid the tedium and subjectivity which affect the marking of traditional exams.
- *Computer software can be used to analyse the effectiveness of the questions.* As well as processing all of the scores, computer software can work out how each question performs, calculating the discrimination index and facility value of each question. This allows the questions which work well as testing devices to be identified, and selected for future exams.
- *Higher-level thinking can be tested.* Multiple-choice exams can move the emphasis away from memory, and towards the ability to interpret information and make good decisions. However, the accusation is often made that such exams seem only to test lower cognitive skills, but this is usually because the questions themselves have not been made more challenging. There are numerous examples where high level skills are being tested effectively.

- *Multiple-response can be used, as well as multiple-choice.* Multiple-response is where more than one option can be correct, with the stem asking (for example) 'Which (one or more) of the following options is correct?' These can go much deeper than simple multiple-choice questions, as some of the 'correct' answers can be less obvious than others, and considerably more thought and knowledge can be required of candidates.
- *Multiple-choice questions can have more than one 'layer'.* For example in computer-based exams, the first layer can ask which is the correct option out of a series, then the next layer can ask *why* this option is the best one, and *why* each distractor is wrong, asking candidates to select the best *reason* in each case. This substantially reduces the 'guess-factor' of the overall question.

Disadvantages

- *The guess factor.* In simple multiple-choice questions, students can often gain marks by lucky guesses rather than correct decisions.
- *It is surprisingly hard to write good multiple-choice questions.* What seems like a good question can turn out to be too easy, with most candidates selecting the correct option, not always for a good reason. Conversely, sometimes a distractor can be too distracting, and can cause casualties with even the best candidates.
- *Designing structured questions takes time and skill.* It is harder to design good multiple-choice questions than it is to write traditional open-ended questions. In particular, it can be difficult to think of the last distractor or to make it look sufficiently plausible. It is sometimes difficult to prevent the correct answer or best option standing out as being the one to choose.
- *Black and white or shades of grey?* While it is straightforward enough to reward students with marks for correct choices (with zero marks for choosing distractors), it is more difficult (but not impossible) to handle subjects where there is a 'best' option, and a 'next-best' one, and so on.
- *Where multiple-choice exams are being set on computers, it is necessary to check that the tests are secure.* Students can be ingenious at getting into computer files that are intended to be secret!
- *The danger of impersonators?* The fact that exams composed entirely of multiple-choice questions do not require students to give any evidence of their handwriting increases the risk of substitution of candidates.

Designing multiple-choice exams

1 **Continuously try out questions with colleagues and with large groups of students.** Make sure that you select for exam usage questions where people are selecting correct options for the right reasons – and not because in one way or another the question gives away which is the correct option.

2 **Make sure that distractors are plausible.** If no one is selecting a given distractor, it is serving no useful purpose. Distractors need to represent anticipated errors in students' knowledge or understanding.

3 **Try to avoid overlap between questions.** If one question helps students successfully to answer further questions, the possibility increases of students picking the right options for the wrong reasons.

4 **Avoid options such as 'none of the above' or 'all of the above'.** These options are a let-out for students who find it hard to decide between the other alternatives, and are often chosen by weaker students in surface-thinking mode. Also, it is surprisingly rare for such options to be in fact the correct one, and test-

wise candidates will already have guessed this. To complicate matters, the best students will sometimes spot weaknesses with the option which is intended to be correct, and select 'none of these' because of this.

5 **Avoid where possible the restrictions of being limited to a set number of options.** For example, four-option or five-option questions are often used, even when thinking of the 'last' distractor is difficult, resulting in the option concerned having little real value in the test. It is better when as many distractors as are realistic errors-of-thinking are allowed, so that each item serves a useful purpose.

6 **Pilot questions in formative tests before using them in summative exams.** Ideally, multiple-choice questions that appear in formal exams should be tried-and-tested ones. It is worth consulting the literature on multiple-choice question design and finding out how to assess the discrimination index and facility value of each question from statistical analysis of the performance of substantial groups of students.

7 **Remember that students can still guess.** The marking scheme needs to take into account the fact that all students can score some marks by pure luck! If most of the questions are, for example, four-option ones, the average mark which would be scored by a monkey would be 25 per cent, so the real range lies between this and 100 per cent. It is important that people are indeed allowed to get 100 per cent in such structured exams, and that this does not cause any problems when the marks are blended with more traditional exam formats where written answers in some subjects still attract marks only in the 70s even when they're reckoned to be first-class answers.

8 **Design feedback responses to each option.** Where possible, it is useful to be able to explain to students selecting the correct (or best) option exactly *why* their selection is right. It is even more useful to be able to explain to students selecting the wrong (or less good) options exactly what may be wrong with their thinking. When multiple-choice questions are

computer-marked, it is a simple further step to get the computer to print out (or display on-screen if the exam is computer-based) feedback responses to each student. This practice can equally be applied to formative multiple-choice tests, and to formal multiple-choice exams. Furthermore, the availability of feedback responses to each decision students make lends itself to extending the use of such questions in computer-based learning packages.

9 **Ensure that students are well-practised at handling multiple-choice questions.** Answering such questions well is a skill in its own right, just as is writing open answers well. We need to ensure that students are sufficiently practised, so that multiple-choice exams measure their thinking and not just their technique.

10 **Look at a range of published multiple-choice questions.** For example, in the UK several Open University courses have multiple-choice assignment questions, as well as multiple-choice exams. You may be surprised how sophisticated such questions can be, and may gain many ideas that you can build into your own question design.

11 **Gradually build up a large bank of questions.** This is best done by collaborating with colleagues, and pooling questions that are found to be working well. It then becomes possible to compose a multiple-choice exam by selecting from the bank of questions. If the bank becomes large enough, it can even be good practice to publish the whole collection, and allow students to practise with it. Any student who has learned to handle successfully a large bank of questions can normally be said to have learned the subject well.

12 **Involve students in groups in designing multiple-choice questions.** When students have learned a topic relatively recently, they can still remember the things that confused them at first, and this helps them to design good distractors. The act of designing such questions has high learning payoff, and serves

as good rehearsal for the relevant technique students need for this kind of exam.

13 **When you've got a large bank of questions, there is the possibility of on-demand exams.** Students can then take a multiple-choice test with a random selection of questions from the bank, at any time during their studies, and 'pass' the component involved as soon as they are able to demonstrate their competence with the questions.

5 Essays: in exams and in coursework

In some subjects, assessment is dominated by essay-writing. This has often been the case for a long time, and essays have become a firmly-established form of assessment in traditional (and open-book) written exams. Assessed coursework often takes the form of essays, formerly handwritten but nowadays almost always word-processed. It is well known that essay-answers tend to be harder to mark, and much more time-consuming to assess, than quantitative or numerical questions. There are still some useful functions to be served by including some essay questions in exams or coursework assessments, but perhaps we need to face up to the fact that reliability in marking essays is often unsatisfactory, and refrain from using essays to the extent that they are used at present.

Advantages

- *Essays allow for student individuality and expression.* They are a medium in which the 'best' students can distinguish themselves. This means, however, that the marking criteria for essays must be flexible enough to be able to reward student individuality fairly.
- *Essays can provide students with opportunities to demonstrate their own particular 'take' on a topic.* While this may be an advantage, it is also a disadvantage in that it can turn out to be particularly troublesome to *assess* students' own 'take' fairly and without prejudice.
- *Essays can reflect the depth of student learning.* Writing freely about a topic is a process which can demonstrate understanding and grasp of the material involved.
- *Essay-writing is a measure of students' written style.* It is useful to include good written communication somewhere in the overall assessment strategy. The danger of students in science disciplines, where essays are used less, missing out on the development of such skills is becoming increasingly recognised.
- *Students are relatively familiar with essays.* They've normally done this sort of writing beforehand, but assessors at university level justifiably grumble that students don't seem to have had any real training in structuring essays, particularly when it comes to logical argument and coming to a resounding conclusion.

Disadvantages

- *The assessment of essays is well proven to be unreliable.* Different markers often award the same essay quite different marks, and students are quick to notice such unfairness. Essays are demonstrably the form of assessment where the dangers of subjective marking are greatest. Essay-marking exercises at workshops on assessment show marked differences between the mark or grade that different assessors award the same essay – even when equipped with clear sets of assessment criteria.
- *The validity of essays as an assessment device remains questionable.* Students' knowledge of the subject is only tested to a limited extent, and technique for essay-writing is tested rather better sometimes.
- *Essay-writing is very much an art in itself.* Students from some backgrounds are disadvantaged regarding essay-writing skills as they have simply never been coached in how to write essays

well. For example, a strong beginning, a coherent and logical middle, and a firm and decisive conclusion combine to make up the hallmarks of a good essay. The danger becomes that when essays are over-used in assessment strategies, the presence of these hallmarks is measured time and time again, and students who happen to have perfected the art of delivering these hallmarks are repeatedly rewarded irrespective of any other strengths and weaknesses they may have.

- *Essays take a great deal of time to mark.* Even with well thought out assessment criteria, it can be difficult to 'get into one's stride' applying a marking scheme, and it is not unusual for markers to need to work back through the first dozen or so of the essays they have already marked, as they become aware of the things that the best students are doing with the questions, and the difficulties experienced by other students.

- *'Halo effects' are significant.* If the last essay answer you marked was an excellent one, you may tend to approach the next one with greater expectations, and be more severe in your assessment decisions based upon it.

- *Essays take time to write (whether as coursework or in exams).* This means that assessment based on essay-writing necessarily is restricted regarding the amount of the syllabus that is covered directly. There may remain large untested tracts of syllabus.

- *With coursework essays, it is increasingly difficult to guarantee that the essay is the work of the candidate.* Ready-made essays can be purchased online on just about any subject, or even directly commissioned. Plagiarism is always a possibility, and there is the need to check authenticity by some other means, such as face-to-face questioning to guarantee that the work is the students' own. This adds even more time to what is already a high-burden kind of assessment.

- *Traditional ways of giving students feedback on essays are known to be problematic, and rarely worth the time taken.* Writing comments on students' work is particularly troublesome, in that it is well known that students don't often make good use of the feedback, not least because it often arrives too late, when they've already moved on in their studies. Using the comments function in word-processing 'track-changes' can be much better, however (this is discussed in some detail later in this chapter).

Setting and using essay-type questions

Many of the suggestions given earlier in this chapter about writing traditional exam questions continue to apply – whether essays are to be used as assessed coursework or as exam questions. Some further suggestions are given below.

1 **Help students to see exactly how essays are marked.** Alert students to the credit they gain from good structure and style. One of the best ways of doing this is to involve classes of students in looking at examples of past (good, bad and indifferent) essays, and applying assessment criteria. This can be followed by involving students in peer-assessment of each other's essays, and indeed in self-assessment of their own essays. This helps them to put their own efforts into perspective, and to learn things to emulate (and things to avoid!) by seeing how other students go about devising essays.

2 **Don't leave students to guess the real agenda.** Some essay questions are so open-ended that it is hard for students to work out exactly what is being sought. The authors of such questions will defend their questions by saying 'well, it's important to find the students who know what to do in such circumstances', but the fact remains that it is an aspect of study technique which is being rewarded, rather than mastery of the learning involved in answering the question.

3 **Subdivide essay questions into several parts, each with marks publicly allocated.** This helps to prevent students from straying so

far off the point that they lose too many of the marks that they could have scored.

4 **Give word limits.** Even in exams, it can be useful to suggest to students that an essay answer should lie between (for example) 800 and 1,200 words say for a 30-minute question, and so on. This helps to avoid the quantity-versus-quality issue, which leads some students into simply trying to write a lot, rather than thinking deeply about what they are writing – and it also helps reduce the time it takes to mark the essays.

5 **Be even firmer about word limits in coursework essays sometimes.** For example suggest 'exactly 400 words' with penalties for each word over or under. Using word-processing software it is easy for students to track the length of their essay on-screen as they compose it, and students often enjoy the challenge of 'putting their best foot forward' in this constrained amount of words. Writing to length is an important skill. Besides, it is demonstrably fair if all students are constrained in the same way, as it can be argued that anyone could score more marks if they had more words at their disposal.

6 **Help students to develop the skills required to plan the content for essays.** This is particularly important in those disciplines where students will be more accustomed to handling structured questions and problems. The danger then is that students tackling essay questions in exams spend far too long on them, and penalise themselves regarding time for the rest of the examination. One of the best – and most time-effective – ways of helping students to become better at handling essay questions is to set class or coursework tasks which require students to prepare essay-plans rather than fully finished masterpieces. A concept-map or diagram can show a great deal about the eventual 'worth' of students' essays, and can avoid distraction from the elements of style and structure. Students can put together at least half-a-dozen essay plans in the time it would take them to complete one essay, and making the plans involves far more payoff per unit time in thinking and learning.

7 **Don't assess essays too often.** Any assessment form advantages those students who happen to be skilled at delivering what is being measured. This applies to essays too, and there is a significant danger that those students who happen to become good at planning and writing essays continue to be advantaged time and time again.

8 **Have a clear, well-structured marking scheme for each essay question.** This can save a lot of time when marking, and can help guarantee that students' answers are assessed fairly and consistently. That said, even the most carefully-designed marking schemes for essays always seem to need adjustment as soon as you start marking a batch, as students' answers always range more widely than one anticipated.

9 **Don't assume that longer equals better.** It is often harder for students to write succinctly than to just ramble on. However, students need to be briefed on how best we want them to develop their art in writing concisely.

10 **Help students to improve their technique through feedback.** Consider the range of approaches you can use to give students useful feedback on their essays, including statement banks, assignment return sheets and email messages, and try to minimise the time you spend writing similar feedback comments onto different students' essays.

11 **Let technology help you to give useful feedback.** The track-changes function on word processing software allows you to speed up giving comments when marking on-screen. In particular, the *comments* can be linked visually to the word, phrase or paragraph you're giving feedback on, and allows you to say more than you could squeeze in between the lines of an essay.

12 **Use some class time to get students to brainstorm titles for essays.** This helps them to think about the standard they could anticipate for essay questions in forthcoming exams, and gives them topic areas to base their practice on.

Pause for thought: a chance to assess two essays

Below you can try your hand at assessing two essays on the same title. Students were briefed to discuss the topic of the title in about 700 words. The level can be regarded as a preparatory course for students working towards entering a Foundation-level Course in Technology. One of the two essays below was written by a mature student, and the other by the author of this book, as a foil.

Preferably with a group of colleagues, 'mark' both essays out of 20 marks (making up your own marking scheme as you go along if you wish). Try to work out which was the 'better' of the two essays, and why this is the case. Then compare your marks with those of other people, and don't be surprised if they diverge quite a lot! Next, compare your marking schemes, and see whether it is possible to agree on a scheme which could be claimed to mark these essays reliably and fairly.

Essay 1: Technology made large populations possible; large populations make technology indispensable

The population of every country in the world has increased in the last 150 years, and in some countries the rate of increase has been much greater than in Britain. When populations increase, more food has to be produced to keep these people nourished. More houses have to be built, with increased water supply and facilities for sewage disposal. More schools and hospitals are needed. Forests are cleared and burned to give fertile land to grow crops but if the increase in food production and provision of housing and other facilities does not take place at the same rate as the increase in population, then the standard of living falls.

The life expectation up to about 150 years ago rose slowly from an average of 20 years for early man to the 50s in the 19th century. Today's life expectancy is 70–80 years and is therefore a population increase of 50 per cent. Infant and child mortality has, until now, been high – in 1866 only 40–45 per cent of those aged between 0 and 15 years were expected to survive. Diseases such as cholera, typhoid, tuberculosis and diphtheria took their toll, mainly on the poor living in slums. Improvements in the standard of hygiene and sanitation reduced this rate so that the survival rate of 0–15 year olds increased to between 62 and 75 per cent in 1961 in Britain, but this is still lower in many parts of the world today.

The world population in 3000 BC was about 100 million. This slowly increased to about 350 million in 100 BC. In the Middle Ages the population was steady at around 350–500 million until the Black Death caused a drop to 250 million people. The population then increased rapidly to around 1,000 million in the 1800s and then very rapidly to nearly 4,000 million in the early 1980s. The projected rise is around 6,500 million people by the year 2000.

Darwin stated in his book *The Origin of Species* that 'there is no exception to the rule that every organic being naturally increases at so high a rate that if not destroyed, the earth would soon be covered by the progeny of a single pair'. He also recognised that there are many 'checks to increase' which limit the size of populations. For humans, the checks have included diseases and epidemics as well as famine over which until recent times, man has had very little control, and wars over which he does. Even now, his control is far from complete where diseases are concerned. The degree to which the incidence of fatal diseases such as smallpox, cholera and tuberculosis has been reduced since 1955, has resulted in an enormous increase in population throughout the tropics. With more mouths to feed, the threat of starvation has increased. Starving people are not as well able to work and increase food production as healthy, well-fed people.

The rise in population is exponential and one wonders what the next 'check to increase' can be. Already, shortage of food and water, and wars, are checking the population growth in many parts of the world. A check on the birth rate would enable the increase in food production to catch up and improve the standard of living of those surviving in the poorer parts of today's world.

High technology is an essential component of medicine today and it can have substantial benefits when appropriately used. A positive and accurate diagnosis made quickly with little discomfort and risk, can lead to quick and efficient appropriate management with resulting reduction in mortality and morbidity. Restoring physiological function (by pacemakers, renal dialysis, open heart surgery or joint replacement) can restore patients to a full and near-normal length of life. Powered prostheses for the severely disabled and simpler aids for other disabilities, can enhance the quality of life for years by allowing greater degrees of independence and easier communication.

The world population cannot continue to grow at its present rate, its resources are running out through use as well as destruction. Conservation has to be now; in ten years' time it might well be too late for us all!

Essay 2: Technology made large populations possible; large populations make technology indispensable

At first sight this seems an excellent example of cause and effect. In this case, technology can be regarded as the cause, and large populations the effect. Looking back over human history, populations increased relatively slowly for millions of years, and the growth in population only became alarming in the last hundred years or so – the age of technology.

There are many examples supporting how technology makes large populations possible. Medical science and technology have allowed many former killer diseases to be eradicated, and consequently life expectancy in the developed world has increased more in the last hundred years than in our evolutionary history. Technology has made it possible to sustain large populations. For example, agricultural technology and fertilisers have allowed greater productivity from limited amounts of farmland. It has been possible to convert to agricultural use land that was previously unsuitable.

Large populations have indeed become dependent on technology. In the developed world, transportation (for example) is an essential part of the way we live, and without technology life as we know it would be difficult – if not impossible. In the home, less and less time is spent on basic tasks such as cooking, washing, cleaning and so on. Technology has been used to automate many of these. More and more time is devoted to leisure activities – particularly that of sitting at home and watching one particular form of technology for entertainment and enlightenment: the television set.

So it would appear that large populations have made technology indispensable. However, our planet is of finite size. The resources upon which many forms of technology draw are limited in availability. The amounts of fossil fuels are limited. The amounts of metal ores are limited. The ability of our ecosystem to absorb the toxic products of some forms of technology are limited. In other words, technology itself has limits. There comes a point where greater uses of technology start to produce irreversible changes in our ecosystem. The holes in the ozone layer may be an example of this.

While it has always been recognised that a finite planet can only support a finite population, it has only recently become recognised that our uses of some forms of technology can only take place on a limited scale. Despite the logic of limiting the population of our planet, there has not been any evidence of any real readiness to accept the implications of the steps necessary to limit population globally. Similarly, it seems difficult for people to agree to curb some forms of technology which are becoming life-threatening.

All is not bad news, however. There are some sources of technology which do not have any deleterious effects on our environment. For example, hydroelectricity, solar energy, wind power, tidal power and wave power are all 'free' forms of energy which do not cause toxins to be released into our ecosystem, and potentially allow us to continue to be dependent on various electrical technologies. Other renewable resources can allow us to continue using paper, some liquid fuels, and medicines. Often, the cost of using renewable resources is greater than that of consuming the finite reserves of our planet, but if large populations are to continue to depend on technology, that cost – sooner or later – will have to be accepted.

In conclusion, it is certainly true that technology played a major part in allowing large populations to develop. To sustain such populations, technology will indeed be indispensable – but only if the wisdom of choosing *appropriate* technologies is brought to bear on preserving our ecosystem. Otherwise, technology will eventually make large populations untenable – or large populations will make the continued use of some technologies impossible.

Debrief on the essay-marking exercise

Here are some of the main points which arise when I use this exercise with lecturers or students at workshops on assessment, or on the study-skills side of essay-writing.

1 Marks for Essay 1 vary enormously, from 17/20 to zero.
2 Marks for Essay 2 are generally considerably higher, from 10/20 to full marks.
3 The exercise invariably shows that essays are an unsafe assessment device when it comes to reliability of marking.
4 Essay 1 is stronger than Essay 2 on content, but only really addresses one part of the title. Many markers give this a really low mark saying 'it didn't answer the question' (even though there was not a question, only a title).
5 Essay 2 was deliberately 'crafted' to *read* more easily than Essay 1, yet is largely weak on real content, and this pays off in marks, showing that markers are susceptible to 'wordsmithing' rather than content of the essay.
6 Essay 2, in its own way has a clear beginning (in a way challenging the title), a seemingly logical progression (with the first sentence of each paragraph echoing several words from the title), and a more-definite end, while Essay 1 just 'stops'. Markers often interpret these differences as 'better structure' for Essay 2, justifying their higher marks.

A possible marking scheme

The marking schemes designed by lecturers are often very divergent, showing that even with the best of intentions, the assessment of such essays still has a significant degree of subjectivity associated with it. Also, lecturers tend to include in their marking schemes ingredients such as 'structure', and 'coherence' which need explanation to students. The scheme shown in Table 2.2 was composed by students rather than lecturers. It could be claimed, however, that this is a reasonable approach to assess a fairly large batch of essays with this title, and that each of the two essays would actually score quite similarly, one being stronger on content and the other on structure.

6 Reviews and annotated bibliographies

Anyone who reviews books or articles for journals or magazines will confirm that there's no better way of making oneself look deeply into a book or article than to be charged with the task of writing a review of it! Getting students to write reviews is therefore a logical way of causing them to interact in depth with the information they review. One way of getting students to review a lot of material at once is to ask them to produce annotated bibliographies on a topic area, and to use these as assessment artefacts.

Annotated bibliographies can provide a much better assessed-coursework task than conventional essays. They can't be used in traditional exams, as candidates would not have the required range of materials available to review, but they can be used in open-book exams where it can be ensured that the required range is provided.

Advantages

- *Reviewing is an active process.* Reviewing material gives students a task to do which focuses their thinking, and helps them avoid reading passively, or writing the content out in 'transcribing' mode.
- *Reviews are useful for revision.* When students have reviewed material, the reviews remain useful learning tools in their own right, and may spare students from having to wade through the material on subsequent revision.
- *Reviewing is high on authenticity.* In most careers, the ability to take in, speedily evaluate and prioritise documents and publications is highly valued, and producing annotated bibliographies as a student is excellent practice, in a context where the skills can be developed with the aid of feedback.
- *Reviewing is excellent practice for research.* The literature review element is important both for students working towards higher degrees, and in contributions they make to the research literature. Annotated bibliographies as an assessed task allow them to develop the relevant skills with feedback from tutors and from fellow students.
- *Annotated bibliographies can be high on validity.* They are one of the most valid ways of assessing the extent to which students have got their heads round the literature in a particular area of a discipline.
- *It can be really useful to have tightly word-constrained bibliographies.* This makes the assessment demonstrably fair to students, and rewards them for skills of prioritisation and concise writing.
- *There is less chance of plagiarism or cheating.* Because annotated bibliographies tend to be highly individual, and word-constrained ones may be quite short, any plagiarism or copying would be much more likely to be noticed than in long essays.
- *Annotated bibliographies can be much quicker to mark than essays.* Bibliographies are necessarily much more condensed, even when quite a large field is being addressed.
- *Marking of annotated bibliographies can be much higher in reliability than marking essays.* Partly because annotated bibliographies are tightly focused, the degree of subjectivity in assessing them is reduced significantly. Content is much more important than style.

Table 2.2 A possible marking scheme

Technology made large populations possible:	
Arguments for:	3
Arguments against:	3
Large populations make technology indispensable:	
Arguments for:	3
Arguments against:	3
Mentioning sources	2
Strong introduction	2
Firm conclusion	2
Flow and readability	2
Total	**20**

- *Reviewing involves important cognitive processes.* When students are required to review material from different sources critically, they are necessarily engaged in higher-level skills of comparing, contrasting and evaluating – far beyond passive reading.
- *Reviewing other papers and articles is useful practice for research writing.* Students who will move on to research can benefit from the training involved in writing reviews, and gain skills in communicating their conclusions coherently.
- *Reviewing helps students to develop critical skills.* Getting students to compare and contrast chosen sources helps them think more deeply about the subject matter involved.
- *Compiling annotated bibliographies is a way of requiring students to survey a considerable amount of material.* It also helps them to reduce a large field to a manageable body of notes and references.

Disadvantages

- *Reviews are necessarily quite individual.* For reviews to lend themselves to assessment, it is important that the task should be delineated quite firmly. This may go against the open-ended approach to reviewing which we may wish students to develop.
- *There may not be sufficient books or journal copies!* With large numbers of students and limited library resources, students may find it difficult or impossible to get adequate access to the materials we want them to review. It might be necessary to have particular sets of materials temporarily made 'for reference only' so that their availability is increased while reviewing is in progress.
- *Reviewing individually can be lonely.* Reviewing a range of resources is often best done as a group task rather than an individual one, maximising the benefits that students derive from discussion and debate. It then becomes more difficult to assess individual contributions to such reviews.

Setting assessed review tasks

1 **Promote variety.** Ask students to select their own subject for research, and give them a wide range of topics to choose from. This can, however, limit the reliability of assessment in that it would be unfair if 'easy' topics fared better than more problematic ones when it came to assessing the reviews.

2 **Prompt awareness of audience.** Ask students to write reviews of different kinds of publication (learned journal, subject magazine, next year's students, student newsletter, and so on), so that they become aware of the differences in tone and style of writing which are appropriate for different audiences.

3 **Get students to assess existing reviews.** For example, issue students with a selection of existing reviews, and ask them to identify features of the best reviews, and faults of the worst ones. As always, students learn more

from seeing a range of artefacts of different quality, than from just seeing exemplars.

4 **Help students to see that reviewing is not just a matter of summarising what everyone has said.** You only have to look at book reviews in journals to see how some reviewers make up their contributions by summarising the 'contents' pages of the material that they are reviewing. This is not a high-level intellectual activity.

5 **Decide about credit to be awarded to 'search' tasks.** It is useful to get students both to locate all relevant major resources addressing a field, and to prioritise (for example) the most important or most relevant half-dozen sources.

6 **Consider limiting the parameters.** Getting students to do a short comparative review of two or three important sources can be easier (and fairer) to assess than when the reviews are done without any restrictions. When such

focused review tasks are coupled with a general search, it is possible to measure information retrieval skills as well as the higher-level 'compare and contrast' skills, without the agenda for the latter remaining too wide for objective assessment.

7 **Set a tight word limit for the review.** The art of writing a good, short review is more demanding than writing long reviews. When students' reviews are of equal length, it becomes easier to distinguish the relative quality of their work. However, brief students on how to draft and re-draft their work, to ensure the quality of short reviews. Make sure that students don't adopt the 'stop when you've written a thousand words' approach.

8 **Think about combining collaborative and individual work.** For example, suggest that groups of students do a search collaboratively, and identify the most relevant sources together. Then suggest they write individual reviews of different sources. Finally, consider asking them to share their reviews, then write individual comments comparing and contrasting the sources.

9 **Ask students to look at the same texts, but give them different focuses.** For example, students could look at a series of articles on pollution, and write different reviews of them aimed to be separately useful to conservationists, parents, individualists, those focusing on sustainability, and general consumers.

10 **Encourage qualitative judgement.** Prompt students to write on not only what a book or article is about, but also about how effective it is in providing convincing arguments, and how well it is expressed.

11 **Involve your library or information services staff.** It's a mean trick to send off large groups of students to rampage through the library, without giving notice to the staff there of what you are doing. Discussing your plans with your faculty librarians, for example, gives them a chance to be prepared, and gives opportunities for them to make suggestions and give advice to you on the nature of the task, before you give it to students.

12 **Think hard about resource availability.** Make sure that there won't be severe logjams with lots of students chasing particular library resources. Widen the range of suggested resources. Consider arranging with library staff that any books which will be in heavy demand are classified as 'reference only' stock for a specified period, so that they can remain in the library rather than disappearing on loan.

13 **Consider setting annotated bibliographies as formative group tasks.** This can encourage students to collaborate productively in future information-seeking tasks, and can reduce the drudgery sometimes experienced in tasks such as literature searching. Giving feedback on the reviews can be sufficiently valuable to students to make it unnecessary to couple the task with formal assessment.

14 **Consider making the final product 'publishable'.** Aim to compile collections of the best reviews and annotated bibliographies, for example to use in next year's Course Handbook, or as the basis of an assessed task for next year's students.

15 **Explore the possibility of involving library staff in the assessment.** Library staff may be willing and able to assess annotated bibliographies and reviews in parallel with yourself, or may be willing to provide additional feedback comments to students.

7 Reports

Assessed reports make up at least part of the coursework component of many courses. Report-writing is one of the most problematic study-skills areas in which to work out how to advise students to develop their approaches. The format, layout, style and nature of an acceptable report varies greatly from one discipline to another, and even from one assessor to another in the same discipline. The most common kinds of report that many students write are those associated with their practical, laboratory or field work. Several of the suggestions offered in this section relate particularly to report-writing in science and engineering

Pause for thought: a case study

The task shown below was set to a cohort on a Postgraduate Certificate in Learning and Teaching programme, as a pre-workshop exercise.

Word-constrained preparatory task on assessment: 800 words only

- Please select the *four* sources that you think are the most valuable, on the assessment of students' work and provision of effective feedback to students.
- Rank them in order of *'value'*, '1' being most valuable.
- Turn your thoughts on these into an annotated bibliography, presenting the references as you would list them in a published journal article, arranging them in order of *'worth'*, with the text of your annotated bibliography justifying your inclusion of these four sources, and explaining *why* you put them in the order you have chosen.
- Please email these to the course administrator, so that a print-out of each can be used at the workshop, for peer assessment and review, as a case-study exercise at the workshop.

disciplines, but can readily be extended to other subject areas. Nowadays, more report-writing is drafted online, and giving students feedback using 'track-changes' functions in word-processing software can help them to develop the editing and refining skills needed to lead them to producing high-quality reports.

Advantages

- *Authenticity can be high, as report-writing is a skill relevant to many jobs.* In many careers and professional areas, the ability to put together a convincing and precise report is useful. Assessed report-writing can therefore provide a medium where specific skills relevant to professional activity can be addressed.
- *Reports can be the end product of useful learning activities.* For example, the task of writing reports can involve students in research, practical work, analysis of data, comparing measured findings with literature values, prioritising, and many other useful processes. Sometimes these processes are hard or impossible to assess directly, and reports provide secondary evidence that these processes have been involved successfully (or not).
- *Report-writing can allow students to display their talents.* The fact that students can have more control when they write reports than when they answer exam questions, allows students to display their individual strengths.
- *Report-writing can be developed incrementally.* Students can be encouraged to cooperate in early stages of report-writing, and learn through feedback from each other, before producing final versions to submit for assessment.
- *Report-writing can be turned into a collaborative task.* Where, for example, students have been working in groups on practical or field work, the groups can be required to submit a joint report, and students can help to work together to refine this by using 'Google Docs' where they collaborate online towards the production of their final report.

Disadvantages

- *Unwanted collaboration can be difficult to detect.* For example, with laboratory work, there may be a black market in old reports! Also, when students are working in pairs or groups in practical work, it can be difficult to set the boundaries between collaborative work and individual interpretation of results.

- *Report-writing can take a lot of student time.* When reports are assessed and count towards final grades, there is the danger that students spend too much time writing reports at the expense of getting to grips with their subject matter in a way which will ensure that they succeed in other forms of assessment such as exams.
- *Report-marking can take a lot of staff time.* With increased numbers of students, it becomes more difficult to find the time to mark piles of reports and to maintain the quality and quantity of feedback given to students about their work.

Setting assessed report-writing

1 **Give clear guidance regarding the format of reports.** For example, issue a sheet listing principal generic section headings, with a short description of the purpose and nature of each main section in a typical report. Remind students, when necessary, of the importance of this guidance in your ongoing feedback to their reports.

2 **Get students to assess subjectively some past reports.** Issue students with copies of some good, bad and indifferent reports, and ask them to mark them independently, simply giving each example an impression mark. Then facilitate a discussion where students explain why they allocated the marks in the ways they did.

3 **Get students to assess objectively some past reports.** Issue groups of students with good, bad and indifferent reports, along with a sheet listing assessment criteria and a mark scheme. Ask each group to assess the reports. Then initiate discussions and comparisons between groups.

4 **Make explicit the assessment criteria for reports.** Help students to see the balance between the marks associated with the structure of their reports, and those given to the content and the level of critical thinking and analysis.

5 **Use a whole-class session to get students to design assessment criteria for reports.** Then use at least some of the criteria they come up with in the assessment of their reports. You may be surprised how well students can come up with good criteria, in clear wording.

6 **Ask students for full reports less often.** For example, if during a course students tackle eight pieces of work involving report-writing, ask students to write full reports for only two of these, and ask for summary or 'short-form' or 'memorandum' reports for the remaining assignments. These shorter reports can be structured in note form or bullet points, and can still show much of the evidence of the thinking and analysis that students have done.

7 **Accommodate collaboration.** One way round the problems of collaboration is to develop approaches where students are required to prepare reports in groups – often closer to real life than preparing them individually.

8 **Involve students in assessing each other's reports.** When marks for reports 'count' significantly, it may be desirable to moderate student peer-assessment in one way or another, but probably the greatest benefit of peer-assessment is that students get a good deal more feedback about their work than hard-pressed staff are able to provide. It is far quicker to moderate student peer-assessment than to mark all the reports from scratch.

9 **Consider asking students to write (or word-process) some reports onto pre-prepared pro formas.** This can help where there are significant 'given' elements such as equipment and methodology. You can then concentrate on assessing the important parts of their writing, for example interpretation of data.

10 **Publish clear deadlines for the submission of successive reports.** For example, in the case of practical work, allow only one or two weeks after the laboratory session. It is kinder to students to get them to write up early, rather than to allow them to accumulate a backlog of report writing, which can interfere (for example) with their revision for exams.

11 **Prepare a standard assessment/feedback grid, to return to students with marked reports.**

Include criteria and marks associated with (for example) the quality of data, observations, calculations, conclusions, references and verdicts.

12 **Start students thinking even before the practical work.** For example, allocate practical work in advance of laboratory sessions, and include some assessed pre-laboratory preparation as a prelude to the eventual report. One way of doing this is to pose half a dozen short-answer questions for students to complete before starting a piece of laboratory work. This helps students know what they are doing, rather than follow instructions blindly. It also avoids wasting time at the start of a laboratory session working out only then which students are to undertake each experiment.

13 **Include some questions linked closely to practical or field work in examinations.** For example, tell students that two exam questions will be based on work they will have done outside the lecture room. This helps to ensure that practical work and associated reports don't get forgotten when students start revising for exams.

14 **Get students to design exam questions based on the work covered by their reports.** Set groups of students this task. Allocate some marks for the creativity of their questions. When done over several years, the products could be turned into a bank of questions which could be placed on computer for students to consult as they prepare for exams.

15 **Wherever possible, allow students to use computers in the laboratories and other practical work situations.** Where facilities are available, arrange that students can input their experimental data directly onto a computer or network. Many universities now enable students to write up their reports straight into a word processor alongside the laboratory bench, using a report template on disk. Such reports can be handed in immediately at the end of the laboratory session, and marked and returned promptly.

8 Practical work

Many areas of study involve practical work, but it is often much more difficult to assess such work in its own right; assessing reports of practical work may only involve measuring the quality of the end product of the practical work, and not the work itself, compromising the validity of the assessment. The following discussion attempts to help you to think of ways of addressing the assessment of the practical work itself.

Advantages

- *Practical work is really important in some disciplines.* In many areas of physical sciences for example, practical skills are just as important as theoretical competences. Students proceeding to research or industry will be expected to have acquired a wide range of practical skills.
- *Employers may need to know how good students' practical skills are (and not just how good their reports are).* It is therefore useful to reserve part of our overall assessment for practical skills themselves, and not just the final products of practical work.
- *Practical work is learning-by-doing.* Increasing the significance of practical work by attaching assessment to it helps students approach such work more earnestly and critically.
- *Students can gain a lot of feedback while they do practical work.* They get very rapid feedback just by seeing how the work itself proceeds, and often get even more feedback by watching and talking with fellow students working alongside them.

Disadvantages

- *It is often difficult to assess practical work in its own right.* It is usually much easier to assess the end point of practical work, rather than the processes and skills involved in their own right.

- *Where students are doing practical work alongside each other, it is difficult to assess individual performance.* However, in many situations, working alongside other people is more authentic than working alone, so perhaps this limitation is acceptable enough.
- *Practical work is expensive.* When there are large numbers of students, there is now the tendency to allow independent study (often online) in place of what used to be practical work, and it is therefore not as possible as it used to be to try to assess practical skills directly.
- *It can be difficult to agree on assessment criteria for practical skills.* There may be several ways of performing a task well, requiring a range of alternative assessment criteria.
- *Students may be inhibited when someone is observing their performance.* When doing laboratory work, for example, it can be very distracting to be watched! Similar considerations apply to practical exercises such as interviewing, counselling, advising, and other 'soft skills' which are part of the agenda of many courses.

Questions and suggestions for assessing practical work

It is important to address a number of questions about the nature and context of practical work, the answers to which help to clarify how best to go about assessing such work. First the questions, then some suggestions:

1 **What exactly are the practical skills we wish to assess?** These may include a vast range of important skills, from deftness in assembling complex glassware in a chemistry laboratory to precision and speed in using a scalpel on the operating table. It is important that students know the relative importance of each skill.

2 **Why do we need to measure practical skills?** The credibility of our courses sometimes depends on what students can do when they enter employment. It is often said by employers that students are very knowledgeable, but not necessarily competent in practical tasks.

3 **Where is the best place to try to measure these skills?** Sometimes practical skills can be measured in places such as laboratories or workshops. For other skills, students may need to be working in real-life situations.

4 **When is the best time to measure practical skills?** When practical skills are vitally important, it is probably best to start measuring them relatively early on in a course (after allowing sufficient time for practice or rehearsal), so that any students showing alarming problems with them can be appropriately advised or redirected.

5 **Who is in the best position to measure practical skills?** For many practical skills, the only valid way of measuring them involves someone doing detailed observations while students demonstrate the skills involved. This can be very time consuming if it has to be done by staff, and also can feel very threatening to students.

6 **Is it worth using video-cameras?** This provides a way of going back and spot-checking particular instances of practical skills in action, but could also be inhibiting to students. In any case, tracking down the particular instances to assess may be much too time-consuming in practice.

7 **Is it necessary to establish minimum acceptable standards?** In many jobs, it is quite essential that everyone practising does so with a high level of skill (for example surgery!). In other situations, it is possible to agree on a reasonable level of skills, and for this to be safe enough (for example teaching?).

8 **How much should practical skills count for?** In some disciplines, students spend a considerable proportion of their time developing and practising practical skills. It is important to think clearly about what contribution to their overall assessment such skills should make, and to let students know this.

9 **May student self-assessment of practical skills be worth using?** Sometimes students know better than anyone else how well they are doing practical tasks, but they can be too hard on themselves when it comes to self-assessing things they have just learned. However, getting students to try to assess their own practical skills can be one way round the impossible workloads which could be involved if staff were to do all the requisite observations. It is much quicker for staff to moderate student self-assessment of such skills than to undertake the whole task of assessing them.

10 **May student peer-assessment of practical skills be worth using?** Involving students in peer-assessment of practical skills can be much less threatening than using tutor assessment. The act of assessing a peer's practical skills is often very good for the peer-assessors, in terms of improving similar skills of their own, and learning from others' triumphs and disasters.

11 **Is it necessary to have a practical examination?** In some subjects, some sort of end point practical test may be deemed essential. Driving tests, for example, could not be wholly replaced by a written examination on the Highway Code.

12 **Reserve some marks for the processes.** Help students to see that practical work is not just reaching a defined end point, but is about the processes and skills involved in doing so successfully.

13 **Ask students to include in their reports 'ways I would do the experiment better next time'.** This encourages students to become more self-aware of how well (or otherwise) they are approaching practical tasks.

14 **Add some 'supplementary questions' to report briefings.** Make these questions that students can only answer when they have thought through their own practical work. For example, students can be briefed to compare their findings with a given published source, and comment on any differences in the procedures used in the published work from those they used themselves.

15 **Design the right end products.** Sometimes it is possible to design final outcomes which can only be reached when the practical work itself is of high quality. For example, in chemistry, the skills demonstrated in the preparation and refinement of a compound can often be reflected in the purity and amount of the final product.

9 Portfolios and e-portfolios

Building up portfolios of evidence of achievement is becoming much more common in higher education, to allow a range of kinds of evidence to be presented for assessment. There is a tendency nowadays to use e-portfolios, allowing students to build them up online, often on particular dedicated software platforms, and to work both independently and collaboratively while building them up. It has to be said, however, that e-portfolios are very difficult to mark fairly, not least because it is difficult to get a feel for 'the whole thing' in the same way as can be done with a physical portfolio.

Typically, portfolios are compilations of evidence of achievement, including major pieces of students' work, feedback comments from tutors, and reflective analyses by the students themselves. It seems probable that in due course, degree classifications will no longer be regarded as sufficient evidence of students' knowledge, skills and competences, and that profiles will be used increasingly to augment the indicators of students' achievements, with portfolios to provide in-depth evidence. Probably the most effective way of leading students to generate portfolios is to build them in as a significant part of a course, attracting commensurate weight in overall assessment. Here, the intention is to alert you to some of the more general features to take into account when assessing student portfolios. You may yourself also be thinking about building your own portfolio of evidence of your teaching practice, and can build on some of the suggestions below to make this process more effective and efficient.

Advantages

- *Portfolios tell much more about students than exam results.* They can contain evidence reflecting a wide range of skills and attributes, and can reflect students' work at its best, rather than just a cross-section on a particular occasion.
- *Portfolios can be high on validity.* It is possible to assess appropriate evidence of achievement relating more directly to intended learning outcomes, than (for example) can be achieved just with written exams.
- *Portfolios can be strong regarding authenticity.* The content of a portfolio can be directly relevant to the context of real-world employment for which students may be preparing.
- *Portfolios can reflect development.* Most other forms of assessment are more like 'snapshots' of particular levels of development, but portfolios can illustrate progression. This information reflects how fast students can learn from feedback, and is especially relevant to employers of graduates straight from university.
- *Portfolios can reflect attitudes and values as well as skills and knowledge.* This too makes them particularly useful to employers, looking for the 'right kind' of applicants for jobs.

Disadvantages

- *Portfolios take a lot of looking at!* It can take a long time to assess a set of portfolios. This applies whether the portfolios are electronic or paper-based, or a mixture of the two. The time problem extends beyond assessment; even though portfolios may contain material of considerable interest and value to prospective employers, it is still much easier to draw up interview shortlists on the basis of paper qualifications and grades. However, there is increasing recognition that it is not cost-effective to skimp on time spent selecting the best candidate for a post. This is as true for the selection of lecturers as for the selection of students for jobs. Lecturers are increasingly expected to produce hard evidence of the quality of their teaching and research, as well as to demonstrate how they teach, to those involved in their appointment.
- *Portfolios are much harder to mark objectively: reliability of assessment can be a problem.* Because of the individual nature of portfolios, it is harder to decide on a set of assessment criteria which will be equally valid across a diverse set of portfolios. This problem can, however, be overcome by specifying most of the criteria for assessing portfolios in a relatively generic way, while still leaving room for topic-specific assessment.
- *Portfolios are difficult to assess online.* There is a tendency towards using e-portfolios, as nowadays it is often easier to build these up online or on a computer, but when trying to assess them on-screen it is hard to keep in mind the overall scope of the 'bigger picture', and this becomes a serious impediment to make judgements between portfolios which may be quite different in nature.
- *The ownership of the evidence can sometimes be in doubt.* It may be necessary to couple the assessment of portfolios with some kind of oral assessment or interview, to authenticate or validate the origin of the contents of portfolios, particularly when much of the evidence is genuinely based on the outcomes of collaborative work.

Designing and assessing portfolios

1 **Specify or negotiate intended learning outcomes clearly.** Ensure that students have a shared understanding of the level expected of their work.

2 **Propose a general format for the portfolio.** This helps students demonstrate their achievement of the learning outcomes in ways which are more easily assembled.

3 **Specify or negotiate the nature of the evidence which students should collect.** This makes it easier to assess portfolios fairly, as well as being more straightforward for students.

4 **Specify or negotiate the range and extent of the evidence expected from students.** This helps students plan the balance of their work effectively, and helps them avoid spending too much time on one part of their portfolio while missing out important details on other parts.

5 **Don't underestimate the time it takes to assess portfolios.** Also don't underestimate their weight and volume if you have a set of them to carry around with you!

6 **Prepare a pro forma to help you assess portfolios.** It is helpful to be able to tick off the achievement of each learning outcome, and make decisions about the quality of the evidence as you work through a portfolio.

7 **Use post-it notes to identify parts of the portfolio you may want to return to.** This can save a lot of looking backwards and forwards through a portfolio in search of something you know you've seen somewhere!

8 **Consider using post-it notes to draft your feedback comments.** You can then compose elements of your feedback as you work through the portfolio, instead of having to try to carry it all forward in your mind till you've completed looking at the portfolio.

9 **Put a limit on the physical size of the portfolio.** A single box file is ample for most purposes, or a specified size of ring-binder can provide guidance for the overall size.

10 **Give guidance on audio or video elements.** Where students are to include video or audiotapes, it is worth limiting the duration of the elements they can include. Insist that they wind the tapes to the point at which they want you to start viewing or listening, otherwise you can spend ages trying to find the bit that they intend you to assess.

11 **Provide interim assessment opportunities.** Give candidates the opportunity to receive advice on whether the evidence they are assembling is appropriate.

12 **Quality not quantity counts.** Students should be advised not to submit every piece of paper they have collected over the learning period, otherwise the volume of material can be immense.

13 **Get students to provide route maps.** Portfolios are easier to assess if the material is carefully structured, and accompanied by a reflective account which not only outlines the contents but also asserts which of the criteria each piece of evidence contributes towards.

14 **Get students to provide a structure.** Portfolio elements should be clearly labelled and numbered for easy reference. If loose-leaf folders are used, dividers should be labelled to enable easy access to material. All supplementary material such as audiotapes, videos, drawings, computer programs, tables, graphs, and so on should be appropriately marked and cross-referenced.

15 **Be clear about what you are assessing.** While detailed marking schemes are not really appropriate for portfolios, it is still necessary to have clear and explicit criteria, both for the students' use and to guide assessment.

16 **Structure your feedback.** Students may well have spent many hours assembling portfolios and may have a great deal of personal investment in them. To give their work a number marks only (or pass/fail) may seem a small reward. Consider using an assessment pro forma so that your notes and comments can be directly relayed to the students, particularly in cases where required elements are incomplete or missing.

17 **Encourage creativity.** For some students, this may be the first time they have been given an opportunity to present their strengths in a different way. Hold a brainstorming session about the possible contents of portfolios, for example, which may include videos, recorded interviews, newspaper articles, and so on.

18 **Provide opportunities for self-assessment.** Having completed their portfolios, a valuable learning experience in itself is to let the

students assess them. A short exercise is to ask them: 'In the light of your experience of producing a portfolio, what do you consider you did especially well, and what would you now do differently?'

19 **Assess in a team.** If possible set aside a day as a team. Compose your comments about each portfolio, and then circulate them round for others to add to. In this way, students get feedback that is more comprehensive, and assessors get to see a more diverse range of portfolios.

20 **Set up an exhibition.** Portfolios take a long time to complete and assess. By displaying them (with students' permission) their valuable experience can be shared.

21 **Think about where and when you will mark portfolios.** They are not nearly as portable as scripts, and you may need equipment such as video or audio playback facilities to review evidence. It may therefore be helpful to set aside time where you can book a quiet, well-equipped room where you are able to spread out materials and look at a number of portfolios together. This will help you get an overview, and makes it easier to get a feel for standards.

10 Presentations

Giving presentations to an audience requires substantially different skills from writing answers to exam questions, or composing word-processed answers to coursework assignments. Also, it can be argued that the communications skills involved in giving good presentations are much more relevant to professional competences needed in the world of work. It is particularly useful to develop students' presentations skills if they are likely to go on to research, so that they can give effective presentations at conferences. It is therefore increasingly common to have assessed presentations as part of students' overall assessment diet.

Pause for thought about portfolios as an assessment approach

Think of an element of your own curriculum where it would be useful to consider getting students to prepare a portfolio of evidence for assessment. Think through your own responses to the following questions about this possibility.

1. What is the principal intended learning outcome that you have in mind?
2. What do you think are the relative merits of e-portfolios versus paper-based ones?
3. What are the main elements you would suggest that students include in their portfolios?
4. Can you make available to students a range of past portfolios, allowing them to see for themselves strengths of good ones, and weaknesses of poor ones?
5. When it comes to assessment, which would be the key things to assess in a portfolio?
6. What advice would you give to students regarding the structure, format and size of their portfolios?
7. What can you do, in a reasonable timescale, to give students at least some feedback regarding how their portfolios are coming along?
8. Approximately how long do you estimate students should spend making their portfolios?
9. Would it be useful to get students themselves to self-assess their portfolio, and include their self-assessment as one of the ingredients of their portfolios?
10. Approximately how long do you think you will have to assess each portfolio?
11. Are there other people you can involve in the assessment of the portfolios?
12. What additional learning outcomes may the portfolios lend themselves to?

Advantages

- *There is no doubt whose performance is being assessed.* When students give individual presentations, the credit they earn can be duly given to them with confidence.
- *High on authenticity.* Students are very likely to need the skills involved in preparing and delivering effective presentations throughout their subsequent careers.
- *Reliability of assessment can be good,* particularly when tutor-assessment is coupled with peer-assessment. Although the actual marks may vary when a number of assessors take part, the rank order of different presentations is usually established quite well.
- *Validity can be high.* Whether the assessment criteria relate to the actual delivery or to the work done preparing a presentation, what is measured is fairly directly evidence of achievement of the relevant intended outcomes.
- *Students take presentations quite seriously.* The fact that they are preparing for a public performance usually ensures that their research and preparation are addressed well, and therefore they are likely to engage in deep learning about the topic concerned.
- *Presentations can also be done as collaborative work.* When it is less important to award to students individual credit for presentations, the benefits of students working together as teams, preparing and giving presentations, can be realised.
- *Useful reflection can be caused by getting students to self-assess their own presentations.* This helps them to internalise their strengths and weaknesses. However, students tend to be 'too hard' on their own presentations, and it is best that any self-assessment does not contribute too strongly to the overall assessment if presentation marks count towards an award.
- *Where presentations are followed by question-and-answer sessions, students can develop some of the skills they may need in oral examinations or interviews.* Perhaps the most significant advantage of developing these skills in this way is that students can learn a great deal from watching each other's performances.

Disadvantages

- *With large classes, a round of presentations takes a long time.* This can be countered by splitting the large class into groups of (say) twenty students, and facilitating peer-assessment of the presentations within each group on the basis of a set of assessment criteria agreed and weighted by the whole class.
- *Some students find giving presentations very traumatic!* However, it can be argued that the same is true of most forms of assessment, not least traditional exams.
- *At least some evidence is transient.* Accompanying resources such as slides or handout materials can be retained, but the presentation itself can all to easily vanish if not recorded. Should an appeal be made, unless there are recordings, there may be insufficient evidence available to reconsider the merit of a particular presentation. With modern technology however, it is relatively straightforward and inexpensive to routinely record a round of presentations, and banks of recorded presentations can (with students' consent) be used as rehearsal peer-assessment activities, helping students to get their heads round the criteria being applied to their forthcoming presentations.
- *Presentations cannot be anonymous.* It can prove difficult to eliminate subjective bias. However, where several assessments are made of a given presentation, such as when peer-assessment is involved, any bias on the part of a single assessor is compensated for to some extent.

• *When students are involved in peer-assessing a series of presentations, there can be 'drift' in the standards demonstrated.* Later presenters may have learned a great deal from observing earlier ones, and either the quality of presentations may increase quite markedly over the series, or the earlier presentations may be disadvantaged by later higher scores. It may be necessary to compensate in some way for this 'drift' when reviewing the scores for the overall series.

Assessing presentations

1 **Be clear about the purposes of student presentations.** For example, the main purpose could be to develop students' skills at giving presentations, or it could be to cause them to do research and reading and improve their subject knowledge. Usually, several such factors may be involved together, and can contribute accordingly towards the overall assessment of presentations.

2 **Make the criteria for assessment of presentations clear from the outset.** Students will not then be working in a vacuum and will know what is expected of them.

3 **Get students involved in formulating the assessment criteria.** This can be done either by allowing them to negotiate the criteria themselves or by giving them plenty of opportunities to interrogate criteria you share with them.

4 **Ensure that students understand the weighting of the criteria.** Help them to know whether the most important aspects of their presentations are to do with the *way* they deliver their contributions (voice, clarity of expression, articulation, body language, use of audio-visual aids, and so on) or the *content* of their presentations (evidence of research, originality of ideas, effectiveness of argument, ability to answer questions, and so on).

5 **Give students some prior practice at assessing presentations.** It is useful, for example, to give students a dry run at applying the assessment criteria they have devised, to one or two presentations on video. The discussion which this produces usually helps to clarify or improve the assessment criteria.

6 **Let the students have a mark-free rehearsal.** This gives students the chance to become more confident and to make some of the more basic mistakes at a point where it doesn't count against them. Constructive feedback is crucial at this point so that students can learn from the experience.

7 **Involve students in the assessment of their presentations.** When given the chance to assess each other's presentations they take them more seriously and will learn more from the experience. Students merely watching each other's presentations tend to get bored and can switch off mentally. If they are evaluating each presentation using an agreed set of criteria, they tend to engage themselves more fully with the process, and in doing so learn more from the content of each presentation.

8 **Ensure that the assessment criteria span presentation processes and the content of the presentations sensibly.** It can be worth reserving some marks for students' abilities to handle questions after their presentations.

9 **Make up grids using the criteria which have been agreed.** Allocate each criterion a weighting, and get all of the group to fill in the grids for each presentation. The average peer-assessment mark is likely to be at least as good an estimate of the relative worth of each presentation as would be the view of a single tutor doing the assessment.

10 **Be realistic about what can be achieved in a given time.** It is not possible to get twelve five-minute presentations into an hour, as presentations always tend to overrun. It is also difficult to get students to concentrate for more than an hour or two on others' presentations. Where classes are large, consider breaking the audience into groups, for example dividing a class of 100 into four groups, with students presenting concurrently in different rooms, or at different timetabled slots.

11 **Think about the venue.** Students do not always give of their best in large, echoing tiered lecture theatres (nor do we!). A more intimate flat classroom is less threatening particularly for inexperienced presenters, especially those who are rather nervous about presenting.

12 **Consider assessing using videos.** This can allow the presenters themselves the opportunity to review their performances, and can allow you to assess presentations at a time most suitable to you. Viewing a selection of recorded presentations from earlier rounds can be useful for establishing assessment criteria with students. This sort of evidence of teaching and learning is also useful to show external examiners and quality reviewers.

13 **Start small.** Mini-presentations of a few minutes can be almost as valuable as 20-minute presentations for learning the ropes, especially as introductions to the task of standing up and addressing the peer group.

14 **Check what other presentations students may be doing.** Sometimes it can seem to students that everyone is including presentations in their courses. If students find themselves giving three or four within a month or two, it can be very demanding on their time, and repetitious regarding the processes.

11 Vivas – oral exams

Viva-voce ('live voice') exams have long been used to add to or consolidate the results of other forms of assessment, and indeed were the main form of assessment before written exams became endemic in some cultures. They normally take the form of interviews or oral examinations, where students are interrogated about selected parts of work which nowadays they have had assessed in other ways. Such exams are often used to make decisions about the classification of degree candidates whose work straddles borderlines. Usually more than one assessor is present, and may ask most of the questions, with the other(s) at least serving as witnesses if needed.

Advantages

- *Vivas can be regarded as strong on validity.* It can be argued that questioning students orally is one of the most direct ways of allowing them to demonstrate evidence of achievement of many kinds of intended learning outcomes.
- *Vivas can cause students to do a lot of learning.* Because it is usually the case that 'anything could be asked', students will often do a substantial amount of revision to prepare themselves for such events.
- *The skills needed for successful vivas are close to skills students need throughout their careers.* Being able to respond at minimal notice to penetrating questions is useful for employment interviews, and being questioned in live contexts such as media interviews and committee meetings.
- *Vivas are useful checks on the ownership of evidence.* They are good when authenticity needs to be tested. It is relatively easy to use a viva to ensure that students are familiar with things that other forms of assessment seem to indicate they have learned well.
- *Vivas can be useful when searching for particular things.* For example, vivas have long been used to help make decisions about borderline cases in degree classifications, particularly when the written work or exam performance has for some reason fallen below what may have been expected for particular candidates.
- *Candidates may be examined fairly.* With a well-constructed agenda for a viva, a series of candidates may be asked the same questions, and their responses compared and evaluated.
- *It can be useful to use vivas more widely than just at critical points in final assessment.* Sadly, for

most vivas as used at a critical stage to check things at a 'final' assessment, students have not had much opportunity to hone and polish relevant skills, so it is worth considering using vivas more widely but less formally to allow students to develop the appropriate skills without too much depending on their performance.

Disadvantages

- *Some candidates never show themselves well in vivas.* Cultural and individual differences can result in some candidates underperforming when asked questions by experts and figures of authority.
- *The speed of response can be too critical in vivas.* Students who are more hesitant, but who are thinking more deeply about the answer to a question can be disadvantaged in vivas, compared with students whose response is more immediate.
- *Vivas can be regarded as 'sudden death' elements of assessment.* While written exams are often 'sudden death' in nature, a viva which goes wrong can be much more traumatic for the student concerned, who may revisit the event for a long time wishing with hindsight that better responses had been given to the questions asked.
- *The agenda may 'leak'.* When the same series of questions is being posed to a succession of students, it is quite difficult to ensure that candidates who have already been examined aren't able to commune with friends whose turn is still to come.
- *The actual agenda covered by a viva is usually quite narrow.* Vivas are seldom good as measures of how well students have learned and understood large parts of the syllabus.
- *The lack of anonymity can bring its own problems.* Lecturers assessing viva performance can be influenced by what they already know about the students' work. However, it is possible to use lecturers who don't know the students at all, or to include such lecturers in a viva panel.

Planning and using vivas

1 **Remind yourself what the viva is for.** Purposes vary, but it is important to be clear about it at the outset. For example, the agenda could include one or more of the following: confirming that the candidates did indeed do the work represented in their dissertations, or probing whether a poor examination result was an uncharacteristic slip, or proving whether students' understanding of a particularly important part of a subject reached acceptable levels.

2 **Prepare your students for vivas.** Explain to them what a viva is, and what they will normally be expected to do. It helps to give them opportunities to practise. Much of this they can do with each other without your help, but they may need you to start them off on the right lines, and to check now and then that their practice sessions are realistic.

3 **Think about the room layout.** Sitting the candidate on a hard seat while you and your fellow-assessors sit face-on behind a large table is guaranteed to make the candidate tremble! If possible, sit beside or close to the candidate. Where appropriate provide students with a table on which to put any papers they may have brought with them.

4 **Think about the waiting room.** If candidates are queuing together for long, they can make each other even more nervous. If you're asking the same questions of a series of students (in some situations you may be *required* to do this for fairness), the word can get around about what you're asking.

5 **Prepare yourself for vivas!** Normally, if you're a principal player at a viva, you will have read the student's work in some detail. It helps if you come to the viva armed with a list of questions you may ask. You don't have to ask all of them, but it helps to have some ready! Normally, you may need to have a pre-

viva discussion with other members of the examining panel, and you need to be seen to have done your homework.

6 **Prepare the agenda in advance, and with colleagues.** It is dangerously easy (and unfair to students) for the agenda to develop during a series of interviews with different students. Prepare and use a checklist or pro forma to keep records. Memory is not sufficient, and can be unreliable, especially when different examiners conducting a viva have different agendas.

7 **Do your best to put the candidate at ease.** Some students find vivas very stressful, and it improves their confidence and fluency if they are greeted cheerily and made welcome at the start of a viva.

8 **When vivas are a formality, indicate this.** When students have done well on the written side of their work, and it's fairly certain that they should pass, it helps to give a strong hint about this straightaway. It puts students at ease, and makes for a more interesting and relaxed viva.

9 **Ensure there are no surprises.** Share the agenda with each candidate, and clarify the processes to be used. You are likely to get more out of candidates this way.

10 **Ask open questions which enable students to give full and articulate answers.** Try to avoid questions which lead to minimal or 'yes/no' replies.

11 **Don't ask questions which are too long or complex.** It can be hard for candidates to remember, in the heat of the moment, the thrust of a long complex question. It is best instead to use a series of shorter questions, gradually probing deeper when the subject is complex. Alternatively, it can be useful to have a long question printed out on paper or on a card, and to give this to the candidate to study for a moment or two before inviting a response.

12 **Let students do most of the talking.** The role of an examiner in a viva is to provoke thought and prompt candidates into speaking fluently about the work or topics under discussion, and to spark off an intellectual dialogue. It is not to harangue, carp or demonstrate the examiner's intelligence, or to trick candidates!

13 **Prepare to be able to debrief well.** Write your own notes during each viva. If you are dealing with a series of such events, it can become difficult to remember each feedback point that you may want to give to each student. Vivas can be very useful learning experiences, but much of the experience can be lost if time is not set aside for a debrief. Such debriefing is particularly useful when students will encounter vivas again.

14 **When debriefing, ask students for their opinions first.** This can spare them the embarrassment of having you telling them about failings they already know they have. You may also find useful food for thought when students tell you about aspects of the vivas that you were unaware of yourself.

15 **Be sensitive.** Vivas can be traumatic for students, and they may have put much time and effort into preparing for them. Choose words carefully particularly when giving feedback on aspects which were unsuccessful.

16 **Be specific.** Students will naturally want to have feedback on details of things they did particularly well. As far as you can, make sure you can find something positive to say even when overall performance was not good.

17 **Consider recording practice vivas on video.** This is particularly worthwhile when one of your main aims is to prepare students for more important vivas to follow. Simply allowing students to borrow the recordings and look at them in the comfort of privacy can provide students with useful deep reflection on their performance. It is sometimes more comfortable to view the recordings in the atmosphere of a supportive student group.

18 **Run a role-play afterwards.** Ask students to play both examiners and candidates, and bring to life some of the issues they encountered in their vivas. This can allow other students observing the role play to think about aspects which they did not experience themselves.

19 **Plan for the next step.** Get students to discuss strategies for preparing for their next viva, and

ask groups of students to make lists of 'dos and don'ts' to bear in mind next time.

20 Get students to produce a guidance booklet about preparing for vivas and taking part in them. This may be useful for future students, but is equally valuable to the students making it as a way of getting them to consolidate their reflections on their own experience.

12 Student projects

In many courses, one of the most important kinds of work undertaken by students takes the form of individual projects, often relating theory to practice beyond the college environment. Such projects are usually an important element in the overall work of each student, and are individual in nature.

Advantages

- *Project work gives students the opportunity to develop their strategies for tackling research questions and scenarios.* Students' project work often counts significantly in their final year degree performance, and research opportunities for the most successful students may depend primarily on the skills they demonstrated through project work.
- *Validity can be high.* Project work can lead students to produce evidence of achievement relating to high-level intended-learning outcomes, in a form which relates closely to how such evidence will be assessed in real-world scenarios later in students' careers.
- *Projects can be integrative.* They can help students to link theories to practice, and to bring together different topics (and even different disciplines) into a combined frame of reference.
- *Project work can help assessors to identify the best students.* Because project work necessarily involves a significant degree of student autonomy, it does not favour those students who just happen to be good at tackling traditional assessment formats.

Disadvantages

- *Project work takes a lot of marking!* Each project is different, and needs to be assessed carefully. It is not possible for assessors to 'learn the scheme, and steam ahead' when marking a pile of student projects.
- *The quality of the 'write-up' may mask the actual quality of the project work itself.* At the end of the day, it is usually the written report which is assessed, and it is useful to consider whether other 'triangulating' evidence of achievement may be needed, for example in a viva or interview.
- *It is possible that some candidates may not have done everything themselves.* There remain possibilities of copying or plagiarism, and it may be necessary to have ways of checking that candidates have indeed done what is written up.
- *Projects are necessarily different.* This means that some will be 'easier', some will be tough, and it becomes difficult to decide how to balance the assessment dividend between students who tackled something straightforward and did it well, as opposed to students who tried something really difficult, and got bogged down in it.
- *Reliability of assessment can be questionable.* Different assessors will sometimes award quite different marks for the same project report. This is at least partly down to the fact that different assessors are likely to have quite varying degrees of familiarity with the project topic.
- *Projects are relatively final.* They are usually one-off elements of assessment. When students fail to complete a project, or fail to get a difficult one started at all, it is rarely feasible to set them a replacement one. This means that it is usually important to have intermediate stages where it can be established how candidates are getting on, and whether they need advice or support.

Designing student projects

Setting, supporting, and assessing such work can be a significant part of the work of a lecturer, and the following suggestions should help to make these tasks more manageable. ·

1 **Choose the learning-by-doing to be relevant and worthwhile.** Student projects are often the most significant and extended parts of their courses, and it is important that the considerable amount of time they may spend on them is useful to them and relevant to the overall learning outcomes of the courses or modules with which the projects are associated.

2 **Work out specific learning outcomes for the projects.** These will be of an individual nature for each project, as well as including general ones relating to the course area in which the project is located.

3 **Formulate projects so that they address appropriately higher level skills.** The aims of project work are often to bring together threads from different course areas or disciplines, and to allow students to demonstrate the integration of their learning.

4 **Give students as much opportunity as possible to select their own projects.** When students have a strong sense of ownership of the topics of their projects, they put much more effort into their work, and are more likely to be successful.

5 **Include scope for negotiation and adjustment of learning outcomes.** Project work is necessarily more like research than other parts of students' learning. Students need to be able to adjust the range of a project to follow through interesting or important aspects that they discover along the way. Remember that it is still important to set standards, and the scope for negotiation may sometimes be restricted to ways that students will go about accumulating evidence to match set criteria.

6 **Make the project briefings clear, and ensure that they will provide a solid foundation for later assessment.** Criteria should be clear and well understood by students at the start of their work on projects, and the specifications of the evidence of achievement of the outcomes should link well to the assessment criteria to be used.

7 **Keep the scope of project work realistic.** Remember that students will often have other kinds of work competing for their time and attention, and it is tragic when students succeed with project work, only to fail other parts of their courses to which they should have devoted more time alongside their projects.

8 **Liaise with library and information services colleagues.** When a number of projects make demands on the availability of particular learning resources or information technology facilities, it is important to arrange this in advance with such colleagues, so that they can be ready to ensure that students are able to gain access to the resources they will need.

9 **Ensure that a sensible range of factors will be assessed.** Assessment needs to relate to work that encompasses the whole of the project, and not be unduly skewed towards such skills as writing up or oral presentation. These are likely to be assessed in any case in other parts of students' work.

10 **Collect a library of past projects.** This can be of great help to students starting out on their own projects, and can give them a realistic idea of the scope of the work likely to be involved, as well as ideas on ways to present their work well.

11 **Arrange staged deadlines for projects.** It is very useful for students to be able to receive feedback on plans for their project work, so that they can be steered away from going off on tangents, or from spending too much time on particular aspects of a project.

12 **Allow sufficient time for project work.** The outcomes of project work may well include that students develop time-management and task-management skills along the way,

but they need time and support to do this. Arrange contact windows so that students with problems are not left too long without help.

13 **Consider making projects portfolio-based.** Portfolios often represent a flexible and realistic way of assessing project work, and allow appendices containing a variety of evidence to be presented along with the more important parts showing students' analysis, thinking, argument and conclusions.

14 **Encourage students to give each other feedback on their project work.** This can be extended to elements of peer-assessment, but it is more important simply to get students talking to each other about their work in progress. Such feedback can help students sort out many of the problems they encounter during project work, and can improve the overall standard of their work.

15 **Think about the spaces and places which students will use to do their project work.** Some of the work may well occur off-campus, but it remains important that students have access to suitable places to write up and prepare their project work for assessment, as well as facilities and support to help them analyse the data and materials they accumulate.

16 **Include a self-evaluation component in each project.** This allows students to reflect on their project work, and think deeper about what went well and where there may have been problems. It can be particularly useful to students to get feedback about the quality of their self-evaluation.

13 Poster displays and exhibitions

When students are asked to synthesise the outcomes of their learning and/or research into a self-explanatory poster (individually or in groups), which can be assessed on the spot, it can be an extremely valuable process. More and more conferences are providing poster display opportunities as an effective way of disseminating findings and ideas. This kind of assessment can provide practice in developing the skills relevant to communicating by such visual means.

Advantages

- *Poster displays and exhibitions can be a positive step towards diversifying assessment.* Some students are much more at home producing something visual, or something tangible, than at meeting the requirements of traditional assessment formats such as exams, essays or reports.
- *Students can be asked to talk about their posters, or answer questions about them.* This further diversifies evidence of achievement of their learning.
- *Skills in producing visual display material can be relevant to many careers, and to presenting research at conferences.* Assessment of posters can have higher validity than (for example) exams and reports, as the assessed artefacts are developed and refined over a period of time, rather than just providing a snapshot of learning evidenced at a single time. Producing visual display materials can help students to develop a wide range of useful, transferable skills.
- *Posters are normally 'word-constrained'.* A considerable amount of judgement is needed in deciding what is important enough to go into the wording on a poster, leading to deeper reflection than sometimes occurs with writing-based assessment formats.
- *Poster displays and exhibitions can provide opportunities for students to engage in peer-assessment.* The act of participating in the assessment process deepens students' learning, and can add variety to their educational experience.

Disadvantages

- *However valid the assessment may be, it can be more difficult to make the assessment of posters or exhibitions demonstrably reliable.* It is harder to formulate 'sharp' assessment criteria for diverse assessment artefacts, and a degree of subjectivity may necessarily creep into their assessment.
- *It is harder to bring the normal quality assurance procedures into assessment of this kind.* For example, it can be difficult to bring in moderation by external examiners, or to preserve the artefacts upon which assessment decisions have been made so that assessment can be revisited if necessary (for example for candidates who end up on degree classification borderlines).
- *It can take more effort to link assessment of this sort to stated intended learning outcomes.* This is not least because poster displays and exhibitions are likely to be addressing a range of learning outcomes simultaneously, some of which are subject-based, but others of which will address the development of key transferable skills.
- *There can be doubts about who did at least some of the work.* Students may get different amounts of help in the production of the final products as shown in their posters.

Planning assessed poster displays and exhibitions

1 **Use the assessment process as a showcase.** Students are often rather proud of their achievements and it can be invaluable to invite others in to see what has been achieved. Think about inviting moderators, senior staff, students on parallel courses, and employers. Gather their impressions, either using a short questionnaire, or verbally asking them a couple of relevant questions about their experiences of seeing the display.

2 **Use posters as a way to help other students to learn.** For example, final year students can produce posters showing the learning they gained during placements. This can be a useful opportunity for students preparing for their own placements to adjust their approaches and base them on others' experiences.

3 **Get students to peer-assess each other's posters.** Having undertaken the task of making posters themselves, they will be well prepared to review critically the work of others. This also provides chances for them to learn from the research undertaken by the whole cohort rather than just from their own work.

4 **Consider asking students to produce a one-page handout to supplement their poster.** This will test a further set of skills, including the ability to prioritise important findings, and can provide all reviewers with an aide-memoire for subsequent use.

5 **Give sufficient time for the debrief.** Lots of learning takes place in the discussion during and after the display. The tendency is to put poster display and exhibition sessions on during the last week of the term or semester, and this can give little time to unpack the ideas at the end.

6 **Make careful practical arrangements.** Large numbers of posters take up a lot of display space, and to get the best effect they should be displayed on boards. Organising this is possible in most universities, for example by borrowing publicity display boards, but it needs to be planned in advance. Allow sufficient time for students to mount their displays, and make available drawing pins, sticky tack, tape, sticky pads, demountable display equipment, and so on.

7 **Spread the peer-assessment.** It can be worthwhile to number the posters and get one half of the group to assess the odd-numbered posters and the other half to assess the even-numbered ones, and average the data which is produced.

8 **Consider getting groups to produce a poster between them.** This encourages collaborative working and can reduce the overall numbers

of posters – useful when student numbers are large. You could then consider getting students within the group to peer-assess (intra) their respective contributions to the group as well as to assess collaboratively the posters of the other groups (inter-peer-group assessment).

9 **Consider linking the display of posters to open days.** Students coming to visit the institution when they are considering applying for courses may well get a good idea about what students actually do on the courses, from looking at posters on display.

10 **Prepare a suitable assessment sheet.** Base this firmly on the assessment criteria for the exercise. Provide space for peers' comments. This paves the way towards plenty of opportunity for peer feedback.

11 **Provide a rehearsal opportunity.** Let the students have a practice run at a relatively early stage, using a draft or mock-up on flipchart paper. Give them feedback on these drafts, and let them compare their ideas. This can help them to avoid the most obvious disasters later.

12 **Let everyone know why they are using poster displays.** This method of assessment may be unfamiliar to students, and to your colleagues. It is therefore valuable if you can provide a clear justification of the educational merits of the method to all concerned.

13 **Brief students really carefully about what is needed.** Ideally, let them see a whole range of posters from previous years (or some mock-ups, or photographs of previous displays) so that they have a good idea about the requirements, without having their originality and creativity suppressed.

14 **Use the briefing to discuss criteria and weighting.** Students will need to know what level of effort they should put into different elements such as presentation, information content, structure, visual features, and so on. If students are not clear about this, you may well end up with brilliantly presented posters with little relevance to the topic, or really dull,

dense posters that try to compress the text of a long report onto a single A1 sheet.

15 **Give students some practical guidelines.** Let them know how many A1 sheets they can have, where their work will be displayed, suggested minimum size of font for text readability, what resources will be available to them in college, and how much help they can get from outsiders such as friends or others who have the knack of producing visually attractive materials.

16 **Attach a budget to the task.** In poster displays, money shows! If you were to give a totally free hand to students, the ones with best access to photocopiers, photographic resources, expensive papers, and so on may well produce better-looking products than students who have little money to spend on their posters or displays (although it does not always turn out this way). Giving a notional budget can help to even out the playing field, as can requiring students to only use items from a given list, with materials perhaps limited to those provided in the institution.

17 **Keep records of poster displays and exhibitions.** Take photographs, or make a short video. It is not possible to retain complete displays and exhibitions, but a handy reminder can be very useful for use when planning the next similar event. Evidence of the displays can also be interesting to external examiners and quality reviewers.

18 **Get someone (or a group) to provide a 'guide booklet' to the exhibition.** This helps the students undertaking this task to make relative appraisals of the different items or collections making up the exhibition as a whole. Producing such a guide could be considered as a separate assessment task, focusing on reviewing skills.

19 **Consider turning it into a celebration as well.** After the assessment has taken place, especially if invited guests have been asked to contribute, it can be pleasurable to provide some refreshments, and make the display or exhibition part of an end-of-term or end-of-course celebration.

14 Dissertations and theses

Students invest a great deal of time and energy in producing dissertations and theses, usually in their final year. Sometimes these arise from the results of their project work. We therefore owe it to them to mark them fairly and appropriately. Students going on to post-graduate study are very likely to need the skills they gain in such work to write longer, more-complex dissertations or theses as a major part of their evidence of achievement to be submitted for Masters degrees and Doctorates, so some of the considerations given in this section also apply there too.

Advantages

- *Dissertations and theses are individual in nature.* There are reduced possibilities regarding plagiarism and cheating compared with many forms of coursework assessment, and a greater confidence that we are assessing the work of individual students, especially when the assessment includes an oral element such as a viva.
- *Literature review is usually an important element.* Besides developing a range of skills of critiquing and summarising, these link forward to future research and related publications.
- *'Sudden-death' assessment can be tempered by allowing staged feedback.* For example, supervisors can provide at least some feedback in advance of the final assessment, such as on literature-review elements, or methodology descriptions and so on.
- *There is usually double or multiple marking.* Because dissertations and theses are important assessment artefacts, more care is taken to ensure that the assessment is as objective as possible.
- *There is usually further triangulation.* External examiners are often asked to oversee the assessment of at least a cross-section of dissertations or theses, and sometimes see all of them. The fact that such triangulation exists is a further pressure towards making the assessment reliable and valid in the first instance.

Disadvantages

- *Assessment takes a long time.* Even more so than with student projects, dissertations or theses are so individual that it is not possible for assessors to 'get into their stride' and forge ahead marking large numbers of these in a given period of time.
- *There is a problem with standards.* Some topics turn out to be much more difficult than others, and this is often not at all obvious until well into the production of the final product. This means that some students may need considerably more support than others.
- *Students working towards dissertations or theses can feel isolated.* There may not be much opportunity for peer-group interaction, particularly when each student has a different topic.
- *In the absence of sufficient feedback along the way, it is perhaps too easy to fail!* Sometimes the students who most need support and feedback may not seek it, and may not come to the attention of those who would have been able to provide it.
- *Such plagiarism and cheating which may still occur can be difficult to detect.* Nowadays when students can easily insert material downloaded from the web, and adjust it sufficiently so as not to be shown up by plagiarism-detection software, it can be hard to be sure of the authorship of at least parts of a dissertation or thesis, especially if there is no face-to-face probing of the material such as at a viva.
- *Assessment can involve subjectivity, and reliability can be compromised.* For example, it is less possible to achieve 'anonymous' marking with large-scale artefacts such as these, as the first

assessor at least is likely to have been supervising or advising the candidate along the route towards assessment.

- *Assessment can be over-dominated by matters of style and structure.* While both of these are important and deserve to contribute toward assessment of dissertations or theses, there is abundant evidence that a well-structured, fluent piece of work where the actual content is quite modest, attracts higher ratings than a less well-structured, somewhat 'jerky' piece of work where the content has a higher quality.

Assessing dissertations and theses

1 **Make sure that the assessment criteria are explicit, clear and understood by the students.** This may seem obvious! However, theses and dissertations are normally very different in the topics and themes they address, and the assessment criteria need to accommodate such differences. Students will naturally compare marks and feedback comments. The availability of clear criteria helps them see that their work has been assessed fairly.

2 **Get groups of students to assess a few past dissertations.** You can't expect them to do this at the same level as is appropriate for 'real' assessment, but you can (for example) issue students with a one-sided pro forma questionnaire to complete as they study examples of dissertations. Include questions about the power of the introduction, the quality and consistency of referencing, and the coherence of the conclusions. It is particularly valuable if this assessment can be debriefed in a group situation, allowing students to learn from each other's views about matters arising in the assessment of this kind of evidence of achievement.

3 **Offer guidance and support to students throughout the process.** Dissertations usually take students quite some time to complete. Students appreciate and need some help along the route. It is worth holding tutorials both individually and with groups. This takes good planning, and dates need to be set well in advance, and published on a noticeboard or handout to students.

4 **Ensure that student support mechanisms are available.** With large class sizes, we cannot afford to spend many hours of staff time with individual students. However, much valuable support can be drawn from the students themselves, if we facilitate ways of them helping each other. Consider introducing supplemental instruction processes, or setting up friendly yet critical student syndicates. Running a half-day workshop with students counselling each other can be valuable.

5 **Beware of the possibility of bias.** Sometimes dissertations involve students writing on topics with a sensitive cultural or political nature. We need to be aware of any prejudices of our own, and to compensate for any bias these could cause in our assessment. Whenever possible, dissertations should be second-marked (at least!).

6 **Do what you can to provide students with equal opportunity regarding selecting their dissertation themes.** Research for some dissertations will involve students in visiting outside agencies, finding materials for experiments, building models, and so on. With resource limitations becoming more severe, students may be forced to avoid certain topics altogether. Try to suggest topics where financial implications are manageable to students.

7 **Be clear about any institutional requirements.** For example, check whether dissertations have to be bound before submission, or whether they will subsequently be made available in library collections. Some institutions have particular requirements regarding margins, page layout, line-spacing and fonts, and even overall word counts.

8 **Help students to monitor their own progress.** It helps to map the assessment criteria in a

way that helps students to keep track of their own progress and achievements. Computer programs are now available which help students work out how they are getting on, and prompt them to the next steps they should be considering at each stage.

9 **When assessing dissertations, collect a list of questions to select from any forthcoming viva.** Even if there is not going to be a viva, such lists of questions can be useful to help you to design the feedback you return to students.

10 **It can be helpful to use post-it notes while assessing dissertations and theses.** These can be placed towards the edges of pages, so that notes and questions written on the post-it notes can be found easily again. They help you avoid having to write directly on the pages of the dissertation or thesis (especially when your questions are found to have been addressed two pages later!).

15 Work-based learning

Increasing use is being made of assessment based on students' performance in the workplace, whether on placements, as part of work-based learning programmes, or during practice elements of courses. HEA (2012) suggests:

> Much traditional assessment tends to focus on remembering and repeating conceptual knowledge and understanding, whereas employability is more likely to be predicated on students' ability to apply that knowledge in different contexts: solving problems, thinking critically, performing in professional settings or analysing case studies.
>
> (HEA, 2012, p. 12)

Often, a variety of assessors are used, sometimes giving rise to concerns about how consistent assessment practice between the workplace and the institution can be assured. Traditional means of assessment are often unsuitable in contexts where what is important is not easily measured by written accounts. Many courses include a placement period, and the increasing use of accreditation of prior experiential learning in credit accumulation systems means that we need to look at ways of assessing material produced by students in work contexts, rather than just things students write up when back at college after their placements.

Advantages

- *The experience itself can be highly authentic.* Students can get a much more realistic impression of the world outside higher education than if they had done all of their learning on-campus. However, the nature of assessment required by educational institutions may sometimes be incompatible with the evidence of work-based experience actually being assessed.
- *Work-based learning can balance the assessment picture.* Future employers are likely to be at least as interested in students' work-related competences as in academic performance, and assessing work-based learning can give useful information about students' competences beyond the curriculum.
- *Assessing placement learning helps students to take placements more seriously.* As with anything else, if they're not assessed, some students will not really get down to learning from their placements.
- *Assessing placement learning helps to make your other assessments closer to practice.* Although it is difficult to assess placement learning reliably, the validity of the related learning may outweigh this difficulty, and help you to tune in more successfully to real-world problems, situations and practices in the rest of your assessment practice.

• *Assessing placement learning can bring you closer to employers who can help you.* It is sometimes possible to involve external people such as employers in some in-college forms of assessment, for example student presentations, interview technique practising, and so on. The contacts you make with employers during placement supervision and assessment can help you to identify those who have much to offer you.

Disadvantages

• *Reliability of assessment can be difficult to achieve.* Placements tend to be highly individual, and students' opportunities to provide evidence that lends itself well to assessment can vary greatly from one placement to another.
• *The playing field may not be at all level.* Some students will have much better placements than others. Some students will have the opportunity to demonstrate their flair and potential, while others will be constrained into relatively routine work practices. Students therefore may not feel that these aspects of their assessment have been approached fairly.

Assessing work-based learning

The following suggestions may help you to strike an appropriate balance between validity and reliability if your assessment agenda includes assessing work-based learning, whether associated with work placements, or arising from a need to accredit prior experiential learning.

1 **Explore how best you can involve employers, professional supervisors and colleagues.** They will need careful briefing, and negotiation may also be required to achieve their full cooperation, as they (like you!) are often very busy people. Ways of involving them include asking them to produce testimonials, statements of competence, checklists, grids and pro formas, or simply to sign off students' own statements of competence or achievement.

2 **Be clear about the purpose of the assessment.** Is the assessment being done to satisfy a funding body, or because it is required by the university, or because the employers wish it to be done? Or is the assessment primarily to aid students' learning? Or is the assessment primarily designed to help students develop skills and experience which will aid their future careers? Clarifying the purposes can help you decide the most appropriate forms of assessment.

3 **Consider the duration of the placement when working out the weighting of the assessment.** For example, if students spend a considerable time on placement, they may expect any related assessment to reflect this. Conversely, the main intended learning outcomes of the placement may be to gain experience and develop transferable skills, and it could be the case that these are not foremost in the overall picture of intended assessment.

4 **Get the balance right.** Work out carefully what proportion of students' overall assessment will be derived from their placements. Decide whether the related assessment should be on a pass–fail basis, or whether it should be attempted to classify it for degrees.

5 **Expect placements to be very different.** If a group of students are spread through a number of companies or organisations, some will have a very good experience of placement, and others through no fault of their own can have an unsatisfactory experience. It is important that factors outside students' control are not allowed to prejudice assessment.

6 **Consider carefully whether a mentor is well placed to assess.** There can sometimes be complex confusions of role if the person who is the professional supporter or friend of the

student whose performance is being assessed is also the person who has to make critical evaluations for assessment purposes.

7 **Decide carefully whether to tutor-assess during workplace visits.** Visiting students on placement certainly gives tutors opportunities to gather data that may be relevant to assessment, but if assessment is on the agenda the whole nature of such visits changes. One way of separating the assessment ethos from the workplace environment is to handle at least some face-to-face meetings with students off site rather than at the workplace.

8 **Consider including the assessment of a work log.** Some professions prescribe the exact form such a log or work diary should take, whereas in other work contexts it is possible for the course team or the students themselves to devise their own formats. Nowadays students may prefer to build these online, which may mean assessing them on-screen. It is often helpful if such logs include lists of learning outcomes, skills, or competences that students are expected to achieve and demonstrate, with opportunities to check off these and add comments as appropriate. It can be even better to encourage students to express as learning outcomes *unanticipated* learning that they discover happening to them during

a placement. Some of these outcomes may be more important than the intended ones.

9 **Ask students to produce a reflective journal.** This can be done online or in traditional ways. This can be a much more personal kind of document, and might include hopes, fears and feelings as well as more mundane accounts of actions and achievements. Assessing reflective journals can raise tricky issues of confidentiality and disclosure, but ways round such issues can be found, particularly if students are asked to submit for assessment edited extracts from their reflective journals.

10 **Consider using a portfolio.** A portfolio to demonstrate achievement at work can include suitably anonymised real products from the workplace (with the permission of the employer) as well as testimonials from clients, patients, support staff and others.

11 **Help to ensure that assessment does not blind students to their learning on placement.** Consider asking students who have completed work placements to write their experiences up in the form of a journal article, perhaps for an in-house magazine or journal. A collection of these can help to disseminate their experiences. Joint articles written with employers are even more valuable, and help make links with employers better.

16 Critical incident accounts

These are particularly used on courses like nursing, education and social work where the students are asked to reflect on their practical and learning experiences, where previously they might have handed in a detailed and sometimes emotional personal reflection. They can also be used for work-based learning, field trips, practical work, and can be an assessed element of large-scale work such as student projects. Critical incident accounts lead students in the direction of structured reflection, where they can link theory and practice and have the benefits for assessors of being faster, and less emotionally demanding to mark. They can be tailored for particular contexts and can be more or less structured by the tutor depending on the level of the programme (as suitable therefore for new undergraduates as for masters students).

A critical incident account can work like this:

1 Students keep a personal diary of their working life on placement, in employment or alongside their learning. This is private and is not handed in so can be as long or as short as they wish and can be in any form (post-its, on a smart phone, in a scruffy diary or whatever the student prefers), and it is the responsibility of the student to maintain it as an aide-memoire.

2 Students are asked within a twelve-week placement, say, to identify two or three occasions when

something important happened and to answer, in a limited number of words per section (perhaps 200 words) questions such as the following:

- What was the context?
- What kinds of interventions did you make?
- What was the theory that you learned on the course underlying your practice and your choices of actions?
- What was the outcome of the intervention for all parties concerned?
- What did you learn from the experience, both about the work and about yourself?
- What you would do differently next time?

The tutor then can assess a critical incident account of around 1,200 words rather than a very detailed reflection or personal diary.

Advantages

- *Can relate strongly to real-world contexts.* This can be a highly authentic form of assessment, linking well to very different kinds of scenario, and developing candidates' skills for real-world problem-solving.
- *Can be high on validity.* They can allow students to present evidence of achievement of some high-level learning outcomes, evidence which otherwise might not have lent itself to being included in assessment.
- *Students can have a significant degree of choice.* Critical incident accounts can cater for student individuality, both in allowing them to choose what sort of incidents to use, and in how to go about the critical reflection they evidence.
- *Students can safely go 'deeper' than most alternative assessments.* Critical incident accounts can be more or less confidential between each student and the assessor.
- *Creativity and originality can be developed.* Since there is no 'correct' or 'best' solution, students can feel free to experiment and develop their evidence of reflection in a personal way.
- *Can help students to 'cut to the chase' in their writing (or speaking).* This can be helped by having word-constraints in place.
- *The word 'else' in briefings can encourage depth of reflection.* For example, suggested questions can address 'what *else* happened?', 'how *else* could this have been done?', 'why *else* was this important?' and so on.
- *Can link to future employability.* Such accounts can provide information on development 'beyond the curriculum' which may be of interest to future employers.
- *Can help students move beyond mere description.* They can be a better way of causing reflection to occur than just writing reflective logs, which often turn out to be much more descriptive than analytical.
- *There can be freedom regarding the timing.* Critical incident accounts can be written at a particular time as a snapshot of thinking and reflection, or can be developed over a period of time allowing second thoughts and further reflection to take place while editing and refining the account.

Disadvantages

- *The reliability (fairness) of assessment can be hard to achieve well.* Incidents inevitably have differing levels of difficulty, so getting students to have comparable experiences can be difficult.

- *Subjectivity of assessment can be a problem.* Different assessors may take quite different views of the approach, depth and content of a given critical incident account.
- *Students in a large cohort, studying on-campus, sometimes find it hard to work out what sort of incident is 'individual enough' to write a critical incident account.* While students on very different work-placements may find it easy to identify appropriate critical incidents, where students' experiences are broadly similar it can be harder to work out how to pitch individuality and creativity.

Using critical incident accounts as assessed work

1 **Show students a range of examples.** It's a good idea to accumulate a bank of critical incident accounts from previous years (with students' permission, and with appropriate anonymisation and possible deletion of very personal elements), providing students rehearsal opportunities to develop skills at handling this assessment format.

2 **Get students to make judgements on some given accounts.** If possible, give students some practice at *assessing* critical incident accounts, and then discussing why they found particular examples better than others.

3 **Decide what criteria you are going to use to assess critical incident accounts.** Balance your choices among a range of possibilities, including 'depth of reflection', 'individuality', 'creative-thinking', 'willingness to be self-critical', and so on.

4 **Get students to work out and prioritise some criteria to assess critical incident accounts.** A group of students will often come up with excellent criteria which you might not have thought of yourself.

5 **Be prepared to 'give and take' in balancing critical incident accounts against given criteria.** One account will often go a long way in connection with some criteria, but hardly touch on others, and it is best to accommodate flexibility in judging the overall strength of each account.

Making formative feedback work

The National Student Survey in the UK since 2005 has repeatedly shown that the areas where students express least satisfaction regarding their experience of final-year university studies are those linked to assessment and feedback. John Cowan, formerly Director of the Open University in Scotland, famously described assessment as the engine that drives learning, to which I would add that feedback is the oil that lubricates the cogs of understanding. Boud (1988, p. 35) would add:

> Assessment methods and requirements probably have a greater influence on how and what students learn than any other single factor. This influence may well be of greater importance than the impact of teaching materials.

And 'feed-forward'?

In practice, most feedback comprises not just commentary about what has been done, but suggestions for what can be done next. In particular, advice about how to improve the next element of work can be particularly helpful to students receiving feedback, especially when this advice is received during the progress of ongoing work, so that adjustments can be made in a progressive manner. It can be worth checking that enough 'feed-forward' is being given, rather than merely feedback on what has already been done. It is also important to help students themselves to distinguish between feedback and feed-forward, and to look carefully for the latter, and regard it as the most useful part, and consciously build upon it as their work progresses. Hounsell (2008) usefully explains feed-forward as follows:

> Feedforward is a strategy that aims to 'increase the value of feedback to the students by focusing comments not only on the past and present…but also on the future – what the student might aim to do, or do differently in the next assignment or assessment if they are to continue to do well or to do better'.
>
> (Hounsell, 2008, p. 5)

What is formative assessment?

This is a highly contested term with no common understanding in the literature. Pickford and Brown (2006), quoting Cowie and Bell, use the following working definition:

> The process used… to recognise, and respond to, student learning in order to enhance that learning, *during learning*' (Cowie and Bell 1999) (their italics).
>
> (Pickford and Brown, 2006, p. 14)

The problem could be considered to be that students receive too much feedback *after* learning, rather than *during* learning, hence their need for much more feed-forward.

What's the difference between formative and summative assessment?

Sadler, who has written extensively about the powerful impact that formative assessment can have on achievement, suggests:

> Summative contrasts with formative assessment in that it is concerned with summing up or summarizing the achievement status of a student, and is geared towards reporting at the end of a course of study especially for purposes of certification. It is essentially passive and does not normally have immediate impact on learning, although it often influences decisions which may have profound educational and personal consequences for the student. The primary distinction between formative and summative assessment relates to purpose and effect, not to timing. It is argued below that many of the principles appropriate to summative assessment are not necessarily transferable to formative assessment; the latter requires a distinctive conceptualization and technology.
>
> (Sadler, 1989, p. 120)

Many years on, Sadler (2010b) suggests that using grades (or marks) in assessment can be problematic, in that some aspects of the grade may be used with good intentions to help students to improve, while other aspects are meant to refer to the standard reached, and the two factors may be confused:

> If a grade is to be trusted as an authentic representation of a student's level of academic achievement, one of the requirements is that all the elements that contribute to that grade must qualify as achievement, and not be something else. The implications of taking this proposition literally turn out to be far reaching. Many elements that are technically nonachievements are routinely incorporated into grades and thereby act as contaminants. A variety of credits and penalties are often included with the intention of helping shape student behaviours or improve their learning.
>
> (Sadler, 2010b, p. 727)

HEA (2012) shares similar reservations about marks, and cautions on the effects of marks and grades as follows:

> Marks, as currently used, are often more a concrete representation of a tutor's broad judgement about a piece of work than they are a conventional numerical measurement. However, we use these marks formulaically in generating grades, artificially combining marks from different sources, which do not have equal weightings, meaning or validity. Thereby, this over-reliance on numbers can obscure learning and achievement in the search for credit equivalence and the end result is divorced from the aims of the original curriculum design.
>
> (HEA, 2012, p. 13)

A number of writers argue that 'pure' formative assessment does not include marks and grades and Sadler concurs with this view:

> A grade therefore may actually be counterproductive for formative purposes. In assessing the quality of a student's work or performance, the teacher must possess a concept of quality appropriate to the task, and be able to judge the student's work in relation to that concept.
>
> (Sadler, 1989)

Sadler (2010c) also suggests:

> Assessment in higher education has two basic functions, facilitating learning, and creating formal records of achievement for student transcripts. Grading is invariably inferential, and carried out within a framework that shapes how scores and grades are produced and interpreted. Two common frameworks are norm referencing and criterion referencing. Regardless of framework, how assessment programs are designed, tasks constructed and student responses marked are crucial in achieving high quality assessment.
>
> (Sadler, 2010c, p. 249)

Nevertheless, many assessors feel that for students, particularly those working to demonstrate capability in live and practical skills, some kind of indication of level of achievement is valuable and that formative assessment is principally a means by which tutors can support the development of their students' understanding and encourage them to progress by providing feedback that is meaningful to the individual.

The role of the tutor in providing formative feedback

The role of the teacher could broadly be described as working to reduce (but not necessarily eliminate) the rate of error production in trial-and-error learning, and thereby to make learning more efficient (Sadler, 1998). Sadler asks what good teachers do in providing feedback to students. He argues that they bring to the task of assessment:

1 Superior knowledge about the content or substance of what is to be learned.
2 A set of attitudes or dispositions towards teaching as an activity, and towards learners, including their own ability to empathise with students who are learning, their desire to help students develop, improve and do better, their personal concern with the validity of feedback and the veracity of their own judgements, and their patterns in offering help.

3 Skill in constructing or compiling tests, in devising tasks, and generally in working out ways to elicit revealing and pertinent responses from students.
4 Evaluative skill or expertise in having made judgements about student efforts on similar tasks in the past.
5 Expertise in framing feedback statements for students.

(Adapted from Sadler, 1998)

Getting students to make use of formative feedback

One of the problems with the term 'feedback' is that there are many ways in which it has traditionally been interpreted. Price et al. (2012) describe the problem thus:

> Although a frequently used term, feedback does not have clarity of meaning. It is a generic term which disguises multiple purposes which are often not explicitly acknowledged. The roles attributed to feedback fall broadly into five, but not entirely delineated discrete, categories: *correction, reinforcement, forensic diagnosis, benchmarking* and *longitudinal development* (feed-forward), the latter being differentiated by a temporal dimension of being forward-looking rather than concerned with work already carried out. These categories act as a nested hierarchy, each building on information provided by the previous category.
>
> (Price et al., 2012, p. 278)

In this *Toolkit*, I adopt the approach (favoured also by Boud and Sadler) that the most important aspect for formative feedback is feed-forward – helping students to build on their strengths and address deficiencies. Sadler (2010a) explains the point of feedback as follows:

> Giving students detailed feedback about the strengths and weaknesses of their work, with suggestions for improvement, is becoming common practice in higher education. However, for many students feedback seems to have little or no impact, despite the considerable time and effort put into its production. With a view to increasing its effectiveness, extensive theoretical and empirical research has been carried out into its structure, timing and other parameters. For students to be able to apply feedback, they need to understand the meaning of the feedback statements. They also need to identify, with near certainty, the particular aspects of their work that need attention.
>
> (Sadler, 2010a, p. 535)

Students tend to be really bad at doing anything constructive with the feedback we give them. Often they are only interested in the mark, and sometimes they don't even bother to read what we have written. When receiving feedback live, they frequently fail to retain what is said to them, apart from when their own views (or worst fears) of how they have performed are confirmed. Sadler argues that getting a clear picture in mind of the characteristics of high quality work is imperative:

> A key premise is that for students to be able to improve, they must develop the capacity to monitor the quality of their own work during actual production, rather than later on. This in turn requires that students possess an appreciation of what high quality work is, that they have the evaluative skill necessary for them to compare with some objectivity the quality of what they are producing in relation to the higher standard, and that they develop a store of tactics or moves which can be drawn upon to modify their own work.
>
> (Sadler, 1989, p. 119)

We need to find ways to help students make good use of the hard work we put into giving them feedback, to interpret it appropriately, to see how the comments and advice they are given links to what they are doing, and to turn this into improvements in competence and knowledge. Sadler proposes that it is crucial that the student works with the feedback s/he receives in order to internalise the standards that are required:

> The indispensable conditions for improvement are that the student comes to hold a concept of quality roughly similar to that held by the teacher, is able to monitor continuously the quality of what is being produced during the act of production itself, and has a repertoire of alternative moves or strategies from which to draw at any given point. In other words, students have to be able to judge the quality of what they are producing and be able to regulate what they are doing during the doing of it.
>
> (Sadler, 1989, p. 121)

Giving formative feedback is not unproblematic. We can't just assume that they know what to do with the commentary we give them; we need to help them engage with it positively and productively. Sadler further describes:

> ... the common but puzzling observation that even when teachers provide students with valid and reliable judgments about the quality of their work, improvement does not necessarily follow. Students often show little or no growth or development despite regular, accurate feedback. The concern itself is with whether some learners fail to acquire expertise because of specific deficiencies in the instructional system associated with formative assessment.
>
> (Sadler, 1989, p. 119)

Using formative assessment to improve student retention

In relatively recent history in UK higher education, high rates of 'wastage' were regarded as a form of quality assurance. 'Look to the right and left of you,' students in their first lecture at university were sometimes told, 'and remember only one of you will achieve a degree'. This brutalist approach certainly weeded out the unconfident and those who didn't really think they belonged in higher education anyway, but didn't do a lot for social justice. Today most academics would hold back from such an approach, but some residual sentiments of that kind still remain in some pockets of traditionalism. However, nowadays staff are more likely to be deeply concerned to maximise the number of students who successfully complete their awards, not only because it is nowadays a key governmental performance indicator in many countries, the ignoring of which can result in financial penalties, but also because they work in values-driven organisations that genuinely care about students as people, not just statistics.

Yorke (2002), who has pioneered research into student retention in the UK, proposes a number of reasons for student non-completion: among these, the lack of formative assessment ranks highly, especially in the early stages of a programme of learning. If students haven't a clue about how they are doing, a negative mindset can easily develop, leading to a downward spiral and ultimate drop-out.

Do students know what we're expecting from them?

A number of studies have suggested that a key issue lies around the management of expectations of students about what studying at degree level implies. For many undergraduate students on degree courses, particularly those studying part-time, balancing paid work, caring responsibilities and studying can lead to a corner-cutting approach, so that only essential tasks are completed. This means in essence that they only do assessed work, and only this if there are heavy penalties for non-completion. Bowl (2003) reported one of the students in her study saying:

> If 25 per cent of your marks is from reading, you've got to try and show that, even if you haven't read. I'm not going to sit there and read a chapter, and I'm certainly not going to read a book. But I'll read little paragraphs that I think are relevant to what I'm writing, and it's got me through, and my marks have been fine. But I can't read. If I read too much, it goes over my head. If I'm writing something, I know what I want to say and I need something to back me up … then I will find something in a book that goes with that. I'm not going to try to take in the whole book just for one little bit. I have my book next to me and then I can pick out the bits. (Jenny, full-time community and youth work student)
>
> (Bowl, 2003, p. 89)

Students in her study also experience worrying levels of lack of clarity about what is expected of them, despite having been given plenty of advice in course documentation:

> The hardship was not understanding. When they give you an assignment and say it was on this handout. But my difficulty is not understanding what to do at first … I think that there's a lack of my reading ability, which I can't blame anyone for. I can only blame myself because I don't like reading. And if you don't read, you're not going to learn certain things. So I suppose that's to do with me … it's reading as well as putting what you read into your essay. You can read it and understand it. I can read and understand it, but then you have to incorporate it into your own words. But in the words they want you to say it in, not just: She said this, and this is the way it should be. The words, the proper language. Maybe it's because I have difficulty pronouncing certain words. I avoid using them as they're not familiar to me. When I'm writing, I find that because I'm not familiar with those words, it's hard to write them … I haven't really gone into it, because I don't want them to say, you're not supposed to be on this course, or anything like that. I've come too far now for them to say that, so I don't like raising the issue. (Helen, brought up in Jamaica)
>
> (Bowl, 2003, p. 90)

It is through feedback dialogue that students should be enabled to gradually put together a picture of the standards they are striving to reach. HEA (2012) suggests that it is well worth developing a shared understanding of standards using feedback as follows:

> Assessment standards are socially constructed so there must be a greater emphasis on assessment and feedback processes that actively engage both staff and students in dialogue about standards. It is when learners share an understanding of academic and professional standards in an atmosphere of mutual trust that learning works best. Active engagement with assessment standards needs to be an integral and seamless part of course design and the learning process in order to allow students to develop their own, internalised conceptions of standards, and to monitor and supervise their own learning.
>
> (HEA, 2012, p. 9)

…where programmes plan for more formative assessment and feedback, there is a better chance that a greater proportion of students pass modules at their first attempt, thereby saving staff time in relation to demand for extra support, resits, appeals and complaints. Improved pass rates and reduced attrition bring obvious financial benefits for institutions and positive outcomes for students.

(HEA, 2012, p. 11)

Using formative feedback to help students develop academic skills

We are used to hearing much about the problems students experience with getting inside the academic discourse and discovering how best to undertake academic *writing* in ways that often don't come naturally to second-chance or late-achieving students. However, there seems to be a real crisis about *reading* among students, and one of the problems emerging about formative assessment is the danger that those very students who are feeling swamped by all the reading required of them, will be the ones who find themselves directed towards yet more reading of formative feedback, whether this is tutor- or peer-initiated. On reading, Coonan (2015) asserts:

> 'Reading' can mean many things, including the demanding process of studying for a degree or one of the activities that students engage in during that study. Yet a connotation of passivity still hangs about our notion of reading, interfering with a recognition that reading scholarly material is very far from being merely receptive or absorptive: rather, it's an active, interrogative dialogue with a work and its argument. However, the active nature of academic reading is not generally well signposted or explained to learners. Many students I encounter, most of whom are postgraduate, have never before encountered the idea of 'active reading' with its attendant practices of questioning, challenging and synthesising, rather than merely absorbing, information.
>
> (Coonan, in Brown, 2015, p. 93)

In the digital age we now live in perhaps we need to reconsider *our* expectations about the amount and nature of reading we require of our students. Colin Robinson argues:

> The literary equivalent of channel surfing replaces the prolonged concentration required to tackle a book. Condensed capsules of digital communication are infecting all forms of reading.
>
> (Robinson, 2013, p. 17)

When less than 10 per cent of the 18–30-year-old population participated in higher education, it may have been reasonable to expect that our students would be likely to have well-developed skills relating to academic reading. With approaching 50 per cent of the 18–30 population in higher education, it should not surprise us that a significant proportion of our students have not attained this level of expertise in reading for academic purposes by the time they come to study with us. Can we *train* all these students to the necessary extent? Or should we perhaps be considering *reducing* our expectations regarding academic reading, and focusing on the *quality* of reading rather than the *quantity or breadth* of reading?

So what's to be done?

Yorke (2002) provides us with confidence that we can actually make a difference to the dismal picture of dropout and perceptions of failure:

> Whereas a higher education institution cannot do much about students' background circumstances, it is probable that there is more academic failure in UK higher education than there should be. There seems to be scope in institutions for improving the ways in which they support students' learning – and hence for reducing the incidence of academic failure. In the end, this comes down to an orientation towards the enhancement of the quality of the student experience.
>
> (Yorke, 2002, p. 39)

There is a case to be made for institutions to consider spending considerable time and resources on students undertaking their first programmes of study to help them understand the purposes of formative feedback and how their own self-beliefs can impact on the ways they receive it. Inevitably this would eat into available time for content delivery, which academic staff no doubt would be unwilling to see slimmed down, but if we are serious about retaining students as a key means of survival in an increasingly competitive world, then tough decisions might have to be made. HEA (2012) suggest:

> The change that has the greatest potential to improve student learning is a shift in the balance of summative and formative assessment. Summative assessment has important purposes in selection, certification and institutional accountability, but its dominance has distorted the potential of assessment to promote learning (assessment for learning).
>
> (HEA, 2012, p. 9)

Quality of feedback

If 'assessment is the engine that drives learning' (John Cowan), then the ways in which we give feedback are important in gearing and lubricating the engine so that maximum effect is achieved from the effort put in by all concerned. This section of the chapter explores a variety of ways in which feedback can be given to students, and includes many suggestions for optimising the usefulness of such feedback.

How can we best give feedback to students? We can select from a wide range of processes, but we also need to address as many as possible of a range of qualities and attributes in our strategy for providing feedback.

For example, feedback needs to be:

* *Timely* – the sooner the better. There has been plenty of research into how long after the learning event it takes for the effects of feedback to be significantly eroded. Ideally feedback should be received within a day or two, and even better almost straightaway, as is possible (for example) in some computer-aided learning situations, and equally in some face-to-face contexts. When marked work is returned to students weeks (or even months) after submission, feedback is often totally ignored because it bears little relevance to students' current needs. Many institutions nowadays specify in their Student Charters that work should be returned within two to three weeks, enabling students to derive greater benefits from feedback. When feedback is received very quickly, it is much more effective, as students can still remember exactly what they were thinking as they addressed each task. Elsewhere (Race, 2014) I have suggested ways to give at least some feedback to students in class at the time they hand in work for marking, *and* that this can save a great deal of time in the marking itself.

- *Intimate and individual.* Feedback needs to fit each student's achievement, individual nature and personality. Global ways of compiling and distributing feedback can reduce the extent of ownership which students take over the feedback they receive, even when the quality and amount of feedback is increased. Each student is still a person.
- *Empowering.* If feedback is intended to strengthen and consolidate learning, we need to make sure it doesn't dampen down learning. This is easier to ensure when feedback is positive of course, but we need to look carefully at how best we can make critical feedback equally empowering to students. We must not forget that often feedback is given and received in a system where power is loaded towards the provider of the feedback rather than the recipient – for example where we are driving assessment systems.
- *Opening doors, not closing them.* In this respect, we have to be particularly careful with the words we use when giving feedback to students. Clearly, words with such 'final language' implications as 'weak' or 'poor' cause irretrievable breakdowns in the communication between assessor and student. To a lesser extent, even positive words such as 'excellent' can cause problems when feedback on the next piece of work is only 'very good' – why wasn't it excellent again? In all such cases it is better to praise exactly what *was* very good or excellent in a little more detail, rather than take the short cut of just using the adjectives themselves.
- *Manageable.* There are two sides to this. From our point of view, designing and delivering feedback to students could easily consume all the time and energy we have – it is an endless task. But also from students' point of view, getting too much feedback can result in them not being able to sort out the important feedback from the routine feedback, reducing their opportunity to benefit from the feedback they need most.

Nicol and MacFarlane-Dick (2006) propose seven principles for good feedback as follows:

Good feedback practice:
1 helps clarify what good performance is (goals, criteria, expected standards);
2 facilitates the development of self-assessment (reflection) in learning;
3 delivers high-quality information to students about their learning;
4 encourages teacher and peer dialogue around learning;
5 encourages positive motivational beliefs and self-esteem;
6 provides opportunities to close the gap between current and desired performance;
7 provides information to teachers that can be used to help shape the teaching.

(Nicol and MacFarlane-Dick, 2006, p. 7)

Perhaps the key word here is in point 4, and is 'dialogue', which resonates well with a sentence from Sadler (2013), included in a quote at the start of this chapter: 'The status of feedback deserves to be challenged on the grounds that it is essentially about telling'.

The suggestions below unpack how you can set about trying to ensure that the feedback you provide for your students addresses the factors listed above. Furthermore, some of the suggestions below are intended to help you to maintain high-quality feedback to your students without consuming inordinate amounts of your precious time and energy.

1 **Try to do more than put ticks.** Tempting as it is to put ticks beside things that are correct or good, ticks don't give much real feedback. It takes a little longer to add short phrases such as 'good point', 'I agree with this', 'yes, this is it', 'spot on', and so on, but such feedback comments do much more to motivate students than just ticks. Think about how students will

feel when they get marked work back. Students can be in states of heightened emotion at such points. If their scripts are covered with comments in red ink (even when it is all praise) it is rather intimidating for them at first.

2 **Avoid putting crosses if possible.** Students often have negative feelings about crosses on their work, carried forward from schooldays. Short phrases such as 'no', 'not quite', 'but this wouldn't work', and so on can be much better ways of alerting students to things that are wrong.

3 **Avoid handwriting if at all possible.** Word-processed feedback, whether on paper or on-screen is much more readable than most people's handwriting, and there's the advantage that one way or another we can keep a copy of it, so we still know what we said to which student.

4 **Consider using 'track-changes' for feedback on work submitted electronically.** Later in this chapter is some discussion of the advantages and disadvantages this can bring.

5 **If handwriting is unavoidable, try to make it legible.** If there is not going to be room to make a detailed comment directly on the script, one way round the problem is to put code numbers or asterisks on the script, and write or print your feedback on a separate sheet. A useful compromise is to put feedback comments on post-it notes stuck to appropriate parts of a script, but it's worth still using a code, asterisk or some such device so that if students remove the post-it notes as they read through their work, they can still work out exactly which points your comments apply to.

6 **Try giving some feedback before you start assessing.** For example, when a class hands in a piece of work, you can issue at once handouts (or web links) of model answers and discussions of the main things that may have caused problems. Students can read such information while their own efforts are still fresh in their minds, and can derive a great deal of feedback straightaway. You can then concentrate, while assessing, on giving them *additional* feedback individually, without going into detail on things that you have addressed in the general discussion comments you have already given them.

7 **Give feedback to groups of students whenever possible.** This helps students become aware that they are not alone in making mistakes, and allows them to learn from the successes and failures of others. Students often learn a great deal more from feedback received by their peers than from the feedback relating to their own work, as they avoid shrugging off praise their peers receive, and are more likely to reflect 'I can do this myself next time'. Similarly, when they see critical comments given to peers, they are quite likely to react 'ah, that's what to avoid in future' rather than become defensive as might have happened when they saw critical comment on their own work.

8 **Let students argue.** When giving one-to-one feedback, it is often useful to allow students the opportunity to interrogate you and challenge your comments (orally or in writing) so that any issues which are unclear can be resolved. It is important to *listen* to them, without jumping in to defend your feedback until you really know what they're arguing about.

9 **Feedback should be realistic.** When making suggestions for improvement of student work, consider carefully whether they can be achieved. It may not have been possible (for example) for students to gain access to certain resources or books in the time available.

10 **Feedback should not be linked to wealth!** Check that you are not giving feedback on the amount of money that was spent on the work you mark, for example when some students can submit work produced by expensive desktop publishing systems, or use photos or colour in diagrams, other students may have no access to such facilities.

11 **Feedback should be honest.** When there are serious problems which students need to be made aware of, feedback comments should not skirt round these or avoid them. It may be best to arrange for individual face-to-face feedback sessions with some students, so you can give any bad news in ways where you can monitor how they are taking it, and provide appropriate comfort at the same time.

12 **Feedback can be given before scores or grades.** Consider whether sometimes it may be worth returning students' work to them with feedback comments but no grades (but having written down your marks in your own records). Then invite students to try to work out what their scores or grades should be, and to report to you in a week's time what they think. This causes students to read all your feedback comments earnestly in their bid to work out how they have done. Most students will make good guesses regarding their grades, and it's worth finding out which students are way out too.

13 **Think about audio files for giving feedback.** Nowadays, voice recorders are affordable, and most mobile phones can be used for this purpose. The audio files can be downloaded onto a laptop or desktop computer, and can be emailed to students, with tutors keeping copies so that they can retrace what they said to whom. Moreover, in some subjects, it is actually quite hard to *write* explanatory comments on students' work. For example, in mathematical problems, it can be quicker and easier to 'talk' individual students through how a problem should be solved, referring to asterisks or code-numbers marked on their

work. Such feedback has the advantages of tone of voice for emphasis and explanation. Another advantage is that students can play it again, until they have fully understood all of your feedback.

14 **Consider giving feedback by email in any case.** Some students feel most relaxed when working at a computer terminal on their own. With email, students can receive your feedback when they are ready to think about it. They can read it again later, and even file it. Using email, you can give students feedback asynchronously as you work through their scripts, rather than having to wait till you return the whole set to a class.

15 **Encourage students to look at the feedback their friends get.** When they see praise, they're likely to think 'ah, I can do this too', rather than just shrug it off (as they might have done with feedback on their own work). When they see criticism, they're likely to think 'ah, this is something I should avoid', rather than get defensive as they might have done with their own feedback. It's important, however, that students look at each other's feedback 'voluntarily', i.e. with fellow-students of their own choice, rather than risk them feeling 'set up'

Feedback and competence development

In Chapter 1, I included a model tracking the development of conscious competence. Feedback is important in all four 'states' represented in the diagram in Figure 2.1. It is worth pausing briefly to reflect on what we mean by 'competence'. Sadler (2013a) offers the following thoughts:

> The competent person makes multi-criterion judgments that are consistently appropriate and situationally sensitive. What is more, the range of situations faced by many professional practitioners is potentially infinite. ... Judgments of competence can properly take place only within complex situations, not in the abstract, and not componentially. They require qualitative appraisals of how well a person 'gets it all together' in a given situation.
>
> (Sadler, 2013a, p. 13)

It can be useful to help learners to become better able to make such 'multi-criterion judgments' by looking at the roles which can be played by feedback in the respective areas of competences they are conscious of, and those they don't yet know about, as well as uncompetences known and unknown.

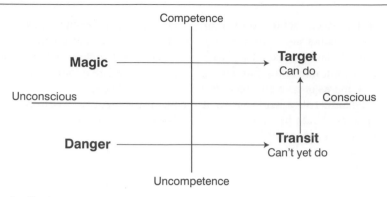

Figure 2.1 Linking feedback to competence development

Feedback addressing conscious competence

Giving students feedback on things they can already do well, and *know* they're already competent at doing, is trickier than may seem obvious! When students *know* that they have done something well, any feedback which smacks of 'faint praise' can be quite damning. We still want it to be used as feed-forward, so that they build on their successes. However, if we wax too lyrical in our praise, it can be seen as condescending. We need to pit our wits towards helping students to take ownership of their successes in this scenario, for example:

> I'm sure you already realise you've done a really good job with this …

or

> Do stop for a moment and think about how well you've done this, and how useful it will be for you to continue to hone these skills – don't lose them!

Feedback addressing conscious uncompetence

We're more practised at giving this sort of feedback. Much of the feedback we routinely give students is directed towards helping them to become better at things they already know they can't yet do well. Bearing in mind how rapidly we all become defensive or prickly when confronted by any feedback which can be regarded as critical, however, we need to be really careful to make feedback on conscious uncompetence acceptable. For example, we can help by giving them suggestions about what to do first in their attempts to move things upwards out of the 'transit' box on the diagram. We can help them prioritise *which* things are worth trying to move, and which are not important enough to bother with.

Feedback addressing unconscious uncompetence

This is by far the most important area for feedback. One of the main points of having assessed coursework is to use this sort of feedback to help students find out much more about what they didn't yet know that they couldn't yet do. In other words, we use feedback to help students to move things out of their danger box and into their transit box, on the way towards the target box.

It could be said that the art of teaching lies in helping students to explore their danger box, and to identify important elements hiding there, bringing them out into the open, then moving them towards conscious competence. As Sadler (2010a) wrote: 'They also need to identify, with near certainty, the particular aspects of their work that need attention'.

The fact that this is an everyday part of helping students to learn does not mean that it is an easy part. For a start, we are now talking about giving feedback addressing *unconscious* uncompetences. Therefore, the first hurdle is gently alerting students to things that they didn't know were there. There is an element of surprise. Some of the surprises will be unpleasant ones – where (for example) students had thought that they were consciously competent in the aspect concerned. It's the 'bad news' box. The good news is that the things identified won't be bad news any more, once moved.

Feedback addressing unconscious competence

This is another surprise box, but this time it's a 'good news' box. For example, part-time mature students bring to their educational experience a wide range of unconscious competences. These are things that they are good at, but don't yet realise how useful and important such things could turn out to be. For example, they're often really skilled at time-management, task-management and multi-tasking. Their life experience has often allowed them to develop skills at handling a number of different agendas at once, and prioritising between competing demands.

Moving these unconscious competences towards the conscious level almost always results in an increase of confidence and self-esteem. If you've just been helped to see that you're actually very good at something that you hadn't ever suspected was among your strengths, would you not feel good about it?

Towards a strategy for choosing feedback processes

Any strategy is essentially a combination of tactics. You can choose your feedback tactics from a wide variety of processes, each with its own advantages and drawbacks in the particular contexts in which you might choose to use it. The pages which follow can be used as starting points for colleagues to explore the pros and cons of their own preferred methods of giving feedback. But don't forget to keep asking students about which feedback processes *they* find most valuable – they can always tell us.

Feedback in writing or print

This is about hard-copy feedback, whether written directly onto students' assessed work, or supplied in writing or print alongside returned work. (We'll explore emailed or online feedback and the use of 'track-changes' shortly; the present section is essentially about old-fashioned feedback, which still happens!) A clear advantage of hard-copy feedback is that it is enduring, and can be viewed and reviewed again by students (and indeed by assessors themselves and quality reviewers). However, a clear *disadvantage* with hard-copy feedback is that it is enduring! A batch of feedback comments to different students can endure quite long enough for each and every inconsistency we make to be used against us in evidence. In the pages which follow, we'll explore half a dozen of the range of processes involving feedback in writing or print. You'll be able to think of other ways of combining these, and alternatives which may have more advantages and fewer drawbacks.

Handwritten comments on (or about) students' assessed work

This is one of the most widely used forms of feedback to students. It includes our written feedback on essays, reports, dissertations, solutions to problems, and so on. Not so long ago, there were few alternatives to this way of giving students feedback on their work, usually accompanied by an assessment judgement of one kind or another.

ADVANTAGES

- Feedback can be personal, individual, and directly related to the particular piece of work.
- Students may regard this sort of feedback as authoritative and credible.
- The feedback can be tailored to justify an accompanying assessment judgement.
- Students can refer to the feedback again and again, and continue to learn from it.
- Such feedback provides useful evidence for external scrutiny, for example external examiners, professional bodies, and so on.

DISADVANTAGES

- Handwritten feedback takes ages to do, and can be hard to read!
- If our handwritten comments are on their work, *we* lose it when we return their work, and can easily forget what we said to whom.
- There may not be enough space, when squeezing handwritten comments between lines or in margins in students' work.
- When critical, handwritten feedback can be threatening because of its authoritativeness.
- It becomes too tempting to degenerate into shorthand – ticks and crosses – rather than to express positive and critical comments.

Post-its stuck to students' work

This is an alternative to handwritten comments, and has a few additional pros and cons.

ADVANTAGES

- Students' work isn't 'defaced', and they can remove the post-its when they've served their purpose.
- The post-its can be stuck at the right place, so as to clearly indicate which part of the work is being referred to.

DISADVANTAGES

- If a detailed comment is needed, a post-it may not be large enough.
- Post-its could get accidentally detached before students get their work back.

Word-processed overall comments on each student's assessed work

This is feedback which you compose, then print out (or email) for each student, summarising your reactions to their work. It may be accompanied by an assessment judgement.

ADVANTAGES

- Such feedback can remain individual, personal and authoritative.
- It is easier to paste in pre-prepared statements, from a bank of such statements you've already prepared.
- When you compose an important new comment for a particular instance, you can copy it to your statement bank for when you may need it again.
- Students can refer to your comments time and time again.

- It is much easier to read than handwriting.
- You can keep copies (paper or electronic) and easily refer to it again.
- It provides useful evidence for external scrutiny.

DISADVANTAGES

- Printed feedback can still be threatening to students when critical.
- It may appear less personal to students than handwritten feedback.
- It is not so easy to link each feedback point to the exact part of the work which caused you to write it.
- The 'cut and paste' elements may show up too strongly to external reviewers, if they have been used too widely.
- It's not so easy to make *emphasis* in word-processed feedback, so that the most important messages stand out from those that are merely routine.

'Track-changes' feedback on work returned to students electronically

Despite the fact that 'track-changes' is normally used in one-to-one editing and feedback (for example on draft theses, dissertations, reports and so on) it seems likely that 'track-changes' feedback is already well on the way towards replacing handwritten comments on students' work in assessment in general. This discussion is about using the 'track-changes' function in word-processing software to give students feedback when marking their work. This is normally when tutors use the 'track-changes' facilities to return to students their original word-processed assignments, duly edited with feedback comments which appear on-screen in another colour. The level of feedback can range from comments providing simple qualitative overall feedback on the whole document or on selected paragraphs or sentences, to very detailed feedback on individual words or phrases. This kind of feedback remains very valuable for large-scale work (essays, dissertations, long reports, drafts of articles for publication and so on).

The other side of 'track-changes' is where deletions, additions, replaced words or phrases can be suggested, and the original author can accept or reject each change in turn, working towards a 'final' version. This is most useful when (for example) supervisors are editing drafts for students to then improve so they can produce a post-feedback edition of their work if they wish (or they can be required to do so as part of the overall assessment process). The 'track-changes' function used in this way can give students feedback about their wording, grammar, spelling, punctuation, but the 'comments' function is more widely used when the main purpose is feedback rather than working towards a better draft.

The discussion below is essentially about a batch of student work being marked with the feedback sent electronically either stage by stage during the marking or when the marking is completed. For feedback synchronously during students' work, and for collaborative work where students can comment on each other's work, 'Google Docs' can be a much richer way for sharing comments, and lead all involved towards improved drafts.

ADVANTAGES

- Comments and changes using 'track-changes' is a way of providing feedback while avoiding defacing students' work by writing on it.
- It is a way of providing the kind of feedback students really want – demonstrably individual feedback on their own particular pieces of work, rather than generic feedback to the whole cohort.
- You can distinguish between 'corrections' and 'comments', as explained above.

- With the 'comments' function you can highlight a whole section and make broad observations – students then appreciate that you have read/understood the broader aspects, and have not just focused on the nitty-gritty errors.
- You can send the edited work back to any student at any convenient time or place as you're assessing their work, rather than having to wait till a whole batch of work is returned. (Caution: you may find your assessing develops during a batch of work, so it can be premature to return too early the first pieces of work you mark.)
- You have the opportunity to edit your feedback before you finally send it – how often have we (when using handwritten feedback) written quite a lot of feedback down, only to find that the student went on to address the point concerned a paragraph or page later!
- Students can open the marked work at a time and place when they're ready, and usually choose to take in your feedback in the relative comfort of privacy.
- You can tailor your feedback to individual students' needs, strengths and weaknesses.
- Students can refer back to your feedback again and again.
- You can keep track of what feedback you have given to which students by saving the marked-up files (except of course where marking is anonymous, but even then you can keep track of which comments you made on which piece of work).
- You can use electronic cut and paste where different students need similar advice, gradually preparing a master copy of a bank of frequently needed comments to select from, and save yourself having to type out such messages more than once.
- Students can reply directly to you *about* your feedback (where marking isn't anonymous).
- Useful evidence of feedback is built up relatively automatically, if needed for external review.
- You can revise comments while marking, for example when it becomes clear that a particular difficulty is widespread in the work of different students.
- Comments on-screen can be far more legible than handwriting, and can still clearly point to the exact part of the student's work being discussed.
- Using the 'next' function, students can work their way systematically through successive changes or comments, seeing where they relate to their original work one at a time, and therefore it is easier (despite the messy overall appearance of loads of comments on the screen) to think about each in turn. They can also back-track to the 'previous' comment or changes when they wish to.
- Students can choose to 'accept' or 'reject' changes, and can choose to 'delete' comments when they wish (though it's worth cautioning them that it's best if they don't delete comments in the heat of the moment if they disagree with them!).
- This way of marking means that you don't have to carry piles of work around with you, and can have the work available online or on a memory stick, and can do some of the marking at any time and at any place when you're at a computer containing the files. This also means you can tackle marking large batches incrementally, rather than being confined to a single marking place.
- Obviously, most of these advantages relate to just 'marking' rather than 'assessing', and you still face the task of making informed judgements about students' work, at least partly on the basis of the feedback comments you have provided, and the changes you might have suggested.
- When you come to making assessment judgements on the overall piece, you can scroll up and down your comments to remind you about your views of the main trends in the work.

DISADVANTAGES

- If there are lots of comments and changes, the feedback can look very intimidating and confusing ('like an overly-critical spider's web' is one reaction!).
- The default setting is usually that comments and changes appear in red! (However, settings on the software can be revised, and green or blue can be much less intimidating. You may have to help students to work out how best to change the settings, as they may have already used track-changes when producing the work in the first place, and this can affect the colour settings they see for your comments.)
- With 'changes' you end up taking responsibility for putting right the student's minor errors, and they become passive recipients of this, without having to take an active role – the text also looks messier than if you suggested the change on a post-it or in a margin comment and left it up to them to do something (active revision).
- Students can only see this feedback when at a computer, and may forget quite a lot of the detail.
- With long pieces of work, students can only see a few comments at a time, and can lose track of general themes in the feedback being offered.
- Comments are usually in the same size of font, so it is harder to make particular words stand out (as you could have done in handwritten comments). However, you've still normally got **bold**, *italic*, underline, and so on to play with, so it is not impossible to make due emphasis apparent when necessary.
- It can be quite tiresome marking a large batch of students' work at a computer.
- It is harder to follow up 'track-changes' feedback face-to-face with a student, as you both need to be able to see the comments together.
- Students (and yourself!) may need a little practice before getting into the swing of using track-changes well.
- Some students may be using different software to that which you're using, or have different versions of the same software. Some students may be using quite different kinds of computer (e.g. Mac versus PC).
- Students without their own computers may have limited access to networked computers, and may then be somewhat rushed when they have opportunities to receive your feedback.
- Students may not treat your feedback as seriously as if it were face-to-face, or on printed or handwritten paper.
- Students are more likely to 'lose' emailed feedback than printed or handwritten feedback; in other words they tend to fail to file it and store it systematically.
- Although a print-out bearing all the changes and comments is possible as a last resort, this can be very hard on the eye.

Model answers or solutions, issued to students along with their marked work

This category covers a wide range of feedback aids, including specimen answers, perhaps supported by 'commentary' notes highlighting principal matters arising with students' work as a whole, worked solutions to calculations or problems, and so on. Model answers or solutions can be provided on paper or online, and the timing can be controlled – e.g. to just after students have submitted their own work.

ADVANTAGES

- Students can use model answers to revisit their own work in self-assessment mode, and can continue to use them as a frame of reference illustrating the standards they are working towards.

- Model answers can save you a lot of time writing individual feedback or explanation to students.
- You can build up a model solution with commentary while you're actually marking a large batch of students' work, putting your remarks into the commentary rather than on individuals' work.
- You can build up model solutions by directly using (with due anonymity) students' work, with their permission of course.
- You can also build up 'how not to do this' examples from students' actual work (but you really do need their permission and blessing to do this).
- They can be issued to students who missed an assignment, or for reference by students who may have been exempted from it.
- They constitute useful evidence of standards and expectations, both for students and for external quality reviewers.

DISADVANTAGES

- Because model answers or solutions are relatively impersonal, some students will not really engage in comparing their own work to them.
- Students who do the assignment equally well overall, but in different ways, may feel that their individuality is not being valued or recognised.
- Students may assume that the model answers represent all that they need to know about the topic on which the assignment was based.
- Students who missed out an important aspect in their own work may not notice the significance of this, and may still need further feedback about their own particular strengths and weaknesses.
- If the same assignment is used again within a year or two, there may be clear evidence that the model answers are still in circulation!

Assignment return sheets

These are normally pre-prepared pro formas, most often a single sheet of paper or web-screen, where you provide detailed written or word-processed, or electronic feedback comments to students on each of a number of assessment criteria applied to their work. Alternatively, these can contain Likert-scale ratings against individual qualities of the work concerned, with columns indicating such judgements as 'really well done', 'quite well done', 'not well done' and so on. A mixture of items with 'free comments' and 'judgements' can be used as appropriate.

ADVANTAGES

- You can plan to address each of the most important or recurring feedback agendas, without having to write out the context, or the relevant criteria, each time.
- Students can compare the feedback they receive with that received by peers, on the basis of each separate criterion if they wish.
- You can copy the assignment return sheets, and keep them for your own records (and for external scrutiny) much more easily than you could keep copies of whole assignments along with your written feedback.
- The essential parts of the feedback agenda can be clarified by the assignment return sheets, giving students a frame of reference for what is expected of them in similar assignments in future.
- The elements of the assignment return sheets can be fine-tuned to reflect the intended learning outcomes associated with the assessed work (particularly welcomed by quality reviewers seeking connections between assessment criteria and published learning outcomes).

DISADVANTAGES

- Not all of the feedback you wish in practice to give to individual students is likely to relate to the anticipated agendas of an assignment return sheet.
- Students may question you about the differences in their scores or grades. (Though this is of course the case in most feedback methods – it just seems to happen more often when different students all have a similar-looking sheet, and are more likely to compare with each other.)
- You may have to find other ways to keep for your own records (and for external review) the individual feedback that you add for students.
- Any pre-prepared agenda is likely to be found to be inappropriate for at least some of the assignments, for example students who do the assignment very well but in an unanticipated way, or students whose work meets the published agenda but where you feel that they still have not actually understood what they are doing (or suspect that plagiarism has occurred).

Word-processed overall class reports on an assignment

These might be issued to a whole (large) group of students, after their work has been marked, along with (or even in advance of) returning to them their marked work. Ideally, such an overall report can be debriefed in a whole-group session with the students. These reports can also be made available online.

ADVANTAGES

- Students can look back at the report again and again as necessary.
- Students can learn from the feedback on mistakes or inadequacies of *other* students' work, and find out from the report about difficulties which were commonly encountered.
- Such reports can save you from having to write repeatedly the same feedback messages in response to commonly occurring mistakes.
- Writing such feedback reports causes you to reflect in some detail on overall student performance in the particular assignment concerned, and you can show this to significant others (for example quality reviewers).
- You could issue a past report to the next cohort of students, alerting them in advance to some things to bear in mind when they tackle a forthcoming similar assessment.

DISADVANTAGES

- Feedback to students is much less personal than is possible using some of the other processes described elsewhere on these pages, and will tend to concentrate on commonly occurring features in the work of the cohort, and may miss out on individuality shown by some of the stronger students.
- Students may think that the only important points they need to bear in mind are contained in the report.
- If some students are likely to submit their work late, you may need to delay issuing the report (or even have to make further adjustments to it), resulting in the main body of students experiencing delay in receiving feedback, and a loss of the 'fresh in mind' dimension when they compare the report with their own work.

Codes written on students' work, debriefed in a whole-group session

For example, instead of writing individual positive or critical comments directly onto students' work, write only a code (a letter, or a number, or a symbol), and alongside compile your 'glossary of codes'on overheads, paper or PowerPoint slides, to use when you debrief the work to the whole group (and to issue as a translation device, so that students can revisit their work and remind themselves of your feedback).

ADVANTAGES

- This can save you a very significant amount of time and energy when 'hand-marking' a set of assignments, as in principle you only need to spell out each common feedback comment once (in your glossary, rather than on their work).
- When addressing common errors or misunderstandings, you can take more time to adjust your feedback messages to make them really understandable.
- It's usually much easier to insert a code letter, number or symbol, in the space available between their lines, than might have been possible to squeeze in the comment you wish to make to a student. This means that students see exactly where the feedback comment relates to their own work.
- Students get their work back without it being covered with feedback wording, which might have looked more threatening (we all tend to see any critical comments first).
- In your debriefing with the whole group, you can go through each of the important codes one at a time, meaning that all of the students to whom the message is directed get the translation of their code at the same moment. This point-by-point debriefing focuses students' attention much more sharply than when general debriefings are given. For example, until you reveal your message, *all* students with a 'W' written once or more on their work will be trying to work out for themselves what that 'W' might mean.

DISADVANTAGES

- It is harder for you to remember which students made which misunderstandings or mistakes (unless you photocopy their work with your codes on it, or make some sort of grid recording the codes used for each student).
- Students may lose the glossary you issue to them, or may not go to the trouble of re-translating your codes when they review their work later.
- The process of debriefing can be boring to the better students who made few of the errors or misunderstandings which you explain to the rest of the cohort.

Face-to-face feedback

Face-to-face feedback can carry with it very high learning payoff for students. It can be memorable, and can help students to change attitudes and approaches. Face-to-face feedback (whether to individuals or groups) carries with it the additional explanation that comes through body language, facial expression, tone of voice, emphasis, and so on. Furthermore, in face-to-face feedback situations, *you* have immediate feedback on how your messages are getting across to students. There is also the opportunity for *dialogue;* students can ask you what you mean by particular comments. You can tell a lot about how they are reacting to your feedback from their expressions, body language, and so on. Moreover, you can *adjust* what you say, and how you say it, to respond to your observations of what is happening.

Face-to-face feedback to whole classes

This includes giving oral feedback to a whole class after having marked their assignments, before or after returning their actual work to them. Alternatively, you can give face-to-face feedback to the whole group about the task immediately after collecting their work from them, but before you've marked it, so that they get at least some feedback on the task as soon as possible, while the task is still fresh in their minds.

ADVANTAGES

- You can give a lot of feedback to a lot of students in a relatively short time.
- Feedback is strengthened by tone of voice, facial expression, body language, emphasis, and so on.
- Students can compare reactions to your feedback, especially when you use some discussion in the process.
- Students can question you, and gain clarification about what you're really getting at when you make a point to the group.
- You can support (and partially evidence) giving feedback to the whole group by issuing a handout summarising the main points you include.

DISADVANTAGES

- Feedback is less individual, personal and intimate to students.
- You can only concentrate on principal feedback matters, and can't cover less common feedback issues.
- Students' records or memories of your feedback may be inaccurate and sketchy, and they may not remember the detail when later they look back over their assessed work.
- Students may be so busy thinking about one particular aspect of your feedback, which they know will apply to their particular work, that they miss other elements as you talk.

Face-to-face feedback to individual students

This can include one-to-one appointments with students, individual discussions out of class or in practical settings, and so on.

ADVANTAGES

- Feedback is likely to be found to be personal, intimate and authoritative.
- You can address each individual student's needs, strengths and weaknesses.
- It is often much quicker to talk rather than write or type.
- It is an important feedback mechanism to be able to justify to external reviewers (but of course you'll need evidence to support your claims for it – for example feedback from students *about* your face-to-face feedback with them).

DISADVANTAGES

- One-to-one face-to-face feedback can be extremely threatening when critical.
- Students may become defensive when receiving critical feedback, and you may feel tempted to go in harder to justify the feedback.
- Students can be embarrassed when receiving positive feedback, and this can cause them not to fully benefit from praise.

- It takes a great deal of time to organise individual appointments with each member of large classes.
- There can be even more time wasted between appointments, and with students who don't turn up.
- Students often tend to remember only *some* of a feedback interview with an important person like you, often the most critical element, and this may undermine confidence unduly.
- It becomes impossible to remember exactly what you said to whom, when class sizes are large.

Face-to-face feedback to small groups of students

Such feedback is often timetabled into tutorial sessions, or in group work where students are working on projects or practical tasks. Some of the advantages of face-to-face feedback can be further exploited, and some of the disadvantages of feeding back to individuals are reduced.

ADVANTAGES

- It can be less threatening to students than one-to-one feedback, especially when critical.
- Individuals' needs can be addressed, while still retaining some degree of relative anonymity within the group.
- Students can learn from the detail of feedback to others in the group, and avoid the problems which others have encountered, and put their own work into context.
- You can enter into detailed discussion if the students in the group wish, so that matters arising are followed up in as much – often more – depth than would have happened with individual one-to-one appointments.

DISADVANTAGES

- Students may not take quite as much notice of feedback to them as members of a group, than they would have done to one-to-one feedback.
- It can be hard to remember to include all the feedback matters which are needed by the group as a whole.
- Discussions may get out of perspective, and result in only part of the intended overall feedback agenda being covered by the group session.

Electronic feedback

We've already looked at 'track-changes' feedback under 'writing or in print' as track-changes has become one of the principal ways feedback is now given in situations where formerly handwritten comments were provided, but there are even more possibilities. The range and variety of the use of electronic feedback is one of the fastest growth areas in higher education today. Increasingly, tutors are finding that electronic feedback not only speeds up the delivery of feedback, and aids the effectiveness of reception of feedback, but also assists with generating appropriate evidence for the quality of feedback.

Using computer conferences for overall comments on batches of students' work

Computer conferences provide the option for one-to-many electronic communication for feedback messages which have relevance to the majority of a group of students, along with the choice to go to one-to-one communication for those parts of feedback messages which are more individual or personal.

Just about all the advantages of emailed feedback still apply, except the option of responding individually through the conference to each student's strengths and weaknesses. Even this can, of course, be addressed by adding individualised emails to the computer conference communication.

- Your overall feedback response to an assignment can be sent as it stands to each of many students, who can each receive it when and where it is convenient to them.
- You can save time responding to matters affecting many students, and use some of the time saved to reply separately by email to those students needing more detailed or individual feedback.
- Students can learn from your feedback to *other* issues than the ones which they themselves need to think about.
- Students can reply individually to you about your overall feedback, and (if you structure the conference accordingly) can directly see each other's responses to your feedback, and generate real conference-type discussion of matters arising from an assignment (and of your own assessment and feedback of the assignment).

DISADVANTAGES

- Students may be less inclined to search through a generalised electronic feedback message for elements which apply to their own work.
- Students replying to the conference about your feedback may feel more exposed than when replying directly to you by email. (Of course there is no reason why you should deny them private communication.)

Computer-delivered feedback

This broad category includes the use of (pre-prepared) feedback responses to structured self-assessment questions in computer-based learning packages. Computer-based feedback can be programmed into learning packages online.

ADVANTAGES

- Students can work through online learning materials at their own pace, and within limits at their own choice of time and place.
- Feedback to pre-designed tasks can be received almost instantly by students, at the point of entering their decision or choice into the system.
- Computer-based feedback legitimises learning by trial and error, and allows students to learn from mistakes in the comfort of privacy.
- You can prepare detailed feedback in anticipation of the most likely mistakes or misconceptions which you know will be common among your students.
- Students can view the feedback as often as they need it as they work through the materials online.

DISADVANTAGES

- You cannot easily tell to what extent individual students are benefiting from the feedback you have designed.
- Students who don't understand the feedback responses you have designed may not be able to question you further at the time, in the ways they could have used with emailed or computer-conference-based feedback.
- The 'now you see it, now it's gone' syndrome can affect students' retention of your feedback messages, as students move quickly from one screenful of information to another as they work.

Reducing your load: short cuts to good feedback

Many lecturers report that they spend much more time marking students' work and designing feedback for students than they spend preparing lectures or working with students directly. We've seen throughout this chapter how important assessment and feedback are for students. The following suggestions may help you keep various aspects of your marking and feedback activities to a reasonable proportion of your overall work.

Keep records carefully ...

Keeping good records of assessment takes time, but can save time in the long run. The following suggestions may help you organise your record-keeping.

1 **Be meticulous about keeping records of marks!** However tired you are at the end of a marking session, record all the marks immediately (or indeed continuously as you go along). Then make sure the marks are stored in different places rather than just with the scripts – for example stored online, *and* in a print-out. Then should any disasters befall you (dog eats marksheets, briefcase stolen, house burned down, computer dies, and so on) there is the chance that you will still have the marks even if you don't have the scripts any longer (or vice versa).

2 **Be systematic.** Use class lists, when available, as the basis of your records. Otherwise make your own class lists as you go along. File all records of assessment in places where you can find them again – on more than one computer. With paper-based records it is possible to spend as much time looking for missing marksheets as it took to do the original assessment!

3 **Use technology to produce assessment records.** Keep marks on a grid or spreadsheet on a computer, and consider saving by date as a new file every time you add significantly to it, so you are always confident that you are working with the most recent version. Keep paper copies of each important list as an insurance against disaster! Keep backup copies of files or sheets – even simply scanning or photocopying any handwritten list of marks is a valuable precaution.

4 **Use technology to save you from number-crunching.** The use of computer spreadsheet programs can allow the machine to do all of the subtotalling, averaging and data handling for you. If you are afraid to set up a system for yourself, a computer-loving colleague or a member of systems support staff (or indeed a student!) will be delighted to start you off.

5 **Use other people.** Some universities employ administrative staff to issue and collect in work for assessment, and to make up assessment lists and input the data into computers. Partners, friends and even young children can help you check your addition of marks, and help you record the data.

Reduce your burden ...

Straightforward ways to lighten your assessment and feedback load are suggested below.

1 **Reduce the number of your assignments.** Are all of them strictly necessary, and is it possible to combine some of them, and completely delete others?

2 **Use shorter assignments.** Often we ask for 2,000-, 3,000- or 5,000-word assignments or reports, when a fraction of the length can be just as acceptable. Some essays or long reports could be replaced by shorter reviews, articles, memorandum reports or summaries. Projects can be assessed by poster displays and summary reports instead of long reports, and exam papers can include some sections of short-answer questions and multiple-choice questions, particularly where these could be marked by optical mark scanners, or using computer-managed assessment directly.

3 **Use assignment return sheets.** These can be pro formas which contain the assessment criteria for an assignment, with spaces for ticks/crosses, grades, marks and brief comments. They enable rapid feedback on 'routine' assessment matters, providing more time for individual comment to students when necessary on deeper aspects of their work.

4 **Consider using statement banks.** These are a means whereby your frequently repeated comments can be composed once each, then printed or emailed to students, or put onto transparencies or slides for discussion in a subsequent lecture.

5 **Involve students in self- or peer-assessment.** Start small, and explain what you are doing and why. Involving students in some of their assessment can provide them with very positive learning experiences, and help them tune in to the assessment culture around them.

6 **Mark some exercises in class time using self- or peer-marking.** This is sometimes useful when students, expecting tutor-assessment, have prepared work to the standard that they wish to be seen by you.

7 **Don't count all assessments.** For example, give students the option that their best five out of eight assignments will count as their coursework mark. Students satisfied with their *first* five need not undertake the other three at all then, and students who did not get into their stride in the first couple of assessments can compensate for this.

And when you still find yourself overloaded ...

No one wants to have to cope with huge piles of coursework scripts or files, or exam papers. However, not all factors may be within your control, and you may still end up overloaded. The following wrinkles may be somewhat soothing at such times!

1 **If the work is paper-based, put the great unmarked pile *under* your desk.** It is very discouraging to be continually reminded of the magnitude of the overall task. Put only a handful of scripts or assignments in sight – about as many as you might expect to deal with in about an hour.

2 **Set yourself progressive targets.** Plan to accomplish a bit more at each stage than you need to. Build in safety margins. This allows you some insurance against unforeseen disasters (and children), and can allow you to gradually earn some time off as a bonus.

3 **Make an even better marking scheme.** Often, it only becomes possible to make a really good marking scheme after you've found out the ways that candidates are actually answering the questions. Put the marking scheme where you can see it easily. It can be useful to paste it up with sticky tack above your desk or table, so you don't have to rummage through your papers looking for it every time you need it.

4 **Mark in different places!** Mark at work, at home, and anywhere else that's not public. This means of course carrying a laptop or scripts around as well as your marking scheme (or a copy of it). It does, however, avoid any one place becoming so associated with doom and depression that you develop place-avoidance strategies for it!

5 **Mark one question at a time through all the scripts, at first.** This allows you to become quickly skilled at marking that question, without the agenda of all the rest of the questions on your mind. It also helps ensure reliability and objectivity of marking. When you've completely mastered your marking scheme for all questions, it's fine to start marking whole scripts.

Involving students in their own assessment

Earlier in this chapter, and indeed throughout this *Toolkit*, I've stressed how useful it is to get students *making judgements* on their own work as they're doing it. Nothing affects students more than assessment, yet they often claim that they are in the dark as to what goes on in the minds of their assessors and examiners. Involving students in peer- and self-assessment can let them in to the assessment culture they must survive.

Once more to quote Royce Sadler (2013b):

> For students to become self-sustaining producers of high quality intellectual and professional goods, they must be equipped to take control of their own learning and performance. How can students become better at monitoring the emerging quality of their work during actual production? Opening up the assessment agenda and liberating the making of judgments from the strictures of preset criteria provide better prospects for developing mature independence in learning.
>
> (Sadler, 2013b, p. 54)

Increasingly peer-assessment is being used to involve students more closely in their learning and its evaluation, and to help to enable students really understand what is required of them. It is not a 'quick fix' solution to reduce staff marking time, as it can be quite intensive in its use of lecturer time at the briefing and development stages. It can have enormous benefits in terms of learning gain. The following suggestions may help you get started with student peer-assessment.

Why consider using student peer-assessment?

Introducing student peer-assessment can seem a daunting and hazardous prospect, if you're surrounded by an assessment culture where lecturers undertake all of the assessing. There are, however, several good reasons why the prospect should not be seen as so formidable, and some of these are proposed below.

1 **Students are doing it already.** Students on campus-based courses are continuously peer-assessing in fact. Students studying online on MOOCs may also be required to interact with each other's work and provide feedback to each other, as a condition inherent in gaining credit for their work. One of the most significant sources of answers to students' pervading question: 'How am I doing?' is the feedback they get about their own learning achievements and performances by comparing with those of others. It is true that feedback from tutors is regarded as more authoritative, but there is less such feedback available from tutors than from fellow students. Setting up and facilitating peer-assessment therefore legitimises and makes respectable something that most students are already engaged in.

2 **Students find out more about our assessment cultures.** One of the biggest dangers with assessment is that students often don't really know how their assessment works. They often approach both exams and tutor-marked coursework like black holes that they might be sucked into! Getting involved in peer-assessment makes the assessment culture much more transparent, and students gain a better idea of exactly what will be expected of them in their efforts to demonstrate their achievement of the intended learning outcomes.

3 **We can't do as much assessing as we used to do.** With more students, heavier teaching loads, and shorter timescales (sometimes caused by moves to modularisation and semesterisation), the amount of assessment that lecturers can cope with is limited. While it is to be hoped that our assessment will still be valid, fair and reliable, it remains the case that the amount of feedback to students that lecturers can give is less per student. Peer-assessment, when facilitated well, can be a vehicle for getting much more feedback to students.

4 **Students learn more deeply when they have a sense of ownership of the agenda.** When peer-assessment is employed using assessment criteria that are devised by the students themselves, the sense of ownership of the criteria helps them to apply their criteria much more objectively than when they are applying tutors' criteria to each other's work.

5 **The act of assessing is one of the deepest learning experiences.** Applying criteria to someone else's work, and making informed judgements on it, is one of the most productive ways of developing and deepening understanding of the subject matter involved in the process. 'Measuring' or 'judging' are far more rigorous processes than simply reading, listening or watching.

6 **Peer-assessment allows students to learn from each other's strengths and successes.** Students involved in peer-assessment cannot fail to take notice of instances where the work they are assessing exceeds their own efforts. When this learning-from-each-other is legitimised and encouraged, students can benefit a great deal from the work of the most able in the group.

7 **Peer-assessment allows students to learn from each other's weaknesses.** Students peer-assessing are likely to discover all sorts of mistakes that they did not make themselves. This can be really useful for them, as their awareness of 'what *not* to do' increases, and they become much less likely to fall into traps that might otherwise have caused them problems in their future work.

Getting students to formulate their peer-assessment criteria

As mentioned already, peer-assessment works at its best when students own the assessment criteria. Furthermore, it is important that the criteria are clearly understood by all the students, and their understanding is shared. The best way of developing a set of good criteria is to involve the students from the outset in the process. It is crucial not to put words in students' mouths during this process, otherwise the assessment agenda can revert to academic terminology which students don't understand. The following processes can be used to generate a set of peer-assessment criteria 'from scratch'. I have used this process with groups of nearly 200 students, as well as with more intimate groups of 20 upwards.

It really does not matter what the task that students are going to peer-assess involves. The process below will be described in terms of students peer-assessing 'a presentation', but the process could be identical for generating student-owned assessment criteria for 'an essay', 'a report', 'a poster display', 'an interview', 'an annotated bibliography', 'a student-devised exam paper', and countless other assessment possibilities.

It is possible to go through all of the processes listed below, with a group of over 100 students, in less than an hour. The more often you do this with students, the faster and better you will become at it (and at taking short cuts where appropriate, or tailoring the steps to your own subject, and to the particular students, and so on). Similarly, when students become accustomed to the processes involved, they too become faster and better at working out good criteria.

In practice, you are very unlikely to need to build in all eighteen of the steps outlined in the list below in any given instance of negotiating criteria with a group of students. Usually, at least some of the processes below may be skipped, but it is worth thinking through the implications of all of the stages before making your own decision about which are most relevant to the particular conditions under which you are planning to facilitate peer-assessment.

1 **Illustrating:** Before getting into helping students to formulate any criteria, it can be really useful to give them some food for thought by showing them (say) three short examples (no more than a minute or two each – this is just to set the scene). If presentations are to be discussed, three video snippets of a really good one, a poor one, and an in-between one can open up thoughts about the sorts of things which may be turned into useful criteria. At this stage, it's best not to say which is the good one or the poor one – just let the students themselves begin to sense that there's a range.

2 **Brainstorming:** Ask all students to jot down individually a few key words in response to: 'What makes a really *good* 10-minute presentation? Jot down some of the things you would look for in an excellent example of one.'

3 **Sharing:** Get students to work in groups. Even in a large lecture theatre, they can work in groups of four or five with their near neighbours. Alternatively, if students are free to move around the room where the exercise is happening, they can be put into random groups (alphabetical, or by birthday month, or allowed to form self-selecting groups). Ask the groups to share and discuss for a few minutes *all* of their ideas for a good presentation.

4 **Shortlisting and prioritising:** Ask the groups to make a shortlist of (say) 'the most important *five* features of a good 10-minute presentation'. It can be useful to ask groups to jot down the chosen five features on separate post-its. Then ask the groups to shuffle the post-its in order of 'importance' or 'value', with the top one in position '1', next in '2' and so on.

5 **Editing:** Get the groups to look carefully at the wording of each item on their shortlisted features. For example, tell them that when they report back an item from their list, if you can't tell exactly what it means, you will ask them to tell you 'what it *really* means is …'. Maybe mention that some of the more academic words such as 'coherence', 'structure' and 'delivery' may need some translation into everyday words (maybe along the lines of 'hangs well together, one point following on logically to the next', 'good interest-catching opening, logical order for the middle, and firm, solid conclusion', and 'clearly spoken, well-illustrated, backed-up by facts or figures'). However, don't put too many words of any kind into students' minds, let them think of their own words.

6 **Re-prioritising:** Remind the groups about the shortlisting process, and to re-sort their five chosen features into order of priority if necessary. The order may have changed during the editing process, as meanings became clearer.

7 **Turning features into checklist questions:** Suggest that the groups now edit each of their features into a question format. For example, 'was there a good finish?', 'how well was the material researched?', and so on. New post-its containing the checklist questions can be stuck onto the existing ones describing the features. The point of this is to pave the way for a checklist of criteria that will be more straightforward as a basis for making judgements.

8 **Collecting the most important questions in the room:** Start collecting 'top' feature-questions. Ask each group in turn for the thing

that came top of its list. Write these up, one at a time, on a slide or flipchart, so that the whole class can see the emerging list of checklist questions. Where one group's highest-rating point is very similar to one that has already been given, either put a tick beside the original one (to acknowledge that the same point has been rated as important by more than one group), or (better) adjust the wording slightly so that the checklist question reflects *both* of the sources equally. Continue this process until each of the groups has reported its top checklist question.

9 **Fleshing out the agenda:** Now go back round the groups (in reverse order) asking for 'the second-most-important thing on your list'. At this stage, the overlaps begin to occur thick and fast, but there will still emerge new and different checklist questions based on further features identified by the groups. Use ticks (maybe in a different colour from the overlaps of top-rated questions) to make the degree of concurrence visible to the whole group as the picture continues to unfold. With a large class, you may need to use more than one slide or flipchart-sheet, but it is important to try to keep all of the agenda that is unfolding visible to the whole class. If using flipcharts this may mean posting up filled flipcharts where everyone can see them, or with slides switching backwards and forwards to help the whole group keep track of the emerging picture.

10 **Any other business?** If the degree of overlap has increased significantly, and after gaining all the second-round contributions, the flow of new ideas has slowed down, it is worth asking the whole group for 'any fairly important things that still aren't represented on your list'. Usually, there will be a further two or three significant contributions at this stage.

11 **Numbering the agenda:** When all of the checklist questions have been noted down, number them. Simply write numbers beside each checklist question, in the order that they were given. During this stage, if you notice that two checklist questions are more-or-less the same, it can be worth asking the class whether you can clump them together.

12 **Weighting individually:** Ask students to work individually again next. Ask them to weight each checklist question, using an agreed total number of marks. Choosing the total number needs care! If there are ten checklist questions, 100 marks would be too tempting regarding the possibility of some students just giving each checklist question ten marks, and avoiding the real business of making prioritising decisions again. Thirteen checklist questions and sixty marks works better, for example. Ask every student to ensure that the total marks number adds up to the agreed figure. Legitimise students regarding ignoring any checklist questions that they individually don't think are important: 'If you think it's irrelevant, just score it zero.' Similarly allow them to give a high weighting for anything they think is really important.

13 **Recording everyone's weighting publicly:** The next stage is to record everyone's marks on the slides or flipcharts. This means starting with checklist question number 1, and inserting beneath it *everyone's* marks-rating. It's worth establishing a reporting-back order round the room first, so that every student knows who to follow (and encouraging students to nudge anyone who has lost concentration and is failing to give you a score!). 'Can you shout them out as fast as I can write them up?' usually keeps everyone (including you) working at speed.

14 **Discussing divergent views:** Then go through all of the remaining checklist questions in the same way. Don't worry that sometimes consecutive scores for the same checklist question will be quite divergent. When this happens, it will be a rich agenda for discussion later, and if you're writing the scores up in the same order each time, it's not too hard to pinpoint the particular individual who gave an unusually high or low rating to any checklist question. You can, for example, ask the student who rated checklist question 8 highest to argue briefly with the student who rated it lowest, and see what the causes of the divergence may be.

15 **Averaging:** Next, average out all the scores. If there are students with calculators in the group, the average rating may be forthcoming from the group without any prompting. Otherwise, it's usually possible to do some averaging and rounding up or down to the nearest whole number just intuitively by looking at the numbers. Ask the whole group, 'Does checklist question 7 get a five or a six please? Hands up those who make it a five?' and so on.

16 **Shedding weak checklist questions:** Look back at the whole range of checklist questions and ratings. At this point, there will usually be one or more checklist questions that can safely be dropped from the agenda. They may have seemed like a good idea at the time to some of the students, but the visible low ratings tell their own story.

17 **Confirming ownership:** 'Are you all happy to proceed with the averaged-out version of the ratings, and with these checklist questions?' is the question to ask next. Mostly, there will be no dissent. Just occasionally, a student with a different view of the ratings may wish to speak out against the consensus. It is worth then offering that any individuals who feel strongly about the ratings can choose to be peer-assessed by their own idiosyncratic rating scales, but that these must now be shared with the whole group for approval. Students rarely wish to do this, particularly if the feeling of ownership of the set of weighted checklist questions is strong in the group as a whole.

18 **Administrating:** Turn the checklist questions into a grid, with the checklist questions down the left-hand side, and the weighting numbers in a column alongside them, with spaces for students to write in their peer-assessment ratings. If students are going to be asked to peer-assess several instances of the task involved (for example maybe ten short presentations), the grids could be marked up so that students used the same grid for the successive presentations (see Figure 2.2). Alternatively, if the peer-assessment grids are going to be used for a small number of assessments (for example, where all students mark three essays or reports, and each of theirs is to be marked by three students), it is worth having separate sheets, with a column for individual feedback comments relating to the score awarded for each of the checklist questions (see Figure 2.3).

The list of processes above may appear daunting, but in fact it is quite a lot easier to do in practice than it is to write out a description of it! Also, some of the steps are in fact very quick to do. Furthermore, as the culture of peer-assessment becomes better known to students, they themselves become better at generating and weighting criteria, and more skilled at applying them well.

Setting up self-assessment tutor dialogues

Think of the following scenario. A piece of coursework is to be handed in and tutor-assessed. This could be just about anything, ranging from a practical report, a fieldwork report, a dissertation, and even an essay or set of answers based on a problems sheet.

Imagine that students are briefed to self-assess their efforts at the point of submitting the work for tutor assessment, and are supplied with a pro forma for this self-assessment, of no more than two pages length. Suppose that the pro forma consists of a dozen or so short, structured questions, asking students to make particular reflective comments upon the work they are handing in, and that the principal purposes behind these questions are to:

- cause students to reflect on what they have done;
- give tutors assessing their work additional information about 'where each student is' in relation to the tasks they have just attempted;

Peer-assessment: grid for multiple examples Your name: Date: Session:									
Example being assessed	Mark out of	A	B	C	D	E	F	G	H
Checklist question 1	4								
Checklist question 2	8								
Checklist question 3	4								
Checklist question 4	8								
Checklist question 5	5								
Checklist question 6	5								
Checklist question 7	2								
Checklist question 8	4								
Total	40								

Figure 2.2 Example of a grid where students peer-assess A to H (for example) presentations

Peer-assessment: grid for a single example Your name: Date: Session:			
Example being assessed	Available mark	Score	Feedback comment
Checklist question 1	4		
Checklist question 2	8		
Checklist question 3	4		
Checklist question 4	8		
Checklist question 5	5		
Checklist question 6	5		
Checklist question 7	2		
Checklist question 8	4		
Total	40		

Figure 2.3 Pro forma for individual peer-assessments of (for example) essays or reports, with feedback

- form a productive agenda to help tutors to focus their feedback most usefully;
- save tutors' time by helping them to avoid telling students things about their submitted work, which they know all too clearly already;
- give students a sense of ownership of the most important elements of feedback which they are going to receive on the work they have submitted.

Some ideas for self-assessment agendas

Each of the suggestions below could take the form of a relatively small box on the pro forma, requiring students to give their own reply to the question, but allowing space for tutors to add a sentence or two in response to each student's reply. Sometimes, of course, tutors would wish to (or need to) enclose additional response information on separate sheets – often pre-prepared handout materials dealing with anticipated problem areas or frequently made errors. A reminder: the menu of questions below is exactly that – a menu – from which individual assessors will need to select carefully only a few questions, those which are most relevant to the nature of the assessed task. Also, for every separate task, it is vitally important that the self-assessment questionnaires are patently task-specific, and that students *don't* see the same (or similar) questionnaires more than once. (We all know how 'surface' students' responses become to repetitively used course evaluation questionnaires, and how limited is the value of the feedback we receive from such instruments!)

For each of the questions I include below, I've added a sentence or two about *why* or *when* it may prove useful to assessors and students. Some parts of the menu below are much more obvious than others, and I believe it is the less-common questions that are most likely to set up deep tutor–student dialogue.

- *What do you honestly consider will be a fair score or grade for the work you are handing in?*
  Most students are surprisingly good at estimating the worth of their work. Only those students who are more than 5 per cent out (or one grade point) need any detailed feedback on any differences between the actual scores and their own estimates – saves tutors' time.
- *What do you think was the thing you did best in this assignment?*
  Assessors know soon enough what students actually did best, but that's not the same as knowing what they *think* they have done well. Where both are the same thing there's no need for any response from assessors, but on the occasions where students did something else much better (or did the original thing quite poorly), feedback is vital, and very useful to students.
- *What did you find the hardest part of this assignment?*
  Assessors know soon enough what students do least well, but that's not always the thing they found hardest. When a student cites something that was completely mastered – in other words, the assignment gives no clue that this was a struggle – it is essential that the student is congratulated on the achievement involved, for example a few words such as 'you say you found this hard, but you've completely cracked it – well done!' go a long way.
- *If you had the chance to do this assignment again from scratch, how (if at all) might you decide to go about it differently?*
  This question can save assessors hours! Students usually know what is wrong with the approach they have engaged in. Let them tell you about this! This saves you having to go on at length telling them about it. Moreover, when students themselves have diagnosed the weaknesses in their approach, the ownership of the potential changes to approach lies with them, rather than us having to take control of this.

- *How difficult (or easy) did you find this assignment?*
  Don't use number scales! Provide words or phrases which students can underline or ring. Use student language, such as 'dead easy', 'tough in parts', 'did my head in!', 'straightforward', 'a real pain', 'took longer than it was worth', 'hard but helped me learn', and so on.
- *What was the most important thing that you learned about the subject through doing this assignment?*
  Answers to this question give us a lot of information about the extent to which the assignment is delivering learning payoff to students.
  *What was the most important thing that you learned about **yourself** while doing this assignment?*
  Such a question gives us information about how well (or badly) the assignment may be contributing to students' development of key transferable skills, including self-organisation.
- *What do you think are the most important things I am looking for in this assignment?*
  This question can be sobering for assessors – it can show us how students perceive our activities, and it can often show us a lot about how we are found to be assessing. Students can benefit from feedback on their responses, when their perceptions of the purposes of an assignment have gone adrift.
- *How has doing this assignment changed your opinions?*
  Not all assignments have anything to do with developing students' views, attitudes or opinions, but some do this, and it is important that we acknowledge this when such issues are intentional. Such a question is better than simply asking 'has your opinion changed?', where the expectation is clearly for a 'yes' response.
- *What's the worst paragraph, and why?*
  This question is particularly useful as a feedback dialogue starter when assignments are substantial, such as long reports or dissertations. Students quite often know exactly where they were trying to firm up an idea, but struggling to express it. Their help in bringing to our attention the exact positions of such instances can save us hours in finding them, and can ensure that we have the opportunity to respond helpfully and relevantly to students' needs.
- *What was the most important thing you picked up from my feedback on the **previous** assignment, which you have tried to address in this assignment?*
  This can cause students to actually look back at previous feedback, and indeed to act on it, in a way which might just not have happened at all without a question of this sort.

Conclusions about assessment and feedback

Assessing students' work and getting feedback to them on their progress are the most important things we do for our students. That's why this chapter is the longest in this *Toolkit* – it's the heart of our work. None of the forms of assessment discussed in this chapter is without its merits or its limitations in the context of assessing various facets of the skills, knowledge and performances of students. The challenges caused by greater numbers of students and increased assessment workloads provide an opportunity to make a radical review of the ways we assess our students. The wealth of research evidence now available to use about assessment and feedback, and the salutary warnings about the urgent need to overhaul our approaches, make such a radical review more than just timely. In particular, assessment has grown far too much. We need to increase the quality of it but reduce substantially the amount of assessment, to do our students' learning justice – and to give them time to learn, rather than filling their time with assessment tasks.

The requirement placed upon us to match assessment criteria to intended learning outcomes give us further opportunity to adjust our assessment so that we are attempting to measure that which is important, rather than merely that which is relatively straightforward to measure.

In particular, we must ensure that our attempts to meet these challenges do not lead to a retreat from those forms of assessment which are less cost-effective, but which help students to get due credit for a sensible range of the knowledge and skills they demonstrate. Probably the best way to do our students justice is to use as wide as possible a mixture of the assessment methods outlined above, allowing students a range of processes through which to demonstrate their respective strengths and weaknesses – but as already said, keep assessment much shorter. Moreover, the sixteen assessment methods discussed in some detail in this chapter are only a cross-section of those which could be used. Ideally, for each area of students' learning, we should be asking 'what is the most appropriate way to measure this fairly, validly, and reliably, and how can we make the whole process more manageable for students and indeed for ourselves?'

Finally, we need to ensure that learning is not simply assessment-driven. In this chapter I've argued that presently we have far too much assessment, but that neither the quality nor the diversity of this assessment is right, and there is a significant shortfall in the amount of formative feedback which can help students towards demonstrating their optimum potential in those assessment elements which count most significantly towards their awards. Students are highly intelligent people; if we confront them with a game where learning is linked to a rigid and monotonous diet of assessment, they will learn according to the rules of that game. To improve their learning, we need to improve our game, not least our feed-forward to students.

Chapter 3

Lectures in the digital age

Many argue that the era of lectures has passed, that it is archaic to expect students to sit physically present in the same room as the lecturer, passively listening to and noting what is said, and thereby absorbing content. If you sit at the back of the lecture theatre and watch what students are actually doing on their laptops and mobile devices, it is evident that few students nowadays simply sit and make traditional lecture notes with pens and paper. But look again and see that as well as updating their Facebook pages, students are making mind-maps of what they are hearing, following the structure of the lecture based on previously pasted-up presentations, Googling unfamiliar words or Tweeting about the subject of the lecture (although there are still students absent in all but body from the lecture as there always have been).

(Sally Brown, 2015, p. 56)

Intended outcomes of this chapter

There are more than the usual number of intended outcomes for this chapter, as there as so many different ways in which we need to think about the most public side of our work, large-group sessions with students. When you've looked through this chapter, and applied the most appropriate ideas it contains to your own teaching, you should be better able to:

- gain confidence in preparing and delivering lectures;
- address the changing expectations of students regarding the large-group experience, and their increasing status as 'customers' when paying for higher education;
- adjust your approach to lectures in the light of the changed nature of information availability in the digital age;
- think consciously about how your students learn in lectures, and about ways you can address the principal factors underpinning successful learning in your lectures;
- develop your work with large groups of students so that their learning is more productive in your sessions;
- make effective use of technology in the lecture room, for example to use slides, video-clips and web-links when giving lectures;
- link lectures to study using online resources on the internet and local intranets;
- derive substantial benefits from having some of your lectures peer-observed, and peer-observing others' lectures;
- get and use feedback on your lectures from your students;
- address the fact that large-group teaching is often the most public arena for judgements on the quality of your teaching.

This chapter isn't just for people with the word 'lecturer' in their job title. Indeed, all sorts of people find themselves at the sharp end in the context of a lecture, including graduate teaching assistants, part-time or sessional staff, visiting speakers, professors, researchers, administrators, managers, and so on. I have developed this chapter with five kinds of colleagues in mind:

- those who are new to large-group teaching, and who would appreciate a little help on how best to get started on such work;
- those for whom student class-sizes have expanded recently, and who may wish for some ideas on how to work well with larger groups;
- those who are finding that student expectations regarding large-group teaching have changed dramatically in an age when so much information (including lectures) is freely available online;
- experienced colleagues who simply would like to explore fresh approaches they may wish to try out in their large-group work with students;
- colleagues who used to make extensive use of handout materials in lectures, and are wondering what else they can do when students expect material to be available to them online.

How important is the act of lecturing?

When you are appointed as a 'lecturer', it may seem reasonable to suppose that this is the most important part of your job. This belief is increased when the main specification of your job turns out to be a timetable, with lecture-slots as the principal fixed teaching duties each week. Most people new to lecturing approach their first encounters with the process with some trepidation – some with sheer terror. Indeed, if measurements were taken of pulse rate, palm sweat, and blood pressure during the first few minutes on stage as a lecturer, the results would give every indication of quite a lot of stress. 'But all their eyes are on me!' new lecturers often think to themselves. If you're naturally at home on the stage in a theatre, stage fright won't worry you – you may even enjoy it. However, for perhaps nineteen out of twenty of us, we are not particularly comfortable being the focus of attention of so many eyes. Fortunately, there are many ways to divert students from watching us, and at the same time help them to think about the topics of our lectures. These diversion tactics include:

- using slides and excursions to the web – and even dimming the lights so that what's on the big screen is more easily seen – and we are less visible!;
- giving students things to do during lectures – for example decisions to make about which of three options on-screen would be preferable;
- getting students to discuss an idea with their immediate neighbours for a minute or two, then sounding out the conclusions they have reached.

But it's not enough just to look after our own comfort levels in lectures; we need to be thinking of what's happening in the minds of each and every member of our audience. Some of the diversion tactics listed above do indeed have direct links to helping students to learn.

The history of the lecture stems from times when there were very few books, and the most efficient way of communicating information was to read it out to people, who could take notes of their own, and store it. Although it was indeed possible to communicate information in this way, it was soon recognised that this did not amount to communicating knowledge. Despite the fact that this situation is long gone, most educational systems continue to place considerable value on the lecture situation, not least because it is something that is visible and accountable, and because many lecturers enjoy lecturing! Nevertheless, Ron Barnett (2000) challenges the status of lectures as follows:

> The formal lecture is a refuge for the faint-hearted, both lecturer and students. It keeps channels of communication closed, freezes hierarchy between lecturer and students and removes any responsibility on the student to respond... students remain as voyeurs; the lecture remains a comfort zone... the students' unsettling is held at a distance.
>
> (Barnett, 2000, p. 159)

Exley and Dennick (2004) summarised the tendency (which has continued since then) to create increasingly sophisticated lecture theatres as follows:

> Lecturing is the cornerstone of many undergraduate courses and is believed by many academics to be the only way their subjects can now be taught of increasing numbers of students. Many universities are spending thousands of pounds in refurbishing lecture theatres and updating the technological support and the provision of audio-visual equipment to make this form of teaching more effective.
>
> (Exley and Dennick, 2004, p. 1)

> The technique goes back many hundreds of years, to the monasteries of Europe before the use of printed books, where scholars would travel hundreds of miles to gain access to specific texts. In a scriptorium, a monk at a lectern would read out a book and the scholars would copy it down word for word.
>
> (Exley and Dennick, 2004, p. 3)

Even many years ago, not everyone liked being in lectures. Some jaundiced views about 'the lecture' were included in Brown and Race (2002) as follows:

> 'A talk by someone barely awake to others profoundly asleep' (lecturer in surgery).

> 'Being told something you don't wish to know, by someone who "knows" better than you' (retired teacher).

> 'Actions done by overpaid, out-of-touch, arrogant, middle-class people, living in a world where only education exists' (a student who dropped out of higher education).
>
> (Brown and Race, 2002, pp. 18–19)

As long ago as 1993, in the first edition of Rethinking University Teaching, Diana Laurillard posited:

> Why aren't lectures scrapped as a teaching method? If we forget the eight hundred years of university traditions that legitimises them, and imaging starting afresh with the problem of how best to get a large percentage of the population to understand difficult and complex ideas, I doubt that lectures will immediately spring to mind as the obvious solution. ... Academics will always define the value of the 'inspirational' lecture as though this could clinch the argument. But how many inspirational lectures could you reasonably give in a week? How many could a student reasonably

absorb? Inspirational lectures are likely to be occasional events. Academics as 'students' typically think little of the method.

(Laurillard, 1993, pp. 108–9)

Bill McKeachie reminds us of a tendency few of us will have failed to notice ourselves when sitting in other people's lectures, and goes on to suggest what we may need to aspire to, in order to overcome the problem:

> One of the characteristics of a passive lecture situation in which a lecturer is using few devices to get students to think actively about the content of the lecture is that attention tends to drift. Probably all of us have had the experience of listening to a speaker and finding with a start that we have not heard the speaker for some time because our attention has drifted on to thoughts that are tangential to the lecturer's theme.

(McKeachie, 1994/1951, pp. 56–7)

> Effective lecturers combine the talents of a scholar, writer, producer, comedian, showman and teacher in ways that contribute to student learning. Nevertheless it is also true that few college professors combine these talents in optimal ways and that even the best lecturers are not always on top form.

(McKeachie, 1994/1951, p. 53)

Nowadays, as you will have seen from just a few of the many thoughts about large-group teaching in the literature, quite a lot of doubt hangs over the effectiveness of lectures as a means of helping students to learn, but this is mainly because some lecturers continue to regard lectures as occasions when they perform, and believe this is all that is necessary for their students to learn. Now that all kinds of information technology based curriculum delivery approaches are available, the central role of lectures is even more in doubt.

That said, giving lectures remains one of the most public sides of the work of most higher education lecturers, and attending lectures is part of the life of most campus-based higher education students. However, Hunt et al. (2012) rightly draw attention to the possibility of at least some lectures remaining really valuable:

> It might be argued that a dazzling presentation of well-organised material from a lecturer who is passionate about the subject may be worth a multitude of small-group discussions between students who have yet to gain mastery of the subject matter.

(Hunt et al., 2012, p. 28)

Harland (2012) acknowledges the problem, and wisely suggests that the way forward is to use large-group contexts for what they can do best:

> The lecture continues to be important in the modern university, despite consistent reports that it is an anachronism from a bygone age. It is a method of teaching that attracts a lot of debate, and opinions about the educational effectiveness of the lecture are often polarised. ... I have a suspicion that what underpins most arguments are the past experiences of sitting through lectures that were either enjoyed or endured.

(Harland, 2012, p. 32)

Less lecturing is an easy lesson but a hard one to implement in practice. Nevertheless, academia should consider this idea because at their worst, lectures can end up as nothing more than an exercise in passing on huge amounts of basic factual information that adds little to what is already in a textbook, or could be summarised in a handout. Less lecturing would happen if lectures were only used for what they can do best.

(Harland, 2012, p. 42)

Although some parts of this chapter are specifically about lecturing, most of the suggestions apply to the processes of working with large groups of students. Suggestions in this chapter include ways to help large-group sessions deliver increased learning payoff to students. In effect, I explore many of the ways in which the principles of active, interactive learning can be brought into the lecture theatre or large-group classroom. Some time ago, Ken Bain (2004) suggested that really effective lectures seem to be built on the following approach:

Lectures from highly effective teachers nearly always have the same five features of critical learning... They begin with a question (sometimes embedded in a story), continue with some attempt to help students understand the significance of the question (connecting it to larger questions, raising it in provocative ways, noting its implications), stimulate students to engage the question critically, making an argument about how to answer that question (complete with evidence, reasoning and conclusion), and end with conclusions. The only exceptions? Sometimes the best teachers leave out their own answers whereas less successful lecturers often only include that element, an answer to a question that no one has raised.

(Bain, 2004, p. 107)

Given how important lectures seem to be even now, you may be surprised that in Chapter 2 in this book I addressed assessment even before teaching. My justification is simple enough: students can survive bad lectures, but they may be damaged by bad assessment. Whatever else we do, we need to link assessment well to what students are intended to learn; how they learn it, when they learn it and where they learn it are of much less importance. It is also fair to say that despite the fears that new lecturers have about lecturing, the fears they have about wielding a red pen in assessment mode for the first time are often even more substantial.

Later in the chapter, attention is turned to some of the technologies used by most lecturers, particularly slides. Hunt et al. suggest that technology can be used to promote interactive learning in many ways, not least as follows:

The use of technology in lectures can increase student engagement and support learning in large classes in a number of ways. For example, some teachers use clickers (classroom response systems) to gain immediate audience response during lectures. Clickers can be used to provide the teacher and the students with immediate feedback on in-class quizzes, to poll opinions and to gauge students' understanding of a topic in a non-threatening and engaging way. Clickers are specific-purpose instruments, but mobile phones can also be used in a similar way in conjunction with open-access software.

(Hunt et al., 2012, p. 29)

If lecturing is such a bad idea, why is it still happening so widely?

Sally Brown (2015), a quote from whom opened this chapter, sums up five of the pressures to maintain a status quo that is far from sensible, as follows:

> Despite what we know, transmissive teaching approaches still remain dominant in many institutions today, often for reasons that have little to do with promoting effective learning, including:
>
> 1 The existence within most universities' estates of large rooms designed to accommodate this mode of teaching, which adapt poorly to more discursive modes of learning, particularly when these take the form of raked lecture theatres with fixed rows of teaching in which students are penned immovably for the duration of the lecture. These are normally designed to maximise sight lines for the students looking at the lecturer and to enable students to hear what the lecturer says rather than vice versa;
> 2 Rigidity in the working methods of those who run timetabling within a university that rely on fixed blocks of time (often an hour) and fixed delivery frequencies (e.g. once a week, once a fortnight, etc.). Block delivery, immersive learning, blended experiences and so on are all very difficult to timetable and so sometimes get blocked;
> 3 A static and seemingly immovable academic timetable (at least in the UK) that requires students to start their studies at fixed points in the year, for assessments to take place within examination periods, and that make activities like field trips outside term/semester time problematic;
> 4 The existence within some academics' minds of similarly fixed models of learning, based on how they themselves were taught. Some academics really relish the control a lecture theatre gives them over students who are required to listen to what they are saying, and some don't have the confidence to relinquish this power;
> 5 The existence within some university managers' minds of a risk-averse view of curriculum delivery, that enables them to feel confident that as long as material is covered in lectures, they will not be open to charges of having failed to teach students what they need to know.
>
> (Brown, 2015, pp. 25–6)

The fact is that at least part of the role of the lecturer has now been overtaken by disintermediation. The lecturer is nowadays not a key part in the process of getting information to students in the way that used to be the case. Most of the 'information' is already out there, on the web. But there's so much out there that the lecturer's role is now more about helping students to find and use the best and most appropriate information. This boils down to a change in how we need to approach large-group sessions, and use these occasions for the things that happen best when lots of students are together in the same place at the same time. Despite the reservations I have already expressed about lecturing in the traditional sense, in this chapter, I will explore how large-group sessions can in fact be made very productive in terms of students' learning, by making optimum use of these occasions when students are together. Meanwhile, let's continue our exploration of how to survive as a lecturer by exploring, then hopefully exploding, some more of the myths about lectures.

Why have lectures?

There has been quite a lot written about how ineffective the traditional lecture can be in terms of learning payoff to students. However, we're stuck with slots with large groups on our timetables, so it's worth thinking about how we can make best use of such time. Long ago, the beginning of the culture of giving lectures was probably due to the fact that only the 'lecturer' had the books. When books had to be copied by hand, they were rare and valuable. Now, students can have relatively easy access to all the original books and papers, not to mention a vast amount of further material available on the internet and online intranets, resource collections and databases. So why does the practice of giving lectures continue? There are good reasons and bad ones – let's look at the worst ones first.

Some bad reasons

- To simply respond to some students' expectations that they are going to be taught all they need to know;
- to fill up students' timetables, so that a 'course' or 'programme of study' is seen to exist;
- to fill up your own timetable so that you're seen to be gainfully employed;
- to keep students 'under control';
- because 'that's the way it's always been done here';
- because 'that's what happened to me when I was a student'.

Some better reasons

Even nowadays when students can have their own access to source material, books, and a range of online learning resources, there are still several things that can best be achieved in large-group sessions with classes. Some of the many reasons for continuing to use large-group sessions with students include the following:

- to give students a shared learning experience and provide a focus, where everyone gets together regularly;
- to whet students' appetites, so that they go away and really want to get down to studying;
- to give students the chance to make sense of things they already know;
- to clarify intended learning outcomes, illustrate intended evidence of achievement of the outcomes, and define the standards of students' performance which will be linked to these outcomes;
- to give students the opportunity of learning-by-doing, where they can get feedback from an 'authority' and from each other;
- to add the power of tone of voice, emphasis, facial expression, and body language to printed or on-screen words, helping students to see what's important, and what is not;
- to provide material for later discussion, exploration and elaboration;
- to challenge students preconceptions, assumptions and beliefs;
- to change or develop students' attitudes and perspectives;
- to create occasions when some at least of the students present can 'first see the light' on tricky concepts and ideas, and consolidate this by sharing the experience of 'the light dawning' with fellow students who've not yet seen the light;
- to give large groups of students common briefings for major assessment-related tasks which they are to undertake as they study the subject further.

Many of the above reasons for continuing to give lectures are more concerned with the broad experience of studying than with the activities which students engage in during a particular lecture. However, it is indeed possible to follow up our exploration of learning processes from Chapter 1 to set out to cause students to learn things during a lecture. This can still be achieved, even with very large student groups, by concentrating on what the students themselves actually do during such lectures, and ensuring that the processes relate to effective learning. Let's look next at some ways of achieving this.

Some things students do in lectures

I've asked many hundreds of lecturers what they believe their students do during lectures, and many thousands of students what they really do. As you may expect, many of the things students do during lectures are far from connected to the content of the lectures. Some of the most common things students do in lectures are listed below:

- copying down things from the screen (though nowadays students expect to be able to download what's on the screen onto their own laptops or tablet);
- jotting down verbatim things said by the lecturer (though today's students are loathe to put pen to paper, and may prefer recording the lecture);
- attempting to summarise things discussed by the lecturer;
- gazing out of the windows (if there are any);
- texting, Tweeting, and looking up things on laptops or mobile phones;
- looking at other students, and what's on their laptop or tablet screens;
- worrying because they can't understand what is being talked about;
- watching the clock – waiting for lunchtime, for example;
- doodling, yawning, fidgeting, shuffling, daydreaming – even sleeping;
- reading things that have nothing to do with the lecture;
- listening to or watching a match on a mobile device;
- thinking about coursework soon to be handed in for other subjects;
- actually doing coursework due to be handed in for other subjects;
- worrying about accommodation problems, cash flow problems, relationships;
- feeling generally unwell – hangover, tiredness, flu, time of the month.

(Please continue this list if you wish!)

Only one of the things mentioned so far is a useful learning process in its own right: 'summarising'. This involves processing the content of the lecture, making decisions about the relative importance of different things, and generally making sense of the content of the lecture.

Most of the remainder of the things in the list above are neither productive in terms of learning payoff, nor are they linked to achieving the intended learning outcomes. In particular, copying things down (whether from the screen, or from what has been said) is far from being as useful as people think it is. Most students will admit having been to lectures where they'd copied all sorts of things down (even transcribed verbatim dictated episodes), but without actually thinking about the material at all at the time. They confirm that if they were to be quizzed about the notes they had just copied out, their answer would have to be along the lines, 'sorry, I haven't actually read it yet – ask me again later!' However, this problem is fading away, as students tend not even to try to capture information with a pen nowadays.

In other words, the fact that a large group of students may look very busy writing during a lecture is in itself no indication that any deep learning is occurring then and there. It is true that students will often get down to learning what they have copied later, but that does not alter the fact that during the lecture itself they were in effect wasting their time and energy on processes with no direct learning payoff.

It used to be thought better to actually give students the relevant material as a handout. However, there were problems with handouts, in particular the danger that students believed that they had then already captured the content of the lecture, and could think that they may safely switch off mentally altogether. Now, the expectation is that students should be able to download relevant resource materials, before or after the actual lecture; but the problem remains that they think 'I've got it' when all they have is the information – which all too often remains unprocessed.

Some productive lecture processes

A number of further activities that students can engage in during lectures can be productive in terms of learning. As we saw in Chapter 1, overlapping processes which underpin successful learning are:

- wanting to learn – motivation, interest, enthusiasm;
- needing to learn – seeing the reason for putting in some hard work, gaining a sense of ownership of the intended learning outcomes;
- learning-by-doing – practising, trial and error, learning from mistakes;
- getting feedback on how the learning is going – other people's reactions, comments, seeing tangible evidence for one's achievements, using what has been learned;
- making sense of what has been learned – getting one's head round it;
- deepening learning by putting things into spoken words – talking to each other in the lecture;
- getting a real grip on the subject concerned by making judgements, assessing things.

Below I have tried to link some productive student actions to these central processes:

- becoming excited about the subject, and enthused (wanting);
- wishing to find out more about things discussed (wanting);
- building on what's already known about the topic (wanting, identifying the need);
- seeing why something is important (needing);
- solving problems (learning-by-doing);
- trying out theoretical principles in practice-based examples (learning-by-doing);
- making decisions (learning-by-doing, also assessing);
- explaining things to fellow students sitting nearby (doing, making sense, feedback, verbalising);
- asking questions (verbalising, seeking feedback);
- working out questions to find out the answers to later (preparing to seek feedback);
- prioritising issues and information (making sense, making judgements);
- summarising (making sense, prioritising);
- answering questions (learning-by-doing, verbalising, getting feedback).

As you read the discussion below, think further how you can construct your lectures in ways that directly address these active processes (and help to avoid the occurrence of some of the unproductive processes mentioned earlier).

Causing learning to happen in lecture contexts

To summarise our thinking on how we can use large-group sessions with students to maximise the learning payoff they derive from them, I would like you to think once again about the practical model of learning introduced in Chapter 1, and the underpinning processes: wanting, needing, doing, making sense, feedback, deepening learning by verbalising (speaking) and making judgements (assessing). Next, let's take each of these in turn, and remind ourselves of some of the ways that they can be embraced within the lecture situation. I will explore below some general factors, which I hope will help you think of your own subject-specific ideas for turning your lectures into interactive learning experiences.

Lectures and wanting to learn

Lectures can be a very effective way of arousing curiosity and even creating the want to learn. Lectures can be occasions where the want is rekindled or amplified. Even if this were the only result of a particular lecture, it would be a useful one. Some ways we can attempt to develop students' want to learn and arouse their curiosity include:

- radiating infectious enthusiasm and passion for the subject;
- posing interesting questions which excite students' curiosity;
- helping students to see how much they can already do, increasing their confidence;
- helping students to see 'what's in it for them' – how the material will help them both towards gaining the qualification for which they're studying, and in their later careers and professions;
- illustrating to students that complex problems can often be solved one step at a time;
- clarifying targets, performance standards and intended learning outcomes, so that students can see exactly what they're aiming for;
- helping students to see the big picture by identifying the difference between what they need to know, and those things that are simply nice to know;
- relating materials to be learned to intended learning outcomes and assessment criteria (establishing the need-to-know dimension).

Lectures and needing to learn

While, as hinted at above, wanting to learn is a much happier driving force for the learning process than needing to learn, the latter is much better than nothing. We can use the shared, large-group situation to help our students to see exactly what is entailed in the expected learning outcomes associated with each topic or theme. We can illustrate the kinds of evidence of achievement of these outcomes which will link strongly to forthcoming coursework and exams. Some of the approaches with which we can help students to take ownership of their particular learning needs include:

- explaining exactly the sorts of things students may be required to do to demonstrate their learning of the topics covered by the lecture;
- helping students to see the purpose of the intended learning relating to the lecture, and alerting them to good reasons for working towards becoming competent in particular aspects of the material covered;
- allowing students to see that some parts of the subject content are expected to be hard, but that it will be worthwhile spending an appropriate amount of energy on these parts.

Lectures and learning-by-doing

I've already suggested that simply writing down what is heard or seen during a lecture is not a particularly useful kind of 'doing'. However, there are many other activities that can be used even with hundreds of students sitting tightly in rows, which all connect to 'learning-by-doing'. Here are some possibilities. Students can be helped to:

- make judgements and decisions – for example picking the best option from several alternatives shown on the screen, and working out why other options are less good or even incorrect;
- solve problems – using information given to them verbally or on the screen, or on websites visited live in the lecture;
- think creatively, for example by working out what the most important issues or questions are, using information given by the lecturer, or from their own experience;
- deepen their learning by speaking to each other: engaging in mini-brainstorms for a few minutes with their immediate neighbours, for example working out what they think may be the main issues that need to be addressed in a scenario or case study;
- place given factors in order of importance, prior to a class discussion which shows them whether their prioritising was effective.

Lectures and learning through feedback

The old-fashioned sort of lecture where students were seen and not heard offered little opportunity for learning through feedback. However, the potential which can be derived from feedback in modern large-group learning environments is in fact very high, by facilitating student actions including getting students to:

- compare thoughts with each other regarding decisions they made individually when given options to choose;
- work together in small clusters of two or three, to make decisions, or solve problems, or prioritise the importance of issues, or formulate questions, and so on;
- find out where they stand compared with each other, for example in 'show of hands' episodes where the positions or views of all the members of even the largest group can be surveyed in seconds;
- put things into spoken words, deepening their thinking by explaining things to each other, or arguing with each other;
- attend to feedback from the lecturer on work which has just been assessed, or on past students' efforts at coursework assignments and exam answers;
- receive feedback from the lecturer, on decisions they have reached or options they have selected;
- make judgements on their own learning, for example by doing self-assessment exercises (at their own pace and in their own way), then using feedback briefings and responses designed to let them see how well they had tackled the exercises.

Lectures and making sense of what is being learned

This is perhaps one of the strongest parts of the rationale for having large groups of students together in one place at a given time. The more we can help students to get their heads around key ideas and concepts while they are together, the more worthwhile it is for students to turn up for a lecture. In the lecture, as well as the information on the screen, they have the richness of everything else the lecturer brings to the occasion to help students make sense of things, including tone of voice, body language, emphasis on particular words, pauses for thinking, and 'saying things again in a different way' when it is noticeable that some students haven't yet 'got it'. When the making sense process really works well in a large-group session, it means that the relevant learning is already firmly under way. For anyone missing such a lecture, just catching up from the online resources is a very poor substitute for an active learning occasion. Just some of the things we can try to do in lectures to get their sense-making under way include:

- giving students the chance to explain things to each other – the act of putting an idea into words is often the fastest way to get a real grip on the idea – especially when coupled with feedback;
- helping students to see the big picture – in other words to make sense of what they have already learned, and to see how it links to the things they will study next;
- helping students to find out how successful their learning has been so far – and where the black spots are;
- giving students tasks where they apply what they have learned from previous lectures in the series to new data or scenarios;
- helping students to find out where they stand, for example letting them see how their views and beliefs compare with those of the rest of the group by show of hands episodes in a lecture.

Lectures and learning by verbalising

You will have already seen in the discussion so far that I suggest that students do not simply sit silently through a lecture, but can gain a great deal to deepen their learning by talking – putting things into spoken words – as a means to deepen their thinking. Indeed, people need to talk. If there aren't opportunities for students to speak, and especially if the subject is rather boring or quite difficult, 'chatter' tends to break out anyway. It is therefore best to cause students to talk, and give them the chance every so often to contribute to the proceeding, particularly by talking to those sitting close to them, but also from time to time by asking questions of the lecturer, and answering questions from the lecturer and from each other.

Lectures and learning by making judgements

This is perhaps where large groups of students can be at their most powerful in terms of learning payoff. This is where students can get their heads round the assessment culture which they need to master to succeed. There are all sorts of things we can get students to do in lectures including:

- applying assessment criteria to examples of essays and exam answers, as a way of helping them to make sense both of the subject matter itself and the criteria which will be used in due course to assess their own learning;
- allowing students to be talked through self-assessment of drafts of their own work which they bring to the lecture, to alert them to strengths and weaknesses in their learning;
- helping students to peer-assess each other's work, allowing them to gain feedback from each other's successes and weaknesses, and to improve their own future work on the basis of such feedback;
- asking students to make decisions on (for example) which of several options displayed on the screen is best in a case-study scenario presented by the lecturer, and then gain feedback on the pros and cons of each of the options.

These kinds of activity go far deeper than merely trying to capture what is being shown or said in traditional lectures.

Beginnings, middles and endings

It has been (wryly!) said that a good lecture should involve three stages:

1 tell them what you're going to tell them;
2 tell them it;
3 remind them what you've told them.

Linked to the student-centred model of learning we're now looking at, however, it might be wiser to rephrase this along the following lines:

1 alert students to what they're going to be doing (create the want or the perceived need – explain the intended learning outcomes of the session);
2 help students get down to learning-by-doing – practising, experiencing, talking, judging, and learning by trial and error – and receiving quick feedback on their learning in progress;
3 help students to make sense of what they've gained from their experience of the session, and the feedback they've derived (such as by reminding them of the intended learning outcomes and asking them to self-assess the extent to which they feel they've achieved them during the lecture).

We've already explored stage 2 of the above processes, but it's perhaps worth saying a little more about beginnings and endings.

Beginnings

First impressions are important. Especially at the first lecture with a group, there's no second chance to make a good first impression. It's worth thinking quite hard about how best to spend the first five to ten minutes of any lecture. This is where concentration levels might be relatively favourable, but also when some interruptions from late-comers may be inevitable. Some ways of getting a lecture off to a productive start include:

- expressing the intended learning outcomes for the lecture, for example using words such as:
  - 'by the end of this lecture you'll be able to do the following four things'
  - 'in this lecture, we'll explore three ways of analysing social policy'
  - 'during this lecture, you'll see for yourself how a typical exam answer is marked'
  - 'when you've worked through the examples we'll discuss in this lecture, you'll be able to use the Second Law of Thermodynamics to solve problems'
  - 'after this lecture, you should be able to begin to formulate your own project outline';
- including an early short task such as 'think of what is the most important point you already know about (one topic to be covered)', then gather a few points from volunteers;
- introducing something relevant to the topic which has happened in the last day or two;
- giving a checklist of points that will be covered in the lecture;
- asking one or two short questions based on what students should already know from previous lectures, and warmly receiving replies;
- posing a list of questions that the lecture will address;
- providing the exam questions on two or three past papers, linking to the material they are about to think about in the lecture.

In other words, it's productive to use at least the first part of a lecture to set the agenda for that particular lecture – and also to link the agenda to things that have already been covered, and things to come later on. Human nature being what it is, however, there are good reasons for not just reciting the agenda or intended learning outcomes – it's better if it can be seen on the screen. The reasons for putting the outcomes in print as well as speech include:

- some students may arrive late, and miss the agenda, or disturb others' reception of the agenda;
- if it is possible to have the outcomes visible in a handout, they continue to serve as an agenda right through the session, rather than being subsumed or forgotten as time goes on;
- if the outcomes are presented on one or more slides, it can be useful to return to these from time to time during the session, so that students keep the bigger picture in mind;
- if questions and issues are planted in students' minds, as the answers and solutions evolve during the session, students are more receptive. It's useful to have students searching (even subconsciously) for the knowledge constituting the answers to questions.

Endings

There's no second chance to make a last good impression either! The last thing you want is for the last impressions you create at lectures to be any of the following:

- 'obviously lost it towards the end, rushing to try and get through the material'
- 'I hate is when lecturer over-runs, and I have to rush to the next one only to be late there'
- 'didn't get through what was promised at the beginning'
- 'looked more and more flustered as the time ran out'
- 'just seemed to stop. No conclusion, no ending'.

It's so easy for time to run out, so that we feel our only option is to stop the lecture in mid-flow – not a good idea at all. Saving the last five or even ten minutes for a purposeful ending phase for a lecture pays dividends. For a start, any observer (or appraiser) will then recognise the signs of a structured approach to using lecture situations. Even when time does run out, it's far more important to have a good ending than to 'get through' all of the agenda that has been presented. In other words, cut short some of the middle, and leave room for the ending. This is in fact quite easy to do, when the middle has been centred round student-centred activities that we explored under the 'learning-by-doing' and 'learning through feedback' headings earlier – simply miss out an activity, or cut one a little. And indeed if you're doing a series of lectures, you don't have to 'get through it all' or even 'get through all of the things you promised at the beginning', particularly if something really vital and interesting came up in the middle of the lecture – perhaps sparked off by an important question from a student. In such circumstances, it's well worth explaining towards the end of the lecture 'We'll catch up next time with a couple of things outstanding, as it was really useful to spend some time on (whatever it was)'.

Some ways of coming to a robust, recognisable conclusion include using one or two (not more) of the following:

- go back to the agenda of intended learning outcomes, re-showing a slide containing them, and briefly summarise how each has been addressed (this helps students with the making sense stage of their learning);
- giving students a minute or so, ask all students to jot down the most important thing they wish to carry forward from the lecture. Then ask them to compare with near neighbours. Finally, ask for one or two volunteers to share the thing they'd chosen;

- pick out any unfinished business from the agenda, to be included in a future lecture, or to be diverted to tutorial sessions for in-depth exploration (note that this allows you to turn occasions when time runs out on you into what seems like an intentional strategy);
- formulate a new agenda for the next lecture, to whet students' appetites for what is to come next, and to give them the opportunity to do some preparation for the next lecture;
- set a task for all students to complete before the next lecture, or for them to bring along to forthcoming tutorial sessions;
- present in advance the intended learning outcomes for the next lecture, giving students the opportunity to add focus to their preparatory work or reading.

Any of these techniques is better than simply having an 'any questions?' episode right at the end of a lecture. An open-ended offer to take questions can lead to the majority of students with no particular questions feeling that for them the lecture is over, and the group gradually dissolving into shuffling and movement. Regularly ending by giving students something to do is a useful ploy; it helps to reduce the fidgeting that so often occurs when a lecture is obviously about to wind up – closing of books, rustling of papers, shifting of chairs, and so on. When students need to listen carefully so that they know exactly what a task is, such fidgeting is almost completely avoided.

Planning 50 minutes for learning: an example for discussion

Timetables are usually developed around one-hour slots (even though concentration spans are measured in seconds and minutes, rather than hours). In practice, that boils down to just around 50 minutes by the time entry and exit are taken into account. The possibility of giving a 60-minute lecture (or even of facilitating a 60-minute learning experience) is remote! Suppose you've got a lecture scheduled from 10.00 to 11.00. Students will often have to be in some other lecture or tutorial in the next slot, starting at 11.00 – and many may have already been at something else scheduled from 09.00 to 10.00. If your lecture goes on past 11.00, there may be hundreds of students (and a frustrated colleague) milling around outside the lecture room waiting to get in. Therefore, it's clear that there are advantages in 'reasonable punctuality' – both regarding starting and finishing. Here are some suggestions. Let me say at once, however, that I'm not suggesting an inflexible regime for conducting large-group sessions, merely a frame of reference to apply and customise as the occasion demands.

10.00: (or earlier, if the room is empty): Arrive on the dot – punctuality and professionalism are closely connected in many people's minds. Get your slides ready, especially a title slide for the lecture (so students coming in will know they're at the right place if unsure) and a slide containing your agenda (or list of questions to be considered during the lecture, or intended learning outcomes for the lecture) ready. Check the projector if you're going to use it, clean a board if necessary, and so on. If you're using anything complex, such as simultaneous web links to other venues, audio-visual materials in addition to normal slides, or giving a practical demonstration, and so on, it's worth booking the room from 09.00 (or even earlier) if possible, and doing all this without time pressure. If you can't book the room from 09.00, and have a lot of setting up to do, you can often arrange to do it before 09.00, and arrange with whoever is using the room from 09.00 to 10.00 that your preparations will be guarded.

10.01: Perhaps (if you are quite ready to start) chat with some of the students who arrive first – make them feel good about being punctual. Smile at those who are already there – they often smile back. Try to avoid looking increasingly irritated as students continue to arrive – some will not have been able to arrive any earlier.

10.05: If more than half of the class is there, make a definite start. For example, do the 'beginnings' bits. Reveal the agenda of intended learning outcomes relating to the next 40-odd minutes, and discuss it. Remind the class of the important things they should have remembered from last time. Or tell an anecdote or joke. Ignore as best you can stragglers who arrive late. Leave it to the punctual students to make any noisily arriving latecomers feel resented!

10.10: Enter the 'middle' phase – preferably with a student-centred activity rather than a direct input from you. You can give your input in response to the results of the student-centred activity soon enough. Continue activities, buzz-group discussions, open discussions, and short inputs from you, with no single thing taking more than 10–15 minutes, until about 10.40.

10.40: Take control again, for example by asking for general questions – or if none are forthcoming, asking questions yourself and putting one or two students on the spot (but not unkindly).

10.45: Start doing the 'winding up' bits – go briefly through the intended outcomes again, perhaps this time elaborating on how these are linked to forthcoming assessment criteria; set a task, and so on. Aim to finish at around 10.50.

10.50: Finish! This is best done 'visually', for example by disconnecting your laptop or taking your memory stick out of the fixed computer or logging off, replacing your papers into your case or bag, switching off the projector, cleaning a board if necessary, and so on. However, there are still five more minutes available, if there are pressing questions from the class, and if you want to deal with them at this stage. However, surprising as it may seem, few students are seriously disappointed when a lecture finishes a few minutes early!

10.55: If you've not managed to do so already, definitely finish and walk out! Especially with large groups, it can easily take five minutes for one group of students to leave and another to take their places. This may mean choosing phrases on your way out such as 'Sorry, but I really must go now'; 'Do email me with any problems or questions', 'I'll take this up next week'; 'We'll look further into this on Thursday at the tutorials'; 'Anyone who wants some further help on this, please come along to my room this afternoon after four'.

If you still wish to talk to a few students until 11.00, do it outside the room, so that the next class can (if punctual) walk straight in before 11.00, and your colleague who will be using the room next is given the courtesy of being able to set up in an un-rushed way. Where students do wish to see you individually, the end of a lecture is rarely the best time, and it can be better to have a few slots reserved for students to come and see you. One way of helping students to be punctual in appointments to see you individually is to advertise an 'open hour' when you will be pleased to see them in your room, and to post a 'make your own appointment' sheet (maybe in five-minute intervals) on your door. This gives you the further advantage that you will often be armed with the names of students intending to call to see you – a luxury when dealing with large groups of students where it can otherwise be quite impossible to link names to faces.

Using technologies – old and new

Decades ago, the only equipment to be found in most lecture rooms was a lectern, and perhaps a blackboard. Nowadays, some lecture theatres abound with technology. The simplest technologies still include blackboards (or whiteboards), but most lecture theatres are equipped at least with a networked computer and data projector, and a place to connect your own laptop. Most also have a lectern microphone or a roving one, and controls for the lighting. In this section of the chapter, I'll present various tips on using each of a range of technological tools, all with two main aims in mind: to help you to

1   keep your cool when using technology;
2   design your usage of slides and other audio-visual materials, keeping your students' learning from them firmly in mind.

These tips are dos and don'ts based on views gathered from countless colleagues and students. Some of these suggestions are likely to seem too obvious to deserve stating, but I hope that in each of the lists which follows you'll find at least some which will trigger you to experiment with how you use technology in your lectures.

Working with slides: some 'dos and don'ts'

Data projectors ('beamers' as they're called in some countries) are more-or-less endemic now, displacing overhead projectors and acetate transparencies which were used earlier. Two major advantages of having images on a big screen are that you can face your audience as you speak, and usually the projectors are bright enough so that you do not need to darken the room (but it often improves the visibility of slides if you can switch off the front row of lights while using slides, then switch them back on again when not using slides so that students can see your facial expressions and gestures more clearly).

The following suggestions may help you to make effective use of projected images, whether it's slides, or visits to websites, or other visual and audio-visual materials. Many of the long list of suggestions below relate to what has become almost an endemic presentation medium in lectures –Microsoft's PowerPoint – but apply equally to other media, including one I've seen often recently where someone always says afterwards 'made me a bit seasick' – I've not been tempted to use that one myself.

1   **Know your machine.** Most projectors have a focus control, on the machine itself, but usually also accessible from a remote control (if it's not been stolen). It's well worth your time to take steps to become familiar with the particular machine you're going to work with.

2   **'Freeze' can be really useful.** On some remotes, there's a 'freeze' button which allows you to freeze the image on display at any moment, giving you the opportunity to fiddle with your computer to adjust the next slide or to locate something else you suddenly wish to include, but without your audience having to watch your efforts to do so. Check early on whether you have the option to freeze – if there's no remote you probably haven't. Also remember to 'un-freeze' when you're ready to continue, and avoid the embarrassment of continuing to work looking at the computer screen, while the audience still only see the frozen image you used.

3   **The medium is the message?** Good quality slides can add credibility to your messages. It's worth investing time making your main slides look professional and believable. There's nothing better than sitting in on colleagues' lectures whenever you can, or watching carefully how people use slides and media at conference keynotes and presentations, for giving you ideas you can try out to use media well in your own lectures.

4 **Experiment with fonts.** 'Sans serif' fonts (common ones include Arial, Calibri, Comic MS) tend to be easier to read than 'serif' fonts (those with 'twiddly bits', for example New York, Times New Roman), and some fonts look better than others on particular equipment.

5 **Don't put too much on any slide – particularly 'straight text'.** Font sizes usually need to be '24' or larger to be easily read anywhere in a large teaching room, with main headings considerably larger. Make sure that each slide you prepare will be visible from the back of the largest room you are likely to use, even by someone without good eyesight.

6 **Keep the number of words down.** A good slide only needs to contain the main ideas, not the details. You can add the details verbally as you discuss the main points on the slides. Your own 'crib' notes can then be written onto a paper copy of each slide, or even displayed for your eyes only beside each slide on your laptop display.

7 **Use only the top two-thirds of the available space on most slides.** It can be really irritating to students if they have to move their heads (or stand up) to see the final bullet point you've just revealed at the very bottom of a slide, or to see the labelling of the horizontal axis of a graph on a slide. As soon as you notice students having to move their head positions to see something on one of your slides, it's worth noting down that there's something to adjust before you use the same slide again.

8 **Try very hard not to read out your slides!** Students (and any audience) really hate this. Your students can read much faster than you can speak. People don't like having things read out to them that they can read for themselves. 'Why bother to come to the lecture just to have the slides I have downloaded anyway read out to me?' they may ask.

9 **Sorry, but it *is* a competition!** Your students will no doubt see many different lecturers using slides, and they can't help noticing the differences, and making judgements about which approaches they find most helpful. It's

a good idea, one way or another, to see how your colleagues use slides – some will gladly let you have their slides to play with, but it's even better to see how different colleagues use slides for real, and how their students react to them. Peer observation really comes into its own here.

10 **Give students at least a little time to make notes if they wish.** Normally, you may make your slides available on an intranet or on the web after a lecture so that students can revisit anything they wished to see for longer, but you may need to strike a balance regarding how long you show a particular slide between (a) irritating some students by whipping away the image too quickly and (b) boring other students waiting to move on.

11 **Be prepared (if you're brave enough) to edit and add things to your slides during lectures.** Students are impressed if an important point is added in response to one of their questions, and in practice we often notice mistakes or things missing on slides only at the instant they first appear on the lecture theatre screen!

12 **Gain confidence at linking slides to other media and to websites.** It's fairly straightforward to use 'action buttons' in PowerPoint to start a short video clip, or an audio recording, or to link to a text file, all of which can be contained on your laptop or memory stick. You can also use them to go to hyperlinks to websites, where internet access is assured, and bandwidth is sufficient to allow reasonable quality of projection when so linked. However, when live links are to be used to external content, it's best to have 'Plan B' for when nothing happens. What works perfectly on your own computer in rehearsal isn't certain to work in a strange lecture theatre with hundreds of eyes watching the drama which might ensue. You've got to be ready to move on, quickly and unruffled, when intended happenings just don't happen. (There's more about this later in the chapter.)

13 **Don't cause 'death by bullet point'!** Even though PowerPoint can introduce bullet points to slides in a variety of ways (appear, fly from

left, dissolve, and much more dramatic options in recent editions of the software), bullet points can quickly become tiresome to an audience. It is worth having a good reason for building any slide step by step.

14 **Don't overdo the special effects.** Doing the whole presentation in a single format becomes boring for your audience, but programming a random sequence of slide builds tends to be irritating for you as presenter, as you don't know what build sequence will be produced when you move to your next slide. Similarly, don't go overboard on the snazzy changes from one slide to the next.

15 **Beware of the sun!** This isn't a problem in lecture theatres with no windows, but in many large classrooms there's the danger of sunlight making slides difficult to see, or impossible if the sun actually shines onto the screen. Sometimes then projectors and screens can be moved, or blinds or curtains drawn, but often enough sunlight can impair the quality of a PowerPoint presentation. Blinds consisting of 'vertical strips' seem the most likely to allow annoying strips of sunlight to reach projection screens! Also don't forget that sunlight moves. If you're setting up a teaching room with windows first thing in the morning, you may need to plan ahead for where any sunlight may be later in the day.

16 **Don't forget the conditions appropriate for human sleep!** Turning down the lights, sitting comfortably in the same place for more than a few minutes, and listening to the sound of your voice may be just the right conditions for your audience to drop off, particularly if the images are monotonous or unclear. At least some of your students are likely to have been working nightshifts to fund their education, and others will have been enjoying nightlife, so there are bound to be members of your audience in need of sleep.

17 **Don't import tables, text files and complex flowcharts just because you can.** The fact that you can import such files into a PowerPoint presentation leads many into temptation. These are very often the slides which can't be read from the back (or even from the front). It is normally better to give students such information as files they can download, rather than to try to show it to them on-screen.

18 **Don't use the wrong colours.** Colours that look good on a computer screen don't always show up so well when they are projected. If most of your presentations will be in rooms with natural daylight, it is usually best to stick to dark colours for text, and light (or even white) backgrounds. If you know you're going to be working in a lecture theatre where you have full control of the lighting, you can then be more adventurous, and use light lettering against dark backgrounds (not forgetting that you may be lulling your audience to sleep if you turn down the lights for optimum display).

19 **Don't depend too much on any particular colour.** For example, it sometimes happens that (say) red doesn't actually get projected (because of wiring problems or a projector fault), and if you carefully build up some slides with red for emphasis, your intention is unexpectedly thwarted. It can be useful to have a hidden 'test' slide you can access quickly while you're setting up, to check out that all the colours are displaying as expected – a photo is often enough for this purpose.

20 **Don't use the same slide format for all of your slides.** PowerPoint allows you to switch your whole presentation into different pre-prepared styles, but the result can be that your slides all look too similar to have an optimum learning payoff for your viewers. Vary the layout, colours and backgrounds from time to time, so that each new slide (or short sequence of slides) makes its own impact. (However, there will always be some feedback from the odd person who would have preferred all of your slides to be in exactly the same format – and the odd pedant who decrees that all the slides in the entire institution should use a given institutional background and layout!)

21 **Don't talk to the screen!** In the past times of overhead projectors, it was easy to develop good habits, including looking at the transparency rather than at the screen, thereby

avoiding turning your back on your audience and talking to the screen. With projected images, you may have no alternative but to keep an eye on the screen, but you need to make sure that you talk to your audience. If you can arrange things so that you can look at a computer screen between yourself and the audience, rather than the projection screen, the problem can be partly solved.

22 **Don't go backwards for too long!** If you need to return to a slide you showed much earlier, it really irritates an audience to go backwards through several slides to get there. It is better to temporarily switch the display off, and find the slide you want without your audience seeing every step. The same applies to returning to your original place in your presentation. Even better, in PowerPoint, if you know you wish to go back to slide 23, keying in '23' then 'enter' will take you straight there. It's useful to know which slide you were at before you did this, so that you can go straight back to it after revisiting '23'. Right-clicking gives you the option to return to the previously viewed slide – which is fine if you only revisited '23'. In practice, it's useful to have a printout of your slides, for example six per page, with the numbers clearly marked with felt-tip pen on the printout, so that you can navigate your entire presentation in any order at will. One renowned presenter I've encountered often goes straight to her 'conclusions' slide shortly after starting a lecture, then explains that the next thirty minutes aims to show how these conclusions have been reached, and goes back to where she left off to continue the story. When the 'conclusions' slide comes up again she smiles with satisfaction – and the audience smiles back. Moreover, if audience questions should mean that there was a danger that there might not be time to reach the 'conclusions' slide, she can miss out some less important slides and go straight to that final slide just at the right time.

23 **Don't forget to rehearse your presentation.** With overhead transparencies you always knew what was coming next; with PowerPoint it is all too possible to forget. If you look surprised when your next slide appears, it does not do much for your credibility with your audience.

24 **Don't underestimate the potential of remote controls to surprise you!** Many systems allow you to change slides with a dongle inserted into your computer, and a simple remote which goes backwards and forwards, or to 'blank screen'. Sometimes the remote also carries a laser pointer too, to spotlight actual things on the screen. If a presenter is very nervous (or has a hangover), however, laser pointers wobble disconcertingly, so you need a steady hand to use one with confidence. Some systems have more complex remote controls, where pressing the wrong button can switch the system to something quite different (for example video input, or 'power down the projector altogether'), and can mean that you can find yourself unable to get back to your presentation without losing your cool.

25 **Don't forget to check your spelling.** PowerPoint, for example, can do this for you, but you have to instruct the software appropriately, and avoid teaching the 'custom dictionary' wrong words! Be careful not to let the software replace words automatically, or you will get some strange slides if you are using unfamiliar words.

26 **Don't miss out on seeing your presentation on paper.** Consider printing out your slides, for example six per page. This helps you to get an overview of your presentation, and can often alert you to where to insert an additional slide or two, or to where you've accidentally repeated yourself. You may also spot errors on the printout of your slides that you wouldn't have noticed on your computer screen. It is also useful to have a printout of such pages in front of you as you present, so that you can easily remind yourself of what's on the next slide, and navigate around your presentation at will when needed.

27 **Remember that in extremis, in 'edit' mode, you can still search for a particular word or phrase to return to a particular slide, using 'Find'.** You may need to do this when asked

a question. This can turn out to be quicker and less stressful than going backwards and forwards looking for a particular slide (but not so good as being able to spot the right slide at once, and its number, from a printout of 6-per-page beside you).

28 **Don't neglect to adjust and improve your slides.** It is so easy to alter a set of slides that there's no real excuse for not editing your presentation frequently so that it is always finely tuned to the particular audience and context. The most beneficial additions are often new slides inserted to address frequently asked questions in advance. Just a few minutes spent editing within a day after giving a lecture can allow you to improve the slides more than you might have imagined.

29 **Don't stop watching other people's technique.** This is one of the fastest ways of improving your own presentations. Look for things that work well for other people, and find out how the effects were achieved, then emulate them. More importantly, look for things that don't work or look clumsy, and make sure that you avoid them.

30 **Remember that when students are asked for feedback on your teaching, one of the first things which may come to their minds is their impressions of your slides.** If the slides were interesting, stimulating, not too many, and useful for revision, that will be reflected in their overall feedback.

31 **Don't forget to back up your presentation.** Have it with you on a memory stick as well as on your laptop. When your laptop develops a problem, you can then still get to your presentation through other computers. There is usually a desktop computer in a lecture theatre – but if not, a student may be honoured to grant you use of another laptop.

32 **Don't switch the data projector off!** You may have good reasons to wish to show nothing on the screen from time to time, but switching the machine itself off can be troublesome. Sometimes projectors take ages to cool down, and even longer to warm up after restarting them. In most circumstances, when using PowerPoint, simply press 'B' for black on the keyboard, and the screen will go black. Then 'B' again to restart the display instantly. (Or 'W' for white, if you'd prefer more light around.) An alternative is to insert a 'black' slide, where you wish to stop your audience from looking at the screen. Don't, however, forget where you've placed these, and panic about where your display has gone! Alternatively, the remote control for the projector often has a button for 'blank'.

Live links in lectures

I've already mentioned that these should be used with caution, as delays and unusable links can be really annoying to audiences, and panic-inducing to presenters. With PowerPoint, you can insert hot-links to all sorts of things using the 'Action Buttons' facility. These links can be clicked using the mouse or remote control while on-screen in the lecture theatre, and if a suitable modem connection is up and running, take you straight to the website, or photo, or different PowerPoint presentation, and so on. It is, of course, important to make sure that you can get back to your presentation when you want to. It is sometimes more difficult than you think, as you might need to click an 'X' box at the far top right-hand corner of the screen to do so, and this might not be possible using the particular remote control you're using, or might be quite hard to do with nervous fingers using your mouse or the trackpad on your laptop.

When we link on-screen into web pages, the problem of visibility and readability can become serious. From the back of the room, only the main headings may be seen at all well. This is not to say that you should never show web pages on-screen in lectures; you may simply want students to register the general appearance of some pages so that they are primed to recognise them more readily when they subsequently search them out for themselves. Or we may just want students in the lecture to see a particular graphic, chart, diagram, table or photo, rather than the small-print wording surrounding it.

All this is fine so long as we make our intentions clear at the time. In other words, if we say 'just look at this bit' and point to it with our on-screen cursor or laser pointer, and add 'don't try to read the text here, wait till you've got the web page on your own machine', then no one is likely to become frustrated by what they can't read there in the lecture room. However, the students sitting at the front are still going to be advantaged – or even distracted – by them actually being able to see both the words and the image you're referring to.

'*Now you see it, now it's gone*'

This is perhaps the most significant pedagogic problem associated with using sophisticated technology in lectures to bring to students' eyes images, data, and so on. When we're using a lot of different on-screen images, how much of it all do students remember, five minutes on, or an hour or two on (let alone a week or two on) after our lecture? It's easy enough to give students our PowerPoint slides themselves, but if we're linking to other things such as web pages, we can't guarantee that students will also be able to follow up all the links wherever they are. But the problem of 'now you see it, now it's gone' continues to apply at least to some extent. We know only too well that it's possible to sit at a computer for an hour, totally absorbed, but not really have a firm grip on what we've been learning from it, unless we do more than just browse through some software applications or tour the internet or follow up links.

'*Now you see it, now it is gone altogether!' Don't panic!*

Returning to using technology in lectures, just about everyone I know has tales to tell of when the technology let them down, in front of a large group of students, unexpectedly, and irretrievably. One or more of the following can happen at any time, any of which can take the technological side of your roadshow right off the road:

- a power cut – everything goes dark except the emergency exit lights (and all the students' mobile phones);
- a fire in the building, which means you've got to evacuate Theatre 2, leaving your laptop with all your stuff on it until tomorrow morning, when the fumes that came in through the air conditioning system have been deemed by the Fire Service to have gone again (and they don't care that you needed your laptop as you've got another lecture on the other campus at 16.00 – keep that memory-stick backup in your pocket and not on the lecture theatre console);
- nothing happens when you press the 'next slide' button on the remote control, or 'N' on the keyboard, or 'esc' for escape;
- the bulb blows in the data projector up on the ceiling;
- the server goes down, and you can't log on to the system to restart the projector;
- the computer itself goes down;
- the computer won't talk to the data projector it talked to happily yesterday;
- the image on the big screen is just the top left two-thirds of what's on your laptop screen;
- the website you're connecting to has gone down;
- alerts about your new emails keep coming up on the big screen when you're linked in to the system and the 'pings' are audible to everyone to make sure they all notice the alerts;
- your text messages and incoming Tweets appear on the screen;
- your laptop insists that your machine is at risk and you must update your virus protection software, and imposes the warning every minute or two on top of your PowerPoint slides;
- you can't find the file on your computer, and your memory stick backup has corrupted.

It's enough to put anyone off using anything more than chalk and talk. But it happens. The main thing is to panic only inwardly. Your students will be really attentive now, watching how you rise to the challenges which beset you. One really wants to just sit there and cry, but that's not what you want them to remember.

'Oh, I'll just give it another try' can be famous last words. Sometimes, we know what to do, and that it will work. But we've all been there on those days where someone found, all too slowly, that there was nothing at all that could be done in the time available. It's the technological equivalent of completely forgetting one's lines on-stage, except that there's not usually a helpful prompt from the wings to put one back on track. It is true that on some occasions a helpful student will know what to do and will bail us out.

My best advice, for use in these emergency situations, is to choose one or more of the following tactics, as your strategy for handling the crisis:

- Smile to yourself (through your teeth if necessary), then smile at the students, and get them smiling back at you.
- Think of something for the students to do for five minutes. It's really useful if you always have with you something for the students to do for five minutes. Alternatively, get them discussing and arguing with each other about something you've already done in the lecture. Give them a decision to make, something which they'll have different views about.
- Whatever you get them to do, now's your time for planning what you're going to do next. If what you were going to do next remains dependent upon the technology, it's time to find something else which isn't.
- Remember that it's not going to be an eternity till the end of the session. The time remaining will pass much more quickly for your students if they're engaged in something interesting.
- Perhaps turn the lecture into a question-and-answer session. Ask the students to cluster into small buzz-groups, and for each group to think of a question they'd like the answer to (preferably about the topic you'd been addressing, but not necessarily), and to jot questions down on slips of paper or post-its (it's always really useful to have a pad of post-its with you in any lecture), and pass them down to you at the front. You can then choose some questions you already know the answers to first, and work towards those questions you may wish to throw back at the whole group.
- Accept that there is likely to be some adjusting you'll need to do to your next couple of sessions, to get back on track to covering what you'd hoped to do before things went wrong. The only problem then is if something goes wrong in your only lecture with that group of students, and there are always ways of rescheduling the event if really necessary.

Most lecturers who seem to sail serenely like swans through technical disasters have learned to do so by trial and error. It's always a useful learning experience for us when our plans are thwarted – indeed it can bring us back down to earth, and get us thinking with the students again. But it's uncomfortable and unwelcome, and uses up far more of our energy than we'd like. Therefore, having at least one emergency tactic can be a comfort for us at any time, and a lifesaver now and then.

Peer-observation of teaching and learning

The next part of this chapter is about making the most of what you can learn about lecturing by being observed by colleagues, and (even more sometimes) by observing your own colleagues at work. Many institutions build teaching observation into quality assurance procedures as a matter of routine. In some, however, a stranger in the classroom or lecture theatre is less common, and may even be regarded as threatening.

It's best when peer-observation is mutual, where you observe a colleague, and they observe you (the order doesn't really matter). Even better, it's great when you have three or four different mutual observations going – you learn different things from watching different colleagues' ways of doing things.

It is useful to couple peer-observation of your lectures with self-evaluation of the same lectures. The real benefits come when you combine both for a particular lecture, and after both you, and your observer, have written down your observations and reflections, then sit down together to compare notes, and discuss some of the finer details which may have applied to the particular lecture.

Some institutions use set pro formas for recording observations in peer-review of teaching, but sometimes these are too cumbersome and clumsy for really useful discussions afterwards. A simple pro forma can be much more practicable than a lengthy one, and it's usually best to devise one which really suits your purposes. Even though it's usually called peer-observation, it is every bit as important to watch what works for the students – and what doesn't. A single-side of A4 paper should be more than enough for successful peer-observation, otherwise far too long would be spent scribbling notes, reducing the quality of the actual observation.

A starting point which you can adapt for yourself is the pro forma I offer in Table 3.1. This example is designed to be filled in by the observer during the session – this could be done on a laptop or by jotting onto a printout. However, this can work even better if the lecturer also fills in responses to the same prompts on another copy of the sheet after the event, and then gets together with the observer to compare notes and impressions. Completed sheets like this are evidence of reflection both for the observer and the lecturer too, and can be parts of an ongoing collection, tracking continuing professional development in both cases.

In the specimen pro forma in Table 3.1, the bottom box is almost always the most valuable. Observers learn far more valuable things from watching what is going on in colleagues' classes, than from almost any other source. That is one good reason why observations should always be reciprocated – it's being the observer that is the greatest learning experience.

The suggestions which follow now are intended to help you to see the benefits of taking part in a peer-observation system. In particular, they aim to help you to get the most out of seeing others teach, and getting feedback from colleagues on your own teaching.

1 **Value feedback from your colleagues.** There isn't really a problem in receiving praise from colleagues, except that we tend to shrug it off and fail to really take notice of it and build on whatever we did that caused the praise. It is useful to get used to taking critical feedback from someone you know, as preparation to taking it well from someone you don't know.

2 **Don't allow practising to go wrong.** Sometimes it is even harder to take critical feedback from someone you know than from someone vested with authority from outside. The criticism may be just as valid, however!

3 **Accept observation as normal.** This means that when the practice is really needed, prior to a real quality-audit visit for example, it is much easier to find the time for it to happen. It also means that many of the potential problems will have already been recognised and dealt with.

4 **Make use of opportunities to be observed, in staff development programmes.** The sooner that you become accustomed to the experience of other people watching your teaching performance, the greater becomes your confidence at handling such situations.

5 **Make appropriate use of existing checklists.** Your institution may well have specific checklists relating to key features of lectures or classroom work, on aspects such as 'planning and preparation', 'use of resources', 'involving students', 'responding to individual needs', and so on.

6 **Lead in new colleagues gently.** Avoid the situation of the performances of new staff being observed against a framework of detailed criteria intended for practised and experienced teachers.

7 **Make sure that not all of the emphasis is placed on presentation skills.** Include room for the quality of slides, media elements, and

Table 3.1 Specimen pro forma for recording observations in peer-review of teaching

Peer-observation notes	Room:	Date: Time:
Lecturer:	**Observer:**	**Topic:**
How the lecturer started the session off:	How the class responded to the start of the session:	Other comments about the beginning:
Two things the lecturer did really well: 1 2	How the students responded to these things: 1 2	Other things I noticed about these:
Two things that did not quite work: 1 2	How the students reacted to these: 1 2	Possible suggestions:
Comments about slides and other audio-visual materials used:	How the students responded to the slides and audio-visuals:	Suggestions:
Any topic areas where the students seemed to have particular difficulties:		Possible ways of addressing these students' difficulties:
How the lecturer got the students contributing:	How well the students actually engaged with these things:	Other possibilities?
How the lecturer brought the session to a conclusion:	How the students reacted to this:	Other comments:
What I learned from watching this session, that I can take forward into my own teaching:		

class exercises to be covered in the observation criteria. This can help spread the load, so that colleagues are not overly anxious about their presentation skills.

8 **Remind yourself that in real teaching you are not being observed every second.** While it is possible that some students will notice slips you may make, you are unlikely (fortunately or sadly?) to have the undivided attention of the whole class at any time.

9 **Beware of the possibility of getting into a rut.** When anyone has been teaching a particular topic for a considerable time, it is natural to tend to go on autopilot, and be less aware of what is actually happening during teaching sessions. Teaching observation can act as a powerful aid to refreshing your approach.

10 **Take advantage of team teaching opportunities.** When you are regularly in the position of observing parts of your colleagues' teaching, and vice versa, a considerable amount of automatic staff development occurs as you learn from each other's triumphs and disasters.

11 **It doesn't take long.** Suppose an observer gives you (say) three tips at the end of an hour; this can be very good value compared with just reading a book on teaching practices, where you may not happen to read the things you most need to find out.

12 **When you've observed someone else teach, always give positive feedback first.** Help to put the colleague you are observing at ease by giving the good news first (and indeed making sure there is always some good news!). We are all much more likely to take on board the 'could do betters' if we have received the positive statements first.

13 **Try to give three positives for every one 'could do better'.** Even when there is much to comment adversely on, it is important to give sufficient good news. If people are given too much adverse comment, they may lose track of which are the most important parts of the agenda that they need to address.

14 **When you are observed, treat it as free consultancy.** 'Isn't it wonderful to have a colleague or friend who finds time to engage in an educational conversation with me?' is a much better approach than 'I haven't time for all this practising'.

15 **Take the attitude that all feedback is potentially useful.** Feedback is an important part of everyday learning, and it is constructive to regard any formal observation not so much in terms of the verdicts which may be reached, but in terms of the availability of valuable feedback which they may bring.

16 **Be prepared to receive positive feedback.** In many cultures, there is a sense of embarrassment when receiving praise. This leads people to shrug it off, and to fail to really take on board the value of finding out more about what is regarded as successful. It is worth practising receiving positive feedback, and verbally acknowledging it, and thanking the people who deliver it.

17 **Get practising for receiving negative feedback.** Regard criticism as useful feedback. Avoid the temptations to become hostile, or to justify one's position, or to make excuses for things that were found to be lacking. When critical feedback is felt to have been openly received and taken note of, the people giving such feedback are much more satisfied that their job has been done effectively, than when they are not at all sure that the feedback has been listened to and heeded.

18 **Practise eliciting feedback.** Gain skills in drawing out feedback, and getting the people giving it to clarify it and expand on it when necessary. 'What do you consider the best thing about the way I am handling so-and-so?' and 'What is the first thing about this that you would suggest I try to change?' are the sort of questions that help in this process.

19 **Share feedback on your teaching with your students.** They like to feel involved. Ask them what they think of feedback you've received. Ask them what actions they might suggest that you consider. Explain why you might be doing something different; this could lead to more feedback. And continue to ask for – and value – feedback directly from your students. They know how well you are teaching, and how well others are teaching.

Who make the best lecturers?

Ken Bain (2004) sums this up nicely, and indeed is convergent with many suggestions in this chapter, in the following descriptors of effective college teachers.

The best college teachers:

1 Are willing to spend time with students, to nurture their learning.
2 Don't foster a feeling of power over, but investment in, students.
3 Ensure their practices stem from a concern for learning.
4 Make the class user-friendly by fostering trust.
5 Employ various pedagogical tools in a search for the best way to help each student.
6 Have the attitude that 'there is no such thing as a stupid question'.
7 Ensure that everyone can contribute and each contribution is unique.
8 Do not behave as a 'high priest of arcane mysteries'.
9 Do not make the classroom an 'an arena for expertise, a ledger book for the ego'.
10 Don't expect students to see science as a 'frozen body of dogma' that must be memorised and regurgitated.
11 Foster the feeling that teachers are fellow students/human beings struggling with the mysteries of the universe.

(Adapted from Bain, 2004, p. 135)

How can we move forward and adapt lectures to the twenty-first century?

Earlier in the chapter, I quoted five pressures cited by Sally Brown as causing an unsatisfactory status quo to have remained for far too long regarding large-group teaching. She suggests five movements and structures which nowadays can counterbalance those pressures:

1 Desires by academics and others to be more student-centred and to enable students to negotiate their own fluid pathways through learning programmes;
2 The changing nature of the relationship between students and the universities in which they study, with students expecting (and requiring) more individual control over what and how they are studying, especially in nations where full-cost fees are paid;
3 Movements by senior managers to harness free resources including open educational resources, TED talks and what is offered by Massive Open Online Courses (and variants of these), sometimes for good pedagogic reasons and sometimes for more nefarious ones, including what is often termed 'driving down the unit of resource', i.e. using fewer academics to teach more students more cost effectively;
4 A recognition by educational developers and others that what worked in a pre-digital age just isn't enough at a time when accessing content is easier than ever before, but selecting relevant, appropriate and trustworthy content is a much tougher proposition altogether;
5 Student expectations that multi-tasking and concurrent activities support learning, so that learning experiences can involve multiple facets, with students using digital and social media while in classrooms, studios and labs, and interacting with academics, externals and one another virtually at the same time as undertaking tasks overseen by their teachers.

(Brown, 2015, p. 26)

Making the most of lectures: some practical pointers

This chapter ends with some practical suggestions for helping students to get the most out of your lectures – and for making these occasions more satisfying for yourself too. These tips are designed to optimise the learning potential of lectures, in particular with reference to teaching and learning processes, and to remind you of ways that large-group sessions can pay real dividends to students, not least in the age when they can, if they choose, watch some of the most renowned lectures free of charge online, on TED talks, MOOCs and in many other learning resource materials.

1 **Make the most of opportunities when you have the whole group together.** There are useful benefits of whole-group shared experiences, especially for setting the scene in a new subject, and talking students through known problem areas. Use lectures for things like these that can't happen easily online. Use them as sessions to develop whole-group cohesion, as well as to give briefings, provide introductions, introduce keynote speakers, and hold practical demonstrations.

2 **Make sure that lectures are not just 'transmit–receive' occasions.** Little was ever learned by students just writing down what the lecturer said, or copying down information from screens or boards, and today's students just won't do this anyway. There are more efficient ways of providing students with the information they need for their learning, including the use of handout materials supplied online, textbooks and other learning resource materials.

3 **Be punctual, even if some of your students will be late.** Chat to the nearest students while people are settling in. Ask them 'How's the course going for you so far?' for example. Ask them 'What's your favourite topic so far?' or 'What are the trickiest bits so far?' All the better if you can chat to them by name – this means a lot to most people.

4 **When you're ready to start, capture students' attention.** It's often easier to do this by dimming the lights and showing your first slide, than by trying to quieten down the pre-lecture chatter by talking loudly. Sometimes you might be able to start with a short (no more than 2 minutes) funny video clip, with sound; it's amazing how a hubbub of chatter quells if there's a soundtrack to something

amusing on the screen. Do make sure there's a way of linking the funny clip to the topic however – students don't usually appreciate humour just for the sake of it. Do your best to ignore latecomers. Respect the courtesy of punctuality of those already present, and talk to them.

5 **Make good use of your specific intended learning outcomes for each lecture.** It can be useful to find out how many students think they can already achieve some of these – and adjust your approach accordingly! For example show the slide and ask 'raise two hands if you can do this already, one if you can already do some of it, and none if it's new to you'. Explaining the outcomes at the start of the session can help students to know exactly what they should be getting out of the lecture, serving as an agenda against which they can track their own progress during the minutes which follow.

6 **Help students to place the lecture in context.** Refer back to previous material (perhaps with a very short summary (one slide) of the previous lecture) and explain how they're going to continue on from this shortly.

7 **Work out some questions which the session will address.** Showing these questions as slides near the beginning of the session is a way of helping students to see the nature and scope of the specific learning outcomes they should be able to address progressively as the session proceeds.

8 **Get students learning-by-doing.** Just about any human being gets bored watching and listening for a full hour, so break the session up with small tasks such as problems for students to work out themselves, applying what you've told them, reading extracts from their handout

material, or discussing a question or issue with the students nearest to them. Even in a crowded, tiered lecture theatre, students can be given things to do independently for a few minutes at a time, followed by a suitable debriefing, so that they can compare views and find out whether they were on the right track.

9　**Variety is the spice of lectures.** Make sure that you build into large-group lectures a variety of activities for students, which might include writing, listening, looking, making notes, sketching diagrams, undertaking small discussion tasks, asking questions, answering questions, giving feedback to you, solving problems, doing calculations, putting things in order of importance, and so on.

10　**Find out from students now and then how it is for them.** Show-of-hands questions such as 'raise two hands of you get it, one if you partly get it, and none if it's as clear as mud' can let you know how their learning is going (and give them a chance to move a muscle or two). There are all sorts of such questions you can use, for example 'How many of you can hear me clearly enough?', 'Am I going too fast?', 'Is this making sense to you?' Observe their responses and try to adjust accordingly.

11　**Use lectures to start students learning from each other.** Getting students to work in small groups in a lecture environment can allow them to discuss and debate the relative merits of different options in multiple-choice tasks, or put things in order of importance, or brainstorm possible solutions to problems. After they have engaged with each other on such tasks, you can draw conclusions from some of the groups, and give expert-witness feedback when needed. The important thing, however, is to get them talking to each other about the topic – and once started well, that's likely to continue to happen well beyond the confines of the lecture.

12　**Use lectures to help students polish up things they have already learned.** It is valuable to make full use of the times when all students are together to give them things to do to allow them to check out whether they can still do the things they covered in previous sessions. This can be really useful for alerting students to the important bits which are liable to slip.

13　**Use lectures to help shape students' attitudes.** The elements of tone of voice, facial expression, gesture, emphasis, body language, and so on can be used by lecturers to bring greater clarity and direction to the attitude-forming shared experiences which help students set their own scene for a topic or theme in a subject.

14　**Genuinely solicit students' questions.** Don't just ask 'any questions' towards the end of a class – that's a signal for everyone to stop thinking and start packing up too. Ask for questions much earlier. When a student does ask a question, repeat the question so all students can hear. Treat students' questions with courtesy even if they seem very basic to you, and then answer in a way that doesn't make the questioner feel stupid. It may have taken some courage to ask the question.

15　**Use large-group sessions to identify and answer students' questions.** This can be much more effective, and fairer, than just attempting to answer their questions individually and privately. When one student asks a question in a large-group session, there are often many other students who only then realise that they too need to hear the answer.

16　**If too many questions keep coming from the same few students, vary your technique.** For example, give out post-its, and ask everyone to jot down a question about the topic, then show their post-it to their neighbours. Ask them then to swap post-its randomly for a few seconds. Then ask for someone to read out someone else's question, with the comfort of relative anonymity regarding the question.

17　**Don't waffle when stuck!** Don't try to bluff your way out of it when you don't know the answer to a question you've been asked. Reply that you'll find out the answer to this question before your next lecture with them – students will respect you more for this than for trying to invent an answer. Alternatively, say 'Great question. I don't at this moment know the answer to this. Does anyone here know?' and give someone who does know the chance to shine for a moment. There is usually someone who knows!

18 **Help any shy or retiring students to have equal opportunity to contribute.** Asking students in large groups to write questions, or ideas, on post-its helps to ensure that the contributions you receive are not just from those students who aren't afraid to ask in public. It can be comforting for students to preserve their anonymity in asking questions, as they are often afraid that their questions may be regarded as silly or trivial.

19 **Put energy and effort into making your lectures interesting and stimulating.** A well-paced lecture which has visual impact and in which ideas are clearly communicated can be a motivating shared experience for students. Become comfortable using the available technology in the lecture room in imaginative ways, but don't let technology distract from the learning you are trying to cause.

20 **Use some lecture time to draw feedback from students.** Large-group sessions can be used to provide a useful barometer of how their learning is going. You can ask students to jot down on post-its questions that they would like you to address at a future session, and stick these on the door on their way out so you can collect them easily.

21 **Use whole-class time to explain carefully the briefings for assessment tasks.** It is essential that all students have a full, shared knowledge of exactly what is expected of them in such tasks, so that no one is disadvantaged by any differentials in their understanding of the performance criteria or assessment schemes associated with the tasks.

22 **Only answer questions about assessment in whole-class settings.** When students come up to you at the end with questions about assessment, or see you at other times with such questions, it can be useful to respond 'Very good question. Please jot it down on this post-it, and put your name too, so I can explain the answer to this next time the whole group is

together' (make sure you actually do this, of course). It would be unfair if some students were to know more about assessment than others.

23 **Show students how the assessor's mind works.** This can be done by devising class sessions around the analysis of how past examples of students' work were assessed, as well as by going through in detail the way that assessment criteria were applied to work that the class members themselves have done.

24 **Record yourself on video every now and then.** Review the video to help you see your own strengths and weaknesses, and look for ways to improve your performance. Your keenest critic is likely to be yourself, so don't try to resolve every little habit or mannerism at once, just tackle the ones that you think are most important, little by little. It can also be really useful for a group of colleagues together to look at each other's videos, and offer each other constructive comments. This is excellent practice for any kind of inspection quality assessment procedures which might be coming up.

25 **Use all opportunities to observe other people's lectures.** You can do this not only in your own department, but also at external conferences and seminars. Watching other people helps you to learn both from what others do well, which you might wish to emulate, and from awful sessions where you resolve never to do anything similar in your own classes.

26 **Watch the body language of your audience.** You'll soon learn to recognise the symptoms of 'eyes glazing over' when students are becoming passive recipients rather than active participants. That may signal the time for one of your prepared anecdotes, or better, for a task for students to tackle.

27 **Notice the nodders.** Sometimes, it's really comforting to have at least some members of your audience nodding in agreement when you're emphasising an important point. It makes you feel you are getting your message across. But beware! I once asked someone who had been nodding quite regularly

'Tell me what you think about this please', and she turned out to have been nodding while thinking about something completely different.

28 **Don't feel you've got to keep going for the full time.** Sometimes the class will have done all that needed to be done, with still ten or fifteen minutes in hand. Don't feel you have to waffle on. It may come as a surprise to you, but your students may be quite pleased to finish early occasionally!

29 **Don't feel that you have to get through all of your material.** Even very experienced lecturers, when preparing a new lecture, often overestimate what they can cover in an hour. It is better to cover part of your material well, than to try to rush through all of it. You can adjust future sessions to balance out the content.

30 **Students will give you feedback on what you did, and on what they did.** They don't need to know what you would have done if you'd had more time. Student experience surveys and module evaluation questionnaires are on what they experienced. Make that experience as good as you can.

31 **Come to a timely conclusion.** Become known for your good timing. A large group session should not just fizzle out, but should come to a definite and strong ending. End with a bang and not a whimper. It is really important not to overrun. It is better to come to a good stopping place a few minutes early, than to end up rushing through something important right at the end of the session.

32 **Capture your reflections.** Within a few hours of the lecture, find just five minutes to think through 'two things which worked well, and which I'll do again' and 'two things that didn't quite work this time', and 'what I'll try to do next time to make them work better' or 'something else I'll try next time'. It is useful to jot down short notes in response to these questions, so you can build on them next time you're doing something similar. Do make sure you actually jot such things down somewhere, on paper, on your computer, on your mobile phone; just thinking is not enough, reflective thoughts evaporate away and are lost. (Towards the end of Chapter 7, I offer various suggestions and templates for capturing your reflections on lectures.)

Conclusions

This book is still called *The Lecturer's Toolkit* in its 4th edition, and many of us are still (in some countries) called 'lecturers', and in colleges and universities around the world there are slots on timetables called 'lectures'. Yet as you will have seen from Chapter 2, most 'lecturers' spend far more time designing and implementing assessment, and getting feedback to students on their learning, than merely standing up in front of a large number of them for an hour at a time. It is, of course, just a bit more terrifying for us to stand and talk to a packed auditorium, than to sit down with a pen or keyboard giving students individual feedback on evidence of their learning.

For campus-based students, lectures are milestones on their learning journey, even if they only count for a relatively small proportion of the time they spend studying and producing evidence of their learning. It is our job, however, to make these milestones work. If our lectures are so boring that students don't come along for them, they've missed some milestones, and their journeys and destinations may be in jeopardy. Whereas if we can manage to enthuse them, arouse their curiosity, entertain them now and then (remembering how finite human concentration spans are), we've done the best we can to use large-group contexts to make at least some learning happen.

I hope that the various ideas in this chapter of the Toolkit have increased your confidence regarding what you can do when lots of pairs of eyes are looking at what you do, what you put up on a screen or board, and above all your enthusiasm for the topic concerned. That confidence is important, as large-group teaching is the most public thing we do, and feedback on lectures is regarded as such an important part of the indicators that are gathered to measure the quality of the overall student learning experience.

All that said, lectures can be dreams or nightmares – even for the most experienced and acclaimed of lecturers. Now and again, it is wonderful to be able to say to oneself 'that worked'. But the nightmares are of the things that didn't work, and like cliff-edge paths getting narrower, long journeys with missed travel connections, and all the other things that disturb our sleep now and again, they can come at any time. We need to distance ourselves from the sentiment 'you're only as good as your last gig' that pervades many cultures. The next gig can always be better – we're learning as we go, however experienced we become. That's how learning is, especially in the driving seat.

Chapter 4

Making small-group teaching work

It's really important for students to work, learn and be assessed in small groups, since few nowadays live and work in isolation. To be able to take turns to propose task solutions, to resolve amicably intra-group conflicts and to work with all kinds of people in teams you've not selected yourself are all skills that make not just for better employability, but also for more fulfilling lives. Some but not all people naturally have these capabilities, and all benefit from regular and productive opportunities to hone them, hence the high value of including group tasks in university programmes. But there are no quick fixes: successful group work needs careful briefing, adequate preparation, rehearsal opportunities and the opportunity to interrogate both the task brief and the means of assessment.

(Sally Brown, 2014)

Intended outcomes of this chapter

When you've thought through the suggestions included in this chapter (and tried out the most relevant ones) you should be better able to:

- put small-group teaching into perspective, at a time when it too often seems like an expensive luxury!
- maximise the small-group learning experience for students, in ways they cannot get on their own online or using MOOCs;
- confront some of the behaviours (student ones and tutor ones) which can reduce the success of small-group work;
- decide the optimum size of student groups for particular collaborative tasks you set;
- choose the best way to establish the group membership for your purposes;
- select from a range of processes such as rounds, buzz-groups, syndicates, snowballing, fishbowls, crossovers, brainstorming and pair-dialogues, to help your students to learn productively and actively in small-group environments.

Why is small-group learning so important?

My aim in this chapter is to help colleagues increase the interest and diversity of the processes used in small-group work with students. A common theme running throughout this chapter is the need to help students to participate fully in small-group situations, so that the learning payoff they derive from such occasions is maximised.

Small-group learning is something that only happens when people are together. At a time when so much information is accessed online, actually getting students together in groups is harder (and more expensive) to achieve, and providing a member of staff to lead small-group work in person becomes less possible as class sizes in educational institutions increase, and as financial restraints continue to increase.

There's a problem regarding the attitudes of students and teachers about small-group contexts. Lecturers naturally may think that working with large groups is bound to be much more important than conducting tutorials and seminars, and not worth the considerable time it takes to extend small-group learning experiences to large numbers of students. Students may think that while it's important to be at lectures to find out more about what is to be learned, and how and when evidence of achievement will be assessed, making time to attend small-group sessions is less important, and can be skipped when other things such as preparing assignments come up. Yet there are many important aspects linking to successful learning which can only really occur well in small-group contexts, including:

- much more opportunity to ask questions than in large-group contexts;
- the benefit of being able to compare with peers, and find out how learning is really going;
- the chance to learn by talking and explaining – much deeper learning than that which happens by reading;
- the opportunity to make sense of things from different parts of the curriculum, compared with lectures which tend to spotlight particular parts of a subject.

We're now in an age where so much is available online. Students may rightly think that there's no need to spend a lot of time in small-group contexts simply to get some information to fuel their learning. They can find massive amounts of information online without going anywhere. But the essence of small-group learning is actually very much about the things that can't be gathered online – talking, listening, explaining, interacting, arguing, debating, and learning from fellow students as well as from tutors. 'Much of this can be done online too' is a common reaction, but online collaboration and discussion, while valuable in its own way, can miss many of the really important dimensions of learning. After all, learning starts in small groups – the family – and progresses in relatively small groups in schools, so in many ways small groups can be considered as part of the 'natural' way to learn.

Small-group learning may be more important than we think. When most people think about teaching in universities and colleges, the image that frequently comes to mind is of a large lecture theatre full of students listening intently (or not) to a lecturer in full spate of erudition. Actually, a large proportion of the most meaningful learning in higher education happens when students are working outside lectures, in small groups, in seminars, tutorials, field work, studios, practicals and laboratories, as well as in groups sitting around computers. Moreover, even more learning can be happening in small-group situations beyond timetabled sessions, where students interact spontaneously with each other, and learn from each other. With increasing pressure on us all to deliver the curriculum in ever more efficient and effective ways, the means by which we manage small-group teaching, and harness the potential learning payoff, come under close scrutiny. This chapter is intended to help you to explore how we can do this to best effect.

Group learning is about getting people to work together well, in carefully set up learning environments. The human species has evolved on the basis of group learning. Learning from other people is the most instinctive and natural of all the learning contexts we experience, and starts from birth. Although learning can only be done by the learner, and can't be done 'to' the learner, the roles of other people in accelerating and modifying that learning remain vitally important. Other people can enhance the quality of our learning, and can also damage it. But *which* other people?

We hear much of collaborative learning, as if it's the most natural activity in the world. But it often seems like the least natural, particularly amongst strangers. Sociological research tells us repeatedly that it is human nature *not* to be involved with people we don't know. We might make a mistake, or look stupid, or be attacked. We will, however, get involved with people we do know. We'll help them with their problems and even defend them. One key to working and learning with other people is, therefore, the ability to lower barriers and become friends with would-be strangers, while acknowledging differences and respecting different viewpoints.

Lecturers are likely to spend time prioritising the development of their techniques to work with large groups of students at a time, but much less likely to foreground skills relating to small-group contexts, assuming (often wrongly) that this will be easy enough to manage 'off the cuff'.

Furthermore, much is now said about the value of transferable skills, particularly including oral communication skills, problem-solving skills, interpersonal skills, self-organisation skills, and reflection. Many of these skills can only be learned from, and with, other people, and cannot be developed solely by reading and studying what others have written about them. It is now increasingly accepted that the most important outcomes of education and training are about developing people, and not just what people know or understand. Employers and managers plead for employees who are able to work well with others, and organise themselves. Working in small groups can allow students to embrace a range of interactive and collaborative skills which are often hard to develop in individual study situations whether with print-based or online resources, and impossible to develop in large-group environments such as lectures. The small-group skills are precisely those required in employment and research, where graduates need to be able to:

- work in teams;
- listen to others' ideas sympathetically and critically;
- think creatively and originally;
- formulate and ask questions skilfully;
- gain skills in explaining things fluently and convincingly;
- build on others' existing work;
- collaborate on projects;
- work together online with fellow-learners;
- manage time and processes effectively;
- see projects through to a conclusion;
- cope with the normal difficulties of interactions between human beings.

The last of these may be the most important of all. Learning in groups allows students to develop cohesion with their peers, when classes are becoming so large as to preclude feelings of whole-group identity, particularly under modular schemes where large cohorts of students come together from disparate directions to study together on a unit.

Group learning has never been as important as it now is. Yet we are still in a world where teachers, educators and trainers tend to be groomed in instruction rather than facilitation. Despite the increased status of group learning, there is nothing fundamentally new in people learning together. Some lecturers find working with small groups more anxiety-provoking than lecturing, because of the necessity to work with students as individuals rather than in the anonymity of large groups. Sometimes there are worries about student behaviour, that they might become too challenging, disruptive or unfocused. Otherwise, there are often anxieties about organisational issues, like how to run a number of parallel seminars, based on a single lecture, with several tutors and research assistants working with different groups. This chapter addresses some of the reasons for persevering nevertheless, and offers some practical suggestions on overcoming a wide range of difficulties.

Deciding on group size

How big is a small group? There is no 'right' answer to this question. A skilled lecturer can bring to a really large group many of the human interactions, including peer-interactions, which are characteristic of a well-facilitated small-group session. Someone unskilled in small-group techniques can all too easily continue to 'lecture' to half-a-dozen or fewer learners. A number of choices exist about the selection of group size and group membership, depending on the context of the group work and the nature of the learning outcomes which are intended to be achieved by students working in groups. If assessed work is to be an outcome of group work, it is worth thinking in advance how appropriate credit for the overall product can best be coupled with credit for individual contributions to the product, particularly where there is the possibility of the contributions being unequal.

There are no rights or wrongs to the following suggestions about ways of establishing student groups; basically it is best to make informed decisions (or inspirational leaps) based on the context and the occasion. It is useful to consider group size first.

The choice of group size will often depend on the size of the whole class, as well as on the size, shapes, and facilities available in the rooms in which small-group work is carried out. Sometimes, episodes in small-group format can be conducted even in a large, full lecture theatre, with groups being formed between students sitting close enough to participate together. However, the most important occasions where group size is likely to be crucial involve subdividing the students present at seminars, tutorials and practical classes. Let's go through some of the pros and cons of groups of increasing size, starting with just two members.

Pairs

In some regards a pair is not really a group. It is usually relatively easy to group students in twos – either by allocating the pairs yourself, random methods, or friendship pairs. Advantages include a low probability of passenger behaviour, and the relative ease for a pair to arrange meeting schedules. However, pairs are good for small-scale tasks, where both students know each other well. Pairs can also be useful where a stronger student can help a weaker one. Problems can occur when pairs fall out, or either student is absent, or lazy or domineering. It is normally unwise to use the same pairs for long-term tasks, but useful to ring the changes of constitution of pairs over different tasks. Pairs however only involve two people, and the skills and expertise in any pair are naturally less than when three or more participants are present.

Couples

This of course is a special case of pairs. In any class of students, there are likely to be some established couples. When they work together on collaborative work, the chances are that they will put a lot more into group work than ordinary pairs, not least because being together for many more times than random pairs, they are likely to spend more time and energy on the tasks involved – though there may also be more distractions to contend with. The risks include the possibility of the couple becoming de-stabilised, which can make further collaborative work much more difficult for them.

Threes

Trios can work well, as communication between three people is still easy and work can often be shared out in manageable ways. Trios represent a very popular group size. The likelihood of passenger behaviours is quite low, and trios will often work well together, sharing out tasks appropriately. It is easier for trios to arrange meetings schedules than for larger groups. There can be the advantage of a 'casting vote' when decisions are to be made. The most likely problem is for two of the students to work together better than with the third, who can gradually (or suddenly) become, or feel, marginalised. Threes can be difficult if two gang up on one, and the group is still fairly vulnerable if one member is often absent or when present doesn't take an equal responsibility.

Fours

This is still quite small as a group size. Passenger behaviour is possible, but less likely than in larger groups. When subdividing group tasks, it can be useful to split into pairs for some activities, and single individuals for others. There are three different ways that a quartet can subdivide into pairs, adding variety to successive task distribution possibilities. Fours can be very effective, and can be a good critical mass for sharing out large projects, with opportunities both for delegation and collaboration. Students with different abilities and qualities can play to their own strengths within a foursome, giving each member a chance to contribute something and feel valued. Fours do have a tendency, however, to split into two pairs, and tensions can arise. With four members (or any other even number) there is no possibility of a 'casting vote' if the group is evenly split between two courses of action.

Fives

Fives have many of the advantages of fours, and are a favoured group size for many tasks, not least because of the 'casting vote' opportunity when making decisions. There are sufficient people to provide a range of perspectives, but the group is not of unmanageable proportions. In a group this size, however, a determined slacker may still be able to hide, unless suitable precautions are taken. The possibility of passenger behaviour begins to increase significantly, and it becomes more important for the group to have a leader for each stage of its work. There are many ways that a group of five can subdivide into twos and threes, allowing variety in the division of tasks among its members.

Sixes

The possibility of passenger behaviour is yet more significant, and group leadership is more necessary. The group can, however, subdivide into threes or twos, in several different ways. It is now much more difficult to ensure equivalence of tasks for group members. In discussions, even though the number of available ideas may be greater than with smaller groups, the 'air-time' for each group member is reduced.

Seven to ten or so

Such numbers are still workable as groups, but the larger the number, the greater the possibility of idlers loafing and shy violets being overshadowed by the more vociferous and pushy members of the group. It can be argued that groups of this size are only really viable if a really substantial task is to be undertaken and if considerable support and advice is given on project and team management. Such groups can still be useful for discussion and debate, before splitting into smaller groups for action. Passengers may be able to avoid making real contributions to the work of the group, and can find themselves outcasts because of this. When it is necessary to set up working groups which are larger than six, the role of the leader needs to change considerably. A skilled facilitator is needed to get a large group collaborating well. It can be advantageous for the facilitator to become somewhat neutral, and to concentrate on achieving consensus and agreement rather than attempting to set the direction of the group.

Ways of forming groups

There are many different ways in which you can create groups of students from a larger class. All have their own advantages and disadvantages, and it is probably best to use a mixture of methods so that students experience a healthy level of variety of group composition, and maximise the benefits of learning from and with each other. Strict rules on how to form groups cannot be provided, as such decisions depend so strongly on context and purpose. The following discussion points out some of the advantages and disadvantages of different ways of constituting student group membership.

Groups with some historical or social basis

Friendship groups

If you let students select themselves into their own groups, often strategic, high-fliers will quickly locate each other, then the middle-ability ones will realise what is happening and form groups among themselves, then the last ones left will tend to be the less able and they will clump together through lack of any alternative. Allowing students to arrange themselves into groups has the advantage that most groups feel a sense of ownership regarding their composition. However, there are often some students 'left over' in the process, and they can feel alienated through not having been chosen by their peers. Friendship groups may also differ quite widely in ability level, as high-fliers select to work with like-minded students. This method is effective if you want to be sure that marks resulting from the assessment of group work will be distributed, but is not such a useful method of group selection if you want peers to support each other. It can also be argued that it is a more challenging and important task to learn the skills needed to work with strangers rather than with friends.

Geographical groups

Simply putting students into groups according to clusters as they are already sitting (or standing) in the larger group is one of the easiest and quickest ways of dividing a class into groups. This is likely to include some friendship groups in any case, but minimises the embarrassment of some students who might not have been selected in a friendship group. The ability distribution may, however, be skewed, as it is not unusual for the students nearest the tutor to be rather higher in motivation compared with those in the most remote corner of the room!

Alphabetical (family name) groups

This is one of several random ways of allocating group membership. It is easy to achieve if you already have an alphabetical class list. However, it can happen that students often find themselves in the same group, if several tutors use the same process of group selection. Also, when working with multicultural large classes, several students from the same culture may have the same family name, and some groups may end up as dominated by one culture, which may not be what you intend to occur.

Other alphabetical groups

For example, you can form groups on the basis of the last letter of students' first names. This is likely to make a refreshing change from family-name alphabetical arrangements. Students also get off to a good start in seeing each other's first names at the outset.

Random groups

Many tutors find this to be the easiest and fairest way of selecting groups of students to work together. Using lottery systems or random number generators, students are allocated to the groups in which they are to work. Problems can arise using this method from difficulties with group dynamics, particularly if the students have been given no preparation on how to be a good team member. However, in industrial and commercial contexts, graduates are often required to work in allocated teams, so this may be regarded as good preparation for real life. The following ways of randomising group composition can add variety to student group work.

Number groups

When students are given a number (for example on a class list), you can easily arrange for different combinations of groups for successive tasks, by selecting a variety of number permutations (including using a random number generator if you have one on your computer). Groups of four could be '1–4, 5–8, ... ' for task 1, then '1, 3, 5, 7 and 2, 4, 6, 8, ... ', then '1, 5, 9, 13', and so on.

Class list rotating syndicates

Where a succession of small-group tasks is to be used, say with group size being four, it can be worth making a printed list of the whole class, and starting off by forming groups by writing AAAA, BBBB, CCCC, DDDD, etc. down the list. Next time round, write ABCD, ABCD, ABCD etc., so that everyone is in an entirely new group. Such rotation can minimise the problems that can be caused by the occasional difficult or uncooperative student, whose influence is then spread around, rather than lumbering the same group each time. It is worth, however, avoiding the grouping being too much influenced by any alphabetical factors; all too often students find themselves in alphabetically determined situations, and it is useful to break free of this unwitting constraint in deciding group membership.

Astrological groups

When selecting group membership from a large class, it makes a change to organise the selection on the basis of calendar month of birth-date. Similarly, 'star signs' could be used – but not all students know when (for example) Gemini starts and finishes in the year. This method often leads to groups of somewhat different sizes, however, and you may have to engineer some transfers if equal group size is needed. Participants from some religions may also find the method bizarre or inappropriate.

Crossovers

When you wish to share systematically the thinking of one group with another, you can ask one person from each group to move to another group. For example, you can ask the person with the earliest birthday in the calendar year to move to the next group clockwise round the room, carrying forward the product or notes from the previous group and introducing the thinking behind that to the next group. The next exchange could be the person with the latest birthday, and so on. When doing this, you need to make sure that not too many students end up stuck in the same physical position for too long.

Coded name labels

Often we want to mix students up in a systematic way so they work in small groups of different compositions, and give and receive feedback from many more people than are involved in the group size they are working in at any given time. One way of predetermining a wide variation in group membership is to use sticky labels (or just small pieces of paper) to become each student's name-badge, also bearing a unique code as follows. A three-digit code of a Greek letter, normal letter, and a number can lead to the possibility of all students finding themselves in three completely different groups for successive tasks. Six of each letters and numbers allows an overall group of 36 students to split into different sixes three times, for example, with each student working cumulatively with 15 other students.

Imagine that you have, for example, 25 students, and that the table shown in Figure 4.1 is your sheet of sticky labels, and that you write on them codes of one Greek letter, one normal letter, and one number.

αA1	βA2	γA3	δA4	εA5
αB2	βB3	γB4	δB5	εB1
αC3	βC4	γC5	δC1	εC2
αD4	βD5	γD1	δD2	εD3
αE5	βE1	γE2	δE3	εE4

Figure 4.1 Codes for 25 students

Give these labels out randomly (and ask students to write their names on them, especially when it will be useful for them to become more familiar with each other's names). Then you can use three entirely different group configurations, each with five groups of five, as follows:

- grouping by Greek letters;
- grouping by Latinate letters;
- grouping by numbers.

So, in this example, by the third group each student would have worked with 12 different students from the whole group of 25, and would have encountered entirely different students in each successive group.

Where the group tasks are successive stages of a larger whole, there is no need for whole-group feedback on the first two tasks, because each individual can act as rapporteur on the outcomes of their previous task in the last configuration. This means that everyone is a rapporteur, and each group can benefit from everything which happened in all the groups without the repetition of plenary report-back. You can also make the task at each stage slightly more difficult and ask for a product from the final configuration if desired.

Crossovers are useful in making sure everyone in the group is active and also help to mix students up outside their normal friendship, ethnic or gender groups. It takes a little forethought to get the numbers and letters right for the cohort you are working with. It can be useful to have some templates of the different number–letter combinations, so that you can cut up a sheet of paper or card and give students their individual numbers (this helps avoid the possibility of duplicating numbers when writing them out by hand in the actual session!). You can, however, do crossovers on the spur of the moment using post-it labels and quick calculations. It can also be useful to have 'wildcard' or blank labels for a few of the students, who can be allowed to go into any group when group membership changes.

An alternative to sticky labels as above is to use a pack of playing cards, especially when the total number of students in the room is around 50. You then have a large repertoire of ways of getting them into different group configurations.

Further ways of forming groups

Performance-related groups

Sometimes you may wish to set out to balance the ability range in each group, for example by including one high-flier and one low-flier in each group. The groups could then be constituted on the basis of the last marked assignment or test. Alternatively, it can be worth occasionally setting a task where all high-fliers and all low-fliers are put into the same group, with most of the groups randomly middle-fliers, but this (though appreciated by the high-fliers) can be divisive to overall morale.

Skills-based groups

For some group tasks (especially fairly extended ones), it can be worthwhile to try to arrange that each group has at least one member with identified skills and competences (for example, doing a web search, using a word-processing package, leading a presentation, and so on). A short questionnaire can be issued to the whole class, asking students to self-rate themselves on a series of skills, and groups can be constituted on the basis of these.

Hybrid groups

This is a compromise solution. You may sometimes wish to organise students by ability or in learning teams, and may at the same time wish to help them avoid feeling that they are isolated from everyone they already know. You can permit students to select one other person they would like to work with, and then juggle pairs to ensure some balance of ability. This can work really well, but can be fraught with difficulty, for example, when pair choice is not coincident! It can also make for difficulties if you try to pair up two self-selecting high-fliers with two of the less able students: resentment and conflict can ensue. In order to avoid this problem, one can sometimes pair middle-ability pairs, which make up the bulk, with more able and less able pairs, using one's best judgement on factors such as friendship and cooperative ability. You need to recognise, however, that when group work is assessed, the likely mark achieved by each group can be affected by your choices and may not be seen as fair, even though it works well in adding value to most students' learning experience.

Learning teams

If your aim is to build upon students' prior experience and ability, it is possible to select group members with specific criteria in mind. You might suggest groups form themselves (or are formed by the tutor) into teams which include, for example, one with proven competence in numeracy, one with excellent communication skills, an IT specialist, someone fluent in a language other than English, someone with experience in the world of work, and so on. This provides the opportunity for team members to take account of each other's divergent abilities and to value them. There may be problems with task allocation, however. Do you allocate the task of doing the drawings to the former draughts-person or to the group member who is inexperienced in this kind of work? Do you give the IT tasks to the technophile or the technophobe? The team's marks will be better if the former choice is made, but there may be more learning gain if the novice undertakes the task with guidance from the specialist. Will the team work to its strengths, and achieve the intended outcomes well, or should it be encouraged to work to its weaknesses and maximise the learning payoff resulting from the tasks? If group work is assessed, it is no surprise that teams will do the former. Forming learning teams also relies on the students and tutors having a good knowledge of prior abilities and competence and may take some considerable organisation.

Small-group process techniques

The most significant single enemy of small-group work with students is their non-participation. There is a wide range of small-group processes from which we can select a variety of ways to help students to learn actively. A balanced programme of different kinds of activities can then be devised which will promote learning to the satisfaction of the students themselves, who are likely to benefit from being stretched. Effective small-group techniques help students derive increased learning payoff from the time students spend working together, by:

- enhancing their motivation to learn, by raising interest levels, and helping them see the relevance of the topics they are working with;
- giving them learning-by-doing opportunities, and allowing them to practise relevant activities, and to learn by trial and error in a safe and supportive environment;

- allowing students to gain a considerable amount of feedback from each other, and from the facilitator of the small-group session;
- helping students make sense of things that they are learning together, particularly by explaining things to each other, and making decisions together.

This chapter continues with some suggestions regarding how you may use each of seven different ways of helping students to be participative in group situations. Some lend themselves to large-group situations, and can be ways of helping interactive learning to occur in packed lecture theatres as well as in smaller-group settings.

1 Rounds

Where groups are not too large, say around twenty or fewer, go around everyone in the group and ask them to respond (for example) to a given sentence-starter, or to give a sentence or two about what they want to find out about the topic to be explored. People often use rounds as icebreakers or equally as part of the winding up of a session, when it can be productive to ask students for (for example) 'one thing you learned, one thing you liked, and one thing you did not like'. Try not to make the round too daunting for students. It helps to provide some guidance on what is expected of them (for example, 'I want everyone to give their name and then identify one aspect of the course programme they know nothing about but are looking forward to learning about' or 'let's go round and find out which single aspect of today's session has been most useful for each person'). In big rounds, students can be quite nervous, so make it clear that it's acceptable to say 'pass' and if people at the beginning have made your point, that concurrence with ideas expressed already is sufficient. Alternatively, ask everyone to write down the point they intend to give, for example on post-it notes, and as the round continues stick all the post-it notes on a chart or wall, so that they're all seen to be equally important. Those students who are reticent orally are often less nervous when they've already jotted down the point they wish to contribute.

A drawback with rounds is that it can be boring if the group is large, and the answers are repetitive. Contributions late in the round tend not to be valued as they're adding nothing new, and the contributors can feel their ideas are rejected.

2 Buzz-groups

Give pairs, threes, fours or larger subdivisions of the whole class, small, timed tasks which involve them talking to each other, creating a hubbub of noise as they work. Their outcomes can then be shared with the whole group through feedback, on a flip-chart sheet poster, or otherwise as appropriate. This technique can also work well in large-group lecture situations, though it is not usually appropriate to do more than collect the feedback from selected groups on such occasions, otherwise reporting-back becomes too tedious, repetitive and time consuming. The noise level in a large lecture theatre full of students 'buzzing' can be quite alarming for lecturers used only to the sound of one or two voices at a time, but when it is remembered that a lot of learning-by-explaining and learning through feedback is occurring in such a noisy room, the use of the time spent is certain to be accompanied by significant learning payoff.

Buzz-groups often work best when they're buzzing about several different things at once. For example, in a large-group lecture, provide several buzz-group tasks, and get different groups of students addressing selected tasks. Report-back from buzz-groups is then not tedious or repetitive, and the interest level of the large group can be maintained.

3 Syndicates

This is a term often used to describe activities undertaken by groups of students working to a brief, usually issued by the tutor, but under their own direction. Syndicate activities can take place within the room where a larger group is working, or can be briefed for things that student groups go off and undertake on their own. For example, students in syndicates can be asked to undertake literature searches, debate an issue, explore a piece of text, prepare an argument, design an artefact, prioritise a list of options, prepare an action plan, or many other tasks. To achieve productively, they will need an explicit brief, appropriate resources and a clear description of the intended outcomes.

Specialist accommodation is not always necessary; syndicates can work in groups spread out in a large room, or, where facilities permit, go away and use social areas of the campus or designated areas of the learning resource centre. On crowded campuses, however, don't just assume that students will be able to find somewhere suitable to work. If the task is substantial, the tutor may wish to move from group to group, or may be available on a 'help desk' at a central location, or available by email online at specified times.

It is important to have clear (sometimes quite rigid) deadlines for syndicate report-back, as it can be very tedious when punctual syndicates have to await tardier colleagues before a plenary sharing session can begin. Outcomes from syndicate work may be delivered in the form of assessed work from the group or produced at a plenary meeting of the whole class as report-backs, or poster displays, and so on.

4 Snowballing

This is also known as pyramiding. Start by giving students an individual task of a fairly straightforward nature such as listing features, noting questions, or identifying problems. Then ask them to work in pairs on a slightly more complex task, such as prioritising issues or suggesting strategies. Third, ask them to come together in larger groups, fours or sixes for example, and undertake a task involving, perhaps, synthesis, assimilation or evaluation. Ask them, for example, to draw up guidelines, or to produce an action plan, or to assess the impact of a particular course of action. They can then feed back to the whole group if required.

It can be useful to issue flipchart sheets, and brief the groups to report back using these to present summaries of their outcomes. If several groups are involved in feedback on the same final task, it can become somewhat repetitive, and it is often useful to give separate contributory elements of the overall task to different groups, so that interest levels are maintained during the final report-back stage.

5 Fishbowls

This is a way of allowing a small number of participants to have a discussion in the middle of an area, with other group members observing but not contributing. If starting off a task in 'fishbowl' mode, ask for a small group of up to half a dozen or so volunteers to sit in the middle of a larger circle comprising the rest of the group. Give the inner circle a task to undertake that involves discussion, problem solving or decision-making, with the group around the outside asking as observers. Usually it is worth having an agreed substitution process, to allow someone from the outer circle to take the place of someone in the inner group, but only when both agree on the exchange. Make the task you give the inner circle sufficiently simple in the first instance to give them the confidence to get started. The levels of the tasks can be enhanced once students have had practice and become more confident.

Fishbowling can also be used where several groups have already undertaken a task (or some complementary tasks) in parallel; form the inner circle using one member from each group (a volunteer or a conscript) and start the inner circle processing the findings of the groups. Arrange that substitution can occur when necessary or when useful, for example to allow another group member from the outer circle to come in when the representative already in the inner circle is stuck. This can be a useful method for managing students who are over-dominating a group, because it gives them permission to be the centre of attention for a period of time. After a suitable interval, you can ask others from the outer circle to replace them, thus giving the less vocal ones an opportunity for undisturbed airtime. Fishbowls can also be useful ways of getting representatives from buzz-groups to feed back to the whole group. Some students will find it difficult to be the focus of all eyes and ears, so it is as well not to coerce anyone to take centre stage (although gentle prompting can be valuable). A 'tag wrestling' version can be used, with those in the outer circle who want to join in gently tapping the shoulders of people in the middle whom they want to replace, and taking over their chairs and opportunities of talking. Fishbowls can work well with quite large groups too.

6 Brainstorming

This can be a valuable way of stimulating creative free-thinking and is particularly useful when looking for a solution to a problem or in generating diverse ideas. Start with a question like 'How can we ...?' or 'What do we know about ...?' and encourage the group to call out ideas as fast as you can write them up (perhaps use two scribes on separate boards if the brainstorm flows well). Make it clear that this is supposed to be an exploratory process, so set ground rules along the following lines:

- a large quantity of ideas is desirable, so everyone should be encouraged to input at whatever level they feel comfortable;
- quick snappy responses are more valuable at this stage than long, complex, drawn-out sentences;
- ideas should be noted without comment, either positive or negative: no one should say 'That wouldn't work because ...' or 'That's the best idea we've heard yet' while the brainstorm is in progress as this might make people feel foolish about their contributions or unduly narrow the focus of further contributions;
- participants should 'piggy-back' on each other's ideas if they set off a train of thought;
- 'logic circuits' should be disengaged, allowing for a freewheeling approach.

It can be useful to generate these rules with the group at the start of the brainstorm, and write them up on a flipchart or slides so that everyone remains aware of them.

Alternatives to these ground rules include gathering contributions from everyone in turn, and allowing people to say 'pass' if they have nothing to add at the time. This helps to prevent the products of the brainstorm being unduly influenced by those members of the group who are most vocal or who have most ideas, though it can be argued that this is not brainstorming in the truest sense. The mass of ideas thus generated can then be used as a basis for selection of an action plan, a programme of development, or a further problem-solving task. One of the most effective ways of following up a brainstorm is to get everyone involved in some sort of prioritisation of the products. For example, everyone can be invited to vote for their own top three of the things written up on the flipcharts, maybe giving three points to what they consider to be the most important point, two for the next most important point, and so on. The numbers can then be added up, and a global view of the prioritisation can be seen. It can be useful to get students to vote 'privately' first, so that voting does not become influenced by the initial trends that may be seen as votes begin to point towards favourite items.

7 Pair dialogues: 'Five (or three) minutes each way'

This can be a useful way of getting students to make sense of their own thinking on a topic or an issue, by explaining and articulating their views uninterrupted for a few minutes. Ask students in pairs to take it in turn alternately to speak and to listen, talking without being interrupted for a specified few minutes on a given topic. They might find this quite difficult at first, but it is an excellent way of getting students to articulate their ideas, and also means that the quieter students are given opportunities to speak and be heard in a non-threatening situation.

The art of listening without interrupting (other than with brief prompts to get the speaker back on target if they wander off the topic) is a useful one that many students will need to foster too. The products of such pair work can then feed into other activities.

Leading and following

Student group work, particularly when there is not the presence of a tutor, can depend a great deal on the skills which the group leader brings to bear on the group. However, no amount of leadership can work on its own, without a substantial investment in 'followership' by those who don't happen to be leading at the time. The following discussion highlights some of the important attributes needed to make the most of followership. There will always need to be more followers than leaders. We all know the problems that occur when too many people try to lead a group! The suggestions below may help you to ensure that your leaders have skilled followers. They may also help to optimise the learning that can be achieved through well thought-out following.

1 **Brief groups about the importance of followership.** It can be important to legitimise followership as a vital factor to underpin the success of group work.

2 **Explain that followership should not be regarded as weakness.** When leadership is rotating between group members, they should regard their work when *not* leading as every bit as important as when they are directing the actions of the group.

3 **Accept that followership requires well developed skills and attributes.** For example, patience may be needed. When it takes a little time for the purpose or wisdom of a leadership decision to become apparent, it is sometimes harder to wait for this to happen than to jump in and try to steer the group, or argue with the decision.

4 **More followers than leaders are needed!** It is virtually impossible to have a successful group where all members are adopting leading stances at the same time. Though the credit for successful group work is often attributed to the leader, it is often the followers who actually own the success. It is more than good sense to acknowledge this right from the start of any group-work situation.

5 **Followership is a valuable, transferable key skill.** In all walks of life, people need to be followers at least for some of the time. It can be useful to employ group-work situations to help people to develop skills that will make them good followers in other contexts of their lives and careers.

6 **Good followership is not the same as being 'easily led'.** Being 'easily led' usually is taken to imply that people are led into doing things against their better judgement. Good followership is closer to being easily led when the direction of the task in hand coincides quite closely to individuals' own judgement.

7 **Followership should not be blind obedience!** Encourage group members to think about how they are following, why they are following, for how long they are going to be content with following, and what they are learning through following.

8 **Suggest that group members experiment with a 'followership log'.** This could be private notes to themselves of their experiences of being led, but it is more important to make notes on their feelings as followers than to write down criticisms of the actions of the leaders. Whether the logs are treated as private or shared notes can be decided later by everyone involved in a group.

9 **Legitimise followership notes as authentic evidence of the operation of a group.** Such notes can tell their own stories regarding the relative contributions of members of the group, and the group processes that worked well, and those which worked badly. When it is known that followership records will count towards the evidence of achievement of a group, leadership itself is often done more sensitively and effectively.

10 **Followership is vital training for leadership.** People who have been active, reflective followers can bring their experience of followership to bear on their future leadership activities. Having consciously reflected on the experience of following informs leadership approaches, and makes their own leadership easier for others to follow.

11 **Good followership is partly about refraining from nit-picking.** When people have too strong a desire to promote their individuality, it often manifests itself in the form of expending energy in trying to achieve unimportant minor adjustments to the main processes going on in group work. Good followership involves adopting restraint about minor quibbles, and saving interventions for those occasions where it is important not to follow without question.

What goes wrong in small groups?

Small-group teaching can provide excellent opportunities for participants to get to know each other, come to grips with their subject and learn actively, and yet small-group format classes are often seen by students as of questionable value compared with lectures, online learning and one-to-one sessions. Talking to students, they often express confusion about the tasks involved and uncertainty about their role, as well as lack of confidence about participating. They criticise tutors for inconsistency of approach and treatment, for dis-organisation and lack of structure, and for hogging the sessions with their own views and opinions.

When things go wrong, sometimes it's the fault of the group members themselves. Sometimes the blame can be directed at the facilitator. In this section, I look in turn at some of the most common 'damaging behaviours', and offer for each a few suggestions that can alleviate the problems that can result from them.

Group member behaviours which damage group work

This section looks at a range of student behaviours which can damage or even destroy group work. These are based on the experience of many facilitators. For each of these behaviours, some tactics are offered below as to how facilitators can reduce the effects on group work.

Group members being late

Sometimes lateness is unavoidable, but even then it is seen as time-wasting and disruptive for the group members who have managed to be punctual. Here are some approaches from which facilitators can select, to reduce the problem.

1 **Lead the group towards including an appropriate ground rule on punctuality.** If the group members feel a sense of ownership of such a ground rule, they are more likely to honour it.

2 **Point out that punctuality is related to courtesy.** Remind group members that when one of them is late, it is an act of discourtesy to all the other people who have been kept waiting, including the group facilitator if present.

3 **Lead by example – don't be late yourself!** If the facilitator is late, it is not surprising that group members can fall into bad habits. Your own actions are seen as a reflection of how you value group learning.

4 **Don't be unkind to anyone arriving late.** If students get a bad experience when they arrive late, they're likely not to bother turning up at all next time they are running late. Better late than never. Furthermore, the occasional late-comer might have a really valid, unavoidable reason for being late.

5 **Make the beginning of group sessions well worth being there for.** If group members realise that they are likely to miss something quite important in the early minutes of a group session, they are likely to try harder to be punctual.

6 **Give out something useful at the start of the session.** For example, issue a handout setting the scene for the session, or return marked assignments straightaway as the session starts.

7 **Avoid queuing.** If the place where a group meeting is due to be held is frequently still occupied at the starting time for the group session, it can be worth rescheduling the group for five or ten minutes later, so that a prompt, punctual start can be made then, without those who arrive early having to hang around.

Group members not turning up at all

This is one of the most common complaints made by facilitators. Student non-attendance can have a serious effect on group work, and a variety of approaches (and incentives) can be used to address the problem, including those listed below.

1 **Ensure that it really is worth turning up.** If group members are not getting a lot out of group sessions, they naturally value them less, and this can lead to them being lower priority than they could have been.

2 **Keep records of attendance.** Simply making notes of who's there and who's not gives the message that you're really expecting students to turn up and join in. If keeping records isn't enough, see below …

3 **Assess attendance.** For example, state that 10 per cent of the coursework element of a programme of study will be based solely on attendance. This is one way of making quite dramatic improvements in attendance at small-group sessions. However, the downside of this way of inducing students to attend is that some group members may be there in body but not in spirit, and can undermine the success of the group work.

4 **Issue something during each session.** Students don't like to miss handouts, task briefings, or the return of assessed work. It is important to make missed paperwork available to students who could not have avoided missing a session, but don't be too ready to do so for those who have no real reason for absence.

5 **Cover some syllabus elements only in small-group sessions.** When students know that these elements will be assessed alongside those covered in lectures, and so on, their willingness to attend the small-group sessions increases.

6 **Don't cancel small-group sessions.** Students are quick to pick up the message that something which has been cancelled could not have been too important in the first place. This attitude then spreads to other people's small-group sessions.

Group members not preparing

Group members can get far more out of small-group sessions if they have done at least some preparation for them. However, many teachers and facilitators complain that students still arrive without having thought in advance about what the session will be covering. It is difficult to cause *every* group member to come prepared, and over-zealous attempts to do this are likely to cause unprepared students to decide not to come at all. The following suggestions may help you to strike a workable balance between getting well-prepared students, and avoiding frightening them off.

1   **Help students to structure their preparation.** For example, issuing an interactive online task or handout for them to complete and bring to the forthcoming session is better than just asking them to 'read Chapter 3 of Smith and Jones'. You could ask them to 'research your own answers to the following seven questions using Chapter 3' instead, and leave space beneath each question for them to make notes as they read.

2   **Don't fail to build on their preparations.** If group members go to the trouble of preparing for a session, and then nothing is done with the work they have done, they are discouraged from preparing for the next session.

3   **Try starting each session with a quick quiz.** Ask everyone one or two short, specific questions, and perhaps ask respondents themselves to nominate the recipient of your next question. This is a way of building on the preparation work that students have done, and making sure that everyone is included, rather than just those who are most forthcoming when you ask questions.

4   **Consider asking them to hand in (or send in) their preparatory work sometimes.** This does not necessarily mean that you have to assess the work, but you could sift through them while group members were busy with an activity, to gather a quick impression of who was taking preparation seriously. The fact that you did this occasionally would lead to students not wishing to be found lacking should it happen again, and lead to better levels of preparation.

5   **Get them to peer-assess their preparations sometimes.** This has the advantage that they can find out how their own learning is going, compared with other students. It also helps them learn from feedback from each other, and the act of giving a fellow student feedback is just as useful as receiving feedback.

Group members not doing their jobs

A lot of time can be wasted when group members go off on tangents to their intended tasks, or procrastinate about starting the next stage of their work. Work-avoidance is human nature at least for some of the time for some people! The following approaches may help you to keep your group members on task.

1   **Have clear task briefings in the first place.** It is usually better to have these in print, and for every student to have a copy, or availability to the task online. Oral briefings are quickly forgotten, and are much more likely to lead to deviation from the intended tasks.

2   **Make the first part of a group task relatively short and straightforward.** This can cause a group to gain momentum more quickly, and this can help to ensure that later, more complex tasks are started without undue procrastination.

3   **Specify the learning outcomes clearly.** Show how evidence of achievement of the outcomes links directly to assessment sooner or later. When students know what they should be getting out of a particular activity, their engagement is enhanced.

4 **Set structured tasks, with staged deadlines.** Most effort is expended as the deadline approaches, especially if students will be *seen* to have slipped if their task is not completed by a deadline. Act as timekeeper if you are facilitating group work; gentle reminders such as 'six minutes to go, please' can cause a lot of work to be done.

Group members being disruptive

Group work is often damaged by one or more participants whose behaviour slows down or diverts the work of others. Disruption is more of a problem in small-group contexts than in formal lectures, for example, as it takes less courage to be disruptive in informal settings. Sometimes there is no easy solution for disruptive behaviour, but the following suggestions may help you to solve some such occurrences.

1 **Check that it really is disruption.** If you're a passing spectator to different groups, you may happen to arrive at one particular group just at the moment when one of its members is expressing a strong feeling, or arguing a point relatively forcefully. This may be fine with the other members of the group, and it gives the wrong message if the facilitator assumes the worst.

2 **Find out why a person is being disruptive.** Sometimes there are identifiable reasons for such behaviour, for example when a group as a whole has become dysfunctional, or when the task briefing is being interpreted in different ways by group members.

3 **Watch for the same group member being disruptive repeatedly.** It is then usually worth talking privately to the person concerned, to find out why this may be happening. If this does not improve the situation, it may be necessary to reconstitute the membership of groups for successive tasks, so that the disruptive element is fairly distributed across a wider range of students, rather than a particular group becoming disadvantaged by recurring disruption.

A group member dominating

Domination can be among the most serious enemies of effective group learning. It needs to be handled with considerable sensitivity, as someone 'taking over' the work of a group may be well intentioned.

1 **Get the group to reflect on how it is functioning.** For example, once in a while, give a relatively small task to do as a group, even an exercise which is primarily for light relief. Then when the group has completed it, ask everyone in the group to *think individually* through their answers to questions such as the following:
   - How well do you think you did that as a group?
   - Did someone take the lead, and if so, how did this come about?
   - Who said most?
   - Whose ideas are most strongly present in the solution to the task?
   - Did you always agree with the ideas being adopted by the group?
   - Was there anything you *thought* but didn't actually say?

   This can cause the group to reflect on any elements of domination which may have occurred, and can reduce the tendency for domination in future group activities.

2 **Lead a discussion on the benefits and drawbacks of assertiveness.** Then ask group members to put into practice what they have learned about assertiveness. This can lead to students watching out for each other's assertive behaviours, and reduce the chance of a particular group member dominating for too long.

3 **Confront the dominator privately.** For example, have a quiet word in a break, or before the next group session. Explain that while you are pleased that the dominant group member has a lot to contribute, you would like other students to have more opportunity to think for themselves.

4 **Intervene in the work of the group.**

Sometimes it is helpful to argue politely with a person who seems to be dominating, to alert other group members to the fact that they could be being led off-target by this person. Be careful, however, not to put down the dominator too much – there's little worse for group dynamics than a sullen ex-dominator!

Group facilitator behaviours which can damage group work

There are many ways in which group learning facilitators can damage group work. Sometimes facilitators know about the things they do which undermine the success of group work, but more often they simply are not aware that things could be improved. When facilitators know they have a bad habit, it would be tempting to simply advise 'stop doing it!', but often this could lead to the reply 'yes, but how?' The following list of facilitator 'faults' is rather longer than the students' damaging behaviours already discussed, but it can be argued that facilitators are able to address their own shortcomings even more directly than they can help students to address theirs. As before, each situation is annotated with some suggested tactics for eliminating or reducing the various kinds of damage which can occur.

Facilitator ignoring non-participants

It is tempting to ignore non-participants, hoping either that they will find their own way towards active participation, or that other group members will coax them out of inactivity. Alternatively, facilitators sometimes take the understandable view that 'if they don't join in, they won't get as much out of the group work, and that's really up to them to decide'. However, there are indeed some straightforward steps, from which facilitators may select, to make positive interventions to address the problem of non-participation as and when they see it.

1 **Remind the whole group of the benefits of equal participation.** This is less embarrassing to the non-participants themselves, and can be sufficient to spur them into a greater degree of involvement.

2 **Clarify the group learning briefing.** Place greater emphasis on the processes to be engaged in by the group, and less on the product that the group as a whole is to deliver.

3 **Consider making the assessment of contribution to the work of the group more explicit.** When non-participants know that participation counts, they are more likely to join in.

4 **Confront a non-participant directly.** This is best done tactfully of course. The simple fact that it was noticed that participation was

not enough is often enough to ensure that the situation does not arise again.

5 **Try to find out if there is a good reason for non-participation.** There often is. Sometimes, for example, a non-participant may find it difficult to work with one or more particular people in a group situation, because of pre-existing disagreements between them. It may then be necessary to consider reconstituting the groups, or see whether a little 'group therapy' will sort out the problem.

6 **Explore whether non-participation could be a cry for help.** The act of *not* joining in to the work of a group can be a manifestation of something that is going badly for non-participants, possibly in an entirely different area of their learning or their lives in general.

7 **Check, with care, whether the problem is with the work rather than the group.** Non-participation can sometimes arise because of the nature of the task, rather than being anything to do with the composition or behaviour of the group. For example, if the group-learning task involves something to do with researching the consumption of alcoholic beverages, it is not impossible that someone whose religion forbids alcohol resorts to non-participation.

8 **Check whether non-participation could be a reaction against the facilitator.** If someone does not like the way that *you* are organising some group learning, their reaction could be not to join in.

Facilitator allowing domineers

Domination has already been discussed under the bad habits that group members can engage in, and several tactics have already been suggested there. However, if you *allow* domination, it can be seen as your fault too. The following tactics may include remedies for situations where you notice group learning being undermined by domineers.

1 **Have a quiet word with the domineer.** This is often enough to solve the problem. Having been seen to be too domineering is usually enough to make a domineer stop and think.

2 **Reward those who aren't dominating.** Simply smiling at them while chatting to them can help to get the message across that any 'attention-seeking behaviour' of the domineer isn't really working.

3 **Get the whole group to do a process review.** For example, give them a relatively straightforward collaborative task to do, then ask them all to review who contributed most, why this happened, whether this was fair, and whether this is what they want to happen with the next (more important) group-learning task.

4 **Watch out for why people dominate.** Sometimes, it's because they are more confident, and it's important not to damage this confidence. It can be better to acknowledge group members' confidence and experience, and gently suggest to them that they need to help others to develop the same, by being able to participate fully in the actions of the group.

Facilitator not having prepared adequately

We've already explored some of the tactics that can be used to solve the problem of lack of preparation by group members. This time, the issue is lack of preparation by the facilitator. The short answer is, of course, 'prepare'. However, the results of this preparation need to be visible to group members. The following approaches can help to ensure that group members can see that you are taking group work as seriously as you want them to do.

1 **Make it obvious that you have prepared specially for the group session.** There are many ways of allowing your preparations to be visible, including:
   - issuing an online briefing specifically relating to the group session;
   - coming armed with a handout relating to the particular occasion, rather than just any old handout;
   - having researched something that has just happened, ready to present to the group as material for them to work on;
   - arriving punctually or early, to avoid the impression you were delayed by getting your own act together ready for the session;
   - making sure that you have indeed done anything you promised to do at the last meeting of the group.

2 **Keep records of group sessions, and have them with you.** You would not arrive to give a lecture or presentation without having your notes and resources with you, and doing the same for group sessions gives the message that you take such sessions just as seriously as larger scale parts of your work.

3 **Issue a debriefing document (e.g. online) after the group session, expanding when necessary on particular matters which arose in that particular session.** This can help students to feel that it's worthwhile raising important matters during the session.

Facilitator being too didactic or controlling

This is one of the most significant of the facilitator behaviours which can damage group learning, and experienced facilitators can be the most vulnerable! The quality of group learning is greatly enhanced when students themselves have considerable control of the pace and direction of their own learning.

The following suggestions may alert you to any danger you could be in.

1 **Don't try to hurry group learning too much.** It is particularly tempting, when *you* know very well how to get the group to where it needs to be, to intervene and point out all the short cuts, tips and wrinkles. It is much better, however, for group students to find their own way to their goals, even when it takes somewhat longer to get there.

2 **Remember that every group session is different.** If you're repeating the same session with different groups, there's a tendency to expect more in the later re-runs of the session, and this can rob the students of the thinking time they may need.

3 **Hide your knowledge and wisdom sometimes.** In other words, allow group members to discover things for themselves, so that they have a strong sense of ownership of the result of their actions. As mentioned previously, this may be slower, but leads to better learning. Don't, however, make it show that you are withholding help or advice. When you feel that you may be giving this impression, it is worth declaring your rationale, and explaining that it will be much better for your group students to think it out for themselves before you bring your own experience to their aid.

4 **Allow group students to learn from mistakes.** Tempting as it is to try to stop students from going along every blind alley, the learning payoff from some blind alleys can be high. Help them *back* from the brick wall at the end of the blind alley, rather than trying to stop them finding out for themselves that there is a brick wall there.

5 **Plan processes rather than outcomes.** It is well worth spending time organising the *ways* that group students can work towards their goals, rather than mapping out in too much detail the things they are likely to experience on the way. The achievement of the group learning outcomes will be much more enduring when the group has ownership of the learning journey towards them.

6 **Ask your students.** Many of the things that can go wrong in teaching or training could have been avoided if feedback had been sought on the way. The best way of getting feedback is to ask for it, not just to wait for it. To get feedback on important things (such as whether or not you are being too didactic or controlling) there's no faster way than asking for exactly that.

7 **Learn from selected colleagues.** Feedback from other group-learning facilitators is always useful. However, it is worth going out of your way to seek feedback from colleagues who have a particular gift for making group learning *productive*, and being duly selective in the tactics you add to your own collection.

Facilitator showing lack of cultural sensitivity

This is a serious group-damaging behaviour. In fact, lack of cultural sensitivity can be more obvious and dangerous in small-group situations than in large-group ones. It is also one of the hardest areas to find out about. Few people are brave enough to challenge a group-learning facilitator with this crime! It is useful for even the most skilled group-learning facilitators to undertake a regular self-audit on this issue. The following tactics can help.

1 **Read about it.** There is no shortage of published material on equal opportunities, diversity, cultural issues, and so on. Sometimes when reading this literature, one can be surprised by the thought 'but sometimes I do this too!'
2 **Watch other group-learning facilitators, with this agenda in mind.** See what they do to avoid the pitfalls, and also notice when they fall into them. Work out alternative approaches which could have circumvented such problems.
3 **Don't make assumptions.** It is particularly dangerous to bring to your role of learning facilitator any preconceptions about the different members of your groups, such as those based on gender, age, ethnic group, perceived social status, and any other area where assumptions may be unwise and unfounded. Treating people with equal respect is an important part of acknowledging and responding to individual difference.
4 **Talk to group members individually.** When you are working with a mixed group, for example, it is in your informal, individual conversations with members of the group that you are most likely to be alerted to anything which could be offending individuals' cultural or personal perspectives.
5 **Ask directly sometimes.** It is important to pick your times wisely, and to select people who you believe will be willing to be frank with you if necessary. Rather than asking *too* directly (for example, 'What do I do which could be culturally insensitive?'), it can be useful to lead in more gently, for example, 'What sorts of learning experiences do you find can be damaged by people who are not sensitive enough culturally?', 'How does this happen usually?', and so on.

Facilitator favouring clones!

This happens more often than most people imagine. It is noticed straightaway by everyone *else* in the group! It can go entirely unnoticed by the perpetrator. It is, of course, perfectly human to have 'warmer' or 'more empathetic' feelings and attitudes towards someone who is more like oneself than other people, or who shares significant attitudes, values, and even 'looks'. In particular, teachers of any sort can be flattered and encouraged when they recognise 'a disciple' among a group of people. If you think you could be in danger of indulging in this particular behaviour, think about which of the following approaches may be most helpful to you.

1 **Go clone detecting!** From time to time, think around the types of people who make up learning groups you work with, and test out whether any of them are more like you are (and particularly more like you *were*) than the others. Then watch out for any signs that you could be treating them differently (even if only slightly).
2 **Don't over-compensate.** It is just as dangerous to be too *hard* on clones as to favour them. The person concerned may have no idea at all why you are being harder on them than on other people. The people you might (consciously or subconsciously) regard as clones may have no inkling that they are in this special position! Subconsciously, you could be putting them under the same sort of pressures as you put yourself under long ago, and exacting of them the standards you applied to yourself.

Facilitator talking too much

This is one of the most common of all group-learning facilitator bad habits. However, it is just about the easiest to do something about. The following suggestions should contain all you need to rectify this problem, if you own it.

1 **Remind yourself that most learning happens by doing, rather than listening.** Concentrate on what your group students themselves do during group sessions, rather than on what you do.

2 **Don't allow yourself to be tempted into filling every silence.** In any group process, short episodes of silence are necessary components, space for thinking. When *you* happen to be expert enough to step in with your thoughts, before other people have had time to put theirs together, it is all too easy to be the one to break the silence. What seems to you like a long silence, seems much shorter to people who are busily thinking. Let them think, then help them to put their thoughts into words. When they have ownership of putting together ideas and concepts, their learning is much deeper and more enduring.

3 **Only say *some* of the things you think.** Being the expert in the group (you probably are!), you're likely to know more than anyone else about the topic being addressed. You don't have to reveal all of your knowledge, just some of it. Don't fall into the trap of feeling you have to defend your expertise, or that you need to justify your position.

4 **Don't let *them* let you talk too much!** It's easier for group members to sit and listen to you than to get on with their own thinking. Sometimes, they can encourage you to fill all of the time, and opt for an easy life.

5 **Present some of your thoughts (particularly longer ones) in print.** Use handouts to input information to the group, but not at the expense of getting group members to think for themselves. You can convey far more information in five minutes through a handout than you could in five minutes' worth of talking. People can read much faster than you can speak and, in any case, they can read a handout again and again – they can't replay you speaking (unless they're recording it – and even then, would they *really* replay it all again?).

Facilitator not providing clear objectives

In education and training it is increasingly accepted that objectives, or intended learning outcomes, have a vital part to play in ensuring that learning takes place successfully. This is no less true of small-group work than lectures. Moreover, the absence of clear objectives for group work is only too readily taken by students as a signal that the group work can't really be an important part of their overall learning. The following suggestions may help you to put objectives or statements of intended learning outcomes to good use in facilitating group learning.

1 **Work out exactly what you intend each group learning session to achieve.** It is best to express this in terms of what you intend students themselves to gain from the session. Make sure that the learning outcomes are expressed in language that students themselves can readily understand, so that they see very clearly what they are intended to achieve.

2 **Publish the learning outcomes or objectives in advance.** This allows students to see where any particular group session fits in to the overall picture of their learning. It also helps them to see that their group learning counts towards their assessment in due course.

3 **Clarify evidence of achievement expected.** When students have a clear idea of what they should become able to *show* as a result of a small-group session, they're much more likely to achieve such targets.

4 **Maintain some flexibility.** For example, it is useful to have some further objectives for any group session, designed to cover matters arising from previous sessions, or to address students' questions and needs as identified on an ongoing basis through a programme of study. These additional objectives can be added to the original intentions for the session, and re-prioritised at the start of the session if necessary.

5 **Don't just write the objectives or outcomes – use them!** State them (or display them on a slide, or issue them on a handout) at the start of each and every group session, even if it is continuing to address a list of intended outcomes which were discussed at previous sessions.

6 **Assist students in creating their own objectives.** From time to time, ask them 'what do *you* need to gain from the coming group session?', for example giving them each a post-it note on which to jot down their replies. Then stick the notes on a chart (or wall, or door, or whiteboard), and ask the group to shuffle them into an order of priority, or to group them into overlapping clusters.

A closer look at tutorials

In this chapter so far, we've looked in general terms at the processes of students working together. In this section, let's think of the most common small-group scenario: that of the academic tutorial, where a tutor is present alongside a small number of students. How many students make a tutorial? It used to be the case, in many universities, where a tutorial was either a one-to-one encounter between a student and a tutor, or a tutor working with a group of no more than four or five students. With present-day class sizes, elements that appear on the timetable as 'tutorials' can in some disciplines and in some universities involve significantly larger numbers of students than five.

What's an academic tutorial?

Everyone who is involved in tutorial work with students agrees that there is no clear dividing line between academic and personal tutorials. Academic tutorials are subject-related, while personal tutorials are normally thought of in terms of development of the 'whole student', but either kind of tutorial is likely to spill over into the other domain. In this chapter, I would like to flag this overlap now at the outset, but then focus on aspects of academic tutorials and other kinds of small-group teaching–learning situations, recognising that quite a lot of the discussion can be translated to personal tutorials too.

There is no agreed definition of a tutorial, and this is probably wise, as tutorials should fulfil any one or more different roles. These may include:

- to provide students with opportunities to learn-by-doing, practising applying things that have been covered in lectures, online study, and learning packages;
- to address students' motivation, helping to increase their confidence in their abilities to handle the curriculum successfully;
- to provide students with feedback, from each other as well as from the tutor, helping them to find out more about how their learning is progressing;
- to give teaching staff opportunities to find out what problems students may be encountering with the subjects they are learning;
- to help students to make sense of the concepts they are learning;
- to allow students to ask questions which they may not be able to ask in large-group sessions.

However, the above descriptions do not amount to a definition of a tutorial, but only serve as a description of some of the processes likely to be involved in the sort of tutorials that help students to get to grips with the curriculum.

What's a personal tutorial?

These are usually regarded as one-to-one encounters between a student and a tutor, but where the main purpose is not to extend or deepen the academic understanding of the subjects being studied, but to support the student's learning in a much broader sense. The tutor may be one of the lecturers involved in the student's course, or may be a teaching assistant or research assistant with some tutorial duties. Students are often assigned a 'personal tutor' for the duration of a year of their course, or for their entire time at university. These tutors are normally expected to exercise a counselling or advising role when necessary, on the wide agenda of anything that may be causing concern to their respective students. However, the success of personal tutorial support is, at best, patchy. Some tutors take it very seriously, and put themselves out to get to know their students well, and to remain well briefed on the progress of each student. For many students, however, their personal tutor is just a name.

A result of this situation is that for most students, the majority of personal tutoring happens in the context of the contact they have with academic staff in those teaching–learning situations where the staff–student ratio is low enough for advice and counselling to be available, and that often means in what are intended to be academic tutorials.

What can students do before academic tutorials?

It's often argued by teaching staff that a problem with tutorials is that students just don't do the preparatory work they were intended to undertake before attending tutorials. However well-briefed students are, it seems inevitable that some will turn up without having done any such work, and others will decide to miss the tutorials altogether, feeling guilty that they have not put sufficient time or energy into preparing for them.

Some ways of maximising the probability that students will turn up having engaged with preparatory work include:

- giving work briefings in print (handouts or online) rather than orally; this increases the chance that students not present at the briefing will still see the briefing;
- when using print-based briefings, issuing them on sheets of a particular colour rather than just on white paper; this helps students not to lose such briefings amongst other papers;
- making briefings interactive: for example include some structured questions with spaces for students to write their answers or conclusions in. This makes it much easier to spot who has done some preparation and who has not – and students don't like to be *seen* not to have written something into the spaces;
- arranging that coursework to be handed in for assessment is gathered in at tutorials. This can help to ensure that students attend, if only to hand in their work. It also allows tutorials to be used to discuss problems students may have encountered with the coursework, before they have forgotten exactly what the problems were;
- including in tutorial time activities such as student self-assessment and peer-assessment, depending on preparation that students are required to have done before participating.

It can be worth exploring possibilities of students doing collaborative work before tutorials, such as meeting together (without a tutor) to help identify common problems and questions, to establish an agenda for forthcoming tutorials – or better still, perhaps, for forthcoming large-group sessions.

What can students do during academic tutorials?

It is probably best to start by looking at things that students *shouldn't* be doing in academic tutorials. These include activities with low learning payoff, including:

- making notes just by copying down things said by the tutor, or things shown on the board or screen;
- spending most of the time listening passively, while one or two students dominate the discussion;
- pretending that they understand what is being discussed, rather than admitting to having problems with the material.

There are many varieties of activity with high learning payoff that students can engage in during academic tutorials. These include (but are by no means restricted to):

- solving problems or doing calculations, either individually or collaboratively;
- discussing different perspectives on an issue;
- working out different ways of approaching a problem or case-study situation;
- applying assessment criteria to their own, or each other's work;
- marking examples of past students' assignments or exam answers;
- asking the tutor questions, or working out agendas of matters for future tutorial exploration;
- answering questions posed by each other and by the tutor;
- doing exercises helping them to apply, and make sense of, material covered in lectures;
- linking work they have done in practical sessions to underpinning concepts and models;
- making summaries and checklists to help them distinguish the main points of a subject from the background detail.

Practical pointers for group work

Already in this chapter there are many suggestions for recognising and responding to some of the things that can go wrong with small-group teaching. Some additional tips are included below.

Getting groups started

Once group work has gathered momentum, it is likely to be successful. The greatest challenge is sometimes to get that momentum going. The first few minutes can be crucial, and you will need all of your facilitation skills to minimise the risk of groups drifting aimlessly in these minutes. Take your pick from the following suggestions about getting group work going right from the start of a task.

1 **Foster ownership of the task.** Wherever possible, try to arrange that the members of the whole group have thought of the issues to be addressed by small-group work. When possible, allow members to choose which group task they wish to engage in. When people have chosen to do a task, they are more likely to attempt it wholeheartedly.

2 **Start with a short group icebreaker.** Before getting groups under way with the main task,

it can be useful to give them a short, 'fun' icebreaker so that each group's members get to know each other, relax, and become confident to work with each other. See the next section for some ideas about icebreakers.

3 **Keep the beginning of the task short and simple.** Einstein is attributed with saying 'everything should be made as simple as possible, but no simpler'. Make sure that the first stage of each group task is something that does not cause argument, and does not take significant time to interpret. Once a group is under way, it is possible to make tasks much more challenging.

4 **Don't rely only on oral briefings.** Oral briefings are useful, as they can add the emphasis of tone of voice, facial expression, and body language. However, when *only* oral briefings are given for group-learning tasks, it is often found that after a few minutes different groups are attempting quite different things.

5 **Use printed briefings.** It is useful to put the overall briefing up on a PowerPoint slide, but if groups then move away into different syndicate rooms, they can lose sight (and mind) of the exact briefing. It is worth having cards or slips of paper containing exactly the same words as in the original briefing, which groups can take away with them.

6 **Visit the groups in turn.** It can make a big difference to progress if you spend a couple of minutes just listening to what is happening in a group, chipping in gently with one or two useful suggestions, then moving on. During such visits, you can also remind groups of the deadline for the next report-back stage.

7 **Clarify the task when asked.** Sometimes, groups will ask you whether you mean one thing or another by the words in the briefing. It is often productive if you are able to reply 'either of these would be an interesting way of interpreting the task; you choose which interpretation you would prefer to address'. This legitimises the group's discovery of ambiguity, and can increase the efforts they put into working out their chosen interpretation.

8 **Have an early, brief, report-back from groups on the first stage of their task.** This can help to set expectations that everyone will be required to be ready for later report-back stages at the times scheduled in the task briefing. Any group which finds itself unprepared for the initial report-back is likely to try to make sure that this position does not repeat itself.

9 **Break down extended tasks into manageable elements.** Often, if the whole task is presented to groups as a single briefing, group members will get bogged down by the most difficult part of the overall task. This element might turn out to be much more straightforward if they had already done the earlier parts of the whole task.

10 **Try to control the amount of time that groups spend on successive stages of each task.** It can be useful to introduce a sense of closure of each stage in turn, by getting groups to write down decisions or conclusions before moving on to the next stage in the overall task.

Icebreakers: some ideas

There are countless descriptions of icebreaking activities in books and articles on training; see particularly Jaques (2000). An icebreaker is most needed when members of a group don't already know each other, and when the group is going to be together for some hours or days. Most icebreakers have the main purpose of helping individuals get to know each other a little better. Here are some ideas to set you thinking about what the most appropriate icebreakers could be for your own groups. Some icebreakers can be very quick, acting as a curtain-raiser for the next activity. Others can be extended into larger-scale activities at the start of a major group project. Don't try to rush these. If you're using icebreakers for each of several successive meetings of the same group, remember to keep a note of which you've already used; participants really don't like repetition. Don't, however, use too many icebreakers with the same group of participants, as they might come to resent the time and energy these take, and want to get on with the main business of the forthcoming group tasks.

1 **Triumphs, traumas and trivia.** Ask everyone to think of one recent triumph in any area of their lives (which they are willing to share), and ask them to think of a trauma (problem, disaster, and so on), and something trivial – anything that may be interesting or funny. Then ask everyone in turn to share a sentence or so about each. Be aware that this activity often brings out a lot of deep feelings, so keep this for groups whose members need to know each other well, or already do so.

2 **One-breath introductions – and a surprise.** Ask everyone in turn to use just one breath to say a little about who they are, where they come from, and what they do. (The 'one breath' briefing can be really useful for stopping some people saying too much and boring everyone else!) Then invite everyone to use another breath, if they wish, to share 'something which not many people know about me'. This can be fascinating, and participants often remember the things which emerge from this activity. However, it's best that this second step is voluntary, as there are often one or two participants who don't want to share this sort of thing – or who can't think of anything interesting to share.

3 **What's on top?** This can be a quick way of finding out where the members of a group are starting from. Ask everyone to prepare a short statement (one sentence) about what is, for them, the most important thing on their mind at the time. This helps people to clear the ground, perhaps if they are (for example) worrying about a sick child, or a driving test, and enables them then to park such issues on one side, before getting down to the real tasks to follow.

4 **What's your name?** Ask everyone in turn to say their (preferred) name, why they were called this name, and what they feel about it. This not only helps group members to learn each other's names, but also lets them learn a little about each other's backgrounds, views, and so on. Bear in mind that some people

don't actually like their names much, so make aliases acceptable.

5 **Pack your suitcase.** Ask individuals to list ten items that they would metaphorically pack into a suitcase if they were in a disaster scenario. Emphasise that these items wouldn't have to literally fit into a suitcase, and could include pets, but shouldn't include people. Ask them to mill around a large room, finding a couple of others who share at least two items from their list. This enables them to get into groups of three or four, with plenty to talk about, before you get them started on the actual group work.

6 **What I like, and what I hate.** Ask everyone to identify something that they really like, and something they really loathe. Ask them then to introduce themselves to the rest of the group, naming each thing. This helps people to remember each other's names, as well as to break down some of the barriers between them.

7 **What do you really want?** Ask everyone to jot down what they particularly want from the session about to start, and to read it out in turn (or stick post-it notes on a flipchart, and explain them). This can help group members (and facilitators) to find out where a group is starting from. It can be useful to ask participants to exchange post-its, and read out someone else's post-it.

8 **What do you already know about the topic?** Ask everyone to jot down, on a post-it note, the single most important thing that they already know about the topic that the group is about to explore. Give them a minute or so each to read out their ideas, or make an exhibition of them on a flipchart. This helps to establish ownership of useful ideas within the group, and can help facilitators to avoid telling people things that they already know.

9 **Draw a face.** Ask everyone to draw on a scrap of paper (or post-it note) a cartoon 'face' showing how they feel at the time (or about the topic they're going to explore together). You may be surprised at how many 'smiley faces' and alternatives that can be drawn.

10 **Provide a picture, with small cartoon figures undertaking a range of activities.** Then ask people to say which activity feels closest to the way they feel at the moment (for example, digging a hole for themselves, sitting at the top of a tree, on the outside looking in, and so on). Use this as a basis for getting to know each other through small-group discussion.

11 **Make a junk sculpture.** Give groups of four or five people materials such as newspaper, disposable cups, string, sellotape, plastic straws, and so on. Ask them to design and produce either the highest possible tower, a bridge between two chairs that would carry a toy car, or some other form of visible output. Ask them to think, while on task, about the group processes involved (who led, who actually did the work, who had little to contribute, and so on), then ask them to unpack these thoughts and share in plenary their summarised conclusions about the group processes.

12 **Develop verbal skills.** Ask students in pairs to sit back to back. Give one of each pair a simple line drawing comprising squares, triangles, rectangles and circles. Without letting their partner see the original, ask those holding the drawings to describe what is on the page, using verbal instructions only, so that their partners can draw the original on a fresh sheet of paper. After a fixed time, let them compare the originals with the copies, and ask them to discuss what the task showed them about verbal communication. A similar task can also be designed using plastic construction bricks.

13 **Make a tableau.** Ask groups of about seven or eight students to decide on a theme for their tableau (for example the homecoming, the machine age, playtime) and ask them to compose a tableau using themselves as key elements. Ask each group in turn to 'present their tableau' to other groups, and then to discuss how they went about the task. Photos of the tableaux can add to the fun, but do not use this activity if you feel that group members are likely to be sensitive about being touched by others.

14 **Organise a treasure hunt.** Give each group a map of the training centre or campus, and a set of tasks to complete across the location. For example, task elements can include collecting information from a display area, checking out a reference item via the internet, collecting prices for specific items from the catering outlet, drawing a room plan of a difficult-to-locate study area, and so on. Different groups should undertake the tasks in a different order, so that individual locations (and people) are not mobbed by too many people arriving at the same time. Give a time limit for the treasure hunt, and award prizes for all who complete on time. This activity helps people to get to know each other and their learning environment at the same time.

15 **Which of these are 'you'?** Give everyone a handout sheet (or show a slide) containing (say) twenty numbered short statements about the topic to be explored. Ask each participant to pick out the three that are most applicable to them. Then ask everyone in turn to disclose their top choice, asking the rest to show whether they too were among their own choices.

16 **Interview your neighbour.** Ask participants in pairs to interview each other for (say) three minutes, making notes of key points that they may wish to report back in summary of the interview. Then do a round asking everyone to introduce their neighbour to the rest of the group.

A popular icebreaker: the 'Statements' exercise

The 'statements' exercise has been around a long time, and has been adapted by just about everyone who uses it. A version I often use at workshops is presented here. It is done as 'a short exam' where candidates fill in the sheet containing the grid on their own, and their scores are recorded on a flipchart or whiteboard. The scores usually range widely, with 'don't know' scores anything from zero to around 12. Participants are often quite surprised at how much their interpretations of what seems like a straightforward exercise can diverge.

Next, participants are asked to discuss the exercise with each other (or put into groups of four or five to do so) and adjust their scores based on discussion. The groups can be asked to come to an agreed score, or allow individual members to decide their own scores. The most common 'right' answer is that only four of the statements are true, and only one definitely false, with the remainder being 'don't know', but there are many ways of interpreting the wording, and participants will often be quite eager to justify yet more interpretations of the exercise.

Using the 'Statements' exercise

One way of using this exercise is to set it as an 'exam', issuing the sheet face-downwards to everyone in the room, asking 'candidates' to turn over at the same time, then working individually to follow the instructions on the sheet, advising that 'scores will be taken down shortly', preparing a flipchart or whiteboard with their names and three columns for 'true', 'false' and 'don't know' totals.

The scores are usually very different for respective participants. Feedback can often be given along the lines 'no-one has got the exercise entirely correct' (as is usually the case). It is then worth getting participants into groups of four or five, asking them to discuss the exercise and work towards an agreed score for the exercise. The new scores can then be written in another colour beside participants' names on the flipchart or whiteboard. The numbers in the 'don't know' column have usually risen substantially.

In debriefing the exercise, the 'correct' solution(s) can then be shown, amounting to True = 4, False = 1 and Don't know = 13 (or 4, 2, 12, as statement 18 can be regarded as ambiguous, and can legitimately be regarded as 'don't know' or 'false'). However, individuals or groups can often justify even higher numbers of 'don't know' choices than 13.

Objectives of the exercise can now be discussed, including the following:

- To remind you what it feels like answering someone else's questions, under exam conditions on your own, using just printed words. This is also similar to working online on your own.
- To show how easy it is, under these conditions, to make assumptions.
- To illustrate how most people hesitate to admit 'don't know'.
- To show how quickly assumptions can be broken down when people have the opportunity to talk to each other. This illustrates how useful group work can be to students, and how working alone online can be disadvantageous.
- To show the dangers of long sentences. For example statement 18 is often taken to be true, even though the 'dashed out' phrase is not included in the story.
- To show how crucial the wording of task instructions can be. (Usually, there are at least some participants who have entered ticks rather than crosses on their sheets, and the point can be made that in exams there are often students who, in the heat of the moment, have not actually read the instructions carefully enough.)

In practice, using this particular icebreaker typically takes around an hour, including the debriefing and discussion, but proves popular with participants, and certainly helps them get to know each other. All sorts of variants are possible.

Statements

Given the story below, you have ten minutes to record in the spaces provided beside each statement whether you think it is true, false, or you don't know (mark with an X). Add up your scores in each column when you have finished.

A businessman had just turned off the lights in a store when a man appeared and demanded money. The owner opened the cash register. The contents of the cash register were scooped up and the man sped away. A member of the police force was notified promptly.

	True	False	Don't know
A man appeared after the owner had turned off his store lights.			
The robber was a man.			
The man who appeared did not demand money.			
The man who opened the cash register was the owner.			
The owner scooped up the contents of the cash register and ran away.			
Someone opened a cash register.			
After the man who demanded money scooped up the contents of the cash register, he ran away.			
While the cash register contained money, the story does not state how much.			
The robber demanded money of the owner.			
The robber opened the cash register.			
After the store lights were turned off, a man appeared.			
The robber did not take the money with him.			
The robber did not demand money of the owner.			
The owner opened a cash register.			
The age of the store owner was not revealed in the story.			
Taking the contents of the cash register with him, the man ran out of the store.			
The story concerns a series of events in which only three persons are referred to: the owner of the store, a man who demanded money, and a member of the police force.			
The following events were included in the story: someone demanded money, a cash register was opened, its contents were scooped up, and a man dashed out of the store.			
Totals			

Learning and using names

People in general tend to take more notice of people they know. Your students will take more notice of you if they feel that they know you – and above all , that you know them. This is particularly important when you work with small groups of students, as they are much more likely to expect you to know who they are! Getting their names right is a useful step towards building up the sort of relationship which fosters learning. The following suggestions provide some general advice on how to improve your 'hit rate' of correct name-calling in small-group work.

1 **Learn all the easy names first.** If you have a group with three Peters in, make sure you know them first and which one is which! You then have a three in twenty (say) chance of getting the first name right!

2 **Make a conscious effort to learn three or four names a session.** This way you should build up a reasonable ability to talk to people by name within the first few weeks in small-group work.

3 **Take particular care with difficult names.** If you have names that you find difficult or unusual to say, write them out clearly and check how to say them, then write it phonetically in a way you will recognise over the top. Use the name as often as you can until you've mastered it, regularly checking that you've got it right.

4 **Consider students' feelings.** Think how you feel when someone gets your name wrong – especially someone you would have expected to know it. One of the problems with university teaching is that new students can feel quite anonymous and alone, especially when part of a large class.

5 **Use preferred names.** At the beginning of the course, ask students 'what do you want to be called?' The names they give you will be more accurate than your printed class-lists, and you'll quickly find out whether Victoria wants to be called Vicky, Jaswinder – Jaz, Cedric – Rick, etc.

6 **Use labels.** At early stages it's useful to give students sticky labels to write their names on in bold felt-tip pen. This gives you the chance to call them by the name they prefer – and gives them the chance to start getting to know each other.

7 **Help students to learn each other's names.** In groups with up to about twenty students, try a round as follows: 'Tell us your name, and tell us something about your name'. This can be a good icebreaker, and can be very memorable too, helping people develop association links with the names involved.

8 **Help students to get to know each other better.** An alternative round is to get the students sitting in a circle. Ask one to say his or her name, then the person to the left to say 'I am … and this is …'. Carry on round the circle, adding one name at each stage, till someone goes right round the circle correctly. A further alternative is to ask students to introduce themselves, stating first their names, and then two 'likes' and two 'dislikes', so some memorable details help associate the person with the name.

9 **Use your list of names to quiz students.** To help you to get to know their names, once you have a complete list of the names, ask people from your list at random some (easy) questions, not to catch them out, but to help you to put names to faces.

10 **Consider using place cards.** In situations where small groups of students are sitting in particular places for a while, it is useful to give the students each a 'place card' (a folded A5 sheet of card serves well) and to write their names on both sides of the card, and place the cards in front of them. Cards can be seen at a distance much better than labels. This allows you to address individuals by name, and also helps them to get to know each other.

Conflict in group work

Much has been written about the stages that are quite normal in group work. For example, it is common for groups to progress through stages of 'forming, storming, norming, and conforming' – not necessarily in that particular order! The following suggestions may help you to minimise the dangers associated with conflict in group work, and to maximise the benefits that can be drawn from people who sometimes disagree.

1 **Legitimise conflict.** It is important to acknowledge that people don't have to agree all of the time, and to open up agreed processes by which areas of disagreement can be explored and resolved (or be agreed to remain areas of disagreement). Ensure, however, that the groups have ground rules for conflict resolution, so that they strive to avoid slanging matches and power games.

2 **Establish the causes of conflict.** When conflict has broken out in a group, it is easy for the root causes to become subsumed in an escalation of feeling. It can be productive to backtrack to the exact instance which initiated the conflict, and to analyse it further.

3 **Encourage groups to put the conflict into written words.** Writing up the issues, problems, or areas of disagreement on a flipchart or marker-board can help to get them out of people's systems. Conflict feelings are often much stronger when the conflict is still bottled up, and has not yet been clearly expressed or acknowledged. When something is 'up on the wall', it often looks less daunting, and a person who felt strongly about it may be more satisfied. The 'on the wall' issues can be returned to later when the group has had more time to think about them.

4 **Establish the ownership of the conflict.** Who feels it? Who is being affected by it? Distinguish between individual issues, and ones that affect the whole group.

5 **Distinguish between people, actions and opinions.** When unpacking the causes of conflict in a group situation, it is useful to focus on actions and principles. Try to resolve any actions which proved to cause conflict. Try to agree principles. If the conflict is caused by different opinions, it can help to accept people's entitlement to their opinions, and leave it open to people to reconsider their opinions if and when they feel ready to do so.

6 **Use conflict creatively.** It can be useful to use brainstorming to obtain a wider range of views, or a broader range of possible actions that can be considered by the group. Sometimes, the one or two strong views which may have caused conflict in a group look much more reasonable when the full range of possibilities is aired, and areas of agreement are found to be closer than they seemed to be.

7 **Capture the learning from conflict.** When conflict has occurred, it can be beneficial to ask everyone to decide constructive things they have learned about themselves from the conflict, and to agree on principles which the whole group can apply to future activities to minimise the damage from similar causes of conflict arising again.

8 **Refuse to allow conflict to destroy group work.** You may wish sometimes to tell groups that achievement of consensus is an aim, or a norm, or alternatively you may wish to ask groups to establish only the extent of the consensus they achieve.

9 **Consider arbitration processes.** When conflict is absolutely irresolvable, the facilitator may need to set up a 'court of appeal' for desperate situations. The fact that such a process is available often helps groups to sort out their own problems without having to resort to it.

10 **Make it OK to escape.** When people know that they can get out of an impossible situation, they don't feel trapped, and in fact are more likely to work their own way out of the conflict. It can be useful to allow people to drop out of a group, and move into another one, but only as a last resort. Beware of the possible effects of someone who is seen as a conflict generator entering a group which has so far worked without conflict!

Gender issues in group work

When problems occur in groups due to gender issues, they can be felt more deeply than problems arising from almost any other cause. The following suggestions may help you to avoid some problems of this sort from arising in the first place, or to alert group members themselves to the potential problems, so that they can work round them in their own group work.

1 **Think about gender when forming groups.** There are advantages and disadvantages for single-gender groups, depending on the balance of the sexes, and other issues including culturally sensitive ones. In some cultures, females may be much happier, for religious reasons, working in single-gender groups. However, in other cases it may be helpful in terms of future employment to gently encourage them to get used to working with members of the opposite gender.

2 **Try to avoid gender domination of groups.** This can happen because of majority gender composition of groups. If this is inevitable because of the overall gender balance of the whole group, try to manage group composition so that minority participants don't feel isolated. If it is unavoidable, address the issue directly when setting ground rules.

3 **Decide when single-gender groups might be more appropriate.** For group work on gender-sensitive issues, such as child abuse, it can be best to set out to form single-gender groups.

4 **Require appropriate behaviour.** For group work to be effective, all participants need to behave in a professional way, with standards that would be expected in an effective working environment. Outlaw sexist or offensive behaviour, and emphasise that one person's 'joke' or 'tease' can be another person's humiliation.

5 **Decide when to stick with existing group compositions.** When a set of groups is working well, without any gender-related or other problems, don't just change the group composition without a good reason.

6 **Set ground rules for talking and listening.** It can be useful to agree on ground rules which will ensure that all group participants (irrespective of gender) are heard, and not talked down or over by other participants.

7 **Avoid setting up excessive competition between male groups and female groups.** When there are gender-specific groups, don't egg a group of one gender on, by saying words to the effect 'Come on, you can do better than them' referring to groups of the other gender.

8 **Be sensitive about role assignment.** For example, try to raise awareness about the dangers of tasks being allocated within groups on the basis of gender stereotypes, such as typing or making arrangements being handled by females, and 'heavy' work by males.

9 **Alert groups to be sensitive to leadership issues.** It is often the case that, for example, male members of groups may automatically see themselves as stronger contenders to lead the group than their female counterparts, and put themselves forward. When group members are aware that this is an issue, they are more likely to agree on a more democratic process for deciding who will lead an activity, or who will report back the outcomes.

10 **Avoid sexual preference oppression.** When it is known that group participants have different sexual preferences from the majority of the group, there is a tendency for them to be oppressed in one way or another by the rest of the group. It can be delicate to raise this issue in general briefings, and it may be best to respond to it as a facilitator when it is seen to be likely to occur.

Conclusions

Facilitating small-group learning can easily swallow up all the time we've got, when hundreds of students in a lecture theatre go off into tutorials and seminars and so on. However, it's dangerous to think the small-group side of our job any less important than the lecture theatre, as it's often in the more intimate contexts of small groups that the 'making sense' side of learning really gets going, and all the learning that accompanies students themselves putting things into spoken words, and making judgements on how their learning is going – and how they compare with each other in their learning. Small-group learning is one of the most valuable reasons for going along to a college or university – anyone can watch brilliant on-line lectures on a MOOC these days, and anyone can download masses of excellent information from the web, but that's nothing compared with the learning that happens talking to – and listening to – fellow learners face-to-face in small groups, and sometimes with the lecturer there too. For lecturers, moreover, small-group work can be one of the most pleasurable parts of our lives, not least because we can keep in touch with our students and their triumphs and trials, and we can tune in to who needs that extra bit of guidance and encouragement to help them to succeed.

Chapter 5

Resource-based learning in the digital age

The Open Educational Resources movement has turned the web into a universal educational library of lecture materials and well-produced educational resources, available to all. This is a significant shift for education because it provides access to educational materials to anyone who has Internet access. It is a wonderful democratization of access to resources. But it is not the same as access to education. And learning technologists have to keep alive the vision for what technology-enhanced learning could be.

Being able to read and write never meant you could therefore learn from books. Learners need teachers. As learners we cannot know what it is possible to know, or how to make that journey to what we want to become. We need guidance.

(Diana Laurillard, 2013, pp. xvi–xvii)

Intended outcomes of this chapter

When you've explored the ideas and suggestions in this chapter, you should be better able to:

- set terms such as 'MOOCs', 'online learning', 'open learning', 'independent learning', 'distance learning', 'blended learning', 'flexible learning' and 'e-assessment' in context;
- decide which forms of resource-based learning relate best to your students' needs (for example, print-based, computer-based, e-books, online learning, and so on);
- decide when to adopt existing materials, or adapt them to your purposes, or design new resource-based or online learning materials;
- choose good reasons for developing resource-based learning components in your teaching;
- choose an effective and efficient strategy for developing your own resource-based learning elements;
- interrogate any learning resource materials using an extensive checklist to judge how well they help your students to achieve high learning payoff.

This chapter is primarily about selecting from the wide range of learning resource materials which may be available online, in print, on CD or DVD, and deciding which could be directly relevant to your students' needs. It also suggests ways to go about the complex task of designing learning resources of your own. In particular, however, this chapter aims to arm you with a series of checklist questions to allow you to interrogate critically resource-based learning, so that you work towards achieving high learning payoff when you include resource-based learning in your curriculum.

You may wish to employ resource-based learning materials directly within your own taught course, or use them to constitute independent learning pathways for appropriate parts of your curriculum. You may also be considering implementing any forms of online, blended, open or flexible learning as provision in their own right.

Resource-based learning, in one form or another, is increasingly being used to provide learning pathways within higher education courses in universities, as well as to open up online and distance learning pathways to students outside the universities. MOOCs are just one of the many manifestations of resource-based learning, sometimes built round the particular resource of recorded web-based traditional lectures. In the UK, the amount of online learning has increased dramatically, as universities and colleges are required to cater for larger numbers of students, with increasingly diverse educational backgrounds, in an environment where communication and information technologies impact ever more greatly on all aspects of life, not least teaching and learning. I will start the chapter, however, by reviewing what is meant by some of the principal terms involved in resource-based learning, which itself has become an umbrella term for all sorts of contexts for learning. It could be argued that just about all learning is resource-based, if we include human resources in the picture.

Some terms and buzz-phrases

Several terms are used widely in connection with resource-based learning materials, reflecting the ways in which such materials are employed. Many definitions and descriptors of these terms exist, so it is worth reviewing the meanings of them.

The term *online learning* is now the most endemic descriptor, where some or all learning is done at a computer or terminal linked to the internet, or to an intranet. The term *blended learning* is often used when a combination of online learning and traditional 'taught' components are used on college campuses, training centres and so on.

MOOCs (massive open online courses) are among the most significant manifestations of online learning. These were started by the 'big players' of Harvard and MIT in the United States, who provide free access online to some lectures and learning materials, and allow peer-review of learners' assignments. A feature of many MOOCs is the very large number of learners who enrol on them, though the drop-out rates are often very high, as learners tend to get what they want from a MOOC and then discontinue. Many other institutions are now developing MOOCs, even for smaller numbers of students, sometimes offering relatively traditional assessment opportunities (at a cost) for those who want accreditation – assessment is more expensive than merely providing online resource materials. Mayes and De Freitas (2013) suggest that:

> It seems likely that many of the learners choosing to study on MOOCs are participating in the kind of lifelong learning tradition that has always provided learning for its own sake, rather than learning that leads to qualifications.
>
> (Mayes and De Freitas, 2013, p. 25)

Furthermore, Chris Pegler (2013) comments:

> There has so far been no fee for engagement in a MOOC and relatively relaxed limits on who can participate. Registered students based at institutions offering the MOOC are likely to be significantly outnumbered by open learners who have no affiliation with it. For example in late 2011, an MOOC on artificial intelligence taught by Stanford professor Sebastian Thrun was capped at 160,000 enrolments from 190 countries, while only 200 Stanford students enrolled on campus.

The exceptional class size represents not only massive scale but massive diversity of background and motivation, adding to a distinctive feel of MOOCs as separate from mainstream education. If open education aims to remove barriers to accessing learning activity, MOOCs could be viewed as a high-profile manifestation of this potential.

(Pegler, 2013, p. 152)

The term *distance learning* is often used when students study at a distance from the provider of the materials. The Open University in the UK has long been a major provider of such programmes. Though the Open University is principally located in Milton Keynes, it is unusual for students to actually go there. Most students study at home, at work, or at any other place of their own choice. The Open University provides tutor support for students, using a combination of full-time Open University staff based in various parts of the UK, and a body of part-time tutors, who are often lecturers in conventional colleges and universities. These tutors are used both to provide ongoing support for students studying with the Open University, and to assess students' coursework. Assessment is usually scheduled to submission deadlines for assignments, and students sometimes take formal examinations set by the Open University, usually taking place in examinations centres set up in other universities or colleges. Although the Open University still uses print-based learning packages (which are also widely used as learning resources by other institutions with permission – and sometimes without permission!), increasing use is being made of online provision, with tutors using email to give feedback on assessed coursework. The Open University itself is responsible for assessment standards, setting the coursework and exams, moderating the assessment by part-time tutors, and awarding qualifications to students. Similar models of distance learning are now extensively used in many parts of the world, notably Canada, Australia and New Zealand.

The term *open learning* is often used for study programmes involving distance learning, as described above. Implied in the concept of open learning is the opening up of some or all of the following aspects of freedom to students:

- when they do their learning;
- where they do their learning;
- what they learn;
- at what pace they learn.

There are further degrees of freedom that vary considerably across the range of programmes operating under the umbrella term of open learning. These include whether students:

- need any qualifications before being accepted onto an open learning programme;
- learn completely independently, or can choose to make use of tutor support;
- have any formal mentoring provision to assist them during their studies;
- can start a particular study module or course at any time ('roll-on, roll-off') or have fixed start dates and completion dates (usually dictated by examination arrangements);
- can select which parts of the programme they study, and in which (if any) of the assessed elements of the programmes they participate.

In some distance learning programmes, particularly what remains of relatively traditional correspondence courses, some or all of these choices are available to students. In others, students are constrained by set start dates and assessment dates, and by the structure of the assessments leading to the award of degrees, diplomas or certificates. The term *open learning* is therefore predominantly used to reflect the freedoms available to students regarding where, when, at what pace, and how they actually undertake their studies. There are several other terms which overlap with open and distance learning, including *independent learning, individualised learning, self-study programmes, self-managed learning,* and so on.

The term *flexible learning* can be used in connection with all of the kinds of study programme mentioned so far in this chapter. Flexibility is about when, where, at what place, and by what processes the learning takes place. The concept of flexible learning extends, however, to the inclusion of open learning, or self-study elements within a conventional college-based programme. For example, students may be attending lectures, workshops, practical sessions and tutorials on a college campus, but at the same time studying selected elements of the curriculum more or less under their own steam, usually online, using learning materials to support those parts of their work. The assessment of the flexible learning components may be entirely integrated into the overall assessment of their work, or may be done separately, or any combination of the two.

The term *resource-based learning* embraces the learning materials that are used in distance, open and flexible learning, but equally applies to the learning that is designed to occur *outside* formal lectures or classes in universities and colleges. The common factor is that part or even all of the curriculum is packaged into learning resource materials, from which students learn either individually or in small groups, with some freedom regarding when, where and how fast. The learning resources themselves are designed in many formats, including:

- online computer-based materials, with electronic communication through a local intranet and/or globally through the internet. These may include multimedia computer-based learning materials, including video extracts, audio commentaries, and so on;
- traditional textbooks, journal articles, and so on, often supplied electronically, addressed by interactive *study guides*;
- print-based interactive learning packages can still be used when appropriate.

Pause for thought: choosing a curriculum area for resource-based learning
Imagine that you are planning to turn a particular element of your teaching into resource-based learning mode. Think through your answers to the questions which follow.
1. Why would you choose this particular curriculum area for resource-based learning?
2. Which intended learning outcomes, in particular, lend themselves to resource-based learning?
3. What will be the main benefits to your students of having this area as a resource-based learning element?
4. What will be the benefits to *you* of delivering this particular area in a resource-based learning mode?
5. What have you got already? Which particular resources may you draw upon, to turn an element of your teaching into a resource-based learning element? This could include existing handouts, printed materials, textbook references, and other learning materials which you think could be useful components of a resource-based learning element.
6. What may you need to design yourself?
7. How would you go about starting to design learning resources yourself?

This chapter should provide ideas to help you go about addressing any or all of these questions.

What are the main components of resource-based learning materials?

The principal components of learning materials vary considerably, depending whether the materials are online, computer-based, multimedia, or print-based, and on whether the materials are designed to be self-sufficient learning resources, or to refer out to existing books, papers and articles, or to be used in conjunction with face-to-face learning situations such as lectures, tutorials or practical sessions. However, it is possible to identify some elements which characterise modern resource-based learning materials, and which differentiate them from more traditional forms of print-based resources such as 'straight' textbooks. These elements include:

- statements of the intended learning outcomes, linked to descriptors of the evidence of achievement of these outcomes, which in turn link to assessment criteria;
- elements of subject content. These can be links to extracts from books and articles, but also may be podcast lecture episodes, debates, discussions, demonstrations, wikis, and so on. Just about any kind of content can be used in the context of resource-based learning;
- a tone and style which is often much more user-friendly and informal than in conventional published books and articles;
- structured learning-by-doing elements such as self-assessment questions, tasks, exercises, quizzes, and so on;
- feedback responses on-screen, using audio or video, or in print, to the structured learning-by-doing elements;
- open-ended learning-by-doing activities, such as assignments, exercises, readings and practical tasks, to help students to consolidate the learning they are doing from the materials;
- tutor-marked assignments, online or submitted on paper, often with details of the marking schemes and assessment criteria.

There may additionally be some of the following components:

- guidance regarding prerequisite knowledge or skills, to help students to judge for themselves whether they are equipped to start work with the learning materials;
- study-guide briefings linking to other materials, such as particular sections or chapters of books, journal articles, and so on, often coupled with tasks for students to do while using these resources;
- pre-prepared feedback discussions on tasks which students have undertaken with learning resource materials;
- in the *blended* learning context, links to face-to-face elements of college-based courses, such as lectures, tutorial programmes, and so on;
- study-skills commentaries, to help students undertake their own study of the materials as effectively and efficiently as possible.

In well-designed resource-based learning materials, the content itself is broken up into manageable chunks by the interactive elements. It is important that the content is not simply presented in the same way as in a traditional textbook, but is punctuated by learning-by-doing and feedback episodes, and that this is done frequently throughout the materials rather than merely at the end of an element of learning. Tutor-marked assignments may be used when it is necessary to link students' work on resource-based learning materials into the assessment scheme of a whole course or module, with the purposes being formative, summative or both. There may also be formal exams, online exams, or some exam questions in a wider traditional exam which covers the whole of the syllabus of which part is delivered by resource-based learning, to represent the summative assessment of the syllabus area addressed by the materials.

Adopt, adapt, or start from scratch?

A vast range of resource-based learning elements already exists, particularly online in MOOCs, TED talks, and on websites, spanning all levels of study from introductory to postgraduate. Many online resources are free, and others can be purchased from publishers and commercial materials providers, and accessed or downloaded online. Many learning materials have also been developed in-house in particular university departments, or by specialist producers, and it is often possible to come to site-licence arrangements with the producers to purchase them with the view to adopting them as they stand, or to adapting them to fit a particular course or programme. The following checklist may help you to decide whether to adopt such packages, adapt them, or whether you may need to develop some completely new materials for your students.

- *Are relevant free materials already available?* It is worth searching online, and asking around on discussion lists, and social media.
- *Are recommended, tried and tested materials available for purchase or site-licence?* Others teaching in your discipline may know about these, and library staff can be very well informed about such possibilities.
- *Are the intended learning outcomes of available materials sufficiently close to those of your course?* When the learning outcomes converge well, it is an indicator that it may be possible to use at least parts of the materials as they stand.
- *Will the 'not-invented-here' syndrome come into play?* When learning materials are brought in from external sources, it is sometimes the case that lecturers (or students) do not feel that the materials are as credible as in-house materials or programmes; any dissatisfaction that lecturers may feel with the materials is quickly passed on to students, damaging in turn the students' trust in the materials, and their confidence in the processes of learning from resources.
- *Have you time to develop entirely new materials?* The short answer to this is very likely to be 'no!', but some of the ideas in this chapter may help you to see that where necessary, materials can indeed be developed step by step, and that you may already have quite a lot to start from.

What do you have that you can adapt?

Lecturers usually have a wide range of materials that can be adapted for use in online, open, blended or independent learning scenarios. The materials you already have available may include:

- your existing syllabus specification, including identified learning outcomes;
- your own lecture materials;
- presentation materials you already use;
- handout materials you already provide online or issue directly;
- tasks and exercises you already set your students;
- assignment briefings;
- model answers;
- selections of good, bad and indifferent work by past students (with their permission);

- case-study materials;
- test and exam questions.

In addition to some of these, you may already have some even more important things to draw on, including your own experience of:

- teaching the subject involved;
- addressing students' problems with the subject;
- designing additional resources to help students with particular problems;
- assessing students' learning in the subject.

Many learning resource materials available externally are produced by people who may know the subject involved, but who may lack some of the vital experience regarding teaching, learning and assessing the subject. Not surprisingly, materials that are developed by writers or designers who are not involved directly in teaching a subject rarely work nearly as well as those developed by those with experience of teaching, supporting learning, and assessing students' achievement.

A strategy for designing resource-based learning materials

The following ideas are adapted from a strategy I developed in *500 Tips on Open and Online Learning* (Race, 2005b).

1 **Start by anticipating the evidence of achievement which you intend learners to reach.** At a time when there is such a richness of information available to students, it is important that they themselves know what their targets are to be, and equally important for us to know what exactly we should need to measure in due course in assessment contexts.

2 **With the evidence of achievement firmly in mind, draft the intended learning outcomes.** Express these in a clear, friendly, jargon-free way. It is best to do this by avoiding formal language such as 'the intended outcomes are that students will demonstrate their understanding of ...', but by addressing the outcomes directly to the students who will use the materials. For example, it is useful to use wording along the lines of: 'When you've worked through Section 6 of this package, you'll be able to:
   - explain why ...;
   - list five factors which influence ...;
   - predict when ... is most likely to occur;
   - design a process to enable ... .'
The main aim should be that students will know exactly what they are intended to be able to do when they will have completed their work on each flexible learning element. It is important to avoid words such as 'understand' or 'know', as these don't give students enough detail regarding how they could be expected or required to *demonstrate* their understanding or knowledge.

3 **Think of tasks, activities and exercises which will give students learning-by-doing experience.** Try not to simply use tasks which require students to recall things they have just learned, but rather use tasks which help them to extend and build on their learning as they work through the resource-based learning materials. It is better to draft out twenty tasks, then to use only three in the materials, than to try to make each task good enough at the outset to include in the materials.

4 **Decide which of the tasks you can already** *respond* **to.** For example, if you have thought of a multiple-choice question, you can probably respond separately to students choosing each of the options. A congratulatory response may be appropriate for students who choose the best option (often referred to as the 'key').

More importantly, for each of the other options (the 'distractors') you can probably respond with a direct message to students who make the mistakes or misunderstandings which may have led them to choose any of these distractors. The tasks where you can respond in print (or on-screen in computer-based packages) are the basis of structured self-assessment questions.

5 **Decide which tasks you can't directly respond to.** These could be the tasks where the human judgement of a lecturer or tutor may be necessary to work out what help students may need, or where students will need detailed feedback on what they have done well and on what they may have missed. These tasks may well be best as tutor-marked assignment questions, whether used online or with face-to-face contact where available.

6 **Compose draft feedback responses to the self-assessment tasks.** You will almost certainly want to edit and polish these responses when you have feedback from students on your first run of the learning materials, but it is well worth composing these responses in some detail if necessary before putting together the whole of an element of material.

7 **Link together self-assessment questions and feedback responses.** Check that your feedback responses address as many as possible of the problems which students may have when they attempt the questions.

8 **Link each feedback response forward to the next self-assessment question.** To move students on from your response to one particular self-assessment question, to be ready to attempt the next one, you will usually need to introduce some new ideas or information.

This is an element of the content of your resource-based learning materials, but is best kept concise and relevant, so that it specifically serves to bridge only the gap between that response and the next question. Where the content to be introduced is already available online, you might need to add guidance about which are the important parts, saving learners from spending too long with any content which does not directly relate to the evidence of achievement which they need to become able to show for their learning.

9 **Try out the self-assessment questions and feedback responses with 'live' students.** There is no quicker way of finding out whether the questions and responses will work well, than to use them as class-based exercises in lectures or tutorials, and find out how students react to them. This helps you to select those questions which will work effectively in resource-based learning materials, and to adjust and improve the wording of those which can be made to work with a little attention, and to discard those questions where it may not be straightforward to devise self-sufficient feedback responses.

10 **Develop the tutor-marked assessment components (if you are using such components).** It could be useful here to devise marking schemes, aiming to make it possible for *any* lecturer to mark students' work on these components. Ultimately, you may be able to develop the marking schemes sufficiently that you could get students to self-assess their own work (if you are not needing such assessment data as part of their coursework profiles).

Although the above steps are listed as a sequence, it is best to work on them iteratively, working on one facet of the learning package, then adjusting others to tune them in to what you have done. For example, you can fine-tune your developing learning materials by:

- adjusting learning outcomes to match the evidence of achievement students will need to become able to show, and adjusting the actual self-assessment questions that you devise;
- further adjusting self-assessment questions when you've tried to compose responses to them;
- adjusting the lead-in sections preceding self-assessment tasks when you've seen how the tasks work in practice;

- adjusting the feedback to self-assessment questions when you've seen how the questions work with some live students in a lecture or tutorial;
- developing the tutor-marked components when you see how students are getting on with the self-assessment elements;

and so on.

There is no substitute for student feedback as an aid to developing effective flexible learning materials. However, in the next section of this chapter, I present a checklist which you can use as you write your own materials, but which you can also use to help you to gauge the quality of existing published materials.

The suggestions I offered above relate to designing the learning into learning materials, rather than the technological design of the resource materials. In *Rethinking Pedagogy for a Digital Age* edited by Helen Beetham and Rhona Sharpe (2013), Helen Beetham ends her chapter 'Designing for learning in an uncertain future', by stressing how design for learning needs to link well to different disciplines' cultures, and be based on dialogue, expertise and experience, as follows:

- Design for learning is a skilled practice, rooted in the culture of different subject areas, which involves the capacity to translate educational principles into practical learning tasks, and the confidence to be creative with digital technologies.
- Teachers and learners need access to good examples of design practice, with the appropriate contextual information to appraise and repurpose them.
- Designers need to engage in dialogue – with learners and other designers – about the educational principles that underpin their practice and how best to translate these principles into learning opportunities.
- Educators need a degree of autonomy to design for specific cohorts of learners and to experiment and innovate in their practice.
- The expertise involved in teaching, whether deployed in the design process or in supporting learners to encounter existing designs, must be rewarded and recognised if the profession is to meet the changing needs of learners.

(Beetham, 2013, p. 278)

A quality checklist for resource-based learning materials and processes

When selecting learning resource materials from the plethora which may be on offer, it is useful to know what questions to ask to ensure that they will serve their purpose well. Even more important, when designing new learning resource materials of your own, or adapting those which are already available, it is important to have in mind at all times the ways that the materials are intended to function, and how students will react to them. In the sections that follow, I have identified an extended series of questions to pose, and some clarifications or suggestions arising from many of the questions. Most of the questions can be applied to all the interactive learning material formats, from print-based flexible learning packages to the various forms of online, web-based and computer-based learning formats (adapted from Race, 2005b). There are currently 67 questions in this checklist, and the number grows every time I revisit it.

This checklist is intended to be an interrogation device for elements of resource-based learning, and you may wish to photocopy the pages which follow, so you can write your 'yes', 'no', 'not applicable' or 'not yet' responses to each of the main questions alongside, and action-planning notes for things you might wish to address to ensure that your learning resource materials work well for students and for others involved. For your convenience, I've divided the questions using the following broad headings:

- Intended learning outcomes;
- Structure, and learning design;
- Learning-by-doing – practice, repetition, trial and error;
- In-built structured feedback to students;
- Context and flow: introductions, summaries and reviews;
- The subject matter itself;
- Visual learning – diagrams, charts, pictures, tables, and so on;
- Some further checklist questions.

Note that the shortest section of this checklist is 'the subject matter itself', as normally this is already well addressed in practice, and it is the *other* dimensions of the checklist that can help to identify things that need to be sorted out in any bid to cause effective learning to result from the use of learning resource materials. Also, despite the grouping under these headings, all of these aspects need to be addressed concurrently in practice, and decisions arising from any one question may well affect what you do regarding other questions in this long list.

Intended learning outcomes

1 **Is there a clear indication of any prerequisite knowledge or skills?** If not, you may usefully compose a specification of what is being taken for granted regarding the starting point of the materials. It is particularly important that when flexible learning elements are being used within college-based traditional courses, students should know where the related learning outcomes fit in to the overall picture of their courses.

2 **Do the intended learning outcomes link firmly to the evidence of achievement you wish students to work towards?** Life is too short to include intended outcomes which are peripheral to the main purposes of the element of study involved, as this might 'dilute' students' efforts, and distract them away from what they really need to be focusing upon.

3 **Are the intended learning outcomes stated clearly and unambiguously?** This is where you may wish to 'translate' the stated intended outcomes of particular learning packages, making them more directly relevant to the students who will use them. This can often be done by adding 'for example, …' illustrations showing how and when the intended outcomes will be relevant to their own situations.

4 **Are the intended outcomes presented in a meaningful and friendly way?** (i.e. *not* 'the expected learning outcomes of this module are that the student will …'!). I suggest that it is preferable to write learning outcomes using language such as 'When you've worked through Section 3, you'll be able to …'. It is important that students develop a sense of ownership of the intended learning outcomes, and it is worthwhile making sure that the outcomes as presented to them make them feel involved, and that the expressed outcomes don't just belong to the learning package or module.

5 **Are the intended learning outcomes relevant to your students' needs?** If you're designing materials of your own, such relevance can be under your control. With adopted or published materials, however, it is usual that only *some* of the intended outcomes are directly relevant, and you will need to

spell out to your students exactly which these are, along with advice about whether or not they should spend time on other parts of the materials where the intended outcomes are not directly useful to them.

6 **Do the intended learning outcomes avoid jargon which may not be known to students before starting the material?** It is of course normal for new terms and concepts to be introduced in any kind of learning, but it is best if this is done in ways that avoid frightening off students at the outset. It may remain necessary to include unfamiliar words in the intended outcomes of a learning package, but this can still allow for such words to be explained there and then, legitimising a starting point of 'not yet knowing' such words. Adding a few words in brackets along the lines of '(this means in practice that …)' can be a useful way ahead in such cases.

Structure, and learning design

7 **Is it really *learning* material?** In other words, is it avoiding just being information? Especially in the case of online learning, the danger of just presenting screen after screen of information needs to be avoided. The most common – and most severe – criticism of many online learning materials is that 'it's just an online book!'

8 **How well does the material cater for different learning preferences?** For example, does it range from text, illustrations and use of other media when appropriate? If it's online or computer-based, is it possible to print out appropriate parts easily for students who prefer to study things on paper, or to retain key parts for study offline?

9 **Do the various components provide a complete and effective learning environment?** For example, in online learning situations, are there paper-based materials to work with alongside the on-screen components? Are there suitable opportunities for communication with other students and with tutors, face-to-face or virtually? Are there opportunities for students to receive ongoing feedback on their progress?

10 **Is the material visually attractive, thereby helping students to want to learn from it?** If materials don't *look* good, students' confidence in using them may be compromised. It is however not always possible to choose the materials that *look* best. Sometimes the best-looking materials may be too expensive, or they may not be sufficiently relevant to

learning needs. At the end of the day, it is the materials that *work* best that are cost-effective, so compromises may have to be made on visual attractiveness.

11 **Is the material designed to minimise difficulties for students with disabilities?** In the UK, for example, disabilities legislation requires that 'reasonable adjustments' are built-in to educational provision, in an anticipatory manner. There is a lot of help available on how best to do this, for example TechDis in the UK (see www.techdis.ac.uk) provides a great deal of information and advice on how best to make on-screen learning materials address and cater for a range of disabilities.

12 **Does the material allow differentiation?** In other words, can the material be equally useful to high-fliers who already know a lot about the subject concerned, and to low-fliers who are quite new to the subject? Does it prevent the low-fliers from feeling inferior? Are there suitable pathways through the material for students of different ability or motivation, allowing all to feel they are getting something useful from the material in a given time?

13 **In print-based materials, is there sufficient white space?** In such materials this is needed for students to write their own notes, answer questions posed by the materials, do calculations and exercises which help them make sense of the ideas they have been reading about, and so on. A learning package which allows – or insists on – students writing all over

it, is likely to be more effective at promoting effective learning-by-doing.

14 **In online or computer-based materials, is there plenty of activity?** Students need to be able to practise, try things out, make mistakes, and get feedback from the materials. Their learning is much more linked to what they *do* while working through the materials than merely to what they see on-screen.

15 **In online materials, will students' activity be suitably 'captured'?** With print-based materials this isn't a problem, as students can look again at their attempts at activities and tasks, but with online material, there may not be any record of exactly what they did with such tasks.

16 **Is it easy for students to find their way backwards and forwards?** Can they navigate their way through the materials? This is sometimes called 'signposting' and includes good use of headings in print-based materials, or effective menus in on-screen materials and online learning delivered through virtual learning environments. Either way, well-signposted materials allow students to get quickly to anything they want to consolidate, as well as helping them to scan ahead to get the feel of what's to come.

17 **Can students bookmark things and return to them at will later?** With print-based materials this is easy enough – many students use highlighter pens to remind them of important or tricky bits, or stick post-it notes to pages so they can find them again quickly. Equivalent processes are perfectly possible to arrange in electronic packages.

18 **Is the material broken into manageable chunks?** Students' concentration spans are finite – and shorter in the digital age where social media tend to fragment concentration so often when students are studying on their own. We all know how fickle concentration is at face-to-face training sessions. The same applies when students are learning from resource materials. If an important topic goes on for page after page, or screen after screen, we should not be surprised if concentration is lost. Frequent headings, subheadings, tasks and activities can all help to avoid students falling into a state of limbo when working through learning packages.

19 **Does the material avoid any sudden jumps in level?** A sudden jump can cause 'shut-the-package' or 'log off from the machine' cues to students working on their own. It is just about impossible for authors of learning materials to tell when they have gone one step too far too fast. The first people to discover such sudden jumps are always the students who can't understand why the material has suddenly left them floundering. In well-piloted materials, such difficulties will have been ironed out long before the packages reach their published forms, but too many materials have not allowed for this vital process to happen.

Learning-by-doing – practice, repetition, trial and error

20 **Are there plenty of things for students to *do*?** For example, I suggest that there should be something to do in sight on each double-page spread in print-based materials, or something to do on most screens in online learning materials, before gaining access to the next screen. If we accept that learning mostly happens by practising, making decisions, or having a go at exercises, it is only natural that effective interactive learning materials are essentially packaged-up learning-by-doing.

21 **Is the material encouraging deep learning rather than surface learning?** The key to this is the extent to which students are helped to make sense of what they are doing when they try tasks or answer questions, linking in turn to how relevant the tasks are to the intended evidence of achievement which is the basis of the learning materials. It is therefore important

that students are helped to stop and reflect on their attempts rather than simply press on with further learning-by-doing, except where the activity is primarily designed for practice and repetition.

22 **Is good use made of self-assessment opportunities?** It is important that much of the learning-by-doing leads on to feedback, allowing students to self-assess how well they have answered the questions or attempted the various tasks as they learn. This means that in the best learning materials, the tasks, questions and exercises need to be structured, so that feedback *can* be given to whatever students are likely to do with them.

23 **Are the tasks clear and unambiguous?** In live sessions, if a task isn't clear to students, someone will ask about it, or you'll notice puzzled looks on faces, and clarification will follow. With packaged learning resources, it is crucial to make sure that people working on their own do not have to waste time and energy working out exactly what the instructions mean every time they come to some learning-by-doing. Shortening the sentence length of questions and activities can often make a huge difference to how well students get their heads around the meanings of the tasks.

24 **Are the questions and tasks inviting?** Is it clear to students that it's valuable for them to have a go rather than skip the tasks or activities? In particular with online materials, it is very tempting just to 'click onwards' rather than stop to think about something. It is sometimes an art to make tasks so interesting that no one is tempted to give them a miss, especially if they are quite difficult ones. However, it helps if you can make the tasks as relevant as possible to students' own backgrounds and experiences.

25 **Are the tasks sufficiently important?** Learning-by-doing should not be there simply for its own sake. There should be at least some useful learning payoff associated with each task students attempt. An exception can be when the odd task is included for entertainment rather than for learning – which can be useful when done appropriately.

26 **Is the comfort of privacy used well?** One of the strongest advantages of open learning – whether online or on paper – is that people can be free to learn by trial and error, without the embarrassment of someone like a tutor seeing their mistakes. Self-assessment tasks can allow students to find out whether or not they have mastered something, and gain feedback about how their learning is progressing.

27 **What about students who know they can already do the tasks easily?** If such students are forced to work through tasks they can already achieve perfectly well, they can get bored and frustrated. In print-based materials students will choose to skip these tasks, but in some computer-based materials they can't move on till they have done each task and can find this tedious. It is of course possible to avoid this situation by having diagnostic exercises which allow students who have already mastered something to move further on into the materials without going through all the tasks designed for their counterparts who need them.

28 **In print-based materials, is there enough space for students to write their answers?** In such materials, it is important to get students writing. If they just *think* about writing something, but don't *do* it, they may well forget what they might have written!

29 **In on-screen materials, will students be caused to put fingers to keyboard, or use the mouse?** It is important to ensure that students continue to make decisions, for example by choosing an option in a multiple-choice exercise, so that they can then receive feedback directly relating to what they have just done. Online learning-by-doing can also make good use of drag-and-drop, text entry, number entry, and a wide range of activities with much higher learning payoff than simply moving on to the next screen.

30 **Cumulatively, does the learning-by-doing relate well to students' evidence of achievement of the intended outcomes?** Perhaps one of the most significant dangers of resource-based learning materials is that it is often easier to

design tasks and exercises on unimportant topics, than it is to ensure that students' activities focus on the things that are involved in them achieving the intended learning outcomes. To eliminate this danger, it is useful to check that each and every intended learning outcome is cross-linked to one or more self-assessment questions or activities, so that students get practice in everything that is important.

In-built structured feedback to students

32 **To what extent is feedback to students immediate?** One of the advantages of online learning or computer-based learning packages is that immediate on-screen feedback can appear every time students make a decision, or select an option, or enter a number, and so on. Even in print-based materials, responses to questions and activities can be included elsewhere in the materials (out of sight of the tasks themselves) so that students can quickly check up on whether they were successful when they attempted the tasks.

33 **Does feedback really *respond* to what students have done?** For example, when they have had a go at a self-assessment question, does the feedback they receive give them more than just the correct answer to the question? If students don't give the correct answer to a question, telling them the right answer is of very limited value; students need feedback on what was wrong with their own attempt at answering the question. In open learning materials of all forms, feedback needs to be available to students in predetermined ways, on-screen or in print.

34 **Does the feedback remind students of exactly what they actually did?** Ideally, the original task, question or activity should still be in sight while students view the feedback to what they did with it. With print-based materials, this can be done by reprinting the tasks or questions wherever the feedback responses are located. With on-screen materials, it is best that the task or question – and the choice or decision students made –

31 **Does the learning-by-doing prepare students for future assessment?** When students have worked diligently through an element of resource-based learning, the learning-by-doing they have engaged in should collectively prepare them for any assessments that they are heading towards – whether it be tutor-marked assignments, exams, practical tests, and so on.

remains visible on screen when the feedback responses appear.

35 **Do the feedback responses meet each student's need to find out *'Was I right?'*, *'If not, why not?'*** When students get a self-assessment question or activity right, it is quite straightforward to provide them with appropriate feedback. It's when they get them wrong that they need all the help we can give them. In particular, they need not only to know what the correct answer should have been, but also what was wrong with their own answers. Multiple-choice question formats are particularly useful here, as they allow different students making different mistakes each to receive individual feedback on their own attempts at such questions.

36 **Do feedback responses provide appropriate praise without patronising students?** It's easy enough to start a response on-screen or in print with words such as 'well done'. However, there are many different ways of affirming, and saying 'splendid' may be fine if the task was difficult and we really want to praise students who got it right, but the same 'splendid' can come across as patronising if students felt that it was an easy question. In such cases 'yes indeed' or 'correct' may be more appropriate starting points for confirmatory feedback.

37 **Do feedback responses include something that will help students who got things wrong *not* to feel like complete idiots?** One of the problems of working alone with resource-based learning materials is that

people who get things wrong may feel they arc thc only people ever to have made such mistakes! When a difficult question or task is likely to cause students to make mistakes or to pick incorrect options, it helps them a lot if there are some words of comfort, such as 'this was a tough one!' or 'most people get this wrong at first'.

Context and flow: introductions, summaries and reviews

38 **Is each part introduced in an interesting, stimulating way?** The first few pages of print-based material, and the first screen or two of on-screen material, are critical. There's no second chance to make a good first impression! If students are put off a topic by the way it starts, they may never recover that 'want' to learn it.

39 **Do introductions inspire confidence?** Attitudes are set early in any learning experience. Confidence is perhaps the single most important pre-determinant of success. When students start something feeling that they can indeed succeed, they are much more likely to continue to be motivated even when the material becomes more testing.

40 **Do the introductions alert students to the way the materials are designed to work?** Learning resource materials should not assume that all students have developed the kinds of study-skills needed for resource-based learning – particularly where students are taking responsibility for their own learning. Authors of materials need to share with students the way that they intend the optimum learning payoff to be achieved. When students know *how* they are intended to be learning, there's more chance they'll use suitable approaches.

41 **Are students able to get stuck into the learning quickly?** Despite what's said above about the need to help students to see how the materials are intended to be used, most students want to get straight into actually *doing* something. With print-based materials, introductory study-skills guidance presented at the start can easily be skipped then returned to later, but in on-screen materials it is important not to trap students in such introductions when some of them will be wanting to cut to the chase of the materials.

42 **Are there clear and useful summaries or reviews?** Do these help students to make sense of and consolidate what they have learned? In any good face-to-face session, lecturers take care to cover the main points more than once, and to remind students towards the end of the session about the most important things they should remember. When designing learning resource materials, authors sometimes mistakenly think that it's enough to put across the main points well – and only once! Summaries and reviews are every bit as essential in good learning materials as they are in live sessions.

43 **Do summaries and reviews provide useful ways for students to revise the material quickly and effectively?** A summary or review helps students to identify the essential learning points they should have mastered. Once they have done this, it should not take much to help them retain such mastery, and they may well not need to work through the whole package ever again if they can polish their grasp of the subject just by reading summaries or reviews.

44 **Can summaries provide a fast-track function for high-fliers?** Those students who already have achieved particular intended learning outcomes may only need to remind themselves of those elements of knowledge, rather than work through tasks and exercises they can already achieve. Summaries can be particularly useful to them to check out what they can already do, and move on quickly to parts of the material which will deliver further learning payoff to them.

The subject matter itself

45 **Is it correct?** The best-designed learning materials will be useless if there is anything seriously wrong with the subject matter itself. While it may be perfectly acceptable that the material may be presented in a different way than you may have chosen to use yourself, it is useful to check out that there is nothing that would be mis-learned from the materials.

46 **Is the material readable, fluent and unambiguous?** When students are working on their own, there is no one for them to ask when something is not clear, though virtual communication to a tutor, for example, can compensate for this in online materials. Good learning resource materials depend a lot on the messages getting across. Those people who never use a short word when they can think of a longer alternative, should not be allowed to create learning resource materials! Similarly, short sentences tend to get messages across more effectively than long sentences, particularly on-screen.

47 **Is the material relevant?** For example, does the content of the material keep closely to the intended learning outcomes as stated? It can be all too easy for the creators of learning resource materials to get carried away with their pet subjects, and go into far more detail than is reasonable. This is fine so long as students *know* that they're looking at an optional extra at the time, and can skip it if they wish.

48 **Is the tone 'involving' where possible?** In task briefings and feedback in particular, is there plenty of use of 'you' for the student, 'I' for the author, 'we' for the student and author together? This is a matter of style. Some writers find it hard to communicate in an informal, friendly manner – it is quite different from the style they might use to write journal articles or scholarly texts. There is plenty of evidence that communication works best in learning materials when students feel involved, and when they feel that the learning package is 'talking' to them on the page – or on the screen – in a natural and relaxed way. Of course, where video elements include real talking, this can add to the feeling of involvement.

Visual learning – diagrams, charts, pictures, tables, and so on

49 **Is each non-text component as self-explanatory as possible?** In face-to-face training sessions, students gain all sorts of clues as to what any illustrations (for example on slides) actually mean. The lecturer's tone of voice and facial expressions do much to add to the explanation, as well as the words they use when explaining directly. With learning packages, it is important that such explanation is provided when necessary in print or on-screen.

50 **Do the students know what to do with each illustration?** They need to know whether they need to learn it, label or complete it, to note it in passing, or to pick out the trend, or even nothing at all. In a face-to-face session, when lecturers show (for example) a table of data, someone is likely to ask, 'Do we have to remember these figures?' If the same table of data is included in learning materials, the same question still applies, but there is no one to reply to it. Therefore, good learning resource materials need to anticipate all such questions, and clarify to students exactly what the expectations are regarding diagrams, charts, and so on. It only takes a few words of explanation to do this, along such lines as, 'you don't have to remember these figures, but you do need to be able to pick out the main trend' or 'you don't have to be able to draw one of these, but you need to be able to recognise one when you see one'.

51 **Is it possible to continue to see an illustration, while learning more about what it means?** In print-based materials it helps if explanations are placed while the figure relating to them is

still in sight. With on-screen explanations, it can be useful to continue to show the appropriate figure as a 'thumbnail', so that students still remember what they're making sense of during discussion or explanations. It is then also useful if they can (for example) double-click the illustration on-screen to restore it to its full size while they think again about it at any point.

52 **Is the material sufficiently illustrated?** A sketch can be more useful than 1,000 words. One of the problem areas with some learning materials is that they're written all in words, at the expense of visual ways of communicating important messages. On-screen materials are usually better in this respect, not least because of the relative ease of including pictures and illustrations. However, sometimes they are badly chosen, and small print on the illustrations may not be readable on-screen.

53 **With online materials, will it work on a mobile phone or small tablet?** While many learners may be using laptops or desktop computers with fairly large screen displays, the tendency now is to wish to do at least some studying on the move using mobile devices. Some topics will be quite impossible to adapt to very small screen displays, but others may allow at least parts of materials to be readable on such devices.

Some further checklist questions

54 **Does the material ensure that the average student will achieve the intended learning outcomes?** This of course is one of the most important questions we can ask of any learning element. If the answer is 'no!', it's probably worth looking for a better package.

55 **Will most students be able to work through the material in a reasonable time?** Some things take longer when working under one's own steam – others are quicker that way. It is useful to have a good idea how long it will take on average for students to work through each element of a learning sequence, but to recognise and accept that some will take much longer, and some much less time.

56 **Will the average student *enjoy* using the material?** In some ways this is the ultimate question. When students 'can't bring themselves to log off from the programme on the computer' or 'can't put the package down because it is so interesting to work through it', there's not usually much wrong with the learning materials.

57 **How up to date is the material covered?** How quickly will it date? Will it have an adequate shelf-life as a learning resource, and will the upfront costs of purchasing it or developing it be justified? At a time when digital resources online can advance so fast, and even unpredictably, this question becomes even more important.

58 **Who will do updating when necessary?** With online and computer-based materials, updating can be done quite easily by whoever designed the material, but not necessarily easily by other people using the materials. With print-based materials, updating is likely to involve revising and reprinting elements, but it may be possible to prepare supplementary sheets and handouts to bridge gaps in the short term.

59 **How significant is the 'not invented here' syndrome?** Can you work with the differences between the approach used in the material and your own approach? Can you integrate comfortably and seamlessly the two approaches with your students? If you criticise or put down learning resource materials your students are using, you're quite likely to destroy their confidence in using the material, along with their trust in the credibility of the content of the material as a whole.

60 **Will it be cost-effective?** For example, with physical packages, can students realistically be expected to acquire their own copies? Can bulk discounts or shareware arrangements be made? If the material is computer-based, are the numbers of students involved sufficient to justify the costs of making the material available

to them? Is it suitable for networking, and is this allowed within copyright arrangements?

61 **Can students gain sufficient access to the materials?** This is particularly crucial when large groups are involved. Could lack of access to essential resource materials be cited as grounds for appeal by students who may be unsuccessful when assessed on what is covered by the material? This particularly applies to online or computer-based learning, where students may have to be in particular places to work through the materials, for example at networked terminals in a learning resource centre, or on wifi -nabled laptops. Are part-time students disproportionately disadvantaged in terms of access to equipment?

62 **How best can students integrate the learning payoff they derive from the materials into their overall learning experience?** Does the learning associated with the materials link comfortably to *other* learning formats and situations – for example group work, lectures, work-based learning, and so on? How best will appropriate elements of their learning from the learning materials be further developed and consolidated in other learning situations?

63 **How is the material or medium demonstrably better than the cheapest, or simplest, way of learning the topic?** How does the material make full use of the benefits of flexible learning? Does it really exploit the freedoms which flexible learning can offer?

64 **Will it make learning more efficient?** How will it save students time, or how will it focus their learning more constructively? How will it cause their learning to be deeper and more meaningful?

65 **How suitable will the material be for a range of students?** Will it minimise instances of disadvantaging (for example) people learning in a second language, women students, mature students, technophobic students, and so on? Will it be equally possible for high-fliers and low-fliers to make use of it at their own speeds? Will students who already know a lot about it be able to skip the parts they don't need?

66 **What *additional* outcomes will students derive from using the material?** In other words, what are the *emergent* learning outcomes? For example, will the material help students to develop important key skills alongside learning the subject? For example, will they develop keyboarding skills and computer literacy? Will they develop information tracking and retrieval skills? Will they develop their learning skills in new directions? Are these outcomes assessed? Should they be assessed or not? Could some of these outcomes outweigh the *intended* learning outcomes?

67 **How best will feedback on the effectiveness of the resource material be sought?** What part should be played by peer feedback from colleagues, feedback from student questionnaires, online feedback, observations of students' reactions to the material, and the assessment of students' evidence of achievement of the intended learning outcomes?

Learning from computer screens

Resource-based learning is increasingly dominated by computer-based learning packages, and online learning through intranets and the internet. In all of these contexts, we need to explore how 'learning from screens' is likely to take place effectively. We are relatively accustomed to interrogating 'learning from paper' in the contexts of handouts, books, articles, and so on, even when it is well known that unless there is substantial learning-by-doing and feedback, the learning payoff from paper can be all too minimal. We also know that learning from 'sight and sound of lecturers' can be effective – or not! This section of this chapter looks critically at 'learning from screens', and particularly at some of the questions which can be in students' minds as they confront any particular screenful of a computer-based learning package, or online sequence.

Perhaps the most important indicator that learning from screens is *not* happening successfully is if the student at the keyboard looks for the 'print' command. In short, if someone learning from a computer-based package needs to print something, it is a signal that it was not possible to do everything that may have been intended with it on-screen.

Now in the digital age where the very same screens may easily be used for social media and all sorts of other stimuli, there can be a problem when prompts that there are unread messages on Twitter, Facebook, and ordinary email awaiting, and it can be all too easy to leave an online learning sequence to attend to such messages, sometimes never to return. It can be argued that the ever-increasing plethora of digital stimuli can cause fragmentation of thinking, and may work against integrating learning well.

Some advantages of screens over paper

- *There can be instant feedback on-screen to pre-planned decision-making.* For example, choosing an option in a screen-based multiple-choice question can lead to immediate feedback on whether it was the best option to select, and (more importantly), 'if not, why not?'
- *Feedback can be withheld on-screen until some learning-by-doing has happened.* For example, the feedback to a selection in a multiple-choice question can be withheld in computer-based learning until students have made their choices. In print-based materials, it can be all too tempting to check out the feedback responses before having made a firm choice.
- *Computers can add sound to on-screen feedback.* Where students can use headphones, for example, the benefits of tone-of-voice can be exploited in feedback responses to students' keyboard choices.
- *Computers can also add talking heads when useful.* Sometimes, facial expression and body language can add significantly to explanations. However, if there are limitations with available technology (bandwidth, speeds and so on) it is better to have sound-only and a well-recorded voice than a jerky or blurry talking head.
- *Computers can route students on to what they need next.* For example, if students have succeeded in several on-screen questions, they can be moved on to something which may be more challenging to them (some harder questions), or if they are struggling with the on-screen tasks they can be moved back to some further practice questions.
- *Computer screens are less likely to cause information overload.* Paper, whether in books, articles, or even handouts, tends to get filled up with print. Publishers of books, journals, magazines and newspapers like to fill each page quite full. Only some of the bolder advertisers use (and pay for) 'white space'. The limit of screen size causes at least some economy of information presentation. However, this advantage can only too easily be thrown away by congested screens of information, especially when what is designed to appear on-screen is too closely linked to what might have otherwise been presented on paper.

Some disadvantages of screens compared with paper

- *'Now you see it, now it's gone!'* Visual memory tends to be relatively transient. If something important is on-screen, there is every chance it will evaporate from students' minds after a few more screens of information.
- *Screens are less successful at showing 'the big picture'.* For example, how a particular element of learning links to the wider context can be hard to demonstrate, as screens tend to show a tiny bit at a time, and even when an overall picture, map or flow diagram is used

on-screen to try to show the big picture, users usually skip on until they can find something they can interact with.

- *It can be hard to work out* which *screenfuls are really important.* One screenful may look much like the one before and the next one, but learners may not be aware of those where they really need to slow down and ponder. On paper, the use of headings can make it clearer where to slow down.
- *Screens can't be used anywhere.* Learning from screens is dependent upon being beside a laptop, tablet, smart phone or computer and monitor. That said, smart phones are now found everywhere – but not always able to link to the web, and the screens are small.
- *Screens can't be spread out around a teaching room or learning space as easily as paper.* This means that students can't move around as freely as they could with print-based learning resources. It also means that in a computer room, it's harder to get everyone thinking about exactly the same thing at the same time (where this is desirable) than when a hard-copy handout is issued. That said, in computer labs, it is usually possible for the facilitator to control at will what's on everyone's screen.
- *Computer-based learning resources are often less easy to navigate than paper-based learning resources.* With a book, handout or article, it is easy to flick backwards and forwards to consolidate what has already been learned, and to spy out the landscape of what is to come. It is possible to stick post-its to the edges of important parts as bookmarks. With computer-based learning, this is not always nearly so easy.

Is this screenful actually working?

I've used the word 'screenful' to refer to what happens to be on a computer screen at a particular instant. In well-designed computer-based or online learning sequences, the screen is rarely 'full', but different things appear, move, change, and vanish over a very short period of time, usually in response to something done by the user using a mouse or touch. Nevertheless, it's worth thinking about how a human brain reacts to exactly what's on the screen at a particular instant, and that's the intention in Table 5.1, where I've summarised some questions which could be in the mind of any student confronted with a particular screenful in a resource-based learning context. I've also linked these questions to some of the principal factors underpinning successful learning.

Practical pointers on resource-based learning

The following sets of suggestions on resource-based learning have been updated and adapted from relevant parts of *500 Tips on Open and Online Learning* (Race, 2005b). Many of these suggestions apply equally to the design of online, computer-based or paper-based resource-based learning. The suggestions are in several sets, each addressing a particular aspect of resource-based learning:

- What's most suitable for resource-based learning?
- Blended learning and e-assessment
- Which students are particularly helped?
- Designing new resource-based learning materials
- The internet: harnessing information for learning.

Table 5.1 Interrogating a computer screenful: some questions which could be in students' minds

Questions which could be going through a student's mind	Links to the factors underpinning successful learning
Why am I seeing what's on the screen at this moment? Why is it there? For how long should I look at it? Can I just skip it? Is it just padding? Have I got to do something to move on? Can I move straight on from here?	*Wanting to learn*: could be damaged if there is not a good reason for the screenful being there. *Needing to learn*: the rationale for the screenful's existence should at least confirm what the student needs to get from its presence. *Making sense*: am I intended to slow down and get my head around what's on this screen now, or will it all become clear in due course?
What are the intended learning outcomes associated with this particular screenful? If there aren't any, why is it there at all? What if anything am I supposed to do with what's on the screen? Is this important?	*Wanting to learn*: could be undermined if the purpose of the screenful is not self-evident. Needing to learn: if it's not linked to intended learning outcomes, the message could be that it's not needed, and not important enough to think about. Evidence of achievement: what, if anything, am I supposed to be able to do myself at this point, with this screenful?
What exactly am I supposed to do with this bit? How am I supposed to handle it? Am I intended to be jotting down my thoughts? Are there on-screen tasks for me to do, such as picking options, entering text, entering numbers, clicking boxes, moving objects around on-screen, and so on?	*Learning by doing*: this is addressed when the screenful is an *interactive* one, in one way or another. The *doing* could be practice, learning by mistakes, or more sophisticated, for example requiring quite a bit of thought before action.
Will I be able to get back to this bit if I want to, or need to? How important is this particular bit? If it's important, will I have another chance to think about it, without having to go backwards to find it?	*Making sense*: putting the screenful into perspective is an important part of making sense of it. If it's not clear from the screenful whether it will be important or not, the student may (wrongly sometimes) assume it is not important.
Where does this bit fit into the big picture? Where does it fit into the overall intended learning outcomes? How much will it count in forthcoming assessments?	*Wanting to learn, needing to learn, making sense*: if the screenful does not clearly link to the overall learning programme, the student may decide it's just there 'in passing' and learn very little from it.
How will I tell whether, and when, I've succeeded with this bit? Will I get feedback from the next few screenfuls? Will I have to write down, or key in, something that will lead to later feedback from a tutor? Will I be given something to compare to what I'm asked to do with the screenful?	*Learning through feedback*: the availability of feedback to the student, after doing something with what's on the screen, gives the message that the screenful is important enough to be taken seriously.
Where is this bit leading me towards? *Where is it taking me from?* Can I tell where I'm heading? Am I supposed to remember where I'm heading? Am I supposed to remember where I'm coming from, and what I learned from previous screenfuls? Should I go back and refresh my memory?	*Making sense*: it is easy to get lost in computer-based scenarios. It is perfectly possible to ensure that each screenful has enough context-setting included, so that this danger is minimised. Unfortunately, this 'navigational' agenda is often not addressed well enough.

continued ...

Table 5.1 continued

Questions which could be going through a student's mind	Links to the factors underpinning successful learning
Who else is involved? Will someone be assessing what I've got out of this bit? Am I supposed to be doing this on my own, or am I expected to talk to other students about it? Is anyone watching me? Would I treat it differently if they were?	These questions can link to *all* of the factors underpinning successful learning. Feedback can be forthcoming on-screen, or from a tutor. 'Learning-by-doing' can be coupled to discussing the screenful with fellow students. The additional interaction and feedback can enhance 'wanting to learn' and consolidate the 'needing to learn' agenda, and aid the 'making sense' process.
What else should I be thinking about while this bit is on-screen? Should I be looking at printed resources as I go? Should I be looking at notes I'm making as I go? Do I need to see another screenful, on another screen, at the same time as this one?	These questions can link to *all* of the factors underpinning successful learning, particularly 'making sense'.
What else am I learning from this bit? What am I learning over and above what's on screen at the moment? How important are these other things I'm thinking about? Will they be assessed in some way, and if so, when, how, and by whom? Will I get feedback on these other things I'm thinking about?	These questions can link to all of the processes underpinning successful learning, particularly 'feedback' and 'making sense'. If the further agendas associated with the screenful are interesting, and seen as important, the 'wanting' and 'needing' to learn aspects are also enhanced.
What am I learning about myself? How is this bit helping me to develop as someone who can learn effectively and independently online or from a computer-based resource? How am I developing skills at managing my own learning?	Questions like these involve the 'making sense' aspect of learning, as well as developing receptivity to feedback, and the ability to develop one's own motivation.
So what? If there have not been any good reasons for looking at the screenful after thinking through all of the questions above, is there any reason at all for it being there?	If learners think 'so what?', it usually means that little learning is happening at that moment (unless the intention was to cause them to think 'so what?' and then immediately go on to address that question). This can be a signal to cut that particular screen, or present the information in another way, such as on a handout, or in an accompanying manual. If the screenful is not addressing at least some of the questions listed earlier, it may as well be deleted from the on-screen agenda of the learning package.

What's most suitable for resource-based learning?

It is worthwhile to think about which parts of the curriculum best lend themselves to a resource-based approach, whether online or paper-based. It is useful to start your resource-based learning design with such parts, and perhaps better still to experiment with adapting existing resources covering such curriculum areas towards a resource-based learning format first. The following suggestions show that such starting points can be based on several different considerations, and are often linked to ways that resource-based learning can augment face-to-face programmes.

1 **Important background material.** In face-to-face programmes, a considerable amount of time is often spent near the start, getting everyone up to speed with essential knowledge or skills, to the annoyance of the students who already have these. Making such information the basis of resource-based learning can allow those people who need to cover this material before the whole group starts, to do so in their own time and at their own pace, without holding up the rest of the group.

2 **'Need to know before …' material.** For example, when different students will be attempting different practical exercises at the same time, it could take far too long to cover all the prerequisite material with the whole group before introducing practical work. Designing separate, short resource-based learning elements to pave the way to each practical exercise, can allow these to be used by students just before they need what's in them, so that the practical work can be started much earlier.

3 **'Remedial material'.** In many face-to-face courses, there are problem topics which can hold up a whole class while the difficulties are addressed by lecturers or tutors. This can lead to time being wasted, and frustration for those students who have no problems with the parts concerned. The availability of resource-based learning (whether online, print-based or both) addressing such areas can allow such resources to be used only by those students who need them, in their own time, so that the progress of the whole group is not impeded.

4 **'Nice-to-know' material.** While 'need-to-know' material is more important, resource-based elements can be particularly useful to address 'nice-to-know' material, and giving such material to students without spending too much face-to-face time on it. This allows contact time to be saved for helping students with the really important material, and for addressing their problems. Sometimes the 'nice-to-know' dimension can be carried online, allowing students with time and energy to spare to enjoy it, without it getting in the way of those with less energy or time.

5 **Much-repeated material.** If you find yourself often covering the same ground, perhaps with different groups of students in different contexts or courses, it can be worth thinking about packaging up such material into learning resources. If you yourself get bored with things you often teach, you're not going to pass much enthusiasm for these topics on to your students, and it can be mutually beneficial to invest your energy into creating an alternative flexible learning pathway to cover such material. Furthermore, if you've taught something really often, you're the ideal person to know exactly what needs to go online or into a learning package to give students just the right kinds of feedback on their ongoing learning.

6 **Material which is best 'learned-by-doing'.** Effective resource-based learning is based on students answering questions, and doing tasks and exercises. Therefore it can be a useful starting point to base it on the sorts of activities that you may already be giving your face-to-face students. Standard assignments and activities already in use in traditionally delivered courses and programmes may be adapted quite easily for resource-based usage, and have the strong benefit that they are already tried and tested elements of the curriculum.

7 **Material where students need individual feedback on their progress.** A vital element of successful resource-based learning is the feedback that students receive when they have attempted to answer questions, or had a try at exercises and activities. The kinds of feedback that you may already give your face-to-face students can be packaged up into learning materials. What you say to students looking over their shoulders as they try their hands at tasks and exercises can be just as useful on-screen online.

8 **Material that you don't like to teach!** It can be tempting to turn such elements of the curriculum into learning materials, where students can work on them individually (or in untutored groups), and using face-to-face time more efficiently to address any problems that students find, rather than to teach them from scratch.

9 **Material that students find hard to grasp first time.** In most subjects there are such areas. Developing resource-based learning materials addressing these means that students can go through them on their own, as many times as they need, in the comfort of privacy. 'Struggling to grasp' something is not enjoyable, but much worse when one is *seen* to be struggling. Effectively, the learning resources become their teacher. Students can then work through such materials at their own pace, and can practise until they master the content.

10 **Material which may be needed later, at short notice.** It is often the case that some topics are only really needed by students quite some time after they may have been covered in a course or programme. When such materials are turned into learning resources, students can polish up their grip on the topics involved just when they need to.

Blended learning and e-assessment

Essentially, blended learning is about integrating resource-based learning – particularly online learning – seamlessly into the overall learning experience of students. It could be summarised simply as 'joined-up thinking' regarding curriculum design – easily said, but not often really achieved.

Implementing flexible learning with small groups of students poses few particular problems, provided the learning materials are of good quality, and there is appropriate support for students. However, student numbers continue to grow in college-based courses in many disciplines, and resource constraints have meant that face-to-face time with students has to be more limited than formerly. Learning resource materials can take some of the pressure away, but need to be firmly linked with mainstream teaching, otherwise students may feel that the resource-based elements are peripheral, and fail to invest sufficient energy into getting to grips with those parts of the curriculum. The following suggestions aim to help you to ensure that such pathways and materials are worth the time and effort that is involved in creating them.

1 **Plan to make the most of economies of scale.** If there are hundreds of students, it can become well worthwhile making good use of online learning and appropriate virtual learning environments. It may not be cost-effective to print large numbers of print-based open-learning packages. The same virtual learning environment may extend easily right across the provision of the whole institution – but it then becomes all the more important to choose it well in the first place! Investigate *what it does* – not just how it looks.

2 **Decide which parts of the curriculum to switch to resource-based mode.** Combine the earlier suggestions about which parts of the curriculum lend themselves to resource-based learning with the categories of students likely to benefit from such learning, to work out in the context of your own programme which will be the best parts to use as resource-based elements, maximising the benefits to the most appropriate cross-section of your class.

3 **Work out the best things to do in face-to-face contexts.** It is becoming increasingly common

to use learning resource materials to replace some of the material that was formerly handled in lectures. It is important to put the remaining occasions when a whole group is together to optimum usage. Such usage includes guiding and supporting students who are doing some or most of their learning from learning resource materials.

4 **Make sure that your students don't regard the resource-based learning as an optional extra.** For example, use lecture time to explain to the whole group which learning outcomes are being covered by the learning materials, and what the balance is between what will be covered in class, and the learning that students are required to do on their own. Explain (for example) that if half of the module is being worked on by students in online mode, half of the exam questions will test their achievement of these parts of the module.

5 **Reserve sufficient class time to answer students' questions about the resource-based learning materials.** It can be useful to use large-group time to collect and address problems that students find, and more efficient use of time than trying to deal with students' questions by appointment or in surgery times. Collecting frequently asked questions online, then going through them in a whole-group setting with students can be a useful way of integrating resource-based learning elements properly into the learning programme.

6 **Use lectures to 'spotlight' rather than to 'cover'.** Decide on the really important elements of the course, where it is worth the whole group having a shared learning experience along with the opportunity for questions and discussion. Explain to students which parts you are going to spotlight in this way, and why. This helps them to see that they have the responsibility for learning the parts that are not going to be spotlighted in this way.

7 **Consider using elements of the resource-based learning material as prerequisite for particular lecture sessions.** For example, you can 'require' students to have worked through a particular section of their materials before

attending a specific lecture, and structuring the session such that students who have not done this feel sufficiently disadvantaged or embarrassed that they don't put themselves in such a position in future. However, beware of the consequence of those who have not done the prescribed work failing to turn up at all for large-group sessions.

8 **Consider building into the learning materials short assignments or exercises to be sent in online before a face-to-face session.** This can help to ensure that students keep up with the intended pace. Sometimes you could assess this work or give feedback on it, or simply use it to check how the materials were working.

9 **Turn some lectures into tutorials – or 'flip the classroom' as is now said.** For example, choose particular areas for students to learn with the learning materials, and arrange a follow-up lecture slot that will be devoted to questions and discussion about the material, rather than introducing anything further on such occasions.

10 **Turn some lectures into large-group, interactive learning experiences.** Even though the use of handout materials in large-group settings has decreased dramatically, occasionally *interactive* handouts can be designed for large-group sessions, where the handouts themselves are in effect miniature learning packages, including stated intended learning outcomes, tasks and feedback responses. Such large-group sessions not only build upon the principles of learning-by-doing and learning from feedback, but they also help students themselves to develop approaches which they can extend to working with fully-fledged learning resource materials.

11 **Explain how, and when, the resource-based learning material content will be assessed.** It can be useful to stage some of the assessment somewhat earlier than the end of the course or module, so that some face-to-face time can be reserved for feedback to the class about any significant problems that were found with the

part of the curriculum delivered with learning resource materials.

12 **Consider using online assessment for appropriate parts of the material.** Such assessment can be based on a bank of questions, with each student being given a random selection from the bank on the occasion when they take a test. The tests can be done either in a booked computer laboratory (with invigilation if necessary to minimise possibilities of cheating), or could be networked over a week or two when the purpose of the assessment may be primarily formative. The use of passwords can add to the security of the tests, and the reporting software can save you a considerable amount of time, and avoid you having to do tasks such as marking and making class-score lists manually. Don't forget, additionally, that online assessment can easily be extended to provide feedback to students during or after the test – so make the most of the opportunity to build into the assessment software feedback messages to show students how they have done – and to save you having to explain it all to them later. Online assessment really comes into its own when student numbers are large.

It's worth expanding a little on the possibilities now afforded by online assessment. Fisher et al. (2014) usefully suggest an impressive range of ways technology can support assessment process, and go on to list several types of objective test, as follows:

Ways in which technology can support assessment processes:
- Question generation – for example, random generators, building question banks, etc.
- Question/task presentation and delivery to learners – for example, students sit at the computers to take the test.
- Development of standalone, self-study and self-assessment tools, such as RLOs (reusable learning objects) – these may take the form of self-assessment quizzes or problem-solving tasks.
- Submission of student responses.
- Marking/grading answers.
- Providing automated feedback and further guidance.
- Detecting plagiarism.
- Analysis of (class) grades and generating statistics and evaluation reports.
- Recording and monitoring learner achievement – for example, using ePortfolios.
- Storage of assessments and student attainments for quality assurance purposes.

(Fisher et al., 2014, p. 112)

Types of objective tests:

- Drag-and-drop: click and drag images or words into position on a diagram, map, table, photograph, etc.
- Multiple-choice question: a 'stem' statement or question that has one or more 'correct' responses.
- Fill-in (or select) the blank: missing key words (possibly selected from pull-down lists).
- Hotspot: clicking on a picture or diagram to indicate the answer.
- Knowledge matrix: several MCQs grouped together.
- Matching pairs: matching items in a list of words or statements with items in a second list.
- Pull-down list: a set of statements that are matched with items in a pull-down list.
- Ranking: a list of choices that must be ranked in order numerically. For example: in priority order, which are the more common causes of a subarachnoid hematoma?

(Fisher et al., 2014, pp. 113–14)

Which students are particularly helped?

All sorts of people use resource-based learning in independent-learning mode whether online or paper-based. The following categories of students are included as those who can be particularly helped in different ways. Many parallels may also be drawn to the use of resource-based learning elements in college-based programmes, where similar benefits can be delivered to a variety of constituencies of the student population.

1 **High fliers.** Very able students are often frustrated or bored by traditional class-based programmes, as the pace is normally made to suit the average student and may be much too slow for high-fliers. With resource-based learning, they can speed through the parts they already know, or the topics they find easy and straightforward. They can work through the materials concentrating only on the parts that are new to them, or which they find sufficiently challenging.

2 **Low fliers.** The least able students in a group are often disadvantaged when the pace of delivery of traditional programmes is too fast for them. They can be embarrassed in class situations by being seen not to know things, or not to be able to do tasks that their fellow students have no difficulty with. With resource-based learning, they can take their time, and practise until they have mastered things. They have the opportunity to spend much longer, in the comfort of privacy, than other students may take.

3 **Students with special needs.** For example, people with limited mobility may find it hard to get to the venue of a traditional course, but may have few problems when studying at home. Students with other problems may be able to work through learning materials with the aid of an appropriate helper or supporter. Resource-based learning is increasingly being used to address the particular needs of diverse groups including carers, prisoners, mentally ill people, religious groups, socially excluded people, and so on. Whether the special needs are linked to disabilities or to educational difficulties, resource-based learning can often be more easily adapted to such students than can large-group or small-group teaching.

Not least, the fact that these students can work at their own pace counts significantly. Furthermore, appropriate software can be used to make online learning materials accessible to students with hearing or sight difficulties, where it would sometimes be quite difficult to compensate for their difficulties in live face-to-face teaching.

4 **Anxious students.** Some people are easily embarrassed if they get things wrong, especially when they are seen to make mistakes in large-group settings. With resource-based learning, they have the opportunity to learn from making mistakes, in the comfort of privacy, as they try self-assessment questions and exercises, and learn from the feedback responses accompanying such components of an interactive learning package.

5 **Students with a particular block.** Students who have a particular problem with an important component of a course can benefit from resource-based learning, in that they can work as often as they wish through those parts of the materials designed to give them practice in the topic concerned. It can be useful to incorporate self-assessment exercises, with detailed feedback specially included for those students who have problems with the topic.

6 **Students who like working with computers.** Present-day school leavers love computer games – sometimes they take over their lives. The number of older people who enjoy playing with computers is also growing – there are plenty of 'silver surfers' around now. All such people can extend their pleasure in working with computers to learning intentionally with them.

7 **Students needing to make up an identified shortfall.** For example, in science and engineering programmes, it is often found quite suddenly that some students in a group have not got particular maths skills. Rather than hold up the progress of a whole class, self-study components can be issued to those students who need to get up to speed in the areas involved. When the students have a sense of ownership of the need that these materials will address, they make best use of the materials.

8 **People learning in a second language.** In class situations, such students are disadvantaged in that they may be spending much of their energy simply making sense of the words they hear or see projected on slides, with little time left to make sense of the ideas and concepts. With resource-based learning materials, they can work through them at their own pace without embarrassment, with the aid of a dictionary, or with the help of students already fluent in the language in which the materials are written.

9 **Part-time students.** These are often people with many competing pressures on their time, or with irregular opportunities for studying, perhaps due to shift work, work away from home, or uneven demands being normal in their jobs. Resource-based learning materials allow them to manage their studying effectively, and to make the most of those periods where they have more time to study. It is worth remembering that most full-time university students nowadays are actually working significant hours most weeks to support their education, and are in effect part-time students.

10 **People who don't like being taught!** Surprisingly, such people are found in college-based courses, but there are many more of these who would not consider going to an educational institution. Resource-based learning allows such people to have a much greater degree of autonomy and ownership of their studies.

11 **Students who only want to do part of the whole.** Some students may only want to – or need to – achieve a few carefully selected learning outcomes that are relevant to their work or even to their leisure activities. Many such learners go to MOOCs, where they can pick and choose what they learn. With resource-based learning, they are in a position to select those parts they want to study, whereas in face-to-face courses they may have to wait quite some time before the parts they are really interested in are covered.

As you can see, resource-based learning can be suitable for just about any students, if the context is appropriate. However, students may well need preparation for taking part in resource-based learning, and we may need to research our students' experience, expectations and needs, to help ensure that they will be able to benefit. Beetham (2013) suggests:

> Depending on the task and context, it may be necessary to consider learners'
> 1. Subject-specific experience, knowledge and competence;
> 2. Access needs, including any physical and sensory disabilities;
> 3. Motives for learning, and expectations of the learning situation;
> 4. Prior experience of learning, especially learning in the relevant mode (e.g. online);
> 5. Preferred approaches to learning;
> 6. Social and interpersonal skills;
> 7. Digital and information literacy.

(Beetham, 2013, p. 37)

Designing new resource-based learning materials

The most difficult stage in starting out to design learning resource materials can be working out a logical and efficient order in which to approach the separate tasks involved. Before really getting started on designing such material, it's worth looking back, and asking yourself a few basic questions once more. These include:

- Am I the best person to create this material?
- Have I sufficient experience of being a resource-based learner myself?
- Is there a materials production unit in my institution which can help me?
- Are there any experienced materials editors there whose expertise I can depend upon?
- Might I need graphics design help and support?
- Is there already an institutional house-style for learning resource materials?
- Can someone else produce the learning materials, while I simply supply the raw material and notes on how I want it to work in resource-based learning mode?

If after asking these questions, you decide to press ahead with designing your own materials, the following suggestions should help you to avoid wasting too much time, and particularly aim to help ensure that the work you do is directly related to composing learning material rather than composing yet another textbook.

1 **Don't just start writing subject material.** Resource-based learning materials are much more than just the subject matter they contain, and in particular provide something for learners to *do* rather than just something to read.

2 **Get the feel of your target audience.** The better you know the sorts of people who will be your learners, the easier it is to design learning materials for them. It is worth spending some time on the suggestions given earlier in this book about making profiles of the main groups which will make up your target audience.

3 **Work out carefully the evidence of achievement which will in due course be the basis of assessment.** This can spare you from designing unnecessary parts of the learning materials, and can help to ensure that the materials 'cut to the chase' of the intended learning, rather than going into unnecessary detail.

4 **Express your intended learning outcomes carefully.** It is worth making a skeleton of the topics that your material will cover in the form of learning outcomes, at least in draft form, before designing anything else. Having established the intended learning outcomes,

you are in a much better position to ensure that the content of your learning material will be developed in a coherent and logical order.

5 **Seek feedback on your draft learning outcomes.** Check that they are seen by colleagues to be at the right level for the material you are designing. In particular, check that they make sense to members of your target audience of learners, and are clear and unambiguous to them. Taking time at the outset to express these outcomes clearly and precisely is a useful investment.

6 **Design questions, tasks and activities, firmly based on your intended learning outcomes.** Some of the outcomes may require several tasks and activities to cover them. It is also useful to plan in draft activities that will span two or three learning outcomes simultaneously, to help pave the way towards integrating your learning materials, and linking the outcomes to each other in a joined-up way.

7 **Test your draft questions, tasks and activities.** These will in due course be the basis of the learning-by-doing in your package, and will set the scene for the feedback responses you will design. It is extremely useful to test

these questions and tasks first, with anyone you can get to try them out, particularly learners who may be close to your anticipated target audience. Finding out their most common mistakes and difficulties paves the way towards the design of useful feedback responses, and helps you adjust the wording of the tasks to avoid ambiguity or confusion.

8 **Plan your feedback responses.** Decide how best you will let your learners know how well, or how badly, they have done in their attempts at each of your tasks, activities and questions.

9 **Think ahead to assessment.** Work out which of the questions, tasks and activities you have designed will be useful as self-assessment exercises, where feedback responses can be provided to learners in print in the learning materials, or on-screen if you're designing computer-based or online learning. Work out which exercises need the human skills and experience of a tutor to respond to them, and will usefully become components of tutor-marked assignments.

10 **Map out your questions, tasks and activities into a logical sequence.** Along with the matching learning outcomes, this provides you with a strong skeleton on which to proceed to flesh out the content of your learning materials.

11 **Work out your main headings and subheadings.** It is wise to base these firmly on the things that your learners are going to be doing, reflecting the learning outcomes you have devised. This is much better than devising headings purely on the basis of the subjects and topics covered, or on the original curriculum descriptors you may have started out with.

12 **Consider using question headings.** Any piece of information can be regarded as the answer to one or more questions. Question headings can often alert learners about the purpose of what follows somewhat better than simple topic headings.

13 **Write 'bridges'.** Most of these will lead from the feedback response you have written for one question, task or activity, into the next activity that your learners will meet. Sometimes these bridges will need to provide new information to set the scene for the next activity. It is important to ensure that these bridges are as short and relevant as you can make them, and that they don't run off on tangents to the main agenda provided by the skeleton you have already made. This also ensures that you make your designing really efficient, and save your valuable time.

14 **Write the introductions last.** The best time to write any lead-in is when you know exactly what you're introducing. It is much easier to lead in to the first question, task or activity when you know how it (and the feedback associated with it) fits in to the material as a whole, and when you already know how and why you have arranged the sequence of activities in the way you have chosen. Although you may need to write draft introductions when first putting together your materials for piloting, it is really useful to revisit these after testing out how learners get on with the activities and feedback responses, and to include in the final version of each introduction suggestions to learners about how to approach the material that follows, based on what was learned from piloting.

The internet: harnessing information for learning

For some time, the term 'e-learning' was used in the context of online and computer-based learning, but so much learning uses electronic means now that it's unwise to differentiate between learning and e-learning any more. In the digital age we're now in, so much is accessed electronically in everyday life that it is unwise to draw distinctions between information accessed in 'hard copy' and that on screens, mobile phones or tablets. In a way, the internet is the ultimate resource-based learning resource – but it is actually just providing information unless it is used actively. There is plenty of freedom. People can use it at times of their own choice, in their own ways, at their own pace, and from anywhere that access to it is available to them. But that said, it is not automatically a vehicle for productive and effective learning. Indeed, it is very easy to become side-tracked by all sorts of fascinating things, and to stray well away from any intended learning outcome. The learning payoff can be zero. The suggestions which follow are not intended as starting points for setting out to deliver learning through the internet, but rather to help learners to use the internet to obtain material to use in connection with their studies, such as in assignments they are preparing. The following suggestions may help you to help your students both to enjoy the internet, *and* to learn well from it.

1 **Play with the internet yourself.** Most people do this anyway of course, but it's worth putting yourself in the place of a learner and experience what it feels like setting off to learn something specific from the web. You need to pick up your own experience of how learners feel when tapping into such a vast and varied database with a learning goal in mind, so you can design ways of helping your students to get high learning payoff from using it themselves. Experience for yourself the pleasure of being able to surf the net productively, and also note how easy it is to surf quite aimlessly.

2 **After you've played with it, work with it.** Use the internet to research something yourself. You may well of course have done this often already, but if not, give it a try before you think of setting your students 'search and retrieve' tasks with the internet. Set yourself a fixed time, perhaps half-an-hour or even less. Choose a topic that you're going to search for, preferably something a little offbeat. See for yourself how best to use the search engines, and compare the efficiency of different engines. Find out for yourself how to deal with 4,593 references to your chosen topic, and how to improve your searching strategy to whittle them down to the ten that you really want to use!

3 **Do they need it all?** Decide whether you want your students to use the whole gamut of material on the internet, or a refined and trimmed range of resource materials on an intranet. An intranet is where a networked set of computers talk to each other, often using internet conventions, but where the content is not open to the rest of the universe. If you are working in an organisation which already has such a network, and if your students can make use of this network effectively, there will be

some purposes that will be better served by the intranet. You can also have *controlled* access to the internet via an intranet, such as by using hot-links to predetermined external sites.

4 **Don't just use it as a filing cabinet for your teaching resources!** While it is useful in its own way if your students can have access to your own notes and teaching–learning resources, this is not really *using* the internet or an intranet – it may only provide information after all. Too many materials designed for use in other forms are already cluttering up the internet. If all you intend your students to do is to download your notes and save their own copies, sending them emailed attachments would do the same job much more efficiently.

5 **Think carefully about your intended learning outcomes.** You may indeed wish to use the internet as a means whereby your students address the existing intended outcomes associated with their subject material. However, it is also worth considering whether you may wish to add further learning outcomes, to do with the processes of searching, selecting, retrieving and analysing subject material. If so, you may also need to think about whether, and how, these additional learning outcomes may be assessed.

6 **Give your students specific things to do using the internet.** Choose these tasks so that it is relevant and important for your students to find and use up-to-the-minute data or news, rather than where the 'answers' are already encapsulated in easily accessible books or learning resources.

7 **Give students plenty of choice.** Consider giving them a menu of tasks and activities. They will feel more ownership if they have a significant degree of freedom in their internet tasks. Where you have a group of

students working on the same syllabus, it can be worth letting them choose different tasks, and then communicating their main findings to each other (and to you) using a computer conference, a wiki, or by email.

8   **Let your students know that the process is at least as important as the outcome.** The key skills that they can develop using the internet include designing an effective search, and making decisions about the quality and authenticity of the evidence they find. It is worth designing tasks where you already know of at least some of the evidence you expect them to locate, and remaining open to the fact that they will each uncover at least as much again as you already know about!

9   **Consider designing your own interactive pages.** You may want to restrict these to an intranet, at least at first. You can then use dialogue boxes to cause your students to answer questions, enter data, and so on. Pave the way towards being able to give students feedback about their work on the intranet, helping them to develop parallel skills to bring to their use of the internet itself.

10 **Consider getting your students to design and post some web pages.** This may be best done restricted to an intranet, at least until your students have picked up sufficient skills to develop pages that are worth putting up for all to see. The act of designing their own web pages is one of the most productive ways to help your students develop their critical skills at evaluating materials already on the internet.

11 **Get groups of your students to design a small resource-based learning package themselves.** This can even be turned into an assessment task, with criteria designed to test the quality of the learning material produced (the design, not just the coverage of content). Additionally, if you can get groups peer-assessing each other's resource-based learning materials, they deepen their learning by making judgements while applying such criteria.

Conclusions

In the last three decades, the role of resource-based learning has grown quickly. Gone are the days when the main resources were confined to printed books, handouts, journals and other paper-based forms including hand-written notes made by students in lectures. The internet and possibilities offered by online learning have contributed to the disintermediation of the role of the lecturer as provider and source of information and expertise regarding subject content. Instead, lecturers now need to have other areas of expertise, not least guiding students on how best to get a grip on subject matter, and assessing students' achievements.

Earlier in the chapter I quoted Helen Beetham (2013) on using technology and designing for learning. She concludes the book *Rethinking Pedagogy for a Digital Age* with a challenging message about resource-based learning in the digital age, as follows:

> In facing the uncertainties of the near and more distant future, we can be sure that learners are better off – more resilient – if they have a broad repertoire of capabilities at their fingertips, those closely aligned with academic expertise and professional practice and those they evolved from their digital experiences, along with hybrids of the two. Learners will be well served by tasks, programmes and environments that generate uncertainty, and foster a repertoire of resourceful responses. Educators, too, will have to become more resilient, more adaptive and multi-competent in the various niches that the new education system will open up… This is not a game we can opt out of. Either we are designers of our own futures, or we are having the future designed for us. As educators we must unequivocally place ourselves on the side of self-determination.
>
> (Beetham, 2013, p. 279)

I end this chapter with a 'double-Haiku' specially composed for this edition by Carole Baume (2014), who for many years worked for the UK Open University, who makes the case that the kinds of disintermediation caused by resource-based learning should not be regarded as threatening by the best lecturers:

Poor experts bemoan:
'Disintermediation
Will steal our power.'

Strong experts rejoice:
'Disintermediation
Will empower all.'

Chapter 6

Looking after yourself

It is the mark of an educated mind to be able to entertain a thought without accepting it.

(Aristotle)

Success does not consist of never making mistakes, but in not making the same one a second time.

(George Bernard Shaw)

Sitting in, regularly, on colleagues' sessions is one of the most productive ways to gain ideas to use in your own approaches. You'll find things they do well which you would like to try, and (just as useful) you'll notice things that they do less well which you will decide to avoid if at all possible.

(Phil Race – later in this chapter!)

Intended outcomes of this chapter

When you've dipped into the suggestions offered in this chapter, I hope you will feel able to take more control of some of the following aspects of your overall life in higher education:

- Managing your workload and stress levels;
- Getting the most out of appraisal;
- Making good use of your feedback from students.

While other chapters in this *Toolkit* have been directly or indirectly about looking after your students, most of this one is about ensuring that *you* survive! I am only too aware of the levels of stress that are experienced by many lecturers, due to all manner of causes, many of which are beyond their control, and I hope that the suggestions in this chapter will contain something for everyone, and help to reduce – or at least *manage* – some of the causes and effects of stress. The chapter continues with a discussion about appraisal – how to prepare for it, and how to approach getting the most from it. Finally, I've included a range of suggestions about how you may go about getting feedback from your students, and analyse it to your (and their) advantage.

Managing your workload

Heavier workloads have become a fact of life for most lecturers. Whenever I start a workshop with a post-it task asking lecturers to complete the starter-sentence: 'Teaching would be much better if only I …', up to half of the responses tend to be '…had more time'. However, this is not the best answer to the question. More time isn't what turns a poor lecturer into a better one; it's 'doing better things' that works, and not just 'doing the same things better'. Nonetheless, lecturers feel under increasing pressure, and it seems highly unlikely that this situation will change. Managing your workload may increasingly seem like a balancing act between teaching, research and administration. I hope the following suggestions will help you to adjust your balance if necessary.

1 **Don't waste energy on trying to turn the clock back!** What some people affectionately or wistfully refer to as 'the good old days' are very unlikely to return. One danger is that we spend so much time talking about how much better things once were, that we put even more pressure on the time and energy we have to face today and plan for tomorrow.

2 **Prioritise your own workload.** It is useful to go through all the tasks and roles that you undertake, asking yourself which are the *really* important ones, and which are the ones that would not have significant effects on your students if you were to prune them or abandon them.

3 **Don't ask for permission to streamline your workload.** No-one is likely to respond 'yes'. It's better to ask for forgiveness if anyone notices things you haven't done!

4 **Cut your assessment workload.** This does not mean reduce the quality of your assessment. It is widely recognised that over-assessment is bad for students, and in former times it was all too easy for such patterns of over-assessment to be established. Now may be the time to think again about how much assessment your students really need, and to improve the quality of this, but at the same time significantly reduce its volume. For example, set tightly word-constrained tasks (e.g. 200 words) instead of longer tasks such as essays. And set short exams rather than long ones – you can test students just as well in a well-designed short exam.

5 **Look for more efficient ways of giving feedback to your students.** Many colleagues find that emailed feedback communications end up saving a lot of time, particularly when you can develop your own bank of 'frequently needed responses' and paste them in as needed in individual emails, or better still on a course or module web page.

6 **Don't play 'email-tennis'.** Don't reply individually to each email, and then to each reply to your reply and so on. Post your (well-considered) replies on a bulletin board, reply to the individual questioner along the lines 'Good question. I've posted a reply on…' giving the link, and direct all students to make good use of your responses.

7 **Make good use of learning resource materials.** Students nowadays learn a great deal more from online, and computer-based materials than once was the case. The quality of learning resource materials is improving all the time, and such materials are getting steadily better at giving students opportunities to learn-by-doing, and to learn from healthy trial and error. Materials are getting much better at providing students with feedback on their individual progress and performance. Making the most of such materials can free up valuable face-to-face time with students, so you can deal with their questions and problems in class time, rather than merely giving information to them.

8 **Make good use of your administrative and support staff.** It is easy for us to find ourselves doing tasks which they could have done just as well, and often they could have done them more efficiently than ourselves.

9 **Make better use of feedback from students.** Listen to their concerns, and focus on them, making your own work more useful to them at the same time. They know better than anyone else where their problems lie, so it is worth making sure that your valuable time is spent addressing the right problems.

10 **Keep your materials well organised.** It's well worth the time spent to devote ten minutes after a particular class or lecture updating or improving the slides and activities you may have used on the basis of 'what worked well' and 'what didn't

quite work', so next time you come to the topic you'll be starting from a better place.

11 **Don't carry your entire workload in your mind.** We can only do one thing at a time, so when doing important work such as teaching and assessing students, don't get side-tracked into worrying about the numerous other tasks jostling for your attention.

Managing your stress levels

The lecturer's job can be extremely stressful as budget constraints and increasing class sizes cause staff to be put under increasing pressure to teach longer hours and in possibly unfamiliar ways, and to spend longer hours on assessment and record keeping as well as research. At the same time, students are becoming more diverse and have an ever widening range of requirements and expectations. A significant proportion of staff in higher education become physically ill as a result of stress. If you're not working at your best because of stress, it becomes a vicious circle. There may indeed be very little you can do about many of the causes of stress, but you could be surprised at how much it is possible for us to adapt our responses to stressors. These tips cannot eliminate your stress, but may alert you to some strategies to help you deal with it.

12 **Don't expect to be stressed, just because everyone else seems to be stressed.** It sometimes feels as if stress is infectious, but it doesn't have to be! There are usually some people who manage to keep calm when everyone else is panicking, and you can be such a person.

13 **Get better at recognising the physical signs of stress.** These include raised heart rate, increased sweating, over-anxiety, short temper, manic outbursts, elevated blood pressure, headaches, dizziness, blurred vision, aching neck and shoulders, skin rashes, and lowered resistance to infection. When people are aware that such symptoms may be caused by stress, it helps them to look to their approaches to work to see if the causes of such symptoms may arise from stress. But don't become a hypochondriac; don't look at the list of symptoms above and tell yourself 'I've an aching neck, so I must be stressed!'

14 **Get better at recognising the behavioural effects of stress.** These include increased anxiety, depression, irritability, increased consumption of tobacco or alcohol, sleep disturbance, lack of concentration, and inability to deal calmly and efficiently with everyday tasks and situations.

15 **Get better at helping those around you who are stressed.** It often makes a big difference when one knows one has helped someone feel better about things that are troubling them, and helps one put one's own problems into a healthier perspective.

16 **Increase awareness of how the human body reacts to stress.** Essentially this happens in three distinct stages. 'The alarm reaction stage' causes defences to be set up and increased release of adrenalin. 'The resistance stage' is when the body will resist the stressor, or adapt to the stress conditions. 'The exhaustion stage' results when attempts by the body to adapt have failed, and the body succumbs to the effects of stress.

17 **Don't ignore stress.** There are no prizes for struggling to the point of collapse; indeed, this is the last thing you should be doing. As the symptoms of stress become apparent to you, try to identify the causes of your stress and do something about how you handle them.

18 **Get over the myths surrounding stress.** Research has shown that stress should not be regarded as being the same as nervous tension, and is not always a negative response, and that some people do indeed survive well and thrive on stress. In an education organisation, it is more important to manage stress than to try to eliminate it.

19 **Look to the environmental causes of stress.** These include working or living under extremes

of temperature, excessive noise, unsuitable lighting, poor ventilation or air quality, poorly laid out work areas, and even the presence of vibration. In a your own institution, finding out what other people think of such environmental conditions is a good first step towards adjusting them.

20 **Look to the social causes of stress.** These can include insufficient social contact at work, sexual harassment, racial discrimination, ageism, inappropriate management approaches, unhealthy levels of competition, and conflict between colleagues. Any or all of these, when present, can be addressed and clarified by asking people about their own experiences of similar problems, and talking things through with them.

21 **Look to the organisational causes of stress.** These can include inappropriately heavy workloads, ineffective communication, excessive supervision or inadequate supervision, excess of unnecessary bureaucracy, lack of relevant training provision, undue concern about promotion or reward systems, and unsatisfactory role perceptions. Once identified, all of these causes can be remedied.

22 **Cultivate the right to feel stress, and to talk about it.** Stress is at its worst when it is bottled up and unresolved. It should be regarded as perfectly natural for people's stress levels to vary in the normal course of their work. When stress is something that can be discussed, it is much more likely that the causes will be addressed. Talk about your problems. Actually voicing what is stressing you to a colleague, a line manager, the person you are closest too or even your cat can sometimes improve the situation. As with learning itself, talking through something helps you to sort your head out about it. Bottling it all up through some misplaced sense of fortitude can be dangerous.

23 **Don't be afraid to go to the doctor.** The worst excesses of stress can be helped by short-term medication and medical intervention of some kind. People are often unwilling to resort to a visit to their GP for matters of stress when they wouldn't hesitate to seek help for a physical ailment, or counsel a friend so to do. Don't let such feelings get in the way of finding the kind of support you need.

24 **Take a break.** Often our panics over time management are caused not so much by how much we have to do as whether we feel we have sufficient time to do it in. Try to take a real break from time to time, so as to help you get your workload into proportion. A little holiday or a whole weekend without college work occasionally can make you better able to cope with the onslaught on your return.

25 **When you take a well-deserved break, don't waste it by feeling guilty.** A sensible amount of time off is an essential part of any busy person's time-management and task-management strategy. It also means that when you return to the workload, you tackle it more speedily and efficiently, so the time off has not been at all lost.

26 **Overcome powerlessness with action.** When you are stressed out, it is often because you feel totally powerless in the situation. It can be useful to look at the areas you do have some control over and try to do something about them, however minor. This may not change the overall picture very much, but will often make you feel better.

27 **Try counselling.** Many colleges have someone to whom staff can turn for trained counselling in times of great stress. Otherwise you could look elsewhere through your GP or in the phone book under therapeutic practice or alternative medicine to find someone who can guide and support you through the worst patches. This is often more productive than piling all your stress onto your nearest and dearest who usually have problems of their own – perhaps *you*!

28 **Try not to personalise a situation into hatred and blame.** It is easy to fall into the trap of seeing all your stress as being caused by an individual or group of people who have it in for you. Of course it may be the case but usually high stress situations are caused by cock-up rather than conspiracy!

29 **Avoid compounding the problem.** If things are pretty stressful at work, try to avoid making

important life changes at the same time, such as moving to a different house or starting a family, if these can be deferred for a while.

30 **Try to adopt a long-term perspective.** It can be really hard to project into the future and to review current stress as part of a much larger pattern, but if you can do it, it helps. Much of what seems really important now will pale into insignificance in a few weeks', months' or years' time. Easier said than done, but stress is nothing new; 'Let nothing scare you. All is fleeting…Let nothing trouble you' wrote St Teresa of Avila, 1515–82.

Managing your appraisal

Most universities and colleges in the UK have in place appraisal programmes that link directly into the overall mission of the institution, the local plans of the school or department, the needs of each individual, and (far from least) the experience of students themselves. For people who have never been appraised, the process may seem intrusive and threatening. Yet many people look forward to appraisal as an opportunity to get some feedback on how they are doing, and indeed to showcase to significant others some of the evidence of success they have built up. Sadly, however, many people coming into universities, especially from commerce, local government or industry, may have somewhat negative experiences of appraisal, which in some contexts is used very much as a management tool to control staff.

How is appraisal organised?

Often the person chosen to appraise you will be your nearest line manager. Ideally it will be someone who knows your work and the context you work in, and also be in a position to make decisions and act on the agreements you make within the performance review process. In some universities, it is possible for you to choose your own appraiser; in others you are allocated an appraiser and it is then not normally possible for you to reject the institution's choice. As far as possible, many institutions try to respect specific requests for you to be appraised by someone of the same gender or ethnic group as yourself, but this is not always feasible or seen to be desirable. Often there is a pre-appraisal meeting lasting ten to fifteen minutes in which appraiser and appraisee have the chance to set the agenda for the actual appraisal, which then allows time for the appraisee to think about the desired focus of the meeting and to prepare some pre-appraisal documentation.

Pause for thought: setting the scene for your appraisal
1. Find out who is likely to be your appraiser when the time comes.
2. Make some enquiries about the specific processes that you are likely to find in your own appraisal; jot down the main points as an aide-memoire.
3. Find out if appraisers and appraisees are expected to undertake training before they undertake an appraisal, and if so, what is involved in this training.
4. Talk to colleagues who have some experience of being appraised, and work out whether the process seems to happen uniformly in different parts of your institution, or whether there are significant differences from one department to another.
5. Ask a few colleagues what was the most useful thing they got out of their own appraisals, and note down your main conclusions.

What sorts of questions may you be asked?

Many institutions have a standard pro forma which can be used in preparing for appraisal. Questions could include:

- What areas of your work do you feel you can associate with a sense of achievement?
- What evidence can you supply to demonstrate your achievements (e.g. student evaluations, comments from peer observations, reports from external assessors)?
- What development activities proved particularly worthwhile, and how have you been able to build upon these in your own work?
- Which activities and goals that you had planned to undertake have fallen by the wayside?
- What are the particular reasons for these unfulfilled aims?
- What support have you received from your line manager and other colleagues during the period under review?

You are also likely to be asked to look forward to the next year and identify:

- your provisional goals for the next twelve months;
- your anticipated developmental needs over the coming period;
- any training or special support you are likely to require to enable you to fulfil your plans;
- what might interfere with your plans to achieve, and what strategies you can adopt to prevent this happening.

If no appraisal pro formas are supplied, it is still a good idea for the appraisee to prepare short notes under such headings to provide areas for discussion.

Pause for thought: getting your act together for appraisal

Rehearse answers to some of these questions:

- What areas of your work do you feel you can associate with a sense of achievement?
- What evidence can you supply to demonstrate your achievements (e.g. student evaluations, comments from peer observations, reports from external assessors)?
- Which activities and goals that you had planned to undertake have fallen by the wayside?
- What are the particular reasons for these unfulfilled aims?
- What support have you received from your line manager and other colleagues during the period under review?
- What additional support may have proved helpful?

Your appraisal interview

During your appraisal you should try to review as honestly as you can how well you feel you are doing and where you need to develop. You should not try to sweep your problems away under the carpet, nor should you be afraid to blow your own trumpet about the things of which you have a right to be proud. At the end of the interview, the appraiser should draw the process to a close by summarising briefly what has been said and then should guide you towards drawing up a set of realistic, specific and measurable goals for the next year, with timescales attached and recognition of the training, support and resources that are likely to be needed to help you to achieve them. If your appraiser does not do this for you, then you will need to make sure that you do it yourself anyway.

In many institutions it is normal for a report to be written on the appraisal meeting. Often, this is written by the appraisee and then signed with or without comments by the appraiser. After the appraisal interview, the appraisal report will then provide a useful reference document for the work of the year to come. There is also normally a system in place by which training needs identified during the process are fed into an institution-wide professional development programme.

> **Pause for thought: preparing *your* agenda for appraisal**
>
> Think through some of the following 'starters' as possible ingredients you might wish to use to steer your appraisal usefully.
>
> - My personal goals for my teaching this year are:
> - My other work-related goals are:
> - The resources and support I will need to help me do this include:
> - Training and staff development that could help me achieve my goals include:
> - What could get in the way of achieving these goals is:
> - I will know if I have achieved my goals when:
> - The evidence I can use to demonstrate such achievements is likely to include:

General suggestions on preparing for your appraisal

Appraisal can be a strong positive power for the good when it is used developmentally to ensure that individuals and groups review their own achievements, build on achievements, set realistic goals for the future and think about how what they are doing fits into their whole institutional programme. The following tips aim to guide you away from allowing appraisal to become merely a tiresome formality, and towards it being an active and dynamic means of coordinating your work and getting the best from yourself and the institution

1 **Prepare thoughtfully for your review.** Try to ensure that you have a clear idea prior to the review, of the areas you aim to focus on. After all, it's your appraisal and it's up to you to get the most you can out of the occasion. If you skimp on the preparation, your appraiser may well take cues from you and also take the process less seriously than it deserves.

2 **Try to see both sides of the process.** If you're preparing for review, think about how it feels to be in your appraiser's position, so that you can help your appraiser to make the process positively developmental. See the appraiser as a guide and support for your process of self-review, rather than as an interrogator who is trying to catch you out.

3 **Collect evidence of achievement.** Bring to the review, or make a list of, concrete examples of outcomes that you have achieved, so that any successes or progress you claim can be backed up with examples. For example, you might bring along one or more of the following:
- student feedback data;
- printouts of your students' achievements;
- examples of your effective organisational and administrative skills;
- copies of a few letters and memos from internal and external colleagues who have acknowledged your efforts.

You can also tell your reviewer about:
- examples of your dealing with problems;
- your contributions to strategic decisions;

- your promotion of the effective work and reputation of your department or institution. You might like to collect these in a loose-leaf folder with material easily referenced so you can refer to specific elements within the appraisal without too much difficulty in finding them.

4 **Regard the review as an opportunity.** Make it an occasion where you can raise all the important issues you haven't had time to discuss earlier. Have a mental shopping list of training you would like agreement that you can undertake, or aspects of your job description that you would like to develop further. You may be able to negotiate time or resources for professional training of various kinds. You might wish to gain approval for your participation in local or national activities relevant to your work. Remember that professional development need not involve high expenditure. Opportunities may exist for you to undertake personal development through work-shadowing, self-instruction and the use of online and print-based staff development resource materials without large outlays of cash.

5 **Talk to colleagues who've been through it all before.** Each appraisal scheme is different, and it's helpful to tune in to the way your own scheme works in practice. Ask colleagues what was most helpful to them regarding preparation, and what they got out of the whole process. Also ask them for any things they would have tackled differently armed with hindsight.

6 **Review your own performance objectively.** Don't over-claim success, or downgrade your own achievements. Try to analyse what has gone well, and why, as well as what has been less successful, and why. In your preparation, ask colleagues who are not involved in your appraisal to help you realistically evaluate how you are doing. Ask them to help you remember the good parts that might have slipped your memory as well as to give you dispassionate accounts of the perhaps traumatic occurrences that you regard as having gone badly.

7 **Don't be artificially modest.** Without being boastful, you can use appraisal as an opportunity to celebrate the things of which you are proud. Often people are not fully aware of what individuals have done, and how much of a cooperative activity has in fact been the responsibility of one person. It is amazing how often an appraiser will say, 'I never realised that you are involved in so many areas'.

8 **Be realistic about your part in areas that have not been successes.** There's no need to shoulder all the blame for anything that went wrong, but the performance review is a chance to analyse how much responsibility you bear for the projects that have not succeeded, or for any deadlines that have been missed. This is the time for you to learn from the mistakes of the past and look forward to the next era. Avoid seeing your review as raking over old ground or digging up past errors and mistakes. Use it as a chance to reflect and to learn from what went wrong or did not work. Do not use this part of your review to criticise other colleagues or dwell on things over which you (or your manager) have little control (particularly a lack of resources).

9 **Write your own private reflective log after your appraisal.** Even if you have already produced a more formal report for your appraiser to sign off as part of the appraisal process, it can be helpful to have a more personal record of your own to refer back to. This can include how you felt when discussing your successes or failures, and notes to yourself about how you will go about following up your commitments arising from the review, and things to bear in mind to make the next occurrence of appraisal smoother.

10 **Remember that it is *your* review.** Don't allow it to become a one-way process, with your reviewer doing most of the talking. Use it as a proactive opportunity to address your own working life. See your review as the most appropriate occasion to renegotiate (if necessary) your job description and make it more interesting or rewarding. If you regard the staff review process as a tokenistic activity

in which your manager is simply going through the motions, then that is what it is likely to become.

11 **Use a part of your review to discuss institution-wide issues that concern you.** These might include equal opportunity matters, health and safety issues, particular problems often faced by students, or your concerns about teaching, learning and assessment. The review process often provides a rare chance for you to have the undivided attention of your line manager.

12 **Try to think of appraisal as a process and not an event.** Don't regard the date of your appraisal interview as the be-all and end-all of appraisal. It may be quite a crucial date, but it is only a milestone on a continuing journey.

13 **Finish the review with an agreement as to what will happen next.** Normally this will involve a confidential written record of the review, together with an agreed action plan that includes deadlines and responsibilities for both you and your line manager. Make sure that you know who is doing what before the end of the meeting. Make notes in your diary so you can follow up agreed actions in due course. Contact your reviewer if you don't feel an agreed activity has actually been set in train or had any outcome.

14 **Review the review process.** If you feel that you have been short-changed by your reviewer because you felt rushed, not listened to, or not taken seriously, say so and do not countersign the formal record of the review or action plan. If you are happy with the way things have been done, make this clear too so that your reviewer, in turn, can use your satisfaction as evidence in his or her own review.

Managing your feedback from students

The consumer's view is being sought more and more, and with students increasingly paying for their tuition, the student voice needs to be taken into account more than ever. Evidence of student feedback is one of the things that anyone reviewing the quality of your teaching is certain to ask to see, especially when student satisfaction as measured in national surveys, such as the National Student Survey in the UK, is a significant ingredient in the formation of league tables about various aspects of the overall standing of an institution.

The most serious danger is that from the students' point of view, giving feedback can become a chore. Then the act of giving feedback may not be taken seriously. The value of obtaining feedback is undermined whenever there is a feeling that the purpose is merely 'to be seen to be obtaining feedback'. The purpose of feedback should not merely be to make things better next time round. Giving feedback can itself be turned into part of the learning experience – particularly when feedback is the result of group discussions. In this section, I would like to point to four questions we should be asking ourselves at each stage of feedback processes:

- Are students developing a feeling of ownership of the feedback they give? (Or is it just clicks on an online survey, or ticks and jottings on someone else's questionnaire!)
- Are we getting the feedback we *need* from students? (Or are we only getting the answers to *our* questions, rather than the things that students need to be telling us?)
- Is giving feedback a learning experience in itself? (In other words, are students led into some deep and useful thinking about their studies, in the process of providing us with feedback?)
- How are we planning to give students the results of their feedback? (If they see that we're not actually taking any notice of their feedback, they're not likely to cooperate with our future attempts to procure feedback from them.)

Feedback on your lectures

There are many ways of getting feedback about the effectiveness of your lecture programme. Some are very simple, and require no special effort on your part.

Body language

You can find out a great deal about how your classes are going by keeping an eye on the ways your students are behaving. You can usually tell the difference between 'eyes glazing over' (or asleep!) and 'eyes which are interested and alert'. However, you can't *always* tell. Some students develop the art of appearing to be interested and alert when they're actually neither! There are of course body language traits that can alert you to unproductive processes – shuffling, chattering, fidgeting, and so on.

Coursework

Often, it's only when you assess the coursework associated with a particular topic that you fully discover how the students' learning *really* went. This can give you the opportunity to use further large-group teaching occasions to address what you've found out about the general state of the group's learning achievements. (It will be too late, of course, to do anything about discoveries about your students' learning which will become all too apparent when you mark their exam scripts – but such feedback remains useful for next time round regarding teaching the same topics.)

Informal comments from particular students

Often, you'll have opportunities to talk informally to some of the students – for example those who happen to come up and ask you questions, or those you meet in other contexts such as labs, studios or fieldwork. However, the feedback you get from these students may not be representative of the feelings of the whole group – the students who ask you questions may be the keenest ones, or the boldest. Any students experiencing real problems with the content of your sessions may not wish to give you any clue that they're not yet 'with you' in their grasp of what is being learned.

Peer feedback

Until relatively recently, there used to be too much privacy attached to our performances with large groups in lecture rooms. Now, most institutions of higher education have some sort of policy on peer observation, sometimes quite informal, but still very useful. Sitting in, regularly, on colleagues' sessions is one of the most productive ways to gain ideas to use in your own approaches to working with large groups. You'll find things they do well which you would like to try, and (just as useful) you'll notice things that they do less well which you will decide to avoid if at all possible. It is really useful if you can identify one or two colleagues where you can develop peer feedback into something really useful, where you mutually and regularly give each other honest and constructive comments about how the sessions are going. Many institutions now use peer-observation of teaching to help lecturers not only to develop their approaches, but also to prepare themselves for any external scrutiny of the quality of their teaching.

If you are heading towards any kind of inspection of the sort where someone from another institution may observe you at work with large groups, it can be very useful to rehearse the situation by getting one or two other lecturers – maybe from other disciplines – to observe you quite formally as preparation. This helps you to become accustomed to the presence of outsiders, and also to become more aware of the things that you do that are most effective and interesting.

Feedback from seeing yourself teach

Making your own video is easier than you may think! You can choose the room, time, class, and position that you place the camera or mobile phone, and when you switch it on and off, and no one but you needs to see the video (though it is even more useful if you get a colleague or friend to watch it with you). It can be even better to get a colleague, or a student, to operate a camera, and follow you around and zoom in to show details of your expression or of the visual aids you may use. You can derive a substantial amount of feedback about your own performance just by watching yourself. You can even get a surprising amount of useful feedback just from making a sound recording of you in action.

Stop, start, continue

A quick and versatile method of gaining feedback – especially from large groups of students – is to give them post-it notes, and ask them to write the three headings 'stop', 'start', and 'continue' on them as shown in Figure 6.1.

You can then ask the class a question along any one of the following lines:

- under each heading, jot down what you'd like *me* to do in future sessions on this course … or …
- tell me what *you'd* like to stop doing, start doing, and continue doing as we go further in this course … or …
- simply write down anything you'd like to tell me under each of the three headings.

Stop …	Start …	Continue …

Figure 6.1 Student feedback

A variety of feedback mechanisms

Feedback can be gathered from students in many different ways, including from:

- interviews with individual students;
- feedback activities with groups of students;
- solicited feedback from large groups of students (for example using the 'stop, start, continue' agenda on post-it notes in large-group lectures, as mentioned above);
- questionnaires online or on paper;
- using clickers in large-group sessions, to get quick responses about how a particular module is going, with students retaining the comfort of anonymity in their responses;
- student representation on programme boards;
- informally (for example through tutorials, seminars, one-to-one chats with students in lab work, studios, field work);
- students' exam performance (but then it's too late for some!);
- students' coursework performance (and particularly from *their* reactions to our own feedback to them);
- information which may be forthcoming from external observers who may be able to discuss with students their experience of courses, e.g. moderators and examiners.

This chapter continues with some illustrations of the advantages and disadvantages of a number of approaches to eliciting feedback from students.

Some limitations of questionnaires

Because it's easy to administer, the questionnaire has become the dominant method of seeking feedback. Unfortunately, it's also easy to fall into the temptation to produce statistics based on questionnaire responses. If 84 per cent of students think Dr Smith's lectures are brilliant, we're inclined to ignore the 16 per cent who don't – but they may have very good reasons for disliking the lectures. The problem is not so much with gathering feedback by questionnaire, but with the ways feedback is processed and collated. Some of the factors which limit the value of questionnaire feedback are listed below.

1 **The 'ticky-box' syndrome on paper-based questionnaires, and 'clicking-on' with online ones.** People become conditioned to make instant responses to questions. Getting through the questionnaire quickly becomes a virtue, and quite often the questions are not read properly. Responses are made on a surface level of thinking rather than as a result of reflection and critical thinking. (This is not a problem on those occasions where instant reaction is what is wanted, but the feedback we gather is not usually analysed on that basis.)

2 **Performing dogs syndrome.** Many people filling in questionnaires tend to want to please! They can usually tell which responses will please the people giving them the questionnaire, and the people whose work is involved in the issues covered by the questionnaire. If they like the people, they are likely to comment favourably on things, rather than use them to show their real views.

3 **The grudgers.** If one way or another you've upset some students, or bored them, or ignored them, when it comes to giving feedback they may tend to tick more of the 'negative' choices.

4 **Lost learning opportunities.** Question-naires are often used after an event rather than during it. This tends to minimise any real learning outcomes of the process of

completing questionnaires. The sense of ownership is reduced, when students don't see how their responses will be of any direct benefit to themselves, and may only help their successors.

5 **The 'WYSIWYG' syndrome** (what you see is what you get). Questionnaires produce feedback on the particular issues covered – but often *not* on other important issues. There is a tendency to design questionnaires which will give positive feedback, and to avoid asking those questions where there is every possibility of critical replies.

6 **'Blue, rosy and purple' questionnaires.** A major limitation of most questionnaires is that responses are coloured by how people *feel* at the moment of filling them in. If the same questionnaire were used a few days later, some responses may be completely different. Yet the results are often statistically analysed as though they reflected permanent, considered reactions to questions and issues, rather than fleeting, transient reactions.

7 **'Conditioned response' questionnaires.** When the same questionnaire format is used repeatedly, students can become very bored, and may revert to answering many of the questions in the same way as they have often done previously. Feedback then is not specific to the particular occasion when the questionnaire is being used, and at best represents overall feelings rather than specific responses.

8 **'Death by questionnaire'.** Especially when there is an 'official' survey (as with the NSS in the UK), many institutions try to sample in advance the tone of the feedback which will be produced, resulting in too many questionnaires issued too often. This is worse when the questionnaires are badly designed in the first place, and when nothing ever seems to happen as a result of the feedback that is given.

Some advantages of questionnaire feedback

Despite all the reservations presented above, there are some significant advantages associated with gathering student feedback through questionnaires. The best ways of using questionnaires therefore depend on using the advantages deliberately, while at the same time minimising the effect of the drawbacks.

- Feedback questionnaires can be anonymous: this allows students the chance at least of giving negative feedback without the embarrassment of giving it publicly.
- Feedback questionnaires can be quick, especially online: many things can be covered in a few minutes.
- Feedback from questionnaires is amenable to statistical analysis: this is an advantage – but as we've mentioned, a dangerous one!
- Feedback from questionnaires can be fed into institutional review and quality procedures. Most institutions have some such processes in operation, and an obvious ingredient is of course feedback from students.
- Questionnaires can be used on a 'deeper' level: it's possible, for example, to get students to go through a questionnaire *twice*. The first time they can be briefed to respond as they feel, the second time they can be asked to respond as they would *like* to feel. This can help to get over the problem of different students preferring different things – the gap between 'how it is' and 'how you'd like it to be' is often more important – and more revealing – than students' reactions just to 'how it is'.

Some ideas on structured questions

Structured (or 'closed') questions are of several types including the following:

Ticking boxes or putting marks on scales

This is often done using 'agreement measures' and can be done with contrasting dimensions at opposite sides of a form, see Table 6.1.

One of the things which can go wrong with such scales is when the factors at each end turn out *not* to be opposites. Furthermore, if an odd number of columns is used (as in the example shown), the middle column represents 'safe middle ground', and can cause students to put their responses there when they can't decide whether something is interesting or boring, and so on. It can be argued that it is better to force them to make a decision by having an even number of columns. Then, those students who *really* think that something is midway between the extremes have to make a conscious decision, for example to put their tick or cross on the central line.

'Usefulness' measures

Various features of the teaching methods or processes can be mentioned at the left-hand side of a pro forma, with boxes for 'very useful', 'quite useful' and 'not useful' to tick. The dimensions can include such things as: online resources, slides, worked examples done in class, for example, see Table 6.2.

Table 6.1 Example of an 'agreement measures' questionnaire

	Strongly agree	Agree	Neither agree nor disagree	Disagree	Strongly disagree	
Boring						Interesting
Too fast						Too slow
Audible						Inaudible
Slides easy to read						Slides hard to read
Aims made clear						Aims hard to work out
I learned a lot						I didn't learn anything
My questions answered						My questions unanswered
Enjoyable						Not enjoyable
Well worth turning up for						Not worth turning up for

Table 6.2 Example of a usefulness measures questionnaire

Feature	Very useful	Quite useful	Not useful
Online resources			
Module web pages			
Practice quizzes			
Large-group sessions			
Small-group sessions			
Independent learning			
Slides in lectures			
In-class exercises			
Peer assessment tasks			

Table 6.3 Example of an agreement measures questionnaire

	Strongly agree	Quite agree	Disagree	Strongly disagree
I find your lectures stimulate me to further work				
I remain switched-off for most of my time in your lectures				
I am clear about the intended learning outcomes of each part of this module				
I don't really know what is expected of me in this subject				
I find it easy to ask questions in your lectures				
I find parts of this subject very hard to understand				

Statements with 'agreement' measures

A series of statements can be checked against boxes such as 'strongly agree', 'more-or-less agree', 'disagree', 'strongly disagree', for example. The statements can usefully be both positive and negative, to ensure that respondents don't fall into the pattern of agreeing (or disagreeing) with everything they see. Part of such a questionnaire could be as shown in Table 6.3.

Number-gradings

This is another form of structuring students' responses, by asking them to enter numbers to indicate their feelings with regard to a statement or an issue, e.g. 5 = most useful, 4 = very useful, 3 = quite useful, 2 = of limited use, 1 = of little use, 0 = of no use.

'More', 'Just right', 'Less' boxes

These could be used (for example) for students to record their feelings about the things they do in tutorials, for example see Table 6.4.

Table 6.4 Example of more, just right, and less

Processes used in tutorials	More of this please	Just right, thanks!	Less of this please
Practising problem solving			
Seeing worked examples done			
Working through case-study materials			
Asking questions of the lecturer			
Being asked questions by the lecturer			
Having marked homework discussed individually			
Having marked practical work returned and discussed			
Seeing examples of assessment criteria			
Using assessment criteria directly to mark own or others' work			
Practising addressing previous exam questions, then marking them			

Prioritising

This sort of structure helps overcome the 'ticky-box' syndrome, as it causes students to think more deeply about issues. For example, they can be asked to enter '1' against the best feature of Dr Smith's classes, '2' against the next best, and so on. My recommendation regarding getting students to prioritise teaching attributes remains 'keep it as simple as possible'. Questions and choices need to be clear and unambiguous. This method can also be used to find out which topics in a subject area students find the most difficult, for example see Table 6.5.

Some ideas for open questions

Open questions allow each student to respond freely to set areas. While such questions can overcome some of the limitations I have mentioned regarding structured questions, if the questionnaires are paper-based, the fact that students are entering their responses in their own handwriting can be a deterrent against them expressing negative or critical views, where they may feel that they could be traced and

Table 6.5 Example of a prioritising questionnaire

Physical chemistry: rank the topics below from '1' (the one you find most straightforward) to '8' (the one you find most difficult)	Your ratings
Electrochemistry	
Chemical kinetics	
Thermodynamics	
Phase equilibria	
Colloid chemistry	
Spectroscopy	
Photochemistry	
Mass transfer	

Table 6.6 Example open questions

Two things I like best about your classes: 1 2
Two things I like least about your classes: 1 2
This module would be better for me if you could:
The three topics I found most difficult to make sense of in this module are: 1 2 3

maybe even penalised as a result. Online questionnaires can be used anonymously – but then students may not think the results will be treated as seriously as if their names were on the questionnaire. See Table 6.6.

Computer-analysed feedback

Many software packages exist which allow student feedback to be gathered, and statistically analysed. Students can be asked a series of multiple-choice (pick *one* of these…) or multiple-response (pick *one or more* of these…) questions, and their choices of entry can be recorded by the computer, enabling statistical analysis to be done on the responses from large groups of students. The feedback can be made anonymous, or students' names can be used. It is probably best to use such feedback approaches where a record is kept of which students have given their feedback, but the individual responses are analysed on an anonymous basis. Students are more likely to give feedback using such software, particularly if the process of gathering the feedback can be made more interesting for the students giving it, for example by providing on-screen responses back to students on the basis of some of the choices they make, for example 'sorry you didn't like this', 'glad this worked for you', 'thanks, we'll bear this in mind in future' and so on.

Computer-gathered feedback is not restricted to multiple-choice questions. Open-ended questions can also be included, and the software can sort and print out lists of the responses of a whole class of students to any particular question. Open-ended feedback of this sort, when gathered by computer, may be more reliable than when given in handwriting, as students may feel less under threat regarding their views being noticed and used against them!

Suggestions on ways of using questionnaires

I've been quite critical about some of the most common methods used to seek and analyse student feedback, and have referred to many of the things which can go wrong with such methods. Next, however, I offer a range of suggestions for developing some of these methods further, taking into account the risks, and aiming to optimise the potential benefits, both to ourselves and to our students.

1 **Consider making the use of questionnaires private to individual members of staff.** For feedback about lectures (or tutorials, or lab work) I think it best that each lecturer designs and uses his/her individual questionnaire, and obtains feedback for his/her own use privately. This doesn't mean, however, that the forms are to be filled in 'privately' by students – it may well be better to use them as an agenda for group feedback.

2 **Make questionnaires 'short and often, not long and once'.** Any feedback form should be short enough not to bore or alienate students. A good guide may be that it should be possible for a group to complete the form in a few minutes or so. This means separate forms for lectures, tutorials, and so on.

3 **Use questionnaires for formative rather than summative feedback whenever possible.** Seek feedback during a programme, so that something can still be done about matters emerging. Feedback after completion of a programme is still useful, but is not seen by students as so valuable as when they have the chance to suggest changes they themselves will benefit from directly.

4 **Employ questionnaires for a wide range of matters to do with presentation, style and approachability.** These aspects of, for example, lecturing, can be gathered in the private mode suggested above. Individual questionnaire components can be selected/composed by each staff member to search for comment about issues that may be of particular concern to the lecturer concerned.

5 **Consider 'more public' questionnaires for general issues, and for summative feedback.** These can be used to measure feedback relating to non-personal variables, such as:
   - relative workload of different topics or modules;
   - perceived relevance of topics as seen by students;
   - relevance of practical work to theory, as seen by students;
   - balance of lectures, tutorials and other teaching/learning contexts.

This 'more public' sort of questionnaire is more likely to have value when used towards the end of a course or module, and to gather summative feedback, which can be used in reviewing the course or module prior to the next time it will be delivered.

6 **Structured questionnaires can have the advantage of anonymity.** Even if using a mixed questionnaire containing open-ended questions as well, you may decide to issue the structured and open-ended parts separately because of this factor.

7 **Try to avoid surface thinking.** Students – and anyone else involved – get bored if they have long questionnaires to complete, and the decisions or comments they make become 'surface' rather than considered ones. Even though students may be able to respond to a structured questionnaire of several pages in relatively few minutes, the fact that a questionnaire *looks* long can induce surface response behaviour.

8 **Consider the visual appearance of your questionnaires.** Go for a varied layout, with plenty of white space, so that it does not look like a solid list of questions. Use a mixture of response formats, such as deletions or selections from lists of options, yes/no choices, tick-boxes, graduated scales, and so on – make it *look* interesting to complete.

9 **For every part of the questionnaire, have definite purposes, including positive ones.** Don't ask anything that could prove to be superfluous or of passing interest only. Ask about positive experiences as well as searching for weaknesses.

10 **Plan your evaluation report before you design your feedback questionnaire.** It helps a great deal if you know exactly how you plan to collate and use the responses you will get from your questionnaires. Working out the things you hope to include in your report often alerts you to additional questions you may need to include, and (particularly) to superfluous questions which would not actually generate any information of practical use to you.

11 **Make each question simple and unambiguous.** If students' interpretations of the questions vary, the results of a survey are not valid enough to warrant statistical analysis of any sort. In particular, it's worth ensuring that in structured questions, students are only required to make decisions involving a single factor.

12 **Ask yourself 'what does this question really mean?'** Sometimes, your reply to yourself will contain wording which will work better in your questionnaire than the original idea you started with.

13 **Avoid safe middle ground in scales.** For example, the scale 'strongly agree, agree, undecided, disagree, strongly disagree' may give better results if the 'undecided' option is omitted, forcing respondents to make a decision one way or the other (or to *write* 'can't tell' on the questionnaire, which then has the validity of a conscious decision).

14 **Be aware that some respondents will make choices on the basis of those they think they are expected to make.** Many respondents set out to 'please' the person gathering the feedback, possibly thinking of possible recriminations if critical selections may be traced back to their authors.

15 **Keep prioritising questions short and simple.** For example if students are asked to rank seven factors in order of value (or importance), it may be easy enough to analyse the best and worst choices, but difficult to make a meaningful analysis of 'middle ground'.

16 **Pilot your draft questionnaire.** There is no better way to improve a structured questionnaire than to find out what students actually do with it! Use short print runs for any paper-based questionnaires, and trial online ones with small groups first, and edit as you find out more about what gives useful feedback and what doesn't.

17 **Remember that students' responses can be influenced by their mood at the moment of answering the question.** Ideally, you may wish to balance out this source of variation in one way or another, for example by issuing a similar questionnaire at another time, and comparing responses, or by including some alternative questions in other parts of your questionnaire which 'test' the same agenda so you can be alerted to inconsistency in responses due to swings of mood.

18 **Don't leave big spaces in paper-based questionnaires for students to fill in their replies.** You can compensate for this restriction later with 'any other comments?' space. If students' responses are necessarily short, you are more likely to get easily interpreted answers to your questions, which helps make statistical analysis more fruitful. Similarly in online questionnaires, it's best not to have fixed box-sizes on-screen, but to allow the box to expand where students feel like being more expansive than expected in their replies.

19 **Decide whether you want the questionnaire to be anonymous, optional or respondent-known.** With responses involving handwriting, there is always the possibility of tracing respondents, and students may respond differently with this possibility in mind. With computer-based open-ended questionnaires, this dimension is simplified, but not entirely overcome if log-in data could be used to trace respondents.

20 **Resist pressures to over-use standard questionnaires.** This applies equally to structured or open-ended versions or mixed-mode questionnaires. Students quickly get bored with identical questionnaires, and are likely to fall into a standard mode of response, where there is considerable 'echo effect' carried forward from previous decisions and responses. The most useful feedback data is normally generated by specially produced questionnaires relating to a specific course or subject, or a particular aspect of the teaching and learning in that subject.

21 **Try to get a good response rate.** When questionnaires are filled in during contact time, you are more likely to get everyone's views. If questionnaires are taken away by students to be sent back later, there is a tendency to get lower response rates, and the students who

actually go to the trouble of responding may not be representative of the whole group. With online questionnaires, some institutions offer random 'prizes' for a few of those completing them.

22 **Give students some free-ranging questions.** For example, it's worth considering asking them, 'What other questions should be included in future editions of this questionnaire?' and inviting them to supply their own answers to the questions they think of. Such data is unsuitable for any statistical purposes, but is valuable in qualitative analysis of feedback from students.

23 **Work out how you are going to analyse the data from open-ended questions.** Sometimes a transcript collecting all responses to a question is necessary before the gist of the feedback can be discerned accurately. In other circumstances, counting the number of times something is mentioned in students' responses can be a valuable process.

24 **Don't accumulate piles of uninterpreted questionnaire data!** It's best to make a deliberate effort to produce a summary report (even if only for your own private use) for each set of data. A pile (or online file) of feedback responses quickly becomes out of date as new developments are implemented in courses. Also, it is worth showing students that you take the data seriously enough to analyse it straightaway.

Feedback from interviews with students

Interviews with students can be a valuable source of feedback. However, interviewing students is costly in terms of time and effort; the following suggestions may help you to make it a cost-effective process.

1 **Prepare your agenda carefully.** To enable you to analyse and collate the feedback you get from students, it is important that they are all asked the same questions in the same way. It is all too tempting to develop the agenda on the basis of the replies of the first few students, so it is usually worth piloting your question list on a few students (not necessarily from the group to be targeted) before starting on a set of 'real' interviews.

2 **Link interviews with other means of getting feedback from students.** If you are already using (or planning to use) structured or open-ended questionnaires, you may find it worthwhile to work out what *else* you will be particularly looking for in feedback from interviews.

3 **Consider the merits of using interviews to follow-up questionnaire feedback.** When you have already analysed questionnaire responses by students, you may be able to pinpoint a few issues where you want to ask students more detailed or more personal questions about their experiences with a subject or a course.

4 **Consider the alternative possibility of using preliminary interviews to establish the agenda for feedback questionnaires.** This would probably not take the form of interviews with the whole group, but with a representative selection of students.

5 **You may not be able to interview the whole group.** Decide how you are going to select the students you choose to interview. There are many possibilities, each with its own advantages and drawbacks. For example, you could select randomly by name or student number, or you could make a representative selection including high-performers, middle-range-performers and low-achievers in related assessments, or you could ask for volunteers (not, however, the most representative of the possibilities).

6 **Remember that some students may be quite anxious.** Any kind of interview may feel to students as if there is an assessment dimension present, and this may cause them to be restrained especially when it comes to expressing dissatisfaction.

7 **Ask questions which lead students to answer rather than to refrain from comment.** For example, asking students 'was there anything you found unsatisfactory?' may be less fruitful than asking 'what was the thing you liked least about the way this module was taught?'

8 **Don't lead your witnesses!** It is one thing to ensure that students feel free to answer questions, but another to lead them towards the answers you want, or the answers they may think you want. 'Do you like the way I used lots of graphics on my slides?' is an obvious example of a leading question!

Feedback from groups of students

Students may be more forthcoming in a group, and you could consider posing the questions (maybe as a handout), leaving the group to come to decisions about how the students wished to answer them, then return to hear their answers. Students have the safety of being able to report minority views or controversial views, without the student who actually speaks such responses having to 'own' the view reported. Group interviews can actually save a considerable amount of time compared with solo interviews, and allow students to compare and contrast their own perspectives. Students in groups can also be helped to prioritise or sequence in order of importance their responses, making their feedback even more valuable. Group interviews can also be used to get students to clarify or explain issues or responses which at first may be unclear.

This can be more useful than feedback from individuals, for the following reasons:

- Feedback from groups captures discussion, reflection and debate. This is more useful than only having the reactions of individual students.
- A group can present negative feedback with less embarrassment than an individual. Individuals can be more forthcoming in making inputs in a group, when their feedback is then rendered more or less anonymous within the group.
- Group feedback is likely to range more widely. Where a questionnaire is used as an agenda for group feedback, the group is more likely to be willing to go beyond the agenda.

It's essential to make good notes when interviewing groups of students! After four or five interviews, you may have a good idea of the general nature of responses to your questions, but you could have lost a lot of the specific detail. More recent interview happenings tend to 'drown' earlier ones in one's memory.

Conclusions

The aspects of 'looking after yourself' discussed in this chapter are not, of course, the end of the story. A further important topic is reflecting on your teaching – in some ways this is the most personal and powerful way of looking after yourself, and there's a lot about this in the final chapter in this *Toolkit*.

However, there are many other people who can help you to look after yourself. You may be lucky enough to have a great mentor – or you may be able to find one for yourself. It's really useful to have someone to turn to on those days where challenges seem just too challenging – and indeed on those occasions when you're so pleased with something you've done you're just burning to tell someone who will also be pleased. More widely, don't be so busy that you lose touch with friends. Sometimes talking about things entirely unrelated to your job can be very restoring. In fact – just keep *talking*. Like learning in general, putting things into spoken words helps us to get our heads around things. Even when things are difficult, 'telling the tale' to different people often both gets it out of your system, and reduces the significance of a problem. When talking, however, don't forget to *listen* to replies and advice. You may not want to take particular advice, but it's good to have people offering it, as you can then select. If you cut people off while giving advice, they won't keep giving it.

And keep *writing* as well. Make notes to yourself, keep a reflective log or diary, if this helps you pin down problems and challenges. Sometimes it's just a relief to have 'put it on the wall' (not publicly) in your own words somewhere. Make some of your writing much more public – there's nothing so good for helping us consolidate our thinking about teaching than to turn some of the better bits of our work into publications, to share what we've learned more widely. There's more about this in the next chapter too. At the end of the day, though, the very best person to look after yourself can only be *you*.

Chapter 7

Challenges and reflections

It is simply madness to keep doing the same things, and expect different results.

(attributed to Albert Einstein)

Intended outcomes of this chapter

When you've explored the ideas in this chapter, and tried out the most appropriate ones in the context of your own teaching, you should be better able to:

- Address some of the many challenges facing professionals in post-compulsory education nowadays.
- Reflect productively on your teaching, and accumulate valuable evidence of reflection.

The first part of the chapter is about challenges you may experience, and the chapter ends with a fairly detailed section on reflection, and building your evidence of reflection as part of your ongoing professional development. The chapter ends with some quite detailed reflective checklists you may find useful as a starting point for capturing your thinking about your teaching and associated activities, and for building on hindsight as you continue to work with students.

Firstly, however, it is useful to collect our thoughts on the kinds of 'madness' we need to guard against, in the light of the Einstein maxim which started this chapter.

Present 'madnesses' include:

- Lecturing, in the traditional way. (Students don't now expect to write notes, and often don't come with pens.) Ways of avoiding this madness were discussed in some detail in Chapter 3.
- Spending hours hand-writing feedback comments on students' work. (Students take little notice, and get feedback too late.) Ways around this were proposed in Chapter 2.
- Marking essays. (Reliability of essays as an assessment method is notoriously poor.) Problems with essay-marking were highlighted in Chapter 2.
- Marking huge piles of exam scripts. (Written exams only measure what comes out of pens, we need to assess what's in heads.) Concerns about traditional exams were addressed in Chapter 2.
- Ignoring the fact that students can get to some of the best 'content' in the world by themselves, at no charge, on their laptops, tablets and mobile phones. The role of resource-based learning was discussed in detail in Chapter 5.

We've got to stop wasting our time and energy doing these 'mad' things, and focus our expertise on helping students to become excellent learners, getting feedback to them in ways that work much better than old-hat written comments, and transforming assessment into something which causes learning, not just attempting to measure snapshots of what has been memorised. Presently, too many staff waste much of their time and energy trying to do things that don't work, and will never work.

On to seven more challenges...

Seven challenges facing teachers in higher education

The first part of this chapter is about some of the more challenging aspects of being a lecturer. Many challenges have already been addressed in earlier chapters in this *Toolkit*, particularly ones relating to assessment, feedback, making lectures inspiring, and small-group teaching, but this section addresses briefly some wider challenges. You may indeed already have found your own ways of addressing at least some of these challenges. Some may be more serious than others, depending on your subject area, the ethos of teaching in your institution, the nature of your student body, and many other factors. The questions addressed here are:

- How can we foster good academic conduct, and discourage students from plagiarism and cheating?
- How can we motivate and engage students, when many have numerous competing pressures on their time?
- How can we provide educational experiences that are inclusive and non-discriminatory to students with disabilities?
- How can we foster cross-cultural capability among our students and staff, working with international students and staff in a global environment?
- How can we provide a coherent approach to the student experience, offering a programme-level approach?
- How can I go about showing how excellent my teaching has become?
- How can I use my pedagogic work to get published?

As you can see from this list, the first five questions are all in one way or another linked to the student experience, but the last two are challenges about your own pedagogic development, and working towards getting this celebrated either through professional recognition for excellent teaching, or getting your work into print in an appropriate way.

I How can we foster good academic conduct, and discourage students from plagiarism and cheating?

Much has been made of the supposed substantial growth in plagiarism since it has been so much easier to do it in recent years. Formerly students intent on copying had at least to copy out others' texts, but nowadays cutting and pasting from online sources can make the act of using others' work without attribution very easy. Specialist software packages like Turnitin can be helpful both in deterring students from doing it (particularly when teachers demonstrate how plagiarism can be detected) and for helping students, especially those with hazy understandings of what comprises plagiarism, to understand the concept of what is counted as plagiarism, and what is acceptable attribution to the work of others.

Plagiarism has become one of the most significant problems which coursework assessors find themselves facing. Indeed, the difficulties associated with plagiarism are so severe that there is considerable pressure to retreat into the relative safety of traditional unseen written exams once again, and we are coming round full circle to resorting to assessment processes and instruments which can guarantee authenticity but at the expense of validity. However, probably too much of the energy which is being put into tackling plagiarism is devoted to *detecting* the symptoms and punishing those found guilty of unfairly passing off other people's work as their own. After all, where are the moral and ethical borderlines? In many parts of the world, to quote back a teacher's words in an exam answer or coursework assignment is culturally accepted as 'honouring the teacher'. When students from these cultures, who happen to be continuing their studies in the UK, find themselves accused of plagiarism, they can be surprised at our attitude. Prevention is better than the cure. We need to be much more careful to explain exactly what is acceptable, and what is not. While some students may indeed deliberately engage in plagiarism, many others find themselves in trouble because they were not fully aware of how they are expected to treat other people's work. Sometimes they simply do not fully understand how they are expected to cite others' work in their own discussions, or how to follow the appropriate referencing conventions.

It is also worth facing up to the difficulty of the question, 'where are the borderlines between originality and authenticity?' In a sense, true originality is extremely rare. In most disciplines, it is seldom possible to write anything without having already been influenced by what has been done before, what has been read, what has been heard, and so on. There is, however, another aspect of authenticity – the extent to which the work being assessed relates to the real world beyond post-compulsory education. In this respect, authenticity is about making assessed tasks as close as possible to the performances which students will need to develop in their lives and careers in the real world.

McDowell and Brown (2001) suggest that preventative strategies are far more beneficial than retributive ones, so the focus in recent years has been primarily on both fostering academic literacy, so students know what kinds of behaviours to avoid, and on good curriculum design to offer assignments that are less open to poor academic conduct.

Harder to detect is the work of academic ghost writers, family members and essay mills from whom students can commission original assignments that plagiarism software cannot detect. McDowell and Brown would propose that providing a culture in which students feel well supported may make it unthinkable for students to cheat. Personalising assignments and making students feel more than just a number can contribute to a collective ethos of this kind, but with higher education being for the masses rather than the elite, the sheer volume of assignments being marked makes it harder to review the work of a whole cohort and to offer meaningful individual attention.

Some suggestions regarding minimising the incidence of plagiarism are given below:

1 **Distinguish between malicious and inadvertent plagiarism.** Punitive action may be quite inappropriate when plagiarism is the consequence of students' lack of understanding of acceptable practice regarding citing the work of others.

2 **Debate issues and solutions with the whole class.** Establish ground rules for fair play, and agreed procedures for dealing with any infringements of these ground rules. It is important that such discussions should take place before the first assessment.

3 **Act decisively when you discover copying.** Here I mean copying within a class, rather than from a wider range of online sources. One option is to treat copying as collaborative work, and mark the work as normal but divide the total score by the number of students involved. Their reactions to this often help you find out who did the work first, or who played the biggest part in doing the work. That said, copying within a class is becoming much rarer, as the availability of a plethora of materials on the web are easier to copy from.

4 **Be alert when encouraging students to work together.** Make sure that they know where the intended collaboration should stop, and that you will be vigilant to check that later assessed

work does not show signs of the collaboration having extended too far.

5 **Help students to understand the fine line between collaborative working and practices which the institution will regard as cheating.** Sometimes it can come as a shock and horror to students to find that what they thought of as acceptable collaboration is being regarded as cheating.

6 **Don't underestimate your students!** We only tend to catch those who are not very skilled at plagiarism! Skilled plagiarists will ensure that they make sufficient adjustments to any work they insert into their own, so that plagiarism detection software will not pick it up. It is best to design coursework assignments which do not lend themselves to cheating – and short focused assignments make it more obvious if there has been any foul play.

7 **Anticipate problems, and steer round them by briefing students on what is – and what isn't – plagiarism or cheating.** When collaboration is likely to occur, consider whether you can in fact turn it into a virtue by redesigning the assessments concerned to comprise collaborative tasks for students in groups.

8 **Be aware of cultural differences regarding acceptable behaviour regarding assessed work.** Bring the possibility of such differences to the surface by starting discussions with groups of students. Acknowledge and discuss the extreme pressures to avoid failure which some students may feel themselves subject to. Discuss with students the extent to which emulating their teachers and using their words is acceptable.

9 **Clarify your institution's requirements on fair practice.** The majority of students actually *want* fair play, and can be very rigorous if asked to devise systems to guarantee this. Draw links between the systems and the assessment regulations extant in your university. Make sure that students understand what the regulations mean!

10 **Wherever you can, devise assessments which include reference to students' own activities or experiences.** For a start, they are usually keen to write about these, and less likely to seek material to slot in from elsewhere. You also have the option, if doubt arises, to question them orally about their experiences, and would soon find out if there was a problem.

11 **Keep assessed work word-limits short.** One of the triggers for plagiarism is lack of sufficient time to get started on a long task with a short deadline.

2 How can we motivate and engage students, when many have numerous competing pressures on their time?

Kneale (1997) suggests that students have to budget their time carefully if alongside study they are also nurturing families and undertaking paid work. Sometimes they seek to do the minimum they need to barely pass; this is risky behaviour, sometimes resulting in undershooting their own modest targets. Students tend to invest their energies cannily in activities that have high payoff, so how we design assessment can be crucial in helping students to work wisely, since they often treat marks like money!

Students tend to become demotivated if they think that:

• They are just one individual in a large cohort and no one knows or cares whether they are attending or not;
• Teaching staff are distant and remote, with little interest in individual student achievement and success. This can particularly be the case where the academic culture clearly prioritises research over teaching;
• There are too many artificial hurdles set in their way to prevent their success, particularly in terms of bureaucratic processes designed for the benefit of the institution rather than the student;

- They perceive unfairness and injustice in the ways that students are treated, with some students seemingly treated with favouritism;
- They have too long to wait for feedback on their last piece of work, and then find that the feedback is disappointing.

Laurillard (2013) suggests that technology can help us to keep up with our students, and adapt our approach to teaching appropriately:

> Technology gives teachers much better access to how students discuss and debate in an online forum, to data analytics that describe how they progress through a sequence of learning activities, what they produce in a collaborative wiki, how they reflect on their learning journey in an e-portfolio. If as teachers, we use technology to elicit and make use of this extensive information to remodel our teaching that will be a new task to fit into the teacher's repertoire.
>
> (Laurillard, 2013, p. xviii)

Mayes and De Freitas (2013) hit the nail on the head, and challenge us to remodel the educational enterprise accordingly:

> As technology-enhanced learning tools become truly powerful in their capability, and global in their scope, so it becomes more feasible to remodel the educational enterprise as a process of empowering learners to take reflective control of their own learning.
>
> (Mayes and De Freitas, 2013, pp. 27–8)

The implications of this for us as teachers are that we have to pay much more than lip service to student-centred learning. Learning is in fact *always* student-centred – it's the teaching, feedback and assessment contexts students find themselves in that are sometimes far from being student-centred, particularly in large institutions. Rather than try to get students to 'inhabit' the world of the academic, we need to try to inhabit their world; only a small proportion of our students aspire to become academics, and those who do are often the ones who least need our help and understanding in practice.

3 How can we provide educational experiences that are inclusive and non-discriminatory to students with disabilities?

In many nations there is a legislative requirement for disabled students to be treated equally, with heavy penalties for individuals and institutions which contravene these regulations. There is also a moral duty on us as teachers to ensure that students with disabilities are given equivalent if not identical opportunities to learn and be assessed alongside their peers.

Student attitudes have also changed significantly in recent years, reflecting the tendency for society as a whole to be more aware of rights, and more likely to resort to law if injustice is felt to have happened. Students are more litigious, and even more so when they are paying for their higher education. This greater sensitivity to customer rights is reflected in students' expectations of teaching and learning environments and processes. Furthermore, should lack of appropriate attention to any identified additional need end up by disadvantaging particular students when they come to be assessed, appeals and even legal action can come as no surprise. In the UK, student complaints about various aspects of their higher education increase in number each year, with a significant proportion being complaints about unfair assessment, and the climate has changed to one where it is seen as acceptable to query marks and grades. The amount of time taken sorting out appeals of this sort can be enormous.

Many post-compulsory organisations today are clued-up about how to ensure that their estates are accommodating for students and staff with mobility issues, and visual and hearing impairments, but not all have as well-established ways of supporting students with dyslexia, mental health issues, chronic fatigue syndrome as well as those on the autism spectrum and with Attention Deficit Disorders. Some institutions seem to think that so long as the wheelchair ramps are in place, specialist software is supplied for visually impaired students and the hearing loops are in operation in the lecture theatres, the job is complete. However, other issues that need addressing include:

- Making sure that discriminatory behaviour towards students with disabilities is neither accepted nor condoned in any quarters. Adams and Brown (2006) suggest that fellow students frequently are the locus of discrimination against disabled students and this must robustly be challenged. Inclusivity awareness training can be helpful for all categories of staff encountered by students.
- Ensuring that sufficient budget is made available to provide reasonable adjustments, since shortage of resources can be used as an excuse for individuals to behave in discriminatory ways, and sometimes for disabled students to be excluded. In some nations, funding is made available at a national level and in others, responsible institutions need to budget at a local level.
- Ensuring that appropriate assessment activities are provided for all students. Offering equivalent assessments can provide particular challenges for institutions, since last minute and *ad hoc* arrangements tend to be problematic.

At the start of his seminar paper on 'Rethinking teaching in the context of diversity', Northedge (2003) suggested the following:

> Higher education has faced profound teaching challenges in recent times, as it has delivered a widening range of courses to students of increasingly diverse backgrounds, expectations and levels of preparedness. These challenges call for a more radical shift in teaching than simply incorporating remedial support within existing teaching programmes. This paper argues that neither traditional 'knowledge delivery' models of teaching, nor a purely 'student-centred' approach, adequately addresses the challenges of student diversity. Instead, it proposes an emphasis on the socio-cultural nature of learning and teaching, modelling learning as acquiring the capacity to participate in the discourses of an unfamiliar knowledge community, and teaching as supporting that participation. It explores the challenges faced by students struggling to make meaning in strange intellectual and social surroundings, and outlines ways teachers can structure courses and tasks so that very diverse cohorts of students can progress together in meeting those challenges.
>
> (Northedge, 2003, p. 17)

Brown (2015) argues that:

> Planning reasonable adjustments for students with special needs is so time consuming, it is often best to design in some options at the outset for those who don't see, hear or write easily, and potentially making these available for any students to choose. TechDis (http://www.jisctechdis. ac.uk/) offers superb practical advice on alternative formats and understanding user needs.
>
> (Brown, 2015, p. 117)

We need to remember not to ignore or undervalue the most significant source of expertise in how best additional needs can be addressed – namely the owners of the needs. Students themselves usually know a great deal about any additional need they have lived with over the years. They know what works for them, and what doesn't work for them. We need to keep asking them individually, 'how best can I help you?' in as many contexts as possible – lectures, group work, individual work, practical work, and preparation for assessment. Very often their answers can not only help us to make adjustments which are really effective for them, but can spare us wasting time and energy making changes which we *imagine* are going to be useful but which are often of limited value in practice.

There is now a great deal of knowledge and expertise at recognising and addressing some of the more common causes of additional needs – dyslexia, dyspraxia, and the wide range of physical disabilities. However, *mental health* needs can be much more complex, and harder to address. This general heading in fact covers a very wide range of needs and conditions, ranging from depression, anxiety, Asperger's syndrome, mania, to schizophrenia – any of which can have significant or even profound effects on students' ability to handle various teaching–learning situations. Also, there are the much more common effects which can be regarded as affecting in one way or another students' 'state of mind', including fatigue (often due to working shifts at night to support study) and conditions related to consuming alcohol or other mind-altering agents. Furthermore, most students at some time (and some students for most of the time) are affected by various levels of stress, attributable to a wide range of sources – financial, emotional, self-esteem related, and so on.

Some mental health conditions can be slow-onset, and grow in intensity so gradually that they are not noticed for some time – including by their owners. Other conditions can be precipitated very rapidly by life-changing events or crises. As with other additional needs, mental health needs of most kinds lie on a continuum, ranging from what we would regard as 'normal' (including occasional stress or anxiety) to 'abnormal' requiring expert help and support. Borderlines are very difficult to define.

Perhaps the most important difference between mental health needs and physical ones is that students affected by mental health conditions are *not* necessarily able to give realistic responses to our question, 'how can I best help you with this?' Some students may indeed have a firm grasp on exactly how their additional needs can best be addressed, but others may be quite wrong in their view of what is likely to be best for them. That is why it is so important that anyone whose job is about making learning happen in post-compulsory education at least knows the nearest sources of expert help in addressing the more significant mental health problems – counsellors and other appropriately trained personnel, who invariably have their own links to the specialists who may be needed on occasion.

What adjustments may we be able to make to address mental health needs? While it can be safely assumed that in a lecture theatre full of students, some will at any given time be impeded by one or more mental health needs or conditions, it is quite impossible for a lecturer to know exactly which conditions may need to be addressed. One can't really ask the students to respond to, 'hands up those of you who have mental health problems today please'! However, there are some general ways to respond to the possibility – indeed probability – that in any group of students there will be some mental health needs at any time. An obvious, but nonetheless important, aim is to avoid conflict, temper, distress or highly charged emotional exchanges for all students at all times. For example, it is worth refraining from overreacting to challenging or unexpected behaviours from any students, however irritating they may be to us – and indeed to the rest of the students in a group. While 'normal' students may weather such minor storms perfectly adequately, those with particular mental health needs may get them quite out of proportion.

It is worth aiming to be as approachable as possible, so that students with mental health problems – transient or developing – feel able to come and seek help and advice. In any case, it is really useful to get to know the support systems and mechanisms of your own institution really well, so that you know exactly where to go to find expert help when needed by your students. Getting to know the people providing such support is really useful, and allows you to seek their advice informally before deciding whether a particular student's problem is one which would take you out of your own depth.

I believe that there is a gradual increase in awareness that students with disabilities should not be regarded as 'a problem', and that any of us may only be temporarily 'without disabilities', and that we need to do everything in our power in our educational systems to respond to people just as they are, and allow them to demonstrate what they *can* do, and gain credit for this.

4 How can we foster cross-cultural capability among our students and staff, working with international students and staff in a global environment?

Most universities nowadays seek to recruit both staff and students from around the globe, but all too often cultural differences are seen as problematical rather than an enrichment of the learning environment. Graduates need to be able to work in cross-cultural contexts, and the mobility of academic staff between nations provides important opportunities for co-learning and development. Brown (2015), drawing on the earlier work of Ryan (2000), identifies a number of areas where there clearly are not shared pedagogic understandings and practices which include:

- The extent to which historical texts and previously accumulated knowledge are respected, and how important it is felt to be for students to have original ideas of their own;
- Conceptual understandings of what post-compulsory teaching should comprise and of the nature of the learning partnership; for example, should students rely totally on their teachers for curriculum content or should they be working independently for significant amounts of time?
- The perceived status distance between the teacher and those taught; this is often demonstrated by physical proximity, with teachers mingling with students or conversely keeping well behind a lectern or demonstration bench;
- The extent to which group work, and particularly group assessment, is used and found acceptable;
- How students respond when being asked questions in class in front of their peers, and how comfortable they feel asking their teachers questions;
- The extent to which arguing forcibly and robustly challenging the ideas of others is welcomed, or conversely, how important it is to seek consensus within discussion;
- The acceptability of anyone other than the lecturer undertaking assessment, including concerns about peer assessment;
- The level of formality of relationships between the academic and their students, including how students should address academics, whether they socialise with their teachers outside class and how acceptable it is considered to give and receive gifts.

(after Brown, 2015, pp. 3–6)

Where these divergences are not recognised or acknowledged, problems can arise, and it is important both for institutions as a whole, and the staff who teach to clarify expectations at the outset. Here are six things that teaching staff can do to help foster cross-cultural capability:

1 Ensure that the curriculum topics, case studies and examples are chosen from a range of nations, not just the one in which study is taking place;
2 Provide opportunities for students from different nations to work together in groups, wherever there is a benefit for all from being multi-cultural and potentially multi-lingual;
3 Where assessment practices are likely to be unfamiliar to some students (for example, oral presentations, portfolios, self-assessed reflective tasks), ensure that there are opportunities for

rehearsal before real assessment kicks in, and for students to review examples from previous years' cohorts and to interrogate assessment criteria;

4 Clarify early on what the expectations are of students, about matters including interruptions and interventions in lectures, how questions are best received and answered, what students are expected to do with the content of lectures (question it? memorise it word-for-word? use it to guide further reading and study?);

5 Foster a climate where students are mutually supportive and collegial, rather than working in separate cliques;

6 Timetable assessment activities and other key curriculum events be undertaken thoughtfully, to avoid times when it is likely to be problematic for particular ethnic and religious groups, for example, not requiring students to sit exams late in the day during Ramadan or on the Sabbath.

5 How can we provide a coherent approach to the student experience, offering a programme-level approach?

In small programmes where course teams know one another and their students, it is relatively straightforward to help students believe they are studying on coherent programmes with clear pathways through the curriculum. However, the larger the institution and the cohort, the more likely it is that modules and other curriculum delivery components are designed and delivered in isolation, without clear thinking going into what the overall programme experience is like for the students undertaking them. Too often, the student experience is that subject material in different modules overlaps – or (worse) is contradictory, and the staff delivering the modules are surprised when it comes to their notice how different the approaches are across a range of modules. This has sometimes been caused by much less opportunity than previously for staff to talk to each other informally, and staff feeling under pressure to simply get on with their own modules because of all the other demands made upon their time, not least maintaining or improving their research profile alongside substantial teaching commitments.

Adopting holistic design implies among other things:

*   having strong course leadership, with a clear vision of how the curriculum will be delivered and assessed;
*   balancing the autonomy of individuals to design, deliver and assess elements of the curriculum autonomously, with a need to foreground the lived student experience, ensuring it makes sense to students and encourages them to engage;
*   involving, inevitably, external review of all kinds to focus scrutiny on coherence. This is likely to involve internal and external peers, and sometimes employers, and representatives from professional bodies, but also – and most importantly – student representatives;
*   having some level of stability where it is possible to plan ahead for the full duration of the programme (often three years for a full-time undergraduate degree) without the significant disruption, which is often the case nowadays, to staffing (for example resulting from institutional reorganisation and increased mobility of staff) and avoid disruption arising from significant changes in student numbers (for example when courses or modules are merged or disaggregated).

Coherent approaches to assessment across programmes are particularly important. The UK National Teaching Fellowship Project led by Peter Hartley at Bradford University on 'Programme Level Assessment' (PASS, 2012) set out to focus on redressing a range of problems, including those of not assessing learning outcomes holistically at a programme level, the atomisation of assessment, often resulting in too much summative and not enough formative feedback, and over-standardisation in regulations. Such problems can result in students and staff failing to see the links between disparate elements of the programme, over-assessment and multiple assignments using repetitive formats. Modules, the programme team felt, were often too short for complex learning and this tended to lead to surface learning and 'tick-box mentality'.

The solution developed (PASS, 2012) was to map out assessment activities and assignments across whole programmes and throughout the duration of study, to ensure there is clear progression, and to help students build assessment literacy incrementally, as they develop expertise using a repertoire of assessment methods and approaches, leading to measurable improvements in student achievement and motivation (for more detail see McDowell, 2012).

6 How can I go about showing how excellent my teaching has become?

Several countries have developed awards for teaching excellence. In the UK and Australia, for example, these awards are highly prized and sought after, with competition between individuals to demonstrate their excellence in teaching, and quite intense competition between institutions to show well in league tables of the numbers of their staff whose teaching has been celebrated as outstanding. One such scheme is the National Teaching Fellowship Scheme (NTFS) in parts of the UK (England, Wales and Northern Ireland to date) presently administrated by the Higher Education Academy on behalf of the respective funding councils. It is instructive to look at the criteria proposed for establishing teaching excellence on this particular scheme, as an example of what sort of performance is deemed to be outstanding. Institutions are allowed to put forward up to three nominees for the NTFS each year, and claimants so nominated are then required to submit a word-constrained description of how they meet each of three equally-rated criteria, with guidance notes for each. In 2014, the wording of the criteria and guidance notes was as follows (HEA, 2014):

Criterion 1: **Individual excellence: evidence of enhancing and transforming the student learning experience commensurate with the individual's context and the opportunities afforded by it.**
This may, for example, be demonstrated by providing evidence of:
- stimulating students' curiosity and interest in ways which inspire a commitment to learning;
- organising and presenting high quality resources in accessible, coherent and imaginative ways which in turn clearly enhance students' learning;
- recognising and actively supporting the full diversity of student learning needs;
- drawing upon the results of relevant research, scholarship and professional practice in ways which add value to teaching and students' learning;
- engaging with and contributing to the established literature or to the nominee's own evidence base for teaching and learning.

Criterion 2: **Raising the profile of excellence: evidence of supporting colleagues and influencing support for student learning; demonstrating impact and engagement beyond the nominee's immediate academic or professional role.**
This may, for example, be demonstrated by providing evidence of:
- making outstanding contributions to colleagues' professional development in relation to promoting and enhancing student learning;
- contributing to departmental/faculty/institutional/national initiatives to facilitate student learning;

- contributing to and/or supporting meaningful and positive change with respect to pedagogic practice, policy and/or procedure.

Criterion 3: **Developing excellence: evidence of the nominee's commitment to her/his ongoing professional development with regard to teaching and learning and/or learning support.**
This may, for example, be demonstrated by providing evidence of:
- on-going review and enhancement of individual professional practice;
- engaging in professional development activities which enhance the nominee's expertise in teaching and learning support;
- engaging in the review and enhancement of one's own professional and/or academic practice;
- specific contributions to significant improvements in the student learning experience.

(HEA, 2014, pp. 5–6)

The fact that there are now several hundred successful NTF holders working in institutions around the UK shows that this way of establishing evidence-based practice relating to teaching and learning has now begun to stand alongside the more traditional criteria for academic success of a significant record of published papers in scholarly journals.

Looking at the criteria in the context of much of what has been advocated throughout this book, it could be said that most of the criteria and suggested dimensions of evidence are simply an extension of what could be regarded as good practice by all who teach and support learning, yet with a limited number of awards per year these Fellowships are competed for strongly, and for each winner there are several disappointed aspirants each year. It can therefore be seen that striving for recognition is not without significant risk to morale, and it takes some courage as well as systematic determination to put forward evidence of excellent practice.

7 How can I use my pedagogic work to get published?

A significant challenge for post-compulsory teachers is the high expectation that academics will research as enthusiastically and effectively as they teach, and the evidence sought for the research side of a lecturers' work is the publication of articles, online material and books. Despite various initiatives to balance the rewards attainable from excellent teaching with those linked to successful research outputs, appointment to institutions and promotion within institutions remains significantly linked to publication profiles. While it is possible to have two lives – teaching and research – it is possible to build a publications profile on the basis of pedagogic work with students, and achieve academic recognition at the same time. Managing this aspect of the overall workload for committed teachers can be particularly difficult for those who came into higher education through professional routes such as Law, Nursing, Accountancy and Built Environment staff, since they are less likely to have entered higher education teaching following doctoral studies, than lecturers coming through traditional academic routes, who might well have already developed the skills and attitudes linking to writing successfully for publication.

For teaching colleagues who have a commitment to innovation and being reflective practitioners, one pathway to publications is to focus on the scholarship of teaching (Boyer, 1990), undertaking systematic reviews of their own changing practice, and publish outcomes of associated research into teaching, learning and assessment. Most universities expect academics to publish in peer-refereed journals and this is a valuable route to follow, especially for professionals who might be seeking to undertake a PhD by Publication (Smith, 2015, in preparation) and the range of journals concentrating on higher education pedagogy continues to expand. Other publishing outlets are well worth considering, including writing for internal institutional publications, writing chapters in edited books and contributing to disciplinary pedagogic conference proceedings. It's considered important too to build and consolidate a digital presence, for example through blogging on your own or your institutional website, taking part in global webinars, and using social media like Facebook, LinkedIn and Twitter for professional purposes. I for one regularly send Tweets comprising no more than 140 characters seeking ideas and disseminating my own, and Twitter is now one of my principal means of discovering new scholarly content to underpin my thinking, through links to websites and articles mentioned in other people's Tweets. I hasten to add that Twitter is a source of considerable fun as well, and can easily comprise an effective work-avoidance tactic!

Here are some pointers to help you publish about your own teaching:

- If you are unsure where to start publishing about your teaching, look back at the pedagogic literature that underpins your own practice and see which journals the people who influence you choose for their publications, then read at least three issues of these journals so you can get a feel for the kind of articles that get accepted. The more you read, the more likely you are to get a good idea of what is publishable, what kinds of style, tone and register are acceptable, and what topics are current.
- You can also similarly look at the post-compulsory sector educational texts published by publishers including Sage, Routledge, Open University Press, Palgrave and others, and contact their commissioning editors to find out whether there are edited collections in progress or being considered, relevant to your own work, to which you might contribute.
- Seek out a mentor with whom you can co-publish; this might be a more experienced colleague in your discipline who has published about learning and teaching, or a member of yous institution's academic educational development team, or one of the authors you have identified as a key influence on your practice.
- Review the activities of some of the valuable educational development networks that operate in your country and internationally, and explore whether you can publish with them. Some examples are listed below:
  - the All Ireland Society for Higher Education (AISHE),
  - the Staff and Educational Development Association (SEDA, originally UK but now with members and contacts globally),
  - the Higher Education Research and Development Society for Australasia (HERDSA),
  - the Higher Education Learning and Teaching Association of South Africa,
  - the Professional and Organisational Development Network in Higher Education (POD) in the USA,
  - the Education Quality Improvement Programme (EQUIOP) in Ethiopia,
  - the International Consortium for Educational Development (ICED) network which promotes academic development worldwide, and whose membership spans most of the other organisations in this list.
- Most such organisations publish journals, but additionally less-formal kinds of texts like newsletters and web materials. Such organisations also offer workshops and conferences through which you can meet colleagues with similar interests and then start to engage in a community of practice (Wenger, 1998) which can help you sustain your enthusiasm and support your first steps in publications about learning and teaching.
- Look to the national bodies that foster good practice in assessment, learning and teaching and seek out opportunities to work with them. These include the Irish Higher Education Authority, the UK Higher Education Academy and Australian Learning and Teaching Council.

Getting down to writing and publishing

In terms of actually getting down to writing about your practice, there are many potential things which can get in the way of researching and publishing, but there are also various ways of overcoming such barriers. Table 7.1 sets out some of the difficulties and distracters that academic writers frequently encounter, together with some thoughts on how to surmount them.

Here are some texts that might be particularly helpful in overcoming these challenges:

Black, D., Day, A., Brown, S. and Race, P. (1998) *500 Tips for Getting Published*, London: Kogan Page.
Day, A. (2008) *How to Get Research Published in Journals,* London: Gower.
Dunleavy, P. (2003) *Authoring a PhD: How to plan, draft, write and finish a doctoral thesis or dissertation,* Palgrave Study Guides, London: Palgrave-Macmillan.
Fairbairn, G. and Fairbairn S. (2005) *Writing Your Abstract: A guide for would be conference presenters* Salisbury: APS Publishing.
Kamler, B. and Thomson, P. (2006) *Helping Doctoral Students Write: Pedagogies for supervision,* London: Routledge.
Noble, K. (1989) Publish or perish: what 23 journal editors have to say, *Studies in Higher Education* 14, Issue 1, pp. 97–102.
Sadler, R. (1984) *Up the Publication Road,* Green Guide No 2, Millperra, NSW: HERDSA.
Thomson, P. and Kamler, B. (2013) *Writing for Peer Reviewed Journals*, London: Routledge.

From reflection on action, to reflection in action

I hope that this final part of the *Toolkit* helps you to take charge of your own reflections on your teaching and assessment-related work, and thereby assists in your own continuous development as a professional in higher education. Being an effective university or college teacher means being open to new ideas, learning from experience and being reflective about one's practice. Many professional qualification programmes in higher education teaching and other systems, for example the UK Professional Standards Framework, expect you to demonstrate how reflection continuously enhances your teaching. Similarly institutional appraisal or professional review systems often require you to prepare for the process by undertaking reflection, and producing evidence that you have done so. Even if there are no external pressures for you to reflect, it's nevertheless good practice to do so, either privately or as part of a conversation with peers.

This section offers some templates you can use as a starting point to help you be an effective and reflective practitioner, working always to improve your teaching. I suggest you use the sample questions offered in this section as a framework for your personal professional development, using them as a trigger for composing no more than 200 words in response to any question, each of which may help you to capture your reflective thinking about various key areas of your work. The templates offered here provide a framework that can be readily adapted for your own local and specific context, but overall I suggest that you keep to around 1,000 words per reflective occasion, keeping an electronic or hard copy record so you can go back over time to see how reflection is enhancing your teaching, and equip yourself with ready access to evidence of reflection when this may help you in preparations for appraisal, performance review, and indeed for working towards professional qualifications and applications for other employment possibilities.

The short templates offered below address seven areas worth reflecting upon, and it does not matter in which order you may work with them – this may well depend on circumstances in your own professional life. In each case, it's worth noting the date, venue, and names of other people involved

Table 7.1 How to surmount difficulties and distracters

The problem:	You might try:	What also sometimes works?
You find it really difficult to find time to write up the interesting innovations you are doing.	Setting yourself the task of blogging daily (250 words) to get yourself in the habit of writing regularly. Finding a time that suits you (e.g. very early mornings, late at night, lunch breaks) when you can carve out space for yourself to write about your teaching.	Search out opportunities to participate in academic retreats of the kind offered by SEDA and a variety of other organisations. Organise yourself a retreat where you go away from home to a place with no distractions.
You find writing very isolating and you are not always sure whether you are working on the right lines.	Seeking out a more experienced co-author who will be prepared to help you write your first pieces together, so you can 'learn on the job'.	Your institutional educational/academic development unit may have supportive programmes. You can also set up 'self-help' groups with peers who also want to write, even if you don't share subject specialisms.
You find it easy enough to start to write but never get round to finishing as other priorities intervene.	Identifying a mentor of a fellow author in the same predicament who can help you set and review incremental targets.	Sometimes 'going public' and letting others know your plans for publication provides an incentive to complete. This particularly works when you can involve your manager or appraiser since this then becomes a performance indicator for you.
It seems to take for ever to get started on an article or a chapter.	Not starting at the beginning. It can be best to work out some of the main things you want to say, gradually work towards some conclusions, and only then write the beginning.	There's no second chance to make a good first impression (on editors and referees, as well as on readers). The beginning is best written when you know exactly where it's going to lead.
You don't really know where to place your article once it is finished.	You shouldn't really be in this predicament, since you should identify your target publication before you start writing. But if you are in the position of having written something already and looking for where to publish it, look at the websites of the journals you have under consideration, and very carefully read the author guidelines to identify which best fits what you have written and then rewrite your draft to make sure it fits really well.	The key authorities in the field, that is the people whose work you regularly cite, may be helpful in responding to direct contacts seeking advice, so long as you keep your messages short and to the point and don't expect instant responses. Library colleagues often have an excellent knowledge of the range of publication possibilities in different disciplines.
You don't feel you have enough opportunities to collect data for a formal study.	Looking out for opportunities to contribute to collective studies with others working in the same pedagogic area so you can share data.	Consider different kinds of research, quantitative, qualitative, ethnographic, action research. Make yourself really familiar with different approaches and choose what works best for you in your context.
You are insufficiently familiar with the pedagogic literature in the field.	Treating it like other aspects of your scholarship: use search engines like Google Scholar to identify relevant material and then set yourself targets to read and familiarise yourself with relevant texts. Keep good bibliographical records of what you read (for example, using a system like Endnote) to avoid wasteful subsequent hunting for sources.	Use social media to help you find source material. Ask advice from people you trust. Find a key text and then follow up the sources cited that seem most helpful. Take comfort from the fact that the literature field is so big now that well-published authors often feel that they've only 'scratched the surface' of the literature themselves!

(for example an observer, or a colleague, and so on) so that later you can look back on your growing collection of evidence of reflection and see trends as well as picking out key incidences of reflection which may have proved particularly important in your own professional development. These seven templates are simply offered as starting places for the various contexts involved – the chapter ends with some more detailed pro formas which could be starting places for you to build up evidence of reflection on your teaching.

Using evidence of your reflections

Reflection on action is useful in its own right (Shulman, 1996) and building up evidence of reflection can be very productive to show your professionalism and commitment. Reflection can be captured for any of

I Learning from being observed

This may include teaching in the lecture theatre, classroom, lab, studio, but also other contexts such as observation on a PhD supervision session, one-to-one meeting with a student, or many other contexts.

Date: Place: Name of observer:

- What was the situation, what were you teaching, was the person observing you a peer, a junior colleague, your senior manager, a friend?
- What were your key intended learning outcomes relating to this particular session, and how (briefly) did it fit with the rest of the programme?
- Were there any aspects of the session that you felt could be improved, and how?
- What did you observe about what students were doing in your session?
- What were the key learning points you took away from being observed?
- Was there anything *else* which you learned as a direct result of this session and being observed on this occasion?

2 Learning from watching others

This could include observing others teach, lead seminars, supervise, undertake practical assessments, facilitate an online session and so on.

Date: Place: Name of person you observed:

- What was the situation, what were you watching, was the person you were observing a peer, a junior colleague, your senior manager, a friend?
- Which aspects of practice did you particularly admire and how could you transfer this learning into your own practice?
- Were there any aspects of the session that you felt could be improved, and how?
- Was there anything you noticed which you resolved to try to avoid in future in your own practice?
- What did you notice about student behaviours and engagement within the session?
- What were the key learning points you took away from the observation?

3 Learning from your practices of assessing students

Date: Courses or modules involved:

- What kinds of assessment have you been undertaking (writing and marking traditional exam papers, designing and using computer-based assessment, setting and marking essays and reports, organising and undertaking practical assessments in the lab, studio, workplace, etc.)?
- Which aspects of your assessing are really working well and which are less successful? To what extent is the assessment you are using contributing positively to student learning? Are there any big problems you need to solve?
- Within what parameters are you working? To what extent do you have flexibility in how you assess and to what extent is this dictated by your institution, nation, professional body and so on?
- What steps are you taking (or can you take) to make sure assessment is manageable, and works well to promote students' learning? What guidance can the scholarly literature on assessment offer?
- What have been the results of the changes you have made in your assessment practices, and how best can you measure their impact?

4 Learning from engaging with pedagogic professional development events

Such events could include conferences, workshops, group discussions, webinars, working on a MOOC.

Date of event: Place: Person(s) running the session:

- What kind of session was it you were engaging with (conference, workshop, webinar, MOOC, on-line conversation, etc.)?
- Why did you choose to engage with it, and how did you select this event as being suitable for you?
- What was the key topic involved, and how does this relate to your particular kind of teaching?
- How will you apply (or have you applied) learning from this engagement in your own teaching?
- What further aspects of professional development did this engagement prompt you to take or consider?
- What (if any) unanticipated things did you take away from your experience of this event?

5 Learning from your scholarly reading

Date of reflection: Place: Particular source(s) used:

- What pedagogic texts (books, papers, online resources) have you been using, and where are they located (own texts, borrowed texts, web materials, etc.)?
- Who, or what prompted you to research this area, and how does it link to your own teaching?
- What were the key learning points you took away from your study of these materials?
- In what ways do you plan to use the learning you've taken from this reading, and how will you apply it in your day-to-day work?
- Where will your reading take you next? What references cited in this work do you plan to follow up and read later?

6 Learning from student feedback and evaluation

Date of reflection: Place: Kind(s) of evidence addressed:

- What kinds of student feedback are you using to prompt your reflection (course/module evaluations, national survey results, individual comments from students, postings to course websites, feedback from external examiners' meetings with your students, etc.)?
- What have you learned from the feedback you have received? How does this make you feel? Are you comfortable, disquieted, reassured, disappointed, validated?
- What are you learning from both the positive and critical aspects of student feedback you are reviewing?
- How do you plan to use this feedback to prompt improvements to the ways you teach and assess? What positive steps will you take? Is there literature in the field that can help you?
- How will this feedback impact on your forward planning for curriculum design and delivery? How can you use evidence of subsequent enhancement to demonstrate your professional competence?

7 Learning from occasions when things went wrong, and what you did (or might do next) to improve the situation

Date: Place: Nature of what went wrong:

- What was the context in which you were working? How did you know things were going wrong?
- What steps did you take to improve your practice? What is proving most helpful to address the things which went wrong (advice from colleagues or your mentor, learning from reading around the subject, professional development opportunities, etc.)?
- Where you've already addressed the problem, what was the impact of the steps you took to remediate problems? How did this improve the student experience? How did you know this had had a positive impact?
- Where you've not yet had the opportunity to address the problem, what do you plan to do next time a similar situation arises? How will you monitor to what extent your actions have solved the problem?
- What reactions have you had from colleagues and the students themselves about the changes you made?
- What actions do you plan to take in the future to monitor the effectiveness of the changes and to avoid future problems?

the situations and contexts mentioned in this section, but you can also use reflection of this kind to build into research projects and publications linked to learning, teaching and assessment. If for example you have been exploring how to improve group assessment, can this be fed back to your department or faculty as part of intra-institutional enhancement conversations? Can you work this up into a presentation or poster at a pedagogic conference? Is there enough evidence of impact for you to work it up into a publication? The further reflection that is involved in working towards publication is valuable in its own right, and publications themselves can show to all your professionalism and commitment to enhancing the student experience and being ready to learn by thinking carefully about feedback on things you do in your work.

Towards reflection in action

The templates used above focused on reflection on action – looking at things which happened in the past, analysing them, and planning how to take your own learning forward into future actions. When such reflection becomes second nature and habitual, it is natural to find yourself reflecting *in* action – while you are teaching, while you are watching others, while you are assessing, and so on, and steering what you do on the basis of your reflecting-as-you-go, rather than waiting for particular points to stop and look back. Perhaps this is a description of a fully-fledged reflective practitioner. The next section goes into rather more detail, when you might wish to analyse deeper into what's working well, and anything that is not yet working in your teaching.

Some more detailed questions to help us to evidence our reflection on teaching

Questions which aid deep reflection are rarely single questions, but tend to form clusters. There is often a starter question which sets the agenda, and frequently this is a 'what?' question. Then come the more important ones – the 'how?' questions and the 'why?' questions – and sometimes the '… else?' questions which ask for even deeper thinking and reflection. In general, it seems too obvious to state it, but simple 'yes/no' questions can rarely enable the extent of reflection which can be prompted by more open-ended questions such as 'to what extent …?' Sadly, however, there remain far too many 'closed' questions on student feedback questionnaires, and unsurprisingly the level of student reflection that such questionnaires tend to elicit is limited.

Below are some clusters of questions – 'families' of questions one could say. The first part tends to be a scene-setting starter, and the sub-questions which follow are probing or clarifying questions, intentionally leading towards deeper or more focused reflection. These questions are not in any particular order. A set of questions to aid us to reflect on an element of teaching we have just finished could use some of these as starting points, and usefully add in subject-specific and context-specific questions to help us to flesh out the agenda for reflection.

Such questions can extend to many continuing professional development contexts, appraisal contexts, even a teaching portfolio for lecturers. Whatever the context, however, the quality of reflection which is prompted is only as good as the questions which prompt it. In other words, for optimum reflection, much more care needs to be taken with phrasing the questions than might have been thought necessary.

1 **What did I actually achieve with this element of teaching?** Which were the most difficult parts, and why were they difficult for me? Which were the most straightforward parts, and why did I find these easy?

2 **How well do I think I helped students to achieve the intended learning outcomes related to this element of teaching?** Where could I have improved their achievement? Why didn't I improve it at the time?

3 **What have I got out of doing this element of teaching?** How have I developed my knowledge and skills? How do I see the payoff from doing this element of teaching helping me in the longer term?

4 **What *else* have I got out of doing this element of teaching?** Have I developed other skills and knowledge, which may be useful elsewhere at another time? If so, what are my own *emergent* learning outcomes from doing this teaching?

5 **What was the best thing I did?** Why was this the best thing I did? How do I know that this was the best thing I did?

6 **What worked least well for me?** Why did this not work well for me? What have I learned about the topic concerned from this not having worked well for me? What have I learned about the students through this not having worked well for me? What do I plan to do differently

in future as a result of my answers to the above questions?

7 **With hindsight, how would I go about this element of teaching differently if doing it again from scratch?** To what extent will my experience of this element of teaching influence the way I tackle anything similar in future?

8 **What did I find the greatest challenge in doing this element of teaching?** Why was this a challenge to me? To what extent do I feel I have met this challenge? What can I do to improve my performance when next meeting this particular sort of challenge?

9 **What was the most boring or tedious part of doing this element of teaching for me?** Can I see the point of doing these things? If not, how could the element of teaching have been redesigned to be more stimulating and interesting for me?

10 **Do I feel that my time and effort on this element of teaching has been well spent?** If not, how could I have used my time more effectively? Or should the teaching have been designed differently? Which parts of the teaching represent the time best spent? Which parts could be thought of as time wasted?

11 **How useful do I expect the feedback to be, that I receive on this element of teaching?** Who can give me useful feedback – students, colleagues, assessors? What sorts of feedback do I really want at this point in time? What sorts of feedback do I really *need* at this point in time? What are my expectations of getting useful feedback now, based on the feedback (or lack of it) that I've already received on past teaching I've done?

12 **What advice would I give to a friend about to start on the same element of teaching?** How much time would I suggest that it would be worth putting into it? What pitfalls would I advise to be well worth not falling into?

13 **What are the three most important things that I think I need to do arising from this element of teaching at this moment in time?** Which of these do I think is the most urgent for me to do? When will I aim to start doing this, and what is a sensible deadline for me to have completed it by?

Designing and delivering a teaching element – a reflective checklist

The checklist in Table 7.2 is intended to be a working tool for planning a session, and for revisiting after the session as an aid to learning from experience and fine-tuning planning for future sessions. The questions are intended to be indicative, and you may well decide to adapt the ideas to make your own working tool for session planning. You might well want to shorten the questionnaire a lot, then add in specific questions relating to your own context. You may wish to print out multiple copies of your own questionnaire of this sort, and use them regularly to build up a database of your experience of developing your teaching over a period of time, as evidence of your own reflections. You could turn this into an online tool, filling in your responses and saving a file each time. Despite what I said earlier about the limitations of yes/no questions, the list below uses these, but with the important 'hindsight' element at the right-hand side of the grid. In each case, tick the 'yes', 'not yet', or 'n/a' (not applicable) columns as you plan the session, then return once more to the checklist after the session using the 'Reflections with hindsight after the session' column to help you to decide how best to put into practice what you have learned from the planning you have done.

REFLECTING ON YOUR SESSION

It is very valuable to reflect on each session you lead, and to learn from things which went well, and of course to think about what could have gone better. The main problem with reflecting is that unless some *record* of reflection is made at the time, one's best ideas can just evaporate away again. Table 7.3

Table 7.2 Some questions which may help you plan an element of teaching, then reflect upon it with hindsight

Session title:		Class size:			
Place:		Date:			
Checklist question	Yes	Not yet	n/a		Reflections with hindsight after the session
Drafting your session outline					
Has a good title been chosen for the session? Will this title help to motivate students to turn up for the session rather than just download any relevant materials later? Will this title be 'lived up to' by the session in practice?					
Has the 'rationale' been drafted well? Does it clarify well what the title actually means in practice, and why the session will be important and useful to students?					
Have intended session outcomes been formulated carefully? Are these relevant and achievable? Do these enable students to see exactly what the session will be about? Will these ensure that there are no unwelcome surprises or disappointments for students at the session?					
Has an outline programme or plan been worked out for the session? Does this give enough detail of how the session will unfold? Is the outline programme still flexible enough to allow the session to be fine-tuned at the session itself, to accommodate students' wishes, expectations and emergent needs?					
Setting the venue up					
Is the venue a 'known quantity' to you and to the students?					
Has the room been visited and checked out for size, shape, lighting, equipment, furniture, and so on?					
Is the seating moveable?					
Are the tables (if present) easily moveable?					
Have decisions been made about the initial room layout, e.g. for plenary introductions?					
Have decisions been made about the way that small groups will be accommodated for group-work elements of the session, if relevant?					
Will it be necessary to allow time before the session to set up the room in exactly the required format?					
Will you need a flipchart in the room? Is one there already?					
Are there whiteboards or blackboards in the room, and will you need them?					

continued…

Are data projection facilities in the room?				
Checklist question	Yes	Not yet	n/a	Reflections with hindsight after the session
Is the internet easily available?				
Can you use your laptop for slides, or will you need a memory stick?				
Online resources, and so on				
Have online resources been selected relating to the session?				
Will these be made available in advance of the session?				
Are these intended to be downloaded after the session?				
Will some of these materials be used at stages during the session?				
Will slides be made available to students before the session?				
Will a feedback questionnaire be used relating to the session?				
Getting the session off to a good start				
Will you be finding out what students already know about the topic near the start of the session?				
Will the intended session outcomes be explained clearly near the beginning of the session?				
Will it be possible to fine-tune the intended session outcomes in the light of students' expectations at the start of the session?				
Making it an active learning experience				
Is there an emphasis on students doing things rather than simply listening to people talking at them?				
Is there a suitable variety of tasks, including individual work, small-group work, jotting down questions while watching a video clip, reporting back in plenary, question-and-answer sessions, and so on?				
Have task briefings been thought through carefully so that students will see what they are intended to get out of doing the tasks?				
Will briefings be shown on-screen so that students remain on task during the activities?				
Are the tasks demonstrably linked to the intended session outcomes?				
Bringing the session to a good conclusion				
Have plans been made so that the session can be adjusted if necessary so that it will end on time?				
Has it been decided what the most appropriate 'ending' activity will be for the session?				
After the session				
Is there a process for dealing with students' questions arising from the session?				
Have decisions been made about adjustments to make to future sessions in the light of students' feedback?				

Table 7.3 A starting point for reflection on an element of teaching

Reflection checklist questions	Your responses and action-planning ideas
What particular aspect of this session was the thing that worked best of all? Why did this element work really well? How can I make sure that I capitalise on this in my future sessions?	
What else worked really well at this session? How best can I build in similar features into my future sessions?	
What worked least well at this particular session? Why was this? What can I do in future sessions to minimise the chance that similar things will happen again?	
What surprised me most at this particular session? Why was this unexpected? What would I now do, with hindsight, to address this, if it were to happen again at a future session?	
How well do I now think that I started this particular session? What have I learned about how best to start this particular kind of session? How will I now fine-tune the beginning of a future similar session?	
How well did I explain the intended learning outcomes to students? Which of these outcomes seemed to be most important to them? Are there any I might miss out next time? How best can I, with hindsight, adjust the intended learning outcomes to be more relevant to future students at similar sessions?	
How much did the students turn out to know already, on average? Was this more than I expected or less than I expected? How would I adjust the content of a future session to fine-tune it better to what the students are likely to know already? How best can I find out from them more about what they already know at the start of a similar session in future?	
What was the best thing about the teaching room at this particular session? Why did this really help the session? What can I do to try to ensure that this kind of venue feature will be put to good use in future sessions?	
What was the worst thing about the teaching room at this particular session? What can I do in future to minimise the risk of similar things spoiling a session?	
What was the best thing about the actual students at this particular session? How can I build on this to make future sessions with the same group of students work well? How best can I try to make use of similar strengths among future students?	
What behaviours did the most difficult student show at this particular session? What can I do to address such behaviours at future sessions, if they occur again?	
What was my own best moment at this particular session? Why do I feel good about this particular aspect? What can I do to lead to more such moments at future sessions?	

continued...

Reflection checklist questions	Your responses and action-planning ideas
What is the single most important thing I wish I hadn't done at this session? Why do I feel badly about this? How best can I avoid doing this in future sessions?	
What was the most important thing I learned about the topic of my session on this occasion? How best can I make use of what I learned on future occasions?	
What, with hindsight, would I now miss out of the session? Why would I now choose to miss this out of similar sessions in future?	
What else, with hindsight, do I wish I had been able to include in this particular session? How best can I make time to include something along these lines into future similar sessions?	
What was the most unexpected happening at this session? How well do I now think that I handled this? How might I handle the same sort of thing differently at a future session?	
How well do I think I closed the session? Did I end it with a whimper or a bang?! Was I rushed towards the end of the session, trying to get through everything on the agenda? What would I do next time round, with hindsight, to make sure that a future similar session ended really positively?	
What do I feel about the feedback I have received from students at this session? What will be the most important thing I will do differently next time as a result of this feedback? What will be the most important thing I will do in exactly the same way because of this feedback?	
What was the most hurtful comment or grading in students' feedback? Why do I find this hurtful? Was it justified? Is it really important considering the feedback as a whole? Would it be useful for me to do something different next time round to address this particular aspect of critical feedback?	
What was the most pleasing comment or grading I received in students' feedback? Why does this please me so much? Will it be possible for me to aim to get further similar feedback in future, and how will I adjust a future session to do so?	
What turned out to be the most revealing question on the feedback questionnaire? Why was this? How could I develop the questionnaire to get better feedback next time round?	
How well did students feel that they had achieved the intended learning outcomes at the end of the session? Which outcomes had they achieved best? Were any of the intended outcomes less important than others? How would it be useful, with hindsight, to adjust the intended learning outcomes for a similar session next time round?	
What is the most important thing I have learned about teaching sessions of this kind from this particular experience? How will I put this learning to good use at future sessions?	

can be a starting point for reflecting after running a teaching session, and for capturing your reflections so that you can put them to good use when planning and running future sessions. Of course, it would be quite impracticable to use a table like this for reflecting on more than a few sessions, and you may wish to use just a few questions to reflect on the average session. However, doing a fairly comprehensive reflection now and then is a useful way to build up a collection of evidence of reflection, to allow you to look at the bigger picture of your teaching as it continues to develop.

The questions in Table 7.3 are just indicative ones; you may wish to use these as a starting point towards developing your own personal checklist to use after a session from time to time.

Conclusions

The reflective checklists discussed above bring us to the end of this *Toolkit*, where I hope I've got you thinking productively about all sorts of aspects of the job of 'a lecturer' – in which, as you will have seen, 'lecturing' itself (in the traditional sense) forms only a small part. Everything we do needs to link to student learning – causing it to happen, designing resources to help them learn, giving them feedback on their learning, helping them learn from each other and – the hardest part of our job – measuring evidence of their achievement of the intended learning outcomes which define their programmes of study.

There's a lot of careful work involved in developing one's practice in making learning happen. Sometimes what we do works well, and at other times we learn what we should have done! So what keeps us at it? In my opinion, helping people to learn (including measuring their achievement) is the most satisfying job that exists. It's about making a difference. Just think of the joy on students' faces at graduation ceremonies (and the pride on the faces of their friends and relations). That's what it's all about. And that's just the public side of the pleasure of learning successfully. While I was writing this edition, my granddaughter aged four happened to learn for the first time to ride her bike around our garden without stabilisers. She was ecstatic. So were we all. Succeeding in learning should be one of life's greatest pleasures, and the job of the lecturer is to help bring that to fruition.

References

Adams, M. and Brown, S. (eds) (2006) *Disabled Students in Higher Education: Working Towards Inclusive Learning*, London: Routledge.

Ausubel, D. P. (1968) *Educational Psychology: A Cognitive View,* London: Holt, Rinehard and Winston.

Bain, K. (2004) *What the Best College Teachers Do,* Cambridge, MA: Harvard University Press.

Barnett, R. (2000) *Realizing the University in an Age of Supercomplexity*, Maidenhead: Open University Press.

Beetham, H. (2013) Designing for learning in an uncertain future, in Beetham, H. and Sharpe, R. (eds) *Rethinking Pedagogy for a Digital Age* (2nd edition), London: Routledge.

Beetham, H. and Sharpe, R. (eds) (2013) *Rethinking Pedagogy for a Digital Age* (2nd edition), London: Routledge.

Biggs, J. and Tang, C. (2011) *Teaching for Quality Learning at University* (4th edition), Maidenhead: SRHE & Open University Press.

Black, D., Day, A., Brown, S. and Race, P. (1998) *500 Tips for Getting Published*, London: Kogan Page.

Bloom, B. S., Engelhart, M. D., Furst, E. J., Hill, W. H. and Krathwohl, D. R. (1956) *Taxonomy of Educational Objectives: Cognitive Domain,* New York: McKay.

Boud, D. (1988) (ed.) *Developing Student Autonomy in Learning*, (2nd edition), London: Kogan Page.

Boud, D. and Associates (2010) *Assessment 2020: Seven Propositions for Assessment Reform in Higher Education,* Sydney: Australian Learning and Teaching Council.

Bowl, M. (2003) *Non-traditional Entrants to Higher Education: 'They Talk about People like Me',* Stoke on Trent: Trentham Books.

Boyer, E.L. (1990) *Scholarship Reconsidered: Priorities of the Professoriate*, San Francisco, CA: Jossey-Bass/ The Carnegie Foundation for the Advancement of Teaching.

Brown, S. (2013) The twenty books that influenced educational developers: thinking in the last twenty years: opinion piece, *Innovations in Education and Teaching International,* 50(4): 321–330.

Brown, S. (2014, in press) Five troublesome assessment issues, and some suggestions on how to resolve them, *Journal of Academic Development and Education.*

Brown, S. (2015) *Learning, Teaching And Assessment In Higher Education: Global Perspectives,* London: Palgrave-Macmillan.

Brown, S. and Glasner, A. (eds) (1999) *Assessment Matters in Higher Education: Choosing and Using Diverse Approaches,* Maidenhead: Open University Press.

Brown, S. and Race, P. (2002) *Lecturing – A Practical Guide*, London: Kogan Page.

Brown, S. and Race, P. (2012) Using effective assessment to promote learning, in Hunt, L. and Chalmers, D. *University Teaching in Focus: A Learning-Centred Approach*, Camberwell, VIC, Acer Press, and Abingdon: Routledge.

Bruner, J. S., Goodnow, J. J. and Austen, G. A. (1956) *A Study of Thinking,* New York: Wiley.

Clegg, K. (2002) in Peelo, M. and Wareham, T. (eds) *Failing Students in Higher Education,* Maidenhead: SRHE/ Open University Press.

Coffield, F., Moseley, D., Hall, E. and Ecclestone, K. (2004) *Learning Styles and Pedagogy in Post-16 Learning: A Systematic and Critical Review,* London: Learning and Skills Research Centre available online at www.lsda.org.uk. (For a shorter review, see also Coffield, F., Moseley, D., Hall, E. and Ecclestone, K. (2004) *Should We Be Using Learning Styles? What Research Has to Say to Practice,* London: Learning and Skills Research Centre.)

Coonan, E. (2014) Helping students to read effectively in ways that support learning, in Brown, S. *Learning, Teaching And Assessment In Higher Education: Global Perspectives,* London: Palgrave-Macmillan.

Cowie, B. and Bell, B. (1999) A model for formative assessment, *Assessment in Education* 6(1): 101–116.

Day, A. (2008) How *to Get Research Published in Journals,* London: Gower.

Dunleavy, P. (2003) *Authoring a PhD: How to Plan, Draft, Write and Finish a Doctoral Thesis or Dissertation,* Palgrave Study Guides, London: Palgrave-Macmillan.

Dunn, L., Morgan, C., O'Reilly, M. and Parry, S. (2004) *The Student Assessment Handbook: New Directions in Traditional and Online Assessment,* London: Routledge.

Dweck, C. S. (2000) *Self Theories: Their Role in Motivation, Personality and Development,* Lillington, NC: Taylor & Francis.

Dweck, C. S. (2013) Do you trust in your ability to grow? available online at http://nilofermerchant.com/2013/09/27/do-you-trust-in-your-ability-to-grow/

Engestrom, Y. (2000) quoted in Illeris, K. (ed.) (2009) *Contemporary Theories of Learning,* Abingdon: Routledge.

Exley, K. and Dennick, R. (2004) *Giving a Lecture: From Presenting to Teaching,* Abingdon: Routledge.

Fairbairn, G. and Fairbairn S. (2005) *Writing Your Abstract: A Guide for Would-be Conference Presenters,* Salisbury: APS Publishing.

Fisher, A., Exley, K. and Ciobanu, D. (2014) *Using Technology to Support Learning and Teaching,* Abingdon: Routledge.

Gardner, H. (1993) *Frames of Mind: The Theory of Multiple Intelligences,* New York: Basic Books.

Gardner, H. (2011) *Frames of Mind: The Theory of Multiple Intelligences,* New York: Basic Books.

Gibbs, G. (1999) Using assessment strategically to change the way students learn, in Brown, S. and Glasner, A. (eds) *Assessment Matters in Higher Education: Choosing and Using Diverse Approaches,* Maidenhead: Open University Press.

Gibbs, G. (2010) *Using Assessment To Support Student Learning,* Leeds: Leeds Met Press.

Harland, T. (2012) *University Teaching: An Introductory Guide,* Abingdon: Routledge.

HEA (2012) *A Marked Improvement: Transforming Assessment in Higher Education,* York: Higher Education Academy, available online at http://www.heacademy.ac.uk/assets/documents/assessment/A_Marked_Improvement.pdf

HEA (2014) National Teaching Fellowship Scheme, available online at http://www.heacademy.ac.uk/ntfshome

Hounsell, D. (2008). The trouble with feedback: New challenges, emerging strategies, *Interchange, Spring,* available online at www.tla.ed.ac.uk/interchange.

Hunt, L., Chalmers, D. and Macdonald, R. (2012) Effective classroom teaching, in Hunt, L. and Chalmers, D. (eds) *University Teaching in Focus: A Learner-Centred Approach,* Melbourne: ACER Press and Abingdon, Routledge.

Illeris, K. (ed.) (2009) *Contemporary Theories of Learning,* Abingdon: Routledge.

Jaques, D. (2000) *Learning in Groups* (3rd edition), London: Kogan Page.

Kamler, B. and Thomson, P. (2006) *Helping Doctoral Students Write: Pedagogies for Supervision,* London: Routledge.

Kneale, P. E. (1997) The rise of the 'strategic student': how can we adapt to cope?, in Armstrong, S., Thompson, G. and Brown, S. (eds) *Facing up to Radical Changes in Universities and Colleges,* London: Kogan Page.

Knight, P. and Yorke, M. (2003) *Assessment, Learning and Employability,* Maidenhead: SRHE/Open University Press.

Kolb, D. A. (1984) *Experiential Learning: Experience as the Source of Learning and Development,* Englewood Cliffs, NJ: Prentice-Hall.

Kolb, D. A. (1999) *The Kolb Learning Style Inventory,* Version 3, Boston: Hay Group.

Laurillard, D. (1993) *Rethinking University Teaching, A Framework for the Effective Use of Educational Technology,* London: Routledge.

Laurillard, D. (2013), Foreword in Beetham, H. and Sharpe, R. (eds) *Rethinking Pedagogy for a Digital Age (2nd edition),* London: Routledge.

Lewin, K. (1952) Field theory in social science, in D. Cartwright, (ed.) *Selected Theoretical Papers,* London: Tavistock.

Marsden, R. (2014) Get your own ideas, *The Guardian Weekend Magazine,* 22 March, p. 45–49.

Mayes, T. and de Freitas, S. (2013) Technology enhanced learning, in Beetham, H. and Sharpe, R. (eds) *Rethinking Pedagogy for a Digital Age: Designing For 21st Century Learning* (2nd edition), Abingdon: Routledge.

McDowell, L. (2012) Programme focussed assessment, Bradford: Bradford University available online at http://www.pass.brad.ac.uk/short-guide.pdf

McDowell, L. and Brown, S. (2001) *Assessing Students: Cheating and Plagiarism,* Higher Education Academy. available online at http://www.heacademy.ac.uk/assets/York/documents/resources/resourcedatabase/id430_cheating_and_plagiarism.pdf

McKeachie, W. J. (1994/1951) *Teaching Tips: Strategies, Research and Theory for College and University Teachers,* Lexington, MA: D. C. Heath and Company.

Nicol, D. J. and Macfarlane-Dick, D. (2006) Formative assessment and self-regulated learning: A model and seven principles of good feedback practice, *Studies in Higher Education* 31(2), 199–218.

Noble, K. (1989) Publish or Perish: what 23 Journal Editors have to say, *Studies in Higher Education* 14(1), 97–102.

Northedge, A. (2003) Rethinking teaching in the context of diversity, *Teaching in Higher Education* 8(1), 17.

NUS (2010) NUS Charter on Assessment and Feedback, available online at http://www.nusconnect.org.uk/asset/news/6010/FeedbackCharter-toview.pdf.

PASS (2012) *The Case for Programme Focused Assessment: PASS Position Paper,* available online at http://www.pass.brad.ac.uk/position-paper.pdf

Peelo, M. and Wareham, T. (eds) (2002) *Failing Students in Higher Education,* Maidenhead: SRHE/Open University Press.

Pegler, C. (2013) in Beetham, H. and Sharpe, R. (eds) *Rethinking Pedagogy for a Digital Age* (2nd edition), London: Routledge.

Pickford, R. and Brown, S. (2006) *Assessing Skills and Practice,* London: Routledge.

Price, M., Rust, C., O'Donovan, B. and Handley, K. (2012) *Assessment Literacy,* Oxford: Oxford Centre for Staff and Learning Development (based on the 'ASKe' Project).

QAA (2013) UK Quality Code for Higher Education: Part B: Assuring and Enhancing Academic Quality, available online at www.qaa.ac.uk.

Race, P. (2005a) *Making Learning Happen,* London: Sage.

Race, P. (2005b) *500 Tips on Open and Online Learning,* (2nd edition), London: Routledge.

Race, P. (2010) *Making Learning Happen* (2nd edition), London: Sage.

Race, P. (2014) *Making Learning Happen* (3rd edition), London: Sage.

Race, P., Brown, S. and Smith, B. (2005) *500 Tips on Assessment,* (2nd edition), London: Routledge.

Reynolds, M. (1997) Learning styles: a critique, *Management Learning,* 28(2), 115–133.

Robinson, C. (2013) Writers should take a year off, and give us all a break, *The Guardian,* Review section, 17 August, p. 17.

Rogers, C. (1983) *Freedom to Learn for the 80s*, Columbus, OH: Charles E. Merrill.

Ryan, J. (2000) *A Guide to Teaching International Students,* Oxford: Oxford Centre for Staff and Learning Development.

Sadler, D. R. (1984) *Up the Publication Road,* Green Guide No 2, Millperra, NSW: HERDSA.

Sadler, D. R. (1989) Formative assessment and the design of instructional systems, *Instructional Science* 18(2): 119–144.

Sadler, D. R. (1998) Formative assessment: revisiting the territory, *Assessment in Education: Principles, Policy and Practice* 5(1): 77–84.

Sadler, D. R. (2010a). Beyond feedback: Developing student capability in complex appraisal *Assessment & Evaluation in Higher Education* 35(5), 535–550.

Sadler, D. R. (2010b) Fidelity as a precondition for integrity in grading academic achievement *Assessment and Evaluation in Higher Education* 35, 727–743.

Sadler, D. R. (2010c). Assessment in higher education. in Peterson, P., Baker, E. and McGaw, B. (eds) *International Encyclopedia of Education,* Vol. 3, 249–255, Oxford: Elsevier.

Sadler, D. R. (2011) Academic freedom, achievement standards and professional identity, *Quality in Higher Education,* 17, 103–118.

Sadler, D. R. (2013a) Making competent judgments of competence, in Blömeke, S., Zlatkin-Troitschanskaia, O., Kuhn, C. and Fege, J. (eds) *Modeling and Measuring Competencies in Higher Education: Tasks and Challenges,* Rotterdam: Sense Publishers.

Sadler, D. R. (2013b). Opening up feedback: Teaching learners to see, in Merry, S., Price, M., Carless, D., and Taras, M. (eds) *Reconceptualising Feedback in Higher Education: Developing Dialogue with Students,* London: Routledge.

Sadler, D. R. (2014) The futility of attempting to codify academic achievement standards, *Higher Education* 67, 273–288.

Shulman, L. (1996) Just in case. Reflections on learning from experience, in Wilson, S. M. (2004) *The Wisdom of Practice: Essays on Teaching, Learning and Learning to Teach*, San Francisco, CA: Jossey-Bass.

Skinner, B. F. (1954) *The Science of Learning and the Art of Teaching*, Charlottesville, VA: University of Virginia.

Thomson, P. and Kamler, B. (2013) *Writing for Peer Reviewed Journals*, London: Routledge.

Wenger, E. (1998) *Communities of Practice: Learning, Meaning and Identity,* Cambridge, MA: Harvard University Press, pp. 216–217.

Wierstra, R. F. A. and de Jong, J. A. (2002) A scaling theoretical evaluation of Kolb's Learning Style Inventory – 2, in Valcke, M. and Gombeir, D. (eds) *Learning Styles: Reliability and Validity*. Proceedings of the 7th Annual European Learning Styles Information Network Conference, 26–28 June, Ghent: University of Ghent, pp. 431–440.

Yorke, M. (2002) in Peelo, M. and Wareham, T. (eds) *Failing Students in Higher Education,* Maidenhead: SRHE/ Open University Press.

Index